The History of the UNITED STATES *of* AMERICA
from the Discovery of the Continent

CLASSIC AMERICAN HISTORIANS

Paul M. Angle, GENERAL EDITOR

The History of the UNITED STATES

of AMERICA
from the Discovery of the Continent

by George Bancroft

abridged and edited by Russel B. Nye

THE UNIVERSITY OF CHICAGO PRESS   Chicago & London

The Centenary Edition of *The History of the United States of America from the Discovery of the Continent,* upon which this abridgment is based, was published in six volumes by Little, Brown and Company between 1876 and 1879.

Library of Congress Catalog Card Number: 66-23683
THE UNIVERSITY OF CHICAGO PRESS, CHICAGO & LONDON
The University of Toronto Press, Toronto 5, Canada
Abridged edition © 1966 by The University of Chicago
All rights reserved
Published 1966. Printed in the United States of America

General Editor's Preface

FEW today read the great American historians. Few can. If a reader limited himself to those chosen for inclusion in this series—Prescott, Parkman, Bancroft, McMaster, Moses Coit Tyler, Henry Adams, Nicolay and Hay, and Rhodes—he would find himself straining his eyes eight hours a day for at least a year. This, in the modern world, is an impossible requirement.

Yet that the works of these men should remain unknown is deplorable. Something is better than nothing. From that conviction this series was born. But what should that "something" be? A series of condensations? How can one condense the sixteen volumes of Parkman, or the nine volumes of Henry Adams, into one volume without doing inexcusable violence to the whole? On the other hand, representative selections, each of substantial length, can convey a good idea of point of view, breadth of treatment, narrative skill, and style. This was the method chosen.

After this choice was made, the general editor came across a relevant pronouncement which John Hay made during the serialization of *Abraham Lincoln: A History*. "The only question," Hay wrote to Richard Watson Gilder, editor of the *Century*, "is whether you want the Life to run three years or four. If the former, you must take heroic measures. Leaving out a chapter here and there, or retrenching an adjective, will do no good. . . . You must cut great chunks of topics out. . . . Neither

Nicolay nor I can write the work over again for the purpose of saving a half chapter here and there." Nor, we submit, can anyone else.

The books in this series were designed for reading, not research. All documentation has, therefore, been eliminated. Editors of individual volumes have used their discretion in retaining expository footnotes. Such footnotes as they have added are identified by their initials. The typographical style, punctuation, and spelling of the original texts have been followed.

PAUL M. ANGLE

Editor's Introduction

GEORGE BANCROFT was born in Worcester, Massachusetts, on October 3, 1800, at the opening of the new century that was to work so many changes in the nation he would write about. The Bancrofts were an old New England family, the first one, John, having arrived in 1632. His descendants were for the most part solid farmers and rock-ribbed Calvinists until Aaron, George Bancroft's father, after a heroic struggle to educate himself sufficiently to enter college, graduated from Harvard and entered the Congregational ministry. He served at minor pastorates until called to Old South Church at Worcester in 1783, where he met and married Lucretia Chandler, daughter of a once-powerful Connecticut family that had lost its fortune in the Revolution. Of their twelve children, George was the eighth.

Aaron Bancroft was a gentle, liberal, and educated man, whose children grew up in a household of books, discussion, and ideas. He was so strongly influenced by the new "unitarian" religious doctrines that he finally withdrew from Old South to form a church of his own, the Second Congregational Church of Worcester, which he served as senior pastor until the end of his life. Young George, who showed early signs of interest in books and theology, was sent to Phillips Academy in New Hampshire, though it took every cent the family could provide, where he carried off all the prizes, won scholarships, and passed the entrance examinations for Harvard at the age of thirteen.

At Cambridge Bancroft was befriended by Edward Everett, then a tutor, and the Reverend Andrews Norton, conceded to be one of the most brilliant young men in the Divinity School. Bancroft's life at Harvard was virtually an extension of his career at Phillips; accounted an assiduous and worthy student, the College expected great things of him. Since Harvard had recently initiated a policy of sending a few of its best graduates abroad to study (Everett had been one of them), Bancroft after his graduation in 1817 was chosen to read classics and theology at Göttingen in Germany, where Everett too had gone. He found German university life intensely exciting; working fourteen hours a day, reading voraciously in German, Hebrew, Greek, Latin, and Syriac, he soon impressed the Göttingen faculty with his scholarship. However, his studies began to lead him away from theology toward philosophy, history, and poetry; his prim New England tastes likewise began to change in the free, loose atmosphere of European society. He took the grand tour as other fashionable young men did, met such notables as Byron and Goethe, learned to drink wine and dress with studied care, and wrote a good deal of sentimental, rebellious poetry. After receiving his Doctor of Philosophy degree in 1820, he attended lectures at Berlin and traveled through France and Italy, sailing for home in 1822.

Nearly four years abroad in the brittle, sophisticated society of romantic Europe left young Bancroft a trifle arrogant, more than a little brash, and, he wrote, "quite estranged from my own country and countrymen." He took a post as tutor in Greek at Harvard, and although a good teacher, he was also a notoriously unpopular one. He gave a few sermons as guest minister in pulpits near Cambridge and published a volume of verse in 1823, but he was not particularly successful as either poet or preacher. He seemed unable to focus his undeniably brilliant mind or to apply his store of learning to any specific task; Ralph Waldo Emerson, who had watched his career with interest, noted in his diary, "He hath sadly disappointed great expectations."

But Bancroft had decided on a career. With a friend, Joseph Green Cogswell, also a Harvard and German-trained scholar, he rented a set of farm buildings near Northampton, Massachusetts, called Round Hill Farm and opened a boys' school in the autumn of 1823. The young men, both of whom had been impressed by German and Swiss Gymnasia, hoped to adapt the new European pedagogy of Pestalozzi and Fellenberg to American educational uses. Round Hill School came at exactly the right time, for America was ready for educational experimentation, with both traditional academies and recently established high schools ready to move in new directions. The school opened with twenty-five students, all subjects except French taught by either Bancroft or Cogswell. Three years later the two owned the property outright, had one hundred and twelve students, a staff of twelve instructors, and a sound and fast-rising reputation. Boys came from twelve states, Canada, Mexico, and Brazil; young Ellery Channing went there, James Russell Lowell sent his younger brother Robert, John Lothrop Motley entered in the school's second year. Also at this time (1827) Bancroft met and married Sarah Dwight, from a wealthy Springfield family, and seemed ready to settle down to the life of a successful educator.

Within the next few years, however, it was plain that Bancroft was bored with the schoolmaster's life. He wanted to have more contact with the world, to test himself against its competition—he wanted "collisions with men," he wrote, to challenge him. He wrote long, erudite reviews for the journals, good ones such as the *North American Review*, and entertained hopes of perhaps entering the editorial field himself. He also took to dabbling in Massachusetts politics on the unfashionable Jacksonian side, shocking his conservative Cambridge and Boston acquaintances. Massachusetts politics was in a state of utter confusion, with Whig, Democrat, Anti-Masonic, and Workingmen's parties contending for power. Bancroft found the situation to his advantage, and soon it was more than dabbling. He was nominated for the state senate in 1830 by the Workingmen's party and in 1831 wrote such a strongly pro-Jackson piece for the *North American Review* that it received notice from Jackson's lieutenant, Martin Van Buren.

From what he knew of politics Bancroft believed it offered the stimulation and challenge he desired; Massachusetts party politicians, for their part, needed the kind of intellectual leadership he represented. In 1830 he severed connections with Round Hill and chose, at least tentatively, to take his chances in the political arena. And at some time within the next two years he chose another career, that of historian. In 1834, when the first volume of the *History of the United States from the Discovery of the American Continent* appeared, he also ran unsuccessfully for the Massachusetts General Court on the Anti-Masonic ticket. He was thus well launched on two careers, neither of which he relinquished for a moment over the next forty years.

William Hickling Prescott, Bancroft's friend and fellow historian, wondered how he could "woo the fair muse of history and the ugly strumpet of faction with one and the same breath." Neither career seemed to interfere with the other, for while Bancroft continued to write and publish (Volumes II in 1837 and III in 1839), he also gained increasing influence in Democratic councils. Though his wife's death in 1837 cast a shadow over his successes, he continued his political and historical work with undiminished energy. In 1838, after Van Buren's victory, he was appointed collector of the Port of Boston, the most powerful patronage post in New England. He moved to Boston, a year later married Elizabeth Davis Bliss, a young widow, founded a newspaper called the *Bay State Democrat*, continued to write reviews and articles for the journals, and kept his political fences well mended. Although the Whig victories in 1840 overturned the Massachusetts Democratic machine, he remained one of the party's most effective leaders.

At the national Democratic convention of 1844 Bancroft was instrumental in swinging the Massachusetts delegation to James K. Polk, a service Polk did not forget. Bancroft himself that year accepted the Democratic nomination for governor, an office he had little hope of winning, and after he lost, the Polk administration offered to pay its debt to him with a major appointment. He hoped for a diplomatic assignment to Europe, but instead Polk proposed and Bancroft accepted the position of secretary of the navy. He served the Navy Department for a year and a half, doing a competent job in a post for which he did not feel especially fitted and which he did not especially like. For one thing, he cut through a good deal of encrusted tradition to make needed changes in certain procedures—he abolished flogging, made merit as well as seniority a factor in promotion, and obtain larger naval appropriations from Congress. He also established a school for midshipmen at Annapolis, Maryland, which became the Naval Academy.

In May, 1846, Congress declared that a state of war existed between the United States and Mexico and Bancroft found himself in command of a wartime navy. For a brief time, when he was also acting secretary of war, he was in charge of all military operations on land and sea, a far greater responsibility than he wanted to assume. In autumn of 1846 the opening of two major diplomatic posts in Europe, London and Paris, gave him an opportunity to remind Polk of his original request. He chose London, arriving there in the winter of 1846. The city and the society were pleasant, his duties not onerous, and three years of good manners, good wines, and good talk—with such men as Carlyle, Macaulay, Hallam, Dean Milman, and Lord Morpeth—brought out much of the latent aristocrat in him, whatever his Jacksonian sympathies. At the same time, having observed and even participated in the decision-making processes that made up history, he felt better equipped to write it. "Constant enjoyment of the most refined and cultured society . . . ," he wrote, "the opportunity of observing statesmen and institutions, lords, commoners, and ministers, have at once instructed me and have soothed and benefited me, when I most needed it." After the Whig victories at home in the elections of 1848, Bancroft, knowing he was to be replaced, returned to the United States in 1849.

He chose to live in New York City and settled down at once

to hard work on the *History*, which had lain fallow for almost ten years. Volumes IV and V appeared in 1852, VI in 1854, VII and VIII in 1858 and 1860. During the Civil War he suspended his research to support Lincoln (though he did not trust him at first) but refused to call himself a Republican. After the war, when Andrew Johnson tried to build a coalition party of old Whigs, non-Radical Republicans, and War Democrats, he threw in his political fortunes with the Tennessean. Johnson accepted him into the inner circle of his advisers, and Bancroft wrote almost the whole text of his first message to Congress. Meanwhile he completed and published Volume IX of the *History*, shortly before Johnson offered him the post of minister to Prussia, the one he coveted most of all.

Bancroft and his wife took up residence in Berlin in 1867. Prussia under Bismarck had already taken the first steps toward the unification of the German state, and Bancroft, with his knowledge of German language, history, and literature, was the perfect American representative. He became close friends with Bismarck, and for that matter with nearly all the important statesmen, scholars, and scientists in Germany. The American minister's home soon became the center of social and intellectual life in the diplomatic corps, and Bancroft's salon the most sought-after in Berlin. When the Empire was officially proclaimed in 1871, he remained as United States minister, serving until 1873; then, after six years abroad, his *History* unfinished and the years gaining on him, he asked to be relieved.

Bancroft took up residence in Washington, resumed his work, and published Volume X in 1874. Immediately, he set about revising the ten volumes for the Centenary Edition of 1876 and embarked on his constitutional history, which appeared in 1882. He kept on writing and revising—historical sketches for the newspapers, reviews for the journals, entries for encyclopedias, the re-worked "author's last revision"—but as time crept up he found his pace slackening. He spent more and more time in his rose garden, on letters to old acquaintances, and in long walks in the parks. As early as 1887 his family noted occasional lapses of memory and momentary confusions; each year he read and wrote less and spent more time browsing and dreaming. On January 17, 1891, he died at his Washington home. After services at St. John's Cathedral, the train bore his body back to the town of his birth in the quiet green hills of Massachusetts. Born into the America of Washington and Jefferson, his life spanned more than three-quarters of the independent existence of the nation whose history he wrote, and of which he was a part.

George Bancroft seems to have decided to write a history of the United States in 1832 or early 1833. His choice of history as a profession was not surprising, since contemporary New England considered the historian the equal of the philosopher, theologian, or lawyer. As a youth at Göttingen and Berlin Bancroft had studied under Eichhorn, Heeren, and Boeckh, three of Germany's greatest historical scholars, and the review-essays he wrote for the *North American Review* and other journals between 1826 and 1834 were almost all concerned with historical topics. In a sense, he had already served his apprenticeship as historian when he began, in mid-1833, to take notes for a history of the United States.

The public for which he intended to write expected certain things of historians. First, it asked that history be personalized —that it be "the history of living men," as Carlyle called it, written in terms of those whose decisions and actions had determined the direction of events for good or ill. When Edward Everett later told Bancroft that his *History* dealt with "real, individual, living" characters and not "pasteboard men and women" he could have made no higher compliment. Second, the public expected history to be presented as a dramatic conflict of opposing individuals, forces, or nations; the historian, like the playwright, imposed form and structure on the disorder of events, finding tension, climax, and resolution in the segments of human experience he chose to write about. Third, Bancroft's generation believed that the historian should identify for his reader certain themes by which he could explain the significance of the past; he should find and expose those elements which bound events together and gave them purpose. In Bancroft's words, the historian should locate "a pervading principle" in the past which gave it "continuity and vitality," tracing "events not only to their authors and immediate courses, but to the place they occupy" in the total pattern of history. Fourth, the historian should create in his work a precise sense of the place, time, and atmosphere of the era it treated, providing what Bancroft called "the spirit of the age, the impalpable but necessary essence" of the society of which he wrote. If the historian did this well, those who read of it also lived within it.

Bancroft's ideas about the function of history and the obligations of the historian were contained in two essays written in 1835 and 1855, entitled "The Office of the People in Art, Government, and Religion" (1835) and "The Necessity, the Reality, and the Promise of the Progress of the Human Race" (1855),[1] and in the *History*. The duty of the historian, he wrote in the earlier essay, in broad terms was "to write the changes in humanity" by considering "events in connection with each other . . . , observing the general principles by which that succession is controlled," and by depicting "the *discovery*, the *diffusion*, and the *application* of truth in the histories of men and nations." His study of the past, Bancroft believed, showed that its animating principle was progress—the absolute, all-pervasive plan of God for all things to improve. "When history is viewed from this point," he said, "it is found that humanity is steadily advancing, that the advance of liberty and justice is certain." In the later essay, in addition to explaining in greater detail the implications of the application of the rule of progress to history, he defined more precisely the function of the historian, who, because he found "God visible in history," ranked below only the poet in the hierarchy of knowledge and shared equal rank with the philosopher and theologian. Since history

[1] Collected, with his early essays and reviews, in *Literary and Historical Miscellanies* (New York: Harper & Bros., 1855).

contained all proof of God's intent, the historian examined it to find "sublimer truths" than nature or mind revealed, "the idea of right . . . , the vestiges of moral law . . . , the reality of justice." The historian, then, in Bancroft's view, was both interpreter and prophet, who perceived God's designs in what had happened in the past and deduced from them what might happen in the future. There was unity and totality in the past, because each bit of it was part of a complex of divinely arranged principles by which the affairs of men and universe were controlled and directed. The historian looked in the past to find laws, to find how "events, placed in proper contiguity, become of themselves firm links of a brightly burnished chain, connecting events with causes. . . ."

When he came to apply his ideas to the history of the United States, he refined and focused them on that specific task. Since history, as he wrote in his preface, must have some "great principle of action" to lend continuity and meaning to the narrative, he identified two unifying threads of American history. The first was liberty—he hoped to trace in his volumes how the United States, from a small group of immigrants in an empty, wild continent, grew to become the freest nation on earth. The second was divine providence—he intended to show how the hand of God directed the nation's rise from feeble wilderness colony to "its present happiness and glory," so that it would serve as His model to the world of what a just, peaceful, and free nation should be. The proof of these principles lay in the American past—in the study of that succession of events by which the American colonies, in their march from repression toward liberty, in their advance from scattered settlement toward unified republic, illustrated the progress and unity of humanity under God's direction. His was history in the romantic, optative mood of America's Golden Day.

The first three volumes of the *History* (published in 1834, 1837, and 1839 by Little, Brown, and Company of Boston) comprised a unit covering the years from Columbus' voyage to the opening of the French and Indian War. Throughout the period Bancroft found evidence to show that "the spirit of the colonies demanded freedom from the beginning," that there developed in them a desire for liberty and unity which, by mid-eighteenth century, was authentically native, national, and American. His increasing involvement in politics and public life delayed until 1852 the appearance of Volumes IV and V, which, with Volume VI (1854) constituted a second unit. This carried the narrative from 1748 to May, 1774, concentrating on the growing disintegration of the British colonial system and the corresponding emergence of the colonial drive toward independence. As the time drew near for the culmination of God's plan for "humanity to make for itself a new existence" in the new land, Bancroft narrowed his narrative down to the clear confrontation of liberty with repression, of freedom with tyranny, setting the stage for the final contest. The third unit, Volumes VII (1858) and VIII (1860) treated events only from May, 1774, to July 4, 1776. Here Bancroft traced the current of independence through each colony in turn, moving to a detailed account of the Continental Congress and the final break in Philadelphia, ending with the incandescent words of the Declaration.

Bancroft worked on the last unit, Volumes IX and X, throughout the Civil War, publishing IX, which took the narrative to the French alliance, in 1866. He did not publish Volume X until he returned from Berlin in 1874, finally completing the task he had set for himself exactly forty years before. Despite the fact that it appeared in ten volumes over four decades, the *History* was a single, consistent, whole work, constructed about his lifelong, unshakable belief in God, country, and progress. The entire work was founded on the proposition that the United States of America, under God's direct personal guidance, was inevitably evolving into the perfect state. The critic's joking comment, that Bancroft wrote American history as if it were the history of the Kingdom of Heaven, had a trifle of truth in it.

Bancroft's methods of research and composition were methodical and precise. He did all the research for the first three volumes, but later, as other responsibilities pressed in upon him, he hired secretaries who served as research assistants— young men such as William Sloane and Austin Scott, both of whom became distinguished scholars in their own right. Every word of every volume, however, Bancroft himself wrote or dictated and revised personally, reworking some passages five to ten times. He wrote in a large hand, sometimes no more than six sentences to a page, leaving wide spaces for interlinear additions and revisions. For the greater part of his life he rose at five, stayed at his desk until eight, and returned in mid-afternoon to work again until dusk. In his early years he sometimes worked ten to fourteen hours a day; at age seventy he still put in at least six hours; and in his mid-eighties, when working on his last revision, set his quota at three hundred words per day.

The approach of the hundredth anniversary of the signing of the Declaration of Independence provided Bancroft with an occasion to revise the *History* in its entirety. The original volumes, by this time, had gone through more than twenty editions, and in late 1874 he began a complete revision. The Centenary Edition appeared over three years, 1876–79, reduced from the original ten volumes to six. While still revising the Centenary Edition Bancroft plunged into the writing of his two-volume *History of the Formation of the Constitution of the United States of America*, which appeared after seven years of unremitting labor in 1882. Still not satisfied, he set about combining the constitutional history with the Centenary Edition, so that the *History* would form a complete narrative from Columbus' departure from Spain to the ratification of the Constitution by Rhode Island. The first volume of the last revision, which again reduced the total to six, came out in 1883 and the last in 1886, when Bancroft was eighty-six. He still planned to write a book on Shakespeare, a biography of James K. Polk, a life of Andrew Jackson, and to complete a biography of Martin Van Buren, begun originally as a campaign piece in 1844. Handicapped by failing health and eyesight, and working from forty-year-old notes, he finished only the Van Buren book in 1889, two years before his death. The last revision, however, should stand as his monument.

Bancroft's prose style, in accordance with the tastes of the times, was modelled after the rhetoric of the contemporary oration. The public expected a writer to treat an important topic in a "grand and sublime" style, "sufficiently ornamented," a writer in the *American Quarterly Review* said, "to meet the public expectation." Bancroft's prose therefore employed all the popular devices of public address—the balanced sentence, the extended metaphor, the classical reference, the rhetorical question, the polysyllabic vocabulary—that his readers associated with the "elevated style" of oratory. As his own and the public's taste changed he began trimming his style, "slaughtering adjectives" as he called it, enabling him to reduce his volumes substantially each time he revised them. The text here is that of the Centenary Edition of 1876, marking a half-way point in the development of his style, more direct than the original, yet retaining enough of its rhetorical flourish to be representative of Bancroft's personal prose manner.

The nationalistic impulse that swept through the society of the new United States after the Revolution made the study of their history a matter of vital necessity to Americans. Where the nation came from, how it came to be formed, and how it succeeded in its revolution—these were questions whose answers every citizen needed. A number of histories appeared soon after the war, chiefly concerned with the conflict itself or with the histories of separate colonies, usually based on incomplete or untrustworthy records. Abiel Holmes' *American Annals* (1805) and Benjamin Trumbull's *General History of the United States* (1810) were among the first attempts to treat the history of the country as a unit, but both were little more than chronologies. Editors and critics continued to demand a credible, comprehensive, patriotic history of the United States. To do this, wrote William Hickling Prescott, the country needed a historian who knew "all the minute feelings, prejudices, and peculiar ways of thinking" which made up the American character and who could interpret the nation's origin and destiny in truly American terms.

When George Bancroft's first volume appeared in 1834, therefore, it found a public so eager to welcome it that its success was virtually assured. Almost unanimously, reviewers praised the *Americanness* of his approach, his patriotic zeal, the magnitude of his plan to write the history of this new great nation, as his preface proclaimed, "from the discovery of the American continent to the present time." "If completed as announced," remarked the influential *North American Review*, "Bancroft's *History* will unquestionably forever be regarded both as an American and as an English classic." *The Western Messenger* believed that in Bancroft "our nation has found a fit chronicler of whose work our nation may be proud, and in which mankind ought to rejoice." The *American Quarterly Review* hailed the *History* as "a patriotic and important undertaking . . . of sterling excellence"; the *Christian Examiner* rejoiced that "at last Americans are to have a HISTORY"; and other journals echoed similar sentiments.[2]

Famous men praised the volume in lavish terms. Carlyle admired it from England; Emerson thought it "noble matter, nobly treated"; the great German historian Arnold Heeren wrote that he found it "truly inspired history." Edward Everett read it straight through, stopping only for food and church, to pronounce it "a work that will last while the memory of America lasts"; and Prescott granted Bancroft "a place among the great historical writers of the age."

There were a few criticisms mingled with the praise, identifying certain tendencies in Bancroft's manner of writing history that were to become characteristic as his volumes continued to appear. Emerson did not like "the insertion of a boyish hurrah,

[2] *North American Review*, XL (January, 1835), 99; *Western Messenger*, V (April, 1838), 4; *American Quarterly Review*, XVI (September, 1834), 201; *Christian Examiner*, XVII (November, 1834), 282.

now and then," and Carlyle was not pleased with Bancroft's "didactic theoretic manner" of making history prove something. John Quincy Adams, while admitting the author's "transcendent talents and indefatigable industry," thought his style "diffuse and declamatory," and the *Southern Literary Messenger* not only criticized the "frequent sacrifice of perspicuity to ornamentation" in Bancroft's prose but objected stridently to his strong unionism. There were also those who felt that Bancroft's political partisanship showed through so clearly that his *History* "voted for Jackson."[3]

The American public, however, found Bancroft's approach to American history quite to its tastes. He expressed a whole set of ideas that had long been common currency in America; he expressed them in an exuberant rhetoric that reassured his readers that these ideas were true and enduring; and he documented their origin and existence with what seemed undeniable and exact evidence. As a result, with the appearance of Volume I, Bancroft became the American public's favorite historian of its past and the popular prophet of its future.

The pattern established by the reviews of Bancroft's early volumes varied little over the next forty-odd years as he continued to publish and revise. Both public and reviewers expected certain things from his *History*, which they either praised or criticized, according to their preferences. The North *American Review*, for example, speaking of Volumes IV and V in 1852, remarked on their "fervid spirit of patriotism" and the author's "love of country too exalted to be discriminating." *Harper's Monthly*, reviewing Volume VI in 1855, praised the author for his ability to combine "the fancy of the poet, the insight of the philosopher . . . and the sagacity of the historian," though disapproving his "highly elaborate, intricate" prose. The *Southern Review*, in 1868, attacked Bancroft sharply for what it considered the partisan political bias of Volume IX, accusing him of "cheating the past into the service of the pres-

[3] See Russel B. Nye, *George Bancroft* (New York: Alfred A. Knopf, 1945), pp. 102–4 and *passim* for a summary of these and similar comments.

ent." Henry Adams's review of the tenth and final volume, written in 1875, summarized accurately the general judgment of his work. Despite the "inevitable peculiarities of his literary style," his Jacksonian faith in "the abstract virtues of democracy," and the "restlessness of mind" which characterized his conclusions, Bancroft must still be accounted, Adams concluded, a scholar whose "merit and solid virtue" make him the most respected historian of America.[4]

The matter did not rest with Adams's appraisal, for his generally favorable comments were among the last that Bancroft's *History* enjoyed. By that time, reviewers and readers of American history were already developing considerable sophistication, styles and tastes in historical writing were rapidly changing, and a younger generation of historians was evolving new attitudes toward and different approaches to the American past. The eighties and the nineties were years of drastic re-evaluation of historical theories and reputations and of great alterations in the way history was conceived and written.

In the first place, the writing of history during the latter decades of the nineteenth century became professionalized, academic, specialized. There was no longer a place for the talented, wide-ranging amateur who took all knowledge for his province as Bancroft, Motley, and their fellows did. The historian was more apt to be a professor with an advanced degree who had studied abroad and who specialized in a particular period or kind of history. And history, Charles M. Andrews later told the American Historical Association, was evolving near the turn of the century "higher canons of criticism and interpretation, better balanced judgments, and more rational methods of presentation" than Bancroft and his generation ever possessed.[5]

Furthermore, historians found much to take exception to in

[4] *North American Review*, CLV (April, 1852), 508; *Harper's Monthly*, XI (June, 1855), 117; *Southern Review*, IV (July, 1868), 208; *North American Review*, CCXLVI (April, 1875), 424–32.
[5] Herman Ausubel, *Historians and Their Craft* (New York: Columbia University Press, 1950), p. 77.

Bancroft's over-all concept of the meaning of American history. His central thesis did not lend itself to a satisfactory interpretation of events after 1789; if, as he assumed, the success of the Revolution and the ratification of the Constitution marked the climax of American history, what followed either had to be anticlimactic or merely the continuation of an already determined pattern. The historians who followed out Bancroft's great theme of national unity found it impossible to explain the Civil War, for example, or post-Civil War America, in any but the most forced and simplistic terms. In emphasizing the broad "common spirit" of America, regional historians claimed, Bancroft submerged the variety and multiplicity of American life and the importance of sectionalism in American history in generalities about the wholeness and unity of the nation. In addition, his conviction that the historian gave "order and connection to events" by discerning in them evidences of "the divine power which gives unity to the universe" simply did not fit the temperament of an era more scientifically and less theologically minded than his own—what the age of Emerson had accepted as a rationale for the universe the age of William James would not.[6]

Historians and public alike, then, by the turn of the century had almost completely rejected most of the assumptions on which Bancroft and the romantic school of American historians based their work. History was now divorced from literature, theology, and philosophy; the historian valued scholarly objectivity, reportorial detachment, and verifiable evidence more than he did generalized theory and the grand sweep of knowledge. The need for different and more complex ways of observing and explaining the American past generated at least four new theories which came to dominate historical writing for the next two generations—the "scientific" school of Herbert Baxter Adams and others of the so-called Teutonic group; the imperial

[6] See John Higham (ed.), *The Reconstruction of American History* (New York: Harper Bros., 1962), pp. 17–20, for a useful summary of historical trends in this period.

school of George Lewis Beer, Charles M. Andrews, and C. H. Van Tyne; the "frontier" school of Frederick Jackson Turner and his followers; and somewhat later the economic determinism of Charles A. Beard. By the time of Beard's *Economic Interpretation of the Constitution* (1913) the old romantic history of Bancroft's day was far out of fashion, and his volumes no longer in print.

Because he best exemplified a discredited historical school, and doubtless too because his popularity had made his books almost household fixtures, Bancroft suffered most at the hands of the revisionists. No other American historian, excepting possibly Charles Beard, has ever been so violently attacked by his fellows; for a time it seemed that each of Bancroft's critics tried to outdo the last. Charles Francis Adams thought that Bancroft's "learning and his philosophy cannot be called sound, and his earlier manner something to be forever avoided." Edward Eggleston told the American Historical Association in 1900 that Bancroft had probably repelled more young people from the study of history than any other single influence in America. Charles McLean Andrews characterized his volumes as "haphazard guesses of no scientific validity" based on "ignorance and national bias . . . , nothing less than a crime against historical truth." Sydney G. Fisher dismissed him as nothing more than "a scholarly Weems." Even those compassionate and judicious critics who showed greater understanding of what the older romantic historians had tried to do, such as John Spencer Bassett and John F. Jameson, could find only temperate praise for Bancroft's work.[7]

[7] Charles Francis Adams, "The Sifted Grain and the Grain Sifters," *American Historical Review*, VI (January, 1901), 221; Edward Eggleston, quoted in Ausaubel, *op. cit.,* p. 313; C. M. Andrews, quoted in A. S. Eisenstadt, *Charles McLean Andrews* (New York: Columbia University Press, 1956), p. 405; S. G. Fisher, "The Legendary and Myth-making Process in Histories of the American Revolution," *Proceedings of the American Philosophical Society*, LI (April-June, 1912), 53–75. As late as 1937 Harry Elmer Barnes, *A History of Historical Writing* (Norman: University of Oklahoma Press, 1937), p. 232, wrote of "the pathetic inaccuracy" of Bancroft's theories, claiming that he had done "almost incalculable, if not irreparable damage" to the writing of American history. Jameson, in his

Though Bancroft's kind of historical writing remains unacceptable to today's historians, there has been an increasing tendency to judge his work within the context of his times, and to modify some of the harsh judgments passed upon it by critics of a half-century ago. The majority of historiographers are willing to credit him with certain substantial contributions to the American historical tradition, as well as to recognize what are, from the modern point of view, his shortcomings of theory and methodology. As historians have learned to avoid his errors and excesses, so have they also begun to acknowledge his virtues. Like Prescott, Motley, and Parkman, Bancroft is considered one of the romantic historians who combined literary art with philosophical and cultural theories designed for their times, men who presented versions of historical truth valid for the public for which they wrote and defensible as literary art.[8] Although his cosmic generalities about the meaning of the American past may no longer be taken seriously by historians, yet his place as interpreter of America to itself, in the nineteenth century's golden age of optimism, is secure.

Drawing up a balance sheet on George Bancroft's *History*, one finds on the debit side of the ledger the fact that his deep faith in Jacksonian democracy encouraged him to see liberty and equality everywhere in the American past, including places and times where it did not exist. His equally powerful belief in the divine law of progress in human (and especially American) affairs predisposed him to view the past, present, and

---

History of Historical Writing in America (Boston: Houghton Mifflin Co., 1891), 103–7, while noting Bancroft's "uncritical patriotism" and "turgid eloquence," nevertheless found that he "caught . . . , with sincere and enthusiastic conviction . . . , the ideas of the new Jacksonian democracy," and Bassett, *The Middle Group of American Historians* (New York: Macmillan Co., 1917), pp. 183–84, though critical of Bancroft's "lack of detachment" and "partisan bias," still gave him "undisputed rank as the greatest living historian" of the old school.

[8] See, for example, Michael Kraus, *A History of American History* (New York: Farrar & Rinehart, 1937), pp. 215–39; David Levin, *History as Romantic Art* (Stanford: Stanford University Press, 1959), pp. 25–37 *passim;* and Harvey Wish, *The American Historian* (New York: Oxford University Press, 1962), pp. 70–88.

future with determined and possibly unwarranted optimism.[9] The fervent patriotism which led him to judge the American Revolution as historically second in importance only to the birth of Christ often warped his point of view and distorted the proportions of the *History*—his first four volumes covered 271 years, for example, and the last six 19. His numerous enthusiasms occasionally lured him into long digressions only distantly relevant to the subject at hand (such as two full chapters on German history in Volume X), and his inherent tendency to generalize and moralize often tempted him into insupportable statements and rhetorical oversimplifications. It would be difficult to document his contention that the people of Massachusetts "beyond any other American colony . . . , loved the land of their ancestors" or that at Lexington "with one impulse, the colonies sprang to arms . . . , with one heart the continent cried 'Liberty or Death!' " To the modern reader his great flaw as historian is his desire to improve the occasion, to read into the past what he believed ought to be there. He preferred not to recognize anything which interfered with the working-out of his theory of history or which marred the logic of the grand design he saw immanent in the sweep of the American past. Yet his theme is so great, and his belief in it so sincere, that the reader may forgive if not excuse his zeal.

On the other hand, Bancroft, to his credit, was among the first to emphasize the necessity of original sources and the vital importance of careful, arduous research. After he began to write history, no one who followed him dared neglect his spadework. Bancroft was, of course, the first to open foreign archives to American scholars and, in his constant reference of American events to the current of European affairs, among the first to place American history within its world setting. Despite accu-

[9] For detailed estimates of Bancroft as historian, see Watt Stewart, "George Bancroft" in *The Marcus W. Jernegan Essays in American Historiography* (Chicago: University of Chicago Press, 1937); N. H. Dawes and F. T. Nichols, "Revaluing Bancroft," *New England Quarterly*, VI (June, 1933), 278–93; and Russel B. Nye, *George Bancroft* (New York: Washington Square Press, 1964), pp. 303–10.

sations of New England bias, he did recognize the importance of the South and West in American history; he knew that colonial history was made up of the separate strands of each colony's development; he was the first to trace the gradual welding of the disparate states into a unified nation and to develop a theory to justify it. He tried always to play fair with reputations—such men as Braddock, Howe, Arnold, and Gage received just treatment at his hands, and he judged North, Bute, and others without undue prejudice. He understood the crucial role of British mercantile policy in precipitating the Revolution, and how foreign diplomacy influenced the course and conclusion of the war. He also recognized the importance of ideas as motives and catalysts in history; his analysis in Volume IX, for example, of the English Protestant and Continental Catholic traditions, and how they joined in the Age of Reason, is still by modern standards an amazingly sophisticated exercise in intellectual history.

Bancroft's real strength as historian lay in the sense of drama that he imparted to the materials of history; he planned scenery, introduced characters, and controlled the stream of events as a playwright would, making history live and breathe as few men have succeeded in doing. He saw the American past as a great play, written by God and man together, moving toward a triumphant last act in which the promises of the Christian tradition and the Age of Reason came true. His was essentially philosophical history, resting on a faith in man and trust in God that arose from his religious principles. Democracy was the lodestar of his work, and its bias, if such a powerful conviction can be so called, was that of a man being true to his most deeply held principles. What he saw in the American past was the promise of a better future, for Americans and for mankind, and his *History* traced out its shape.

Contents

The History of the UNITED STATES *of* AMERICA
from the Discovery of the Continent

GEORGE BANCROFT *took approximately fifty years and one million seven hundred thousand words to complete what he first called, in 1834,* The History of the United States from the Discovery of the American Continent. *In its final form, the* History *was organized as follows:*

Part I. *Colonial History, 1492–48*
Part II. *The American Revolution, 1748–82*

Epoch First: *1748–63, The Overthrow of the European Colonial System*

Epoch Second: *1763–74, How Great Britain Estranged America*

Epoch Third: *1774–76, America Declares Itself Independent*

Epoch Fourth: *1776–82, The Independence of America Is Acknowledged*

Part III. *The Formation of the Constitution, 1782–89*

About two-thirds of the whole he devoted to the Revolution, which, to his view, represented a crucial turning point of human history—the colonial period its preparation, the constitutional period its epilogue and fruition. To Bancroft, American history from 1492 to 1789 was a continuous, unified narrative of how a divinely favored people found the meaning of freedom, fought for it in a bitter contest against Old World tyranny, and in the American system of constitutional union fashioned the perfect instrument for its preservation.

Introduction

THE United States of America constitute an essential portion of a great political system, embracing all the civilized nations of the earth. At a period when the force of moral opinion is rapidly increasing, they have the precedence in the practice and the defence of the equal rights of man. The sovereignty of the people is here a conceded axiom, and the laws, established upon that basis, are cherished with faithful patriotism. While the nations of Europe aspire after change, our constitution engages the fond admiration of the people, by which it has been established. Prosperity follows the execution of even justice; invention is quickened by the freedom of competition; and labor rewarded with sure and unexampled returns. Domestic peace is maintained without the aid of a military establishment; public sentiment permits the existence of but few standing troops, and those only along the seaboard and on the frontiers. A gallant navy protects our commerce, which spreads its banners on every sea, and extends its enterprise to every clime. Our diplomatic relations connect us on terms of equality and honest friendship with the chief powers of the world; while we avoid entangling participation in their intrigues, their passions, and their wars. Our national resources are developed by an earnest culture of the arts of peace. Every man may enjoy the fruits of his industry; every mind is free to publish its convictions. Our government, by its organization, is necessarily identified with the interests of the people, and relies exclusively on their attachment for its durability and support. Even the enemies of the state, if there are any among us, have liberty to express their opinions undisturbed; and are safely tolerated, where reason is left free to combat their errors. Nor is the constitution a dead letter, unalterably fixed: it has the capacity for improvement; adopting whatever changes time and the public will may require, and safe from decay, so long as that will retains its energy. New states are forming in the wilderness; canals, intersecting our plains and crossing our highlands, open numerous channels to internal commerce; manufactures prosper along our watercourses; the use of steam on our rivers and railroads annihilates distance by the acceleration of speed. Our wealth and population, already giving us a place in the first rank of nations, are so rapidly cumulative, that the former is increased fourfold, and the latter is doubled, in every period of twenty-two or twenty-three years. There is no national debt; the community is opulent; the government economical; and the public treasury full. Religion, neither persecuted nor paid by the state, is sustained by the regard for public morals and the convictions of an enlightened faith. Intelligence is diffused with unparalleled universality; a free press teems with the choicest productions of all nations and ages. There are more daily journals in the United States than in the world beside. A public document of general interest is, within a month, reproduced in at least a million of copies, and is brought within the reach of every freeman in the country. An immense concourse of emigrants of the most various lineage is perpetually crowding to our shores; and the principles of liberty, uniting all interests by the operation of equal laws, blend the discordant elements into harmonious union. Other governments are convulsed by the innovations and reforms of neighboring states; our constitution, fixed in the affections of the people, from whose choice it has sprung, neutralizes the influence of foreign principles, and fearlessly opens an asylum to the virtuous, the unfortunate, and the oppressed of every nation.

And yet it is but little more than two centuries since the oldest of our states received its first permanent colony. Before that time the whole territory was an unproductive waste. Throughout its wide extent the arts had not erected a monument. Its only inhabitants were a few scattered tribes of feeble barbarians, destitute of commerce and of political connection. The axe and the ploughshare were unknown. The soil, which had been gathering fertility from the repose of centuries, was lavishing its strength in magnificent but useless vegetation. In the view of civilization the immense domain was a solitude.

It is the object of the present work to explain how the change in the condition of our land has been brought about; and, as the fortunes of a nation are not under the control of blind destiny, to follow the steps by which a favoring Providence, calling our institutions into being, has conducted the country to its present happiness and glory.

BANCROFT *believed, as he explained in his 1834 preface to Volume I, that he was doing a number of things not done before by historians of the United States. First of all, he intended to dwell "at considerable length in this first period because it contained the germ of our institutions"; since "the maturity of the nation is but a continuation of its youth," the American colonial period demanded much more careful exploration and elucidation than heretofore accorded to it. Bancroft found there unmistakable evidences of a pervasive "spirit of American liberty," an "active freedom" which led directly to the quest for liberty and unity that in turn culminated in the Revolution. The great theme of his treatment of colonial history was that "the spirit of the colonies demanded freedom from the beginning." He also believed that he had broken new ground (as indeed he had) in his detailed studies of early Virginia, Maryland, and Rhode Island, as well as in his careful analyses of Cromwellian foreign and colonial policy.*

After opening the volume with descriptions of early French, Spanish, and English voyages to the New World, he provided the reader with broad sweeping surveys of Philip's Spain and Elizabeth's England, finally narrowing the focus of his narrative to the two main centers of English colonization, Virginia and New England. Bancroft had very little interest in economic causes in American history, for he saw its meaning primarily as a contest between absolutism and liberty. The importance of the Virginia Company, therefore, which possessed "the first written charter of a permanent American colony," was that its members "first asserted the doctrine of popular sovereignty" and established the foundation for "the superstructure of its liberties."

Colonization of Virginia

THE period of success in planting Virginia had arrived; yet not till changes in European politics and society had moulded the forms of colonization. The Reformation had broken the har-

mony of religious opinion; and differences in the church began
to constitute the basis of political parties. After the East Indies
had been reached by doubling the southern promontory of
Africa, the great commerce of the world was carried upon the
ocean. The art of printing had been perfected and diffused;
and the press spread intelligence and multiplied the facilities
of instruction. The feudal institutions, which had been reared
in the middle ages, were already undermined by the current
of time and events, and, swaying from their base, threatened
to fall. Productive industry had built up the fortunes and extended the influence of the active classes; while habits of indolence and expense had impaired the estates and diminished
the power of the nobility. These changes produced corresponding results in the institutions which were to rise in America.

A revolution had equally occurred in the purposes for which
voyages were undertaken. The hope of Columbus, as he sailed
to the west, had been the discovery of a new passage to the
East Indies. The passion for gold next became the prevailing
motive. Then the islands and countries near the equator were
made the tropical gardens of the Europeans. At last, the higher
design was matured: to plant permanent Christian colonies;
to establish for the oppressed and the enterprising places of
refuge and abode; to found states in a temperate clime, with
all the elements of independent existence.

In the imperfect condition of industry, a redundant population had existed in England even before the peace with Spain,
which threw out of employment the gallant men who had served
under Elizabeth by sea and land, and left them no option but
to engage as mercenaries in the quarrels of strangers, or incur
the hazards of "seeking a New World." The minds of many
persons of intelligence and rank were directed to Virginia. The
brave and ingenious Gosnold, who had himself witnessed the
fertility of the western soil, long solicited the concurrence of
his friends for the establishment of a colony, and at last prevailed with Edward Maria Wingfield, a merchant of the west
of England, Robert Hunt, a clergyman of fortitude and modest

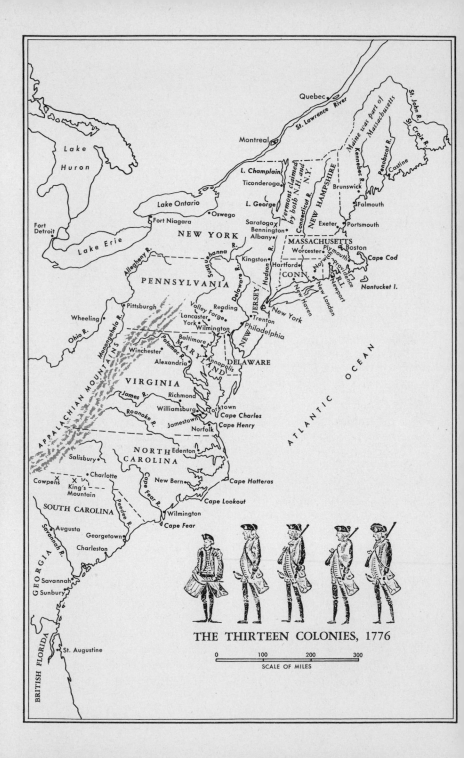

THE THIRTEEN COLONIES, 1776

0   100   200   300
SCALE OF MILES

worth, and John Smith, an adventurer of rarest qualities, to
risk their lives and hopes of fortune in an expedition. For more
than a year, this little company revolved the project of a plantation. At the same time, Sir Ferdinando Gorges was gathering
information of the native Americans, whom he had received
from Waymouth, and whose descriptions of the country, joined
to the favorable views which he had already imbibed, filled him
with the strongest desire of becoming a proprietary of domains
beyond the Atlantic. Gorges was a man of wealth, rank, and
influence; he readily persuaded Sir John Popham, lord chief
justice of England, to share his intentions. Nor had the assigns
of Raleigh become indifferent to "western planting;" which the
most distinguished of them all, "industrious Hakluyt," the historian of maritime enterprise, still promoted by his personal
exertions, his weight of character, and his invincible zeal. Possessed of whatever information could be derived from foreign
sources and a correspondence with eminent navigators of his
times, and anxiously watching the progress of Englishmen in
the west, his extensive knowledge made him a counsellor in
every colonial enterprise.

The king of England, too timid to be active, yet too vain to
be indifferent, favored the design of enlarging his dominions.
He had attempted in Scotland the introduction of the arts of
life among the Highlanders and the Western Isles, by the establishment of colonies; and the Scottish plantations which he
founded in the northern counties of Ireland contributed to the
affluence and the security of that island. When, therefore, a
company of men of business and men of rank, formed by the
experience of Gosnold, the enthusiasm of Smith, the perseverance of Hakluyt, the influence of Popham and Gorges, applied
to James I for leave "to deduce a colony into Virginia," the
monarch on the tenth of April, 1606, readily set his seal to an
ample patent.

The first colonial charter, under which the English were
planted in America, deserves careful consideration. A belt of
twelve degrees on the American coast, embracing the soil from

Cape Fear to Halifax, excepting perhaps the little spot in Acadia then actually possessed by the French, was set apart to be colonized by two rival companies. Of these, the first was composed of noblemen, gentlemen, and merchants, in and about London; the second, of knights, gentlemen, and merchants, in the west. The London adventurers, who alone succeeded, had an exclusive right to occupy the regions from thirty-four to thirty-eight degrees of north latitude, that is, from Cape Fear to the southern limit of Maryland; the western men had equally an exclusive right to plant between forty-one and forty-five degrees. The intermediate district, from thirty-eight to forty-one degrees, was open to the competition of both companies. Yet collision was not probable; for each was to possess the soil extending fifty miles north and south of its first settlement; so that neither might in the beginning plant within one hundred miles of its rival. The conditions of tenure were homage and rent; the rent was no other than one fifth of the net produce of gold and silver, and one fifteenth of copper. The right of coining money was conceded, perhaps to facilitate commerce with the natives, who, it was hoped, would receive Christianity and the arts of civilized life. The general superintendence was confided to a council in England; the local administration of each colony to a resident council. The members of the superior council in England were appointed exclusively by the king; and the tenure of their office was his good pleasure. Of the colonial councils, the members were from time to time to be ordained, made, and removed, according to his instructions. Supreme legislative authority over the colonies, extending to their general condition and the most minute regulations was reserved to the monarch. A duty, to be levied on vessels trading to its harbors, was, for one-and-twenty years, to be wholly employed for the benefit of the plantation; at the end of that time was to be taken for the king. To the emigrants it was promised that they and their children should continue to be Englishmen. Lands were to be held by the most favorable tenure.

The first written charter of a permanent American colony,

which was to be the chosen abode of liberty, gave to the mercantile corporation nothing but a desert territory, with the right of peopling and defending it, and reserved to the monarch absolute legislative authority, the control of all appointments, and a hope of an ultimate revenue. The emigrants were subjected to the ordinances of a commercial corporation, of which they could not be members; to the dominion of a domestic council, in appointing which they had no voice; to the control of a superior council in England, which had no sympathies with their rights; and, finally to the arbitrary legislation of the sovereign. The first "treasurer" or governor of the London company, to whom chiefly fell the management of its affairs, was Sir Thomas Smythe, a merchant zealous for extending the commerce of his country, but without a conception of popular rights, and not in the least inclined by his character to mitigate the authority of the corporation.

The summer was spent by the patentees in preparations for planting a colony, for which the king found a grateful occupation in framing a code of laws; an exercise of royal power which has been pronounced in itself illegal. The superior council in England was permitted to name the colonial council, which was independent of the emigrants whom it was to govern; having power to elect or remove its president, to remove any of its members, and to supply its own vacancies. Not an element of popular liberty was introduced. Religion was established according to the doctrine and rites of the church within the realm; and no emigrant might avow dissent, or affect the superstitions of the church of Rome, or withdraw his allegiance from King James. Lands were to descend according to the laws of England. Not only murder, manslaughter, and adultery, but dangerous tumults and seditions, were punishable by death; so that the security of life depended on the discretion of the magistrate, restricted only by the trial by jury. All civil causes, requiring corporal punishment, fine, or imprisonment, might be summarily determined by the president and council; who also possessed full legislative authority in cases not affecting life or limb. Kindness to the savages was enjoined, with the use of all proper means for their conversion. It was further ordered that the industry and commerce of the respective colonies should, for five years at least, be conducted in a joint stock. The king reserved to himself the right of future legislation.

Thus were the political forms of the colony established, when, on the nineteenth day of December, in the year of our Lord one thousand six hundred and six, one hundred and nine years after the discovery of the American continent by Cabot, forty-one years from the settlement of Florida, the squadron of three vessels, the largest not exceeding one hundred tons' burden, with the favor of all England, stretched their sails for "the dear strand of Virginia, earth's only paradise." Michael Drayton, the patriot poet "of Albion's glorious isle," cheered them on their voyage, saying,

> Go, and in regions far
> Such heroes bring ye forth
>   As those from whom we came;
>   And plant our name
> Under that star
> Not known unto our north.

Yet the enterprise was ill concerted. Of the one hundred and five, on the list of emigrants, there were but twelve laborers, and very few mechanics. They were going to a wilderness, in which, as yet, not a house was standing; and there were forty-eight gentlemen to four carpenters. Neither were there any men with families. Dissensions sprung up during the voyage; as the names and instructions of the council had, by the folly of James, been concealed in a box, which was not to be opened till after the arrival in Virginia, no competent authority existed to check envy and disorder. The superior capacity of Smith excited jealousy; and hope, the only power which can still the clamors and allay the feuds of the selfish, early deserted the colonists.

Newport, who commanded the ships, was acquainted with the old passage, and sailed by way of the Canaries and the West

India Islands. As he turned to the north, a severe storm, in April, 1607, carried his fleet beyond the settlement of Raleigh, into the magnificent Bay of the Chesapeake. The headlands received and retain the names of Cape Henry and Cape Charles, from the sons of King James; the deep water for anchorage, "putting the emigrants in good Comfort," gave a name to the northern Point; and within the capes a country opened, which appeared to "claim the prerogative over the most pleasant places in the world." "Heaven and earth seemed never to have agreed better to frame a place for man's commodious and delightful habitation." A noble river was soon entered, which was named from the monarch; and, after a search of seventeen days, during which the comers encountered the hostility of one savage tribe, and at Hampton smoked the calumet of peace with another, on the thirteenth of May the peninsula of Jamestown, about fifty miles above the mouth of the stream, was selected for the site of the colony.

Thus admirable was the country. The emigrants themselves were weakened by factious divisions. So soon as the council was duly constituted, its members proceeded to choose Wingfield president; and then, as by their instructions they had power to do, they excluded Smith from their body, on a charge of sedition. But the attempt at his trial was abandoned, and by "the good doctrine and exhortation" of Hunt, the man without whose aid the vices of the colony would have caused its immediate ruin, was restored to his station.

While the men were busy in felling timber and providing freight for the ships, Newport and Smith and twenty others ascended the James River to the falls. They visited the native chieftain Powhatan, "the emperor of the country," at his principal seat, just below the site of Richmond. The imperial residence was a village of twelve wigwams! The savages murmured at the intrusion of strangers into the country; but Powhatan disguised his fear, and would only say: "They hurt you not; they take but a little waste land."

About the middle of June, Newport set sail for England.

What condition could be more pitiable than that of the English whom he had left in Virginia? Weak in numbers, and still weaker from want of habits of industry, they were surrounded by natives whose hostility and distrust had already been displayed; the summer heats were intolerable to their laborers. Their scanty provisions had become spoiled on the long voyage. "Our drink," say they, "was unwholesome water; our lodgings, castles in the air: had we been as free from all sins as from gluttony and drunkenness, we might have been canonized for saints." Despair of mind ensued; in less than a fortnight after the departure of the fleet, "hardly ten of them were able to stand;" the labor of completing some simple fortifications was exhausting; and no regular crops could be planted. During the summer, there were not, on any occasion, five able men to guard the bulwarks; the fort was filled in every corner with the groans of the sick, whose outcries, night and day, for six weeks, rent the hearts of those who could minister no relief. Sometimes, three or four died in a night; in the morning, their bodies were trailed out of the cabins, like dogs, to be buried. Fifty men, one half of the colony, perished before autumn; among them Bartholomew Gosnold, a man of rare merits, worthy of a perpetual memory in the plantation, for he was its projector, and his influence had alone thus far preserved some degree of harmony in the council.

Disunion completed the scene of misery. Wingfield, the president, accused of appropriating public stores and designing to abandon the colony, was deposed. Ratcliffe, the new president, possessed neither judgment nor industry; so that the management of affairs fell into the hands of Smith, whose buoyant spirit of heroic daring diffused light amidst the general gloom. In boyhood, such is his own narrative, he had sighed for the opportunity of "setting out on brave adventures;" and, though not yet thirty years of age, he was already a veteran in service. He had fought for the independence of the Batavian republic; as a traveller, had roamed over France; had visited Egypt; had returned to Italy; and, panting for glory, had sought the borders

of Hungary, where there had long existed an hereditary warfare
with the followers of Mahomet. There he distinguished himself
by brave feats of arms, in the sight of Christians and infidels.
At length, in November, 1602, he, with many others, was over-
powered in a sudden skirmish among the glens of Wallachia;
and, as a prisoner of war, was sold "like a beast in a market-
place," and sent to Constantinople as a slave. Removed to the
Crimea, and there subjected to the harshest usage among half-
savage serfs, he rose against his taskmaster, whom he slew in
the struggle; mounted a horse, and through forest paths escaped to Transylvania. There bidding farewell to his companions in arms, he resolved to return "to his own sweet country;" but, on hearing rumors of civil war in Northern Africa,
he hastened, in search of untried dangers, to the realms of
Morocco. At length regaining England, his mind was wholly
mastered by the general enthusiasm for planting states in America; and now the infant commonwealth of Virginia depended
for its life on his firmness. He was more wakeful to gather
provisions than the covetous to find gold; and strove more to
keep the country than the faint-hearted to abandon it. As autumn approached, the Indians, from the superfluity of their
harvest, made a voluntary offering; and supplies were also collected by expeditions into the interior. But the conspiracies
that were still formed to desert the settlement, first by Wingfield, and again by Ratcliffe, could be defeated only after a
skirmish, in which one of the leaders was killed; and the danger
of a precipitate abandonment of Virginia continued to be imminent, till the approach of winter, when the homeward navigation became perilous, and the fear of famine was removed by
the abundance of wild fowl and game. Nothing then remained
but to examine the country.

The South Sea was considered the ocean path to every kind
of wealth. The coast of America on the Pacific had been explored by the Spaniards, and had been visited by Drake; the
collections of Hakluyt had communicated to the English the
results of their voyages; and the maps of that day exhibited a

tolerably accurate delineation of the continent of North America. Yet, with singular ignorance of the progress of geographical knowledge, it had been enjoined on the colonists to seek a communication with the South Sea by ascending some stream which flowed from the north-west. The Chickahominy was such a stream. Smith, though he did not share the ignorance of his employers, was ever willing to engage in discoveries; he not only ascended the river as far as he could advance in boats, but struck into the interior. His companions disobeyed his instructions, and, being surprised by the Indians, were put to death. Alone with his Indian guide, and environed in the woods by Opechancanough and his warriors, he gave himself up as a prisoner; but saved his life by displaying a pocket compass, and explaining its properties to the savage chief. His captors "used him with what kindness they could," listening to his discourse about ships and the manner of sailing the seas; about the earth and the skies, and about his God. They saved him from a warrior who would have taken vengeance on him for the loss of his son; and in the worst winter weather they sent his letters to the English fort on James River. From the villages on the Chickahominy he was escorted through many Indian towns to an audience with Powhatan, who chanced at that time to be on what is now York River. The emperor, studded with ornaments, clad in raccoon skins, proudly lying upon ten or twelve mats, and raised a little above the attendant warriors and women, showed a grave and majestical countenance as he welcomed him with good words and "great platters of sundrie" food; and gave assurance of friendship with a speedy restoration to liberty. After a few days, which he diligently used in inquiries respecting the country, "he was sent home," accompanied by four men, two of whom were laden with maize.

The relation of this adventure by Smith had no sooner reached England than, in the author's absence, it was instantly seized on for the press. These first printed "Newes from Virginia" made famous to English readers the name of Pocahontas, the daughter of Powhatan, a girl "of tenne" or "twelve" "years old, which not only for feature, countenance, and expression, much exceeded any of the rest of his people, but for wit and spirit was the only nonpareil of the country." The captivity of the bold explorer became a benefit to the colony; for he not only had observed with care the country between the James and the Potomac, and had gained some knowledge of the language and manners of the natives, but he established a peaceful intercourse between the English and the tribes of Powhatan. The child, to whom in later days he attributed his rescue from death, came to the fort with her companions, bringing baskets of corn for the garrison.

Restored to Jamestown after an absence of but four weeks, Smith found the colony reduced to forty men; and, of these, the strongest were preparing to escape with the pinnace. This attempt at desertion he repressed at the hazard of his life.

Meantime, the council in England, having received an increase of its numbers and its powers, determined to send out new recruits and supplies; and Newport had hardly returned from his first voyage, before he was again despatched with one hundred and twenty emigrants. Yet the joy in Virginia on their arrival was of short continuance; for the new comers were chiefly vagabond gentlemen and goldsmiths, who soon persuaded themselves that they had discovered grains of gold in a glittering earth which abounded near Jamestown; and "there was now no talk, no hope, no work, but dig gold, wash gold, refine gold, load gold." Martin, one of the council promised himself honors in England as the discoverer of a mine; and Newport believed himself rich as he embarked for England with a freight of worthless earth.

Disgusted at the follies which he had vainly opposed, declining for the moment the office of president, Smith undertook the perilous and honorable office of exploring the Bay of the Chesapeake, and the rivers which it receives. Two voyages, in an open boat, with a few companions, over whom his superior courage, rather than his station as a magistrate, gave him authority, occupied him about three months of the summer, and embraced a navigation of nearly three thousand miles. The slenderness of his means has been contrasted with the dignity and utility of his discoveries, and his name has been placed among the ever memorable men who have enlarged the bounds of geographical knowledge, and opened the way for colonies and commerce. He surveyed the Bay of the Chesapeake to the Susquehannah, and left only the borders of that remote river to remain for some years longer the fabled dwelling-place of a giant progeny. He was the first to publish to the English the power of the Mohawks, "who dwelt upon a great water, and had many boats, and many men," and, as it seemed to the feebler Algonkin tribes, "made war upon all the world;" in the Chesapeake, he encountered a fleet of their canoes. The Patapsco was discovered and explored, and Smith probably entered the harbor of Baltimore. The majestic Potomac especially invited curiosity; and he ascended beyond Mount Vernon and Washington to the falls above Georgetown. Nor did he merely examine the rivers and inlets. He penetrated the territories, and laid the foundation for future beneficial intercourse with the native tribes. The map which he prepared and sent to the company in London delineates correctly the great outlines of nature. The expedition was worthy the romantic age of American history.

On the tenth of September, 1608, three days after his return, Smith was made president of the council. Order and industry began to be diffused when Newport, with a second supply, entered the river. About seventy new emigrants arrived; two of whom were females. The charge of the voyage was two thousand pounds; unless the ships should return full freighted with commodities, corresponding in value to the costs of the adventure, the colonists were threatened that "they should be left in Virginia as banished men." Neither had experience taught the company to engage suitable emigrants. "When you send again," Smith was obliged to write, "I entreat you rather send but thirty carpenters, husbandmen, gardeners, fishermen, blacksmiths, masons, and diggers up of trees' roots, well provided, than a thousand of such as we have."

In 1609, after the departure of the ships, Smith employed his authority to enforce industry. Six hours in the day were spent in work; the rest might be given to pastime. The gentlemen had learned the use of the axe, and had become accomplished woodcutters. "He who would not work, might not eat;" and Jamestown assumed the appearance of a regular place of abode. Yet so little land was under culture that it was still necessary to gather food from the Indians. Thus the season passed away; of two hundred in the colony, not more than seven died. In the spring, the culture of maize was taught by two savages; and thirty or forty acres were "digged and planted."

The golden anticipations of the London company had not been realized; but the cause of failure appeared in the policy, which had grasped at sudden emoluments. Undaunted by the train of misfortunes, the kingdom awoke to the greatness of the undertaking, and designs worthy of the English nation were conceived. The second charter of Virginia, which, at the request of the former corporation, passed the seals on the twenty-third of May, 1609, intrusted the colonization of that land to a very numerous and opulent and influential body of adventurers. The name of Robert Cecil, Earl of Salisbury, the inveterate enemy and successful rival of Raleigh, appears at the head of those who were to carry into execution the grand design to which Raleigh, now a close prisoner in the Tower, had roused the attention of his countrymen. Among the many hundreds whose names followed, were the Earls of Southampton, Lincoln, and Dorset, George Percy, Sir Oliver Cromwell, uncle to the future protector, Sir Anthony Ashley, Sir Edwin Sandys, Si Francis Bacon, Captain John Smith, Richard Hakluyt, George Sandys, many tradesmen, and five-and-fifty public companies of London; so that the nobility and gentry, the army and the bar, the industry and trade of England, were represented.

The territory granted to the company extended two hundred miles to the north, and as many to the south of Old Point Comfort, "up into the land throughout from sea to sea, west and north-west;" including "all the islands lying within one hundred miles along the coast of both seas of the precinct."

At the request of the corporation, the new charter transferred to the company the powers which had before been reserved to the king. The perpetual supreme council in England was now to be chosen by the shareholders themselves, and, in the exercise of the functions of legislation and government, was independent of the monarch. The governor in Virginia, whom the corporation was to appoint, might rule the colonists with uncontrolled authority, according to the tenor of instructions and laws established by the council, or, in want of them, according to his own good discretion, even in cases capital and criminal, not less than civil; and, in the event of mutiny or rebellion, he might declare martial law, being himself the judge of the necessity of the measure, and the executive officer in its administration. If not one valuable civil privilege was guaranteed to the emigrants, they were at least withdrawn from the power of the king; and the company could at its pleasure endow them with all the rights of Englishmen.

BANCROFT *prefaced his account of the voyage of the "Mayflower" with a lenghty history of religious arguments in England during the reign of James and an analysis of the political implications of Calvinism, pointing out that "the enfranchisement of the mind from religious despotism led directly to inquiries into the nature of civil government." The Puritans, he wrote, eventually became "the sole guardians of popular liberty" in an authoritarian England, bringing that precious gift in the "Mayflower" to the shores of New England. Because those "doctrines of popular liberty" which came with them "infused themselves into the lifeblood" of all of Western civilization, Bancroft wrote of the Pilgrims' voyage and subsequent experiences with almost biblical reverence and finality.*

The Pilgrims

AND now the English at Leyden, trusting in God and in themselves, made ready for their departure. The ships which they had provided—the "Speedwell," of sixty tons, the "Mayflower," of one hundred and eighty tons—could hold but a minority of the congregation; and Robinson was therefore detained at Leyden, while Brewster, the governing elder, who was also an able teacher, conducted "such of the youngest and strongest as freely offered themselves." Every enterprise of the pilgrims began from God. A solemn fast was held. "Let us seek of God," said they, "a right way for us, and for our little ones, and for all our substance." Anticipating their high destiny, and the sublime lessons of liberty that would grow out of their religious tenets, Robinson gave them a farewell, breathing a freedom of opinion and an independence of authority such as then were hardly known in the world.

"I charge you, before God and his blessed angels, that you follow me no further than you have seen me follow the Lord Jesus Christ. The Lord has more truth yet to break forth out of his holy word. I cannot sufficiently bewail the condition of the reformed churches, who are come to a period in religion, and will go at present no further than the instruments of their reformation. Luther and Calvin were great and shining lights in their times, yet they penetrated not into the whole counsel of God. I beseech you, remember it,—'tis an article of your church covenant,—that you be ready to receive whatever truth shall be made known to you from the written word of God."

"When the ship was ready to carry us away," writes Edward Winslow, "the brethren that stayed at Leyden, having again solemnly sought the Lord with us and for us, feasted us that were to go, at our pastor's house, being large; where we refreshed ourselves, after tears, with singing of psalms, making joyful melody in our hearts, as well as with the voice, there being many of the congregation very expert in music; and indeed it was the sweetest melody that ever mine ears heard. After this they accompanied us to Delft-Haven, where we went to embark, and then feasted us again; and, after prayer performed by our pastor, when a flood of tears was poured out, they accompanied us to the ship, but were not able to speak one to another for the abundance of sorrow to part. But we only, going aboard, gave them a volley of small shot and three pieces of ordnance; and so, lifting up our hands to each other, and our hearts for each other to the Lord our God, we departed." A prosperous wind soon wafts the vessel to Southampton; and in a fortnight the "Mayflower" and the "Speedwell," freighted with the first colony of New England, leave Southampton for America. But they had not gone far upon the Atlantic before the smaller vessel was found to need repairs, and they entered the port of Dartmouth. After the lapse of eight precious days, they again weigh anchor; the coast of England recedes; already they are unfurling their sails on the broad ocean, when the captain of the "Speedwell," with his company, dismayed at the dangers of the enterprise, once more pretends that his ship is too weak for the service. They put back to Plymouth, "and agree to dismiss her, and those who are willing return to London, though this was very grievous and discouraging." Having thus winnowed their numbers, the little band, not of resolute men only, but wives, some far gone in pregnancy, children, infants, a floating village of one hundred and two souls, went on board the single ship, which was hired only to convey them across the Atlantic; and, on the sixth day of September, 1620, thirteen years after the first colonization of Virginia, two months before the concession of the grand charter of Plymouth, without any warrant from the sovereign of England, without any useful charter from a corporate body, the passengers in the "Mayflower" set sail for a new world, where the past could offer no favorable auguries.

Had New England been colonized immediately on the discovery of the American continent, the old English institutions would have been planted with the Roman Catholic hierarchy; had the settlement been made under Elizabeth, it would have been before activity of the popular mind in religion had conducted to a corresponding activity of mind in politics. The pilgrims were Englishmen, Protestants, exiles for conscience, men disciplined by misfortune, cultivated by opportunities of extensive observation, equal in rank as in rights, and bound by no code but that of religion or the public will.

The eastern coast of the United States abounds in beautiful and convenient harbors, in majestic bays and rivers. The first Virginia colony, sailing along the shores of North Carolina, was, by a favoring storm, driven into the magnificent Bay of the Chesapeake; the pilgrims, having selected for their settlement the country near the Hudson, the best position on the whole coast, were conducted to the most barren part of Massachusetts. After a boisterous voyage of sixty-three days, during which one person had died, they espied land; and, in two days more, cast anchor in the harbor of Cape Cod.

Yet, before they landed, the manner in which their government should be constituted was considered; and, as some were observed "not well affected to unity and concord," they formed themselves into a body politic by a solemn voluntary compact:—

"In the name of God, amen; we, whose names are underwritten, the loyal subjects of our dread sovereign King James, having undertaken, for the glory of God, and advancement of the Christian faith, and honor of our king and country, a voyage to plant the first colony in the northern parts of Virginia, do, by these presents, solemnly and mutually, in the presence of God and one of another, covenant and combine ourselves together, into a civil body politic, for our better ordering and preservation, and furtherance of the ends aforesaid; and, by vitue hereof, to enact, constitute, and frame such just and equal laws, ordinances, acts, constitutions, and offices, from time to time, as shall be thought most convenient for the general good of the colony. Unto which we promise all due submission and obedience."

This instrument was signed by the whole body of men, forty-one in number, who, with their families, constituted the one hundred and two, the whole colony, "the proper democracy," that arrived in New England. Here was the birth of popular constitutional liberty. The middle age had been familiar with charters and constitutions; but they had been merely compacts for immunities, partial enfranchisements, patents of nobility, concessions of municipal privileges, or limitations of the sovereign power in favor of feudal institutions. In the cabin of the "Mayflower," humanity recovered its rights, and instituted government on the basis of "equal laws" enacted by all the people for "the general good." John Carver was immediately and unanimously chosen governor for the year.

Men who emigrate, even in well-inhabited districts, pray that their journey may not be in winter. Wasted by the rough voyage, scantily supplied with provisions, the English fugitives found themselves, at the opening of winter, on a bleak and barren coast, in a severe climate, with the ocean on one side and the wilderness on the other. There were none to show them kindness or bid them welcome. The nearest French settlement was at Port Royal; it was five hundred miles to the English plantation at Virginia. As they attempted to disembark, the water was found so shallow that they were forced to wade; and, in the freezing weather, this sowed the seeds of consumption. The bitterness of mortal disease was their welcome to the inhospitable shore.

Winter was at hand, and the spot for the settlement remained to be chosen. The shallop was unshipped; and it was a real disaster to find that it needed repairs. The carpenter made slow work, so that sixteen or seventeen days elapsed before it was ready for service. But Standish and Bradford, and others, impatient of the delay, determined to explore the country by land. "In regard to the danger," the expedition "was rather permitted than approved." Much hardship was endured; but what beneficial discoveries could be made in the deep sands near Paomet Creek? The first expedition in the shallop was likewise unsuccessful; "some of the people, that died that winter, took the original of their death" in the enterprise; "for it snowed and did blow all the day and night, and froze withal." The men who were set on shore "were tired with marching up and down the steep hills and deep valleys, which lay half a foot thick with snow." A heap of maize was discovered; and further search led to a burial-place of the Indians; but they found "no more corn, nor any thing else but graves."

At length, the shallop was again sent out, with Carver, Bradford, Winslow, Standish, and others, and eight or ten seamen. The spray of the sea froze as it fell on them, and made their clothes like coats of iron. That day, they reached Billingsgate Point, at the bottom of the Bay of Cape Cod, on the western shore of Wellfleet harbor. The next morning, the company divided; those on shore find a burial-place, graves, and four or five deserted wigwams, but neither people, nor any place inviting a settlement. Before night, the whole party met by the seaside, and encamped on land together near Namskeket, or Great Meadow Creek.

The next day, they rose at five; their morning prayers were finished, when, as the day dawned, a war-whoop and a flight of arrows announced an attack from Indians. They were of the

tribe of the Nausites, who knew the English as kidnappers; but
the encounter was without further result. Again the boat's crew
give thanks to God, and steer their bark along the coast for the
distance of fifteen leagues. But no convenient harbor is discovered. The pilot, who had been in these regions before, gives
assurance of a good one, which may be reached before night;
and they follow his guidance. After some hours' sailing, a storm
of snow and rain begins; the sea swells; the rudder breaks; the
boat must now be steered with oars; the storm increases; night
is at hand; to reach the harbor before dark, as much sail as
possible is borne; the mast breaks into three pieces; the sail
falls overboard; but the tide is favorable. The pilot, in dismay,
would have run the boat on shore in a cove full of breakers.
"About with her," exclaimed a sailor, "or we are cast away."
They get her about immediately; and, passing over the surf,
they enter a fair sound, and shelter themselves under the lee of
a small rise of land. It is dark, and the rain beats furiously;
yet the men are so wet, and cold, and weak, they slight the
danger to be apprehended from the savages, and, after great
difficulty, kindle a fire on shore.

The light of morning showed the place to be a small island
within the entrance of a harbor. The day was required for rest
and preparations. Time was precious; the season advancing;
their companions were left in suspense. The next day was the
"Christian sabbath;" and the pilgrims kept it sacredly, though
every consideration demanded haste.

On Monday, the eleventh of December, old style, on the very
day of the winter solstice, the exploring party of the forefathers
land at Plymouth. A grateful posterity has marked the rock
on which they first trod. That day is kept as the origin of New
England, the planting of its institutions. Historians love to
trace every vestige of the pilgrims; poets commemorate their
virtues; the noblest genius has been called into exercise to display their merits worthily, and to trace the consequences of
their enterprise.

The spot, when examined, invited a settlement; and, in a few days, the "Mayflower" was safely moored in its harbor. In memory of the hospitalities which the company had received at the last English port from which they had sailed, this oldest New England colony took the name of Plymouth. The system of civil government had been established by common agreement; the church had been fully organized before it left Leyden. As the pilgrims landed, their institutions were already perfected. "A commonwealth was in the bud." Democratic liberty and independent Christian worship started into being. . . .

The men of Plymouth exercised self-government without the sanction of a royal charter, which it was ever impossible for them to obtain; so that, according to the principles adopted in England, the planters, with an unquestionable property in the soil, had no right to assume a separate jurisdiction. It was therefore in the colonists themselves that their institutions found a guarantee for stability. They never hesitated to punish small offences; it was only after some scruples that they inflicted capital punishment. Their doubts being once removed, they exercised the same authority as the charter governments. Death was, by subsequent laws, made the penalty for several crimes, but was never inflicted except for murder. House-breaking and highway robbery were offences unknown in their courts, and too little apprehended to be made subjects of severe legislation.

"To enjoy religious liberty was the known end of the first comers' great adventure into this remote wilderness;" and they desired no increase but from the friends of their communion. Yet their residence in Holland had made them acquainted with various forms of Christianity; a wide experience had emancipated them from bigotry; and they were never betrayed into the excesses of religious persecution, though they sometimes permitted a disproportion between punishment and crime. In 1645, a majority of the house of delegates were in favor of an act to "allow and maintain full and free toleration to all men that would preserve the civil peace and submit unto government; and there was no limitation or exception against Turk, Jew, Papist, Arian, Socinian, Nicolaitan, Familist, or any other;" but the governor, fearing it would "eat out the power of godliness," refused to put the question, and so stifled the law.

It is chiefly as guides and pioneers that the fathers of the old colony merit gratitude. Through scenes of gloom and misery, the pilgrims showed the way to an asylum for those who would go to the wilderness for the liberty of conscience. Accustomed "in their native land to a plain country life and the innocent trade of husbandry," they set the example of colonizing New England with freeholders, and formed the mould for the civil and religious character of its institutions. Enduring every hardship themselves, they were the servants of posterity, the benefactors of succeeding generations. In the history of the world, many pages are devoted to commemorate the men who have besieged cities, subdued provinces, or overthrown empires. In the eye of reason and of truth, a colony is a better offering than a victory; it is more fit to cherish the memory of those who founded a state on the basis of democratic liberty; the men who, as they first trod the soil of the New World, scattered the seminal principles of republican freedom and national independence. They enjoyed, in anticipation, their extending influence, and the fame which their successors would award to their virtues. "Out of small beginnings," said Bradford, "great things have been produced; and as one small candle may light a thousand, so the light here kindled hath shone to many, yea, in some sort to our whole nation." "Let it not be grievous to you," such was the consolation offered from England to the pilgrims in the season of their greatest sufferings, "let it not be grievous to you, that you have been instruments to break the ice for others. The honor shall be yours to the world's end." "Yea, the memory of the adventurers to this plantation shall never die."

IN WRITING *of the Massachusetts Bay colonists, as he had of the Virginians, Bancroft emphasized the desire for freedom as their major motivation. Since "purity of religion and civil liberty were the objects nearest to the wishes of the emigrants," he found that "freedom and liberty of conscience" formed "the principles and foundation of the charter of Massachusetts" and provided the earliest expression of the American search for freedom.*

The Extended Colonization of New England

AT A very full general court, convened on the twentieth of October [1629] for the choice of new officers out of those who were to join the plantation, John Winthrop, of Groton in Suffolk, of whom "extraordinary great commendations had been received both for his integrity and sufficiency, as being one altogether well fitted and accomplished for the place of governor," was by erection of hands elected to that office for one year from that day; and with him were joined a deputy and assistants, of whom nearly all proposed to go over. The greatness of the undertaking brought a necessity for a supply of money. It was resolved that the business should be proceeded in with its first intention, which was chiefly the glory of God; and to that purpose its meetings were sanctified by the prayers and guided by the advice of Archer and Nye, two faithful ministers in London. Of the old stock of the company, two thirds had been lost; the remainder, taken at its true value, with fresh sums adventured by those that pleased, formed a new stock, which was to be managed by ten undertakers, five chosen out of adventurers remaining in England, and five out of the planters. The undertakers, receiving privileges in the fur-trade and in transportation, assumed all engagements and charges, and after seven years were to divide the stock and profits; but their privileges were not asserted, and nine-tenths of the capital were sunk in the expenses of the first year. There was nothing to show for the adventure but the commonwealth which it helped to found. Of ships for transporting passengers, Cradock furnished two. The large ship, the "Eagle," purchased by members of the company, took the name of "Arbella," from a sister of the Earl of Lincoln, wife to Isaac Johnson, who was to go in it to the untried sorrows of the wilderness. The corporation, which had not many more than one hundred and ten members, could not meet the continual outlays for colonization; another common stock was therefore raised from such as bore good affection to the plantation, to defray public charges, such as maintenance of ministers, transportation of poor families, building of churches and fortifications. To the various classes of contributors and emigrants, frugal grants of land promised some indemnity. In this manner, by the enterprise of the ten undertakers and other members of the company, especially of those who were shipowners, by the contributions of Puritans in England, but mainly by the resources of the emigrants themselves, there were employed, during the season of 1630, seventeen vessels, which brought over not far from a thousand souls, beside horses, kine, goats, and all that was most necessary for planting, fishing, and ship-building.

As the hour of departure drew near, the hearts of some even of the strong began to fail. On the eighteenth of March, it became necessary at Southampton to elect three substitutes among the assistants; and, of these three, one never came over. Even after they had embarked, a court was held on board the "Arbella," and Thomas Dudley was chosen deputy governor in the place of Humphrey, who stayed behind. It was principally the calm decision of Winthrop which sustained the courage of his companions. In him a yielding gentleness of temper, and a never failing desire for unity and harmony, were secured against weakness by deep but tranquil enthusiasm. His nature was touched by the sweetest sympathies of affection for wife, children, and associates; cheerful in serving others and suffering with them, liberal without repining, helpful without reproaching, in him God so exercised his grace that he discerned his own image and resemblance in his fellow-man, and cared for his neighbor like himself. He was of a sociable nature; so that "to love and be beloved was his soul's paradise," and works of mercy were the habit of his life. Parting from affluence in England, he unrepiningly went to meet impoverishment and premature age for the welfare of Massachusetts. His lenient benevolence tempered the bigotry of his companions, without impairing their resoluteness. An honest royalist, averse to pure democracy, yet firm in his regard for existing popular liberties; in his native parish, a conformist, yet wishing for "gospel purity;" in America, mildly aristocratic, advocating a government of "the least part," yet desiring the part to be "the wiser of the best;" disinterested, brave, and conscientious,—his character marks the transition of the reformation into virtual republicanism. The sentiment of loyalty, which he was still intended to cherish, gradually yielded to the unobstructed spirit of civil freedom.

England rung from side to side with the "general rumor of this solemn enterprise." On leaving the Isle of Wight, Winthrop, and the chief of his fellow passengers on board the "Arbella," including the ministers, bade an affectionate farewell "to the rest of their brethren in and of the church of England." "Reverend fathers and brethren," such was their address to them, "howsoever your charitie may have met with discouragement through the misreport of our intentions, or the indiscretion of some amongst us, yet we desire you would be pleased to take notice that the principals and body of our company esteem it our honour to call the church of England, from whence we rise, our deare mother, and cannot depart from our native countrie, where she specially resideth, without much sadnes of heart and many tears in our eyes; blessing God for the parentage and education, as members of the same body, and, while we have breath, we shall syncerely indeavour the continuance and abundance of her welfare.

"Be pleased, therefore, reverend fathers and brethren, to helpe forward this worke now in hand; which, if it prosper, you shall bee the more glorious. It is a usuall exercise of your charity to recommend to the prayers of your congregations the straights of your neighbours: do the like for a church springing out of you owne bowels; pray without ceasing for us, who are a weake colony from yourselves.

"What we intreat of you that are ministers of God, that we crave at the hands of all the rest of our brethren, that they would at no time forget us in their private solicitations at the Throne of Grace. If any, through want of cleare intelligence of our course, or tenderness of affection towards us, cannot conceive so well of our way as we could desire, we would intreat such not to desert us in their prayers, and to express their compassion towards us.

"What goodness you shall extend to us, wee, your brethren in Christ Jesus, shall labour to repay; wishing our heads and hearts may be as fountains of tears for your everlasting welfare, when wee shall be in our poore cottages in the wildernesse, overshadowed with the spirit of supplication, through the manifold necessities and tribulations which may not altogether unexpectedly, nor, we hope, unprofitably befall us."

About seven hundred persons or more—most of them Puritans, inclining to the principles of the Independents; not conformists, but not separatists; many of them men of high endowments and large fortune; scholars, well versed in the learning of the times; clergymen, who ranked among the best educated and most pious in the realm—embarked with Winthrop in eleven ships, bearing with them the charter which was to be the warrant of their liberties. The land was to be planted with a noble vine, wholly of the right seed. The principal emigrants were a community of believers, professing themselves to be fellow-members of Christ; not a school of philosophers, proclaiming universal toleration and inviting associates without regard to creed. They desired to be bound together in a most intimate and equal intercourse, for one and the same great end. They knew that they would be as a city set upon a hill, and that the eyes of all people were upon them. Reverence for their faith led them to pass over the vast seas to the good land of which they had purchased the exclusive possession, with a charter of which they had acquired the entire control, for the sake of reducing to practice the system of religion and the forms of civil liberty, which they cherished more than life itself. They constituted a corporation to which they themselves might establish the terms of admission. They kept firmly in their own hands the key to their asylum, and were resolved on closing its doors against the enemies of its unity, its safety, and its peace.

"The worke wee have in hand," these are Winthrop's words on board the "Arbella" during the passage, "is by a mutuall consent, through a speciall overruling Providence, and a more than ordinary approbation of the churches of Christ, to seeke out a place of cohabitation and consorteshipp under a due forme of government both civill and ecclesiastical. For this wee are entered into covenant with God; for this wee must be knitt together as one man, allways having before our eyes our commission as members of the same body. Soe shall wee keepe the unitie of the spirit in the bond of peace. The Lord will be our God, and delight to dwell among us, as his owne people; wee shall see much more of his wisdome, power, goodness, and truthe, than formerly wee have been acquainted with; hee shall make us a prayse and glory, that men shall say of succeeding plantations, 'The Lord make it likely that of New England.' "

After sixty-one days at sea, the "Arbella" came in sight of Mount Desert; on the tenth of June [1630], the White Hills were descried afar off; near the Isle of Shoals and Cape Ann, the sea was enlivened by the shallops of fishermen; and on the twelfth, as the ship came to anchor outside of Salem harbor, it was visited by William Peirce, of the "Lyon," whose frequent voyages had given him experience, as a pilot on the coast. Winthrop and his companions came full of hope; they found the colony in an "unexpected condition" of distress. Above eighty had died the winter before. Higginson himself was wasting under a hectic fever; many others were weak and sick; all the corn and bread among them was hardly a fit supply for a fortnight. The survivors of one hundred and eighty servants, who had been sent over in the two years before at a great expense, instead of having prepared a welcome, thronged to the new comers to be fed; and were set free from all engagements, for their labor, great as was the demand for it, was worth less than their support. Famine threatened to seize the emigrants as they stepped on shore; and it soon appeared necessary for them, even at a ruinous expense, to send the "Lyon" to Bristol for food.

To seek out a place for their plantation, since Salem pleased them not, Winthrop, on the seventeenth of June, sailed into Boston harbor. The west country men, who, before leaving England, had organized their church with Maverick and Warham for ministers, and who in a few years were to take part in calling into being the commonwealth of Connecticut, were found at Nantasket, where they had landed just before the end of May. Winthrop ascended the Mystic a few miles, and on the nineteenth took back to Salem a favorable report of the land on its banks. Dudley and others, who followed, preferred the country on the Charles River at Watertown. By common consent, early in the next month the removal was made, with much cost and labor, from Salem to Charlestown. But, while drooping with toil and sorrow, fevers consequent on the long voyage, and the want of proper food and shelter, twelve ships having arrived, the colonists kept the eighth of July as a day of thanksgiving. The emigrants had intended to dwell together, but in their distress they planted where each was inclined. A few remained at Salem; others halted at the Saugus, and founded Lynn. The governor was for the time at Charlestown, where the poor "lay up and down in tents and booths round the Hill." On the other side of the river, the little peninsula, scarce two miles long by one broad, marked by three hills, and blessed with sweet and pleasant springs, safe pastures, and land that promised "rich cornfields and fruitful gardens," attracted, among others, William Coddington of Boston in England, who, in friendly relations with William Blackstone, built the first good house there, even before it took the name which was to grow famous throughout the world. Some planted on the Mystic, in what is now Malden. Others, with Sir Richard Saltonstall and George Phillips, "a godly minister specially gifted, and very peaceful in his place," made their abode at Watertown; Pynchon and a few began Roxbury; Ludlow and Rossiter, two of the assistants, with the men from the west of England, after wavering in their choice, took possession of Dorchester Neck, now South Boston. The dispersion of the company was esteemed a grievance; but it was no time for crimination or debate, and those who had health made haste to build. Winthrop himself, "givinge good example to all the planters, wore plaine apparell, drank ordinarily water, and, when he was not conversant about matters of justice, put his hand to labour with his servants."

The enjoyment of the gospel as the dearest covenant that can be made between God and man was the chief object of the emigrants. On Friday, the thirtieth of July, a fast was held at Charlestown; and, after prayers and preaching, Winthrop, Dudley, Isaac Johnson, and Wilson united themselves by covenant into one "congregation," as a part of the visible church militant. On the next Lord's Day, others were received; and the members of this body could alone partake of the Lord's Supper, or present their children for baptism. They were all brothers and equals; they revered, each in himself, the dignity of God's image, and nursed a generous reverence for one another; bound to a healing superintendence over each other's lives, they exercised no discipline to remove evil out of the inmost soul, except the censure of the assembly of the faithful, whom it would have been held grievous to offend. This church, the seminal centre of the ecclesiastical system of Massachusetts, was gathered while Higginon was yet alive; on the sixth of August, he gave up the ghost with joy, for the future greatness of New England, and the coming glories of its many churches, floated in cheerful visions before his eyes. When, on the twenty-third of August, the first court of assistants on this side the water was held at

Charlestown, how the ministers should be maintained took precedence of all other business; and it was ordered that houses should be built for them, and support provided at the common charge. Four days later, the men "of the congregation" kept a fast, and, after their own free choice of John Wilson for their pastor, they themselves set him apart to his office by the imposition of hands, yet without his renouncing his ministry received in England. In like manner, the ruling elder and deacons were chosen and installed. Thus was constituted the body which, crossing the Charles River, became known as the First Church of Boston. It imbodied the three great principles of Congregationalism: a right faith attended by a true religious experience as the requisite qualifications for membership; the equality of all believers, including the officers of the church; the equality of the several churches, free from the jurisdiction of ecclesiastical court or bishop, free from the jurisdiction of one church over another, free from the collective authority of them all.

The civil government was exercised with mildness and impartiality, yet with determined vigor. Justices of the peace were commissioned with the powers of those in England. On the seventh of September, names were given to Dorchester, Watertown, and Boston, which thus began their career as towns under sanction of law. Quotas were settled and money levied. The interloper who dared to "confront" the public authority was sent to England, or enjoined to depart out of the limits of the patent.

As the year for which Winthrop and the assistants had been chosen was coming to an end, on the nineteenth of October, a general court, the first in America, was held at Boston. Of members of the company, less than twenty had come over. One hundred and eight inhabitants, some of whom were old planters, were now, at their desire, admitted to be freemen. The former officers of government were continued: as a rule for the future, "it was propounded to the people, and assented unto by the erection of hands, that the freemen should have power to choose assistants, when any were to be chosen; the assistants to choose from among themselve the governor and his deputy." The rule implied a strong reluctance to leave out of the board any person once elected magistrate; and perhaps also revealed a natural anxiety respecting the effect of the large creation of freemen which had just been made, and by which the old members of the company had abdicated their controlling power in the court; but, as it was in conflict with the charter, it could have no permanence.

During these events, sickness delayed the progress of the settlements, and death often withdrew the laborer from the fruit of his exertions. Every hardship was encountered. The emigrants, miserably lodged, beheld their friends "weekly, yea, almost daily, drop away before their eyes;" in a country abounding in secret fountains, they pined for the want of good water. Many of them had been accustomed to plenty and ease, the refinements, and the conveniences of luxury. Woman was there to struggle against unforeseen hardships, unwonted sorrows; the men, who defied trials for themselves, were miserable at beholding those whom they cherished dismayed by the horrors which encompassed them. The virtues of the lady Arbella Johnson could not break through the gloom; and, as she had been ill before her arrival, grief hurried her to the grave. Her husband, a wise and holy man, in life "the greatest furtherer of the plantation," and by his bequests a large benefactor of the infant state, sank under disease and afflictions; but "he died willingly and in sweet peace," making a "most godly end." Winthrop lost a son, who left a widow and children in England. A hundred or more, some of them of the board of assistants, men who had been trusted as the inseparable companions of the common misery or the common success, disheartened by the scenes of woe, and dreading famine and death, deserted Massachusetts, and sailed for England; while Winthrop remained, "parent-like, to distribute his goods to brethren and neighbors." Before December, two hundred, at the least, had died. Yet, as the brightest lightnings are kindled in the darkest clouds, the general distress did but augment the piety and confirm the fortitude of the colonists. Their earnestness was softened by the mildest sympathy; while trust in Providence kept guard against weakness and despair. Not a trace of repining appears in their records; the congregations always assembled at the stated times, whether in the open fields or under the shade of an ancient oak; in the midst of want, they abounded in hope; in the solitudes of the wilderness, they believed themselves watched over by an omnipresent Father. Honor is due not less to those who perished than to those who survived: to the martyrs, the hour of death was an hour of triumph such as is never witnessed in more tranquil seasons. For that placid resignation, which diffuses grace round the bed of sickness, and makes death too serene for sorrow and too beautiful for fear, no one was more remarkable than the daughter of Thomas Sharpe, whose youth and sex and unequalled virtues won the eulogies of the austere Dudley. Even children caught the spirit of the place; awaited the impending change in the tranquil confidence of faith, and went to the grave full of immortality. The survivors bore all things meekly, "remembering the end of their coming hither." "We here enjoy God and Jesus Christ," wrote Winthrop to his wife, whom pregnancy had detained in England, "and is not this enough? I thank God I like so well to be here, as I do not repent my coming. I would not have altered my course, though I had foreseen all these afflictions. I never had more content of mind."

ONE OF *the strengths of Bancroft's* History *lay in his awareness, unusual for the times, of the importance of what would now be called social, cultural, and intellectual history. Having reached the point in his narrative at which the English colonies in America could be said to have gained permanence and stability, he paused to describe and assess the characteristics of the two major colonial cultures—New England and Virginia—finding in them a common "love of personal independence" and "freedom of conscience" which, he wrote in 1837, "neither distorted by fanaticism, nor subdued by superstition, nor wounded by persecutions . . . , but fondly cherishing the active instinct for personal freedom, secure possession, and legislative power . . . made its dwelling place" in America. Bancroft anticipated Herbert Baxter Adams, John Fiske, and the later school of Teutonic historians by tracing the roots of the New England political tradition back to early British and Germanic origins; Virginians, too, he said in the first edition of Volume II, were more than anything else "Anglo-Saxons in the woods again." Bancroft emphasized constantly the importance of the fact that the great majority of early colonists were Anglo-Saxon, Christian, and Protestant, who brought with them neither monarchy, nor feudalism, nor a state church, nor guilds, nor any of the trappings of European absolutism—"Nothing came from Europe but a free people."*

The United Colonies of New England

. . . A NATION was already planted in New England; a commonwealth was ripened; the contests in which the unfortunate Charles became engaged, and the republican revolution that followed, left the colonists, for the space of twenty years, nearly unmolested in the enjoyment of virtual independence. The change which their industry had wrought in the wilderness was the admiration of their times. The wigwams and hovels in which the English had at first found shelter were replaced by well-built houses. The number of emigrants who had arrived in New England before the assembling of the Long Parliament is esteemed to have been twenty-one thousand two hundred. Two hundred and ninety-eight ships had borne them across the Atlantic; and the cost of the plantations had been almost a million of dollars, a great expenditure and a great emigration for that age. In a little more than ten years, fifty towns and villages had been planted; between thirty and forty churches built; and strangers, as they gazed, could not but acknowledge God's blessing on the endeavors of the planters. A public school, for which on the eighth of September, 1636, the general court made provision, was, in the next year, established at Cambridge; and when, in 1638, John Harvard, a non-conformist clergyman, a church member and freeman of Charlestown, esteemed for godliness and the love of learning, bequeathed to it his library and half his fortune, it was named Harvard College. "To complete the colony in church and commonwealth work," Jose Glover, a worthy minister, "able in estate," and of a liberal spirit, in that same year embarked for Boston with fonts of letters for printing, and a printer. He died on the passage; but, in 1639, Stephen Daye, the printer, printed the Freeman's Oath, and an Almanac calculated for New England; and, in 1640, "for the edification and comfort of the saints," the Psalms, faithfully but rudely translated in metre from the Hebrew by Thomas Welde and John Eliot, ministers of Roxbury, assisted by Richard Mather, minister of Dorchester, were published in a volume of three hundred octavo pages, the first book printed in America, north of the city of Mexico.

In temporal affairs, plenty prevailed throughout the settlements, and affluence came in the train of industry. The natural exports of the country were furs and lumber; grain was carried to the West Indies; fish also was a staple. The art of ship-building was introduced with the first emigrants to Salem; but "Winthrop had with him William Stephens, a shipwright, who had been preparing to go for Spain, and who would have been as a precious jewel to any state that obtained him." He had built in England many ships of great burden, one even of six hundred tons, and he was "so able a man that there was hardly such another to be found in the kingdom." In New England he lived with great content, where, from the time of his arrival, ship-building was carried on with surpassing skill, so that vessels were soon constructed of four hundred tons. So long as the ports were thronged with new comers, the older settlers found full employment in supplying their wants. But now "men began to look about them, and fell to a manufacture of cotton, whereof they had store from Barbadoes." In view of the exigency, "the general court made order for the manufacture of woollen and linen cloth."

The Long Parliament, which met in 1641, contained among its members many sincere favorers of the Puritan plantations. But the English in America, with wise circumspection, feared to endanger their legislative independence. "Upon the great liberty which the king had left the parliament in England," says Winthrop, "some of our friends there wrote to us advice to solicit for us in the parliament, giving us hope that we might obtain much. But, consulting about it, we declined the motion for this consideration, that, if we should put ourselves under the protection of the parliament, we must then be subject to all such laws as they should make, or, at least, such as they might impose upon us. It might prove very prejudicial to us." When the letters arrived, inviting the colonial churches to send their deputies to the Westminster assembly of divines, the same sagacity led them to neglect the summons. Especially Hooker, of Hartford, "liked not the business," and deemed it his duty rather to stay in quiet and obscurity with his people in Connecticut, than to go three thousand miles to plead for Independency with Presbyterians in England. Yet such commercial advantages were desired as might be obtained without a surrender of chartered rights. In 1641, the general court "sent three chosen men into England to congratulate the happy success there, and to be ready to make use of any opportunity God should offer for the good of the country here, as also to give any advice, as it should be required, for the settling of the right form of church discipline there." Of these agents, Hugh Peter was one.

The security enjoyed by New England presented the long desired opportunity of establishing a "body of liberties" as a written constitution of government. In the absence of a code of laws, the people had for several years continued to be uneasy at the extent of power that rested in the discretion of the magistrates. On the other hand, most of the magistrates, and some of the elders, thinking that the fittest laws would arise upon occasions, and gain validity as customs, and moreover fearing that their usages, if established as regular statutes, might be censured by their enemies as repugnant to the laws of England, "had not been very forward in this matter." Now that some of the causes of apprehension existed no longer, the great work of constitutional legislation was resumed; and in December, 1641, a session of three weeks was employed in considering a system which had been prepared chiefly by Nathaniel Ward, of Ipswich. He had been formerly a student and practiser in the courts of common law in England, but became a non-conforming minister; so that he was competent to combine the humane principles of the common law with those of natural right and equality, as deduced from the Bible. After mature deliberation, his "model," which for its liberality and comprehensiveness may vie with any similar record from the days of Magna Charta, was adopted as "the body of liberties" of the Massachusetts colony.

All the general officers of the jurisdiction, including governor, deputy governor, treasurer, assistants, military commander, and admiral, if there should be a naval force, were to be chosen annually by the freemen of the plantation, and paid from the common treasury. The freemen in the several towns were to choose deputies from among themselves; or, "to the end the ablest gifted men might be made use of in so weighty a work," they might select them elsewhere as they judged fittest, who were to be paid from the treasury of the respective towns, and to serve "at the most but one year; that the country may have an annual liberty to do in that case what is most behooveful for the best welfare thereof." No general assembly could be dissolved or adjourned without the consent of the major part thereof. The freemen of every town had power to make such by-laws and constitutions as might concern the welfare of the town, provided they be not of a criminal nature, nor repugnant to the public laws of the country; and that their penalties exceed not twenty shillings for one offence. They also had power to choose yearly selectmen "to order the prudential occasions of the town according to instructions to be given them in writing."

Life, honor, and personal liberty and estate were placed under the perpetual protection of law. To every person, whether inhabitant or foreigner, was promised equal justice without partiality or delay. Every man, whether inhabitant or foreigner, free or not free, that is, whether admitted as a member of the general court of the freemen under the charter or not, had the liberty to come to any court, council, or town-meeting, and there to move any question or present any petition, either by speech or writing. Every officer exercising judicial authority was annually elected; the assistants by the freemen of the whole plantation; the associates to assist the assistants in any inferior court, by the towns belonging to that court; and all jurors, by the freemen of the town where they dwelt. Judicial proceedings were simplified; by mutual consent of plaintiff and defendant, actions might be tried, at their option, by the bench or by a jury; and in criminal trials the like choice was granted to the accused.

Every incident of feudal tenure that would have been a restraint on the possession and transmission of real estate was utterly forbidden; and all lands and heritages were declared free and alienable; so that the land of a child under age, or an idiot, might, with the consent of a general court, be conveyed away. The charter had indeed reserved to the king, by way of rent, one-fifth of the gold and silver that might be mined; but this was a mere theoretical feud, resolving itself into fealty alone. In Massachusetts, all the land was allodial. All persons of the age of twenty-one years, even the excommunicate or condemned, had full power to alienate their lands and estates, and to make their wills and testaments. Children inherited equally as co-partners the property of intestate parents, whether real or personal, except that to the first-born son, where there was a son, a double portion was assigned, unless the general court should judge otherwise. No man could be compelled to go out of the limits of the plantation upon any offensive war. To every man within the jurisdiction, free liberty was assured to remove himself and his family at their pleasure. The grant of monopolies was prohibited, except of new inventions profitable to the country, and that for a short time. Every married woman was protected against bodily correction or stripes by her husband, and had redress, if at his death he should not leave her a competent portion of his estate. Of other nations professing the true Christian religion, all fugitives from the tyranny or oppression of their persecutors, or from famine or wars, were ordered to be entertained according to that power and prudence that God should give; so that the welcome of the commonwealth was as wide as sorrow. On slavery this was the rule: "There shall never be any bond slaverie, villinage, or captivitie amongst us, unles it be lawfull captives taken in just warres, and such strangers as willingly selle themselves or are sold to us. And these shall have all the liberties and Christian usages which the law of God established in Israel concerning such persons doeth morally require. This exempts none from servitude who shall be judged thereto by authoritie." "If any man stealeth a man or mankinde, he shall surely be put to death."

The severity of the Levitical law against witchcraft, blasphemy, and sins against nature, was retained; otherwise, death was the punishment only for murder, adultery, man-stealing, and false witness wittingly to take away any man's life. In the following year, rape was also made a capital crime.

With regard to the concerns of religion, all the people of

God who were orthodox in judgment and not scandalous in life had full liberty to gather themselves into a church estate; to exercise all the ordinances of God; and from time to time to elect and ordain all their officers, provided they be able, pious, and orthodox. For the preventing and removing of error, ministers and elders of near adjoining churches might hold public Christian conference, provided that nothing be imposed by way of authority by one or more churches upon another, but only by way of brotherly consultations.

Such were the most important of the liberties and laws, established at the end of 1641, for the government of Massachusetts. Embracing the freedom of the commonwealth, of municipalities, of persons, and of churches according to the principles of Congregationalism, "the model" exhibits the truest picture of the principles, character, and intentions of that people, and the best evidence of its vigor and self-dependence.

In its main features it was the embodiment of the customs of the colony. The public teaching of all children, the train-bands and the training-field, the town-meeting and the meeting of all the inhabitants for public worship,—these essential elements of early New England public life grew up before their establishment by a superior authority, and, as it were, created the laws for their perpetuation.

Do we seek to trace the New England town to its origin? The vital principle of Teutonic liberty lies in the immemorial usage of the meeting of all the people with the equal rights of each qualified inhabitant to give counsel and to vote on public affairs. The usage still exists, nearly in its pristine purity, in some of the cantons of Switzerland; it has left in the Teutonic race a more profound sense of the need of local self-government than exists elsewhere on the continent of Europe; in England, it is the formative idea of its parliament and of its hundred, and in some narrow measure still survives in the parish. It was saved in many English towns by special agreement with their rulers, through these agreements were warred upon and essentially changed by later and more arbitrary kings. This seminal principle of English liberty scattered itself and took root wherever Englishmen trod the soil of America. The first ordinance for the constitution of Virginia enumerated the divisions of towns, hundreds, and plantations; but there the system was imperfectly developed from the scattered mode of life of the planters and the introduction of the English system of parishes. In New England, the precious seed fell on the best ground for its quickening. Each company of settlers as it arrived, or as it divided from earlier companies, formed a town by themselves, which at once began as by right with taking care of its own concerns. All the electors met annually, and more often if required. They might at any time be called together to treat of any subject that was of interest to them, even if it were but to express an opinion. When business became too complicated to be executed in the public assembly, the annual meeting voted what should be done in the year, and selected men to carry out their votes. When the annual gathering of all the freemen of the corporation gave way to the representative system, each town that had as many as ten freemen might send at least one deputy to what was still called the general court. Thus in Massachusetts, and it was substantially so in all the New England states, the commonwealth was made up of living, integral organizations, in which the people were trained, from the beginning, to feel themselves members of the state and to take their share in public life.

In these early days, there fell under the control of the several towns two subjects, which are now removed from them. The minister, without whom the existence of a town could not be conceived of, was chosen in open town-meeting, and received his support according to the contract that might be made between him and the people. This regulation continued in usage in some of the interior precincts for nearly two centuries.

By the charter all the land of the commonwealth was granted to the freemen of the corporation; but they never laid claim to it for themselves. They sometimes showed their gratitude to benefactors by voting to them lands; but, as the rule, the land

within the limits of a town was granted by the commonwealth
to the individuals who were to plant the town; not in perpetuity,
nor in equal parts, but to be distributed among the inhabitants
according to their previous agreements, or to their wants and
just expectations as judged of by the towns themselves. Each
town made its own rules for the division of them. It was usual to
reserve a large part of the town's domain for such persons as
from time to time should be received as inhabitants; and, in
the mean while, rights to wood, timber, and herbage, in the
undivided lands, attached to all householders. A permanent
community of property in land was never designed or attempted. . . .

There are some who love to enumerate the singularities of
the early Puritans. They were opposed to wigs; they could
preach against veils; they denounced long hair; they disliked
the cross in the banner, as much as the people of Paris disliked
the lilies of the Bourbons. They would not allow Christmas
to be kept sacred; they called neither months, nor days, nor
seasons, nor churches, nor inns, by the names common in England; they revived Scripture names at christenings. The grave
Romans legislated on the costume of men, and their senate
could even stoop to interfere with the triumphs of the sex to
which civic honors are denied: the fathers of New England
prohibited frivolous fashions in their own dress; and their aus-
terity, checking extravagance even in woman, frowned on her
hoods of silk and her scarfs of tiffany, extended the length of
her sleeve to the wrist, and limited its greatest width to half an
ell. The Puritans were formal and precise in their manners;
singular in the forms of their legislation; rigid in the observance
of their principles. Every topic of the day found a place in
their extemporaneous prayers, and infused a stirring interest
into their long and frequent sermons. The courts of Massachusetts respected in practice the code of Moses; the island of
Rhode Island followed for a year or two Jewish precedents; in
New Haven, the members of the constituent committee were
called the seven pillars, hewn out for the house of wisdom. But

these are only the outward forms, which gave to the new sect
its marked exterior. If from the outside peculiarities, which so
easily excite the sneer of the superficial observer, we look to the
genius of the sect itself, Puritanism was Religion struggling for
the People; a war against tyranny and superstition. "Its ab-
surdities," says one of its scoffers, "were the shelter for the noble
principles of liberty." It was its office to engraft the new institution of popular energy upon the old European system of a
feudal aristocracy and popular servitude; the good was permanent; the outward emblems, which were the signs of the party,
were of transient duration, like the clay and ligaments which
hold the graft in its place, and are brushed away as soon as the
scion is firmly united.

The principles of Puritanism proclaimed the civil magistrate
subordinate to the authority of religion; and its haughtiness in
this respect has been compared to "the infatuated arrogance"
of a Roman pontiff. In the firmness with which the principle
was asserted, the Puritans did not yield to the Catholics; and,
if the will of God is 'the criterion of justice, both were, in one
sense, in the right. The question arises, Who shall be the interpreter of that will? In the Roman Catholic Church, the office
was claimed by the infallible pontiff, who, as the self-constituted
guardian of the oppressed, insisted on the power of dethroning
kings, repealing laws, and subverting dynasties. The principle
thus asserted could not but become subservient to the temporal
ambition of the clergy. Puritanism conceded no such power to
its spiritual guides; the church existed independent of its pastor,
who owed his office to its free choice; the will of the majority
was its law; and each one of the brethren possessed equal rights
with the elders. The right, exercised by each congregation, of
electing its own ministers was in itself a moral revolution; religion was now with the people, not over the people. Puritanism
exalted the laity. Every individual who had experienced the
raptures of devotion, every believer, who in moments of ecstasy
had felt the assurance of the favor of God, was in his own eyes
a consecrated person, chosen to do the noblest and godliest

deeds. For him the wonderful counsels of the Almighty had appointed a Saviour; for him the laws of nature had been suspended and controlled, the heavens had opened, earth had quaked, the sun had veiled his face, and Christ had died and had risen again; for him prophets and apostles had revealed to the world the oracles and the will of God. Before heaven he prostrated himself in the dust; looking out upon mankind, how could he but respect himself, whom God had chosen and redeemed? He cherished hope; he possessed faith; as he walked the earth, his heart was in the skies. Angels hovered round his path, charged to minister to his soul; spirits of darkness vainly leagued together to tempt him from his allegiance. His burning piety could use no liturgy; his penitence revealed itself to no confessor. He knew no superior in holiness. He could as little become the slave of a priestcraft as of a despot. He was himself a judge of the orthodoxy of the elders; and if he feared the invisible powers of the air, of darkness, and of hell, he feared nothing on earth. Puritanism constituted not the Christian clergy, but the Christian people, the interpreter of the divine will. The voice of the majority was the voice of God; and the issue of Puritanism was popular sovereignty.

The effects of Puritanism display its character still more distinctly. Ecclesiastical tyranny is of all kinds the worst; its fruits are cowardice, idleness, ignorance, and poverty; Puritanism was a life-giving spirit; activity, thrift, intelligence, followed in its train; and, as for courage, a coward and a Puritan never went together.

It was in self-defence that Puritanism in America began those transient persecutions which shall find in me no apologist; and which yet were no more than a train of mists hovering, of an autumn morning, over the channel of a fine river, that diffused freshness and fertility wherever it wound. The people did not attempt to convert others but to protect themselves; they never punished opinion as such; they never attempted to torture or terrify men into orthodoxy. The history of religious persecution in New England is simply this: the

Puritans established a government in America such as the laws of natural justice warranted, and such as the statutes and common law of England did not warrant; and that was done by men who still acknowledged a limited allegiance to the parent state. The Episcopalians had declared themselves the enemies of the party, and waged against it a war of extermination; Puritanism excluded them from its asylum. Roger Williams, the apostle of "soul-liberty," weakened civil independence by impairing its unity; and he was expelled, even though Massachusetts bore good testimony to his spotless virtues. Wheelwright and his friends, in their zeal for liberty of speech, were charged with forgetting their duty as citizens, and they also were exiled. The Anabaptist, who could not be relied upon as an ally, was guarded as a foe. The Quakers denounced the worship of New England as an abomination, and its government as treason; and they were excluded on pain of death. The fanatic for Calvinism was a fanatic for liberty; and, in the moral warfare for freedom, his creed was his support and his most faithful ally in the battle.

For "New England was a religious plantation, not a plantation for trade. The profession of the purity of doctrine, worship, and discipline, was written on her forehead." "We all," says the confederacy in one of the two oldest of American written constitutions, "came into these parts of America to enjoy the liberties of the gospel in purity and peace." "He that made religion as twelve, and the world as thirteen, had not the spirit of a true New England man." Religion was the object of the emigrants; it was also their consolation. With this the wounds of the outcast were healed, and the tears of exile sweetened. "New England was the colony of conscience."

Of all contemporary sects, the Puritans were the most free from credulity, and, in their zeal for reform, pushed their regulations to what some would consider a skeptical extreme. So many superstitions had been bundled up with every venerable institution of Europe, that ages have not yet dislodged them all. The Puritans at once emancipated themselves from a crowd of observances. They established a worship purely spiritual.

They stood in prayer. To them the elements remained but wine and bread, and in communing they would not kneel. They invoked no saints; they raised no altar; they adored no crucifix; they kissed no book; they asked no absolution; they paid no tithes; they saw in the priest nothing more than a man; ordination was no more than an approbation of the officer, which might be expressed by the brethren, as well as by other ministers; the church, as a place of worship, was to them but a meeting-house; they dug no graves in consecrated earth; unlike their posterity, they married without a minister, and buried the dead without a prayer. Witchcraft had not been made the subject of skeptical consideration; and, in the years in which Scotland sacrificed hecatombs to the delusion, there were three victims in New England. Dark crimes, that seemed without a motive, may have been pursued under that name; I find one record of a trial for withcraft, where the prisoner was proved a murderess.

On every subject but religion, the mildness of Puritan legislation corresponded to the popular character of Puritan doctrines. Hardly a nation of Europe has as yet made its criminal law so humane as that of early New England. A crowd of offences was at one sweep brushed from the catalogue of capital crimes. The idea was never received that the forfeiture of life may be demanded for the protection of property; the punishment for theft, for burglary, and highway robbery, was far more mild than the penalties imposed even by modern American legislation. The habits of the young promoted real chastity. The sexes lived in social intimacy, and were more pure than the recluse. Of divorce I have found no example; yet a clause in one of the statutes recognises the possibility of such an event. Divorce from bed and board, the separate maintenance without the dissolution of the marriage contract,—an anomaly in Protestant legislation, that punishes the innocent more than the guilty,—was abhorrent from their principles. The sanctity of the marriage-bed was protected by the penalty of death; a penalty which was inexorably enforced against the adulteress and her paramour. If in this respect the laws were more severe, in another they were more lenient than modern manners approve. The girl whom youth and affection and the promise of marriage betrayed into weakness was censured, pitied, and forgiven; the law compelled the seducer of innocence to marry the person who had imposed every obligation by the concession of every right. The law implies an extremely pure community; in no other could it have found a place in the statute-book.

The benevolence of the Puritans appears from other examples. Their thoughts were always fixed on posterity. Domestic discipline was highly valued; the law was severe against the undutiful child; it was also severe against a faithless parent. Till 1654, the laws did not permit any man's person to be kept in prison for debt, except when there was an appearance of some estate which the debtor would not produce. Even the brute creation was not forgotten; and cruelty towards animals was a civil offence. The sympathies of the colonists were wide; a regard for Protestant Germany is as old as emigration; and during the thirty years' war the people of New England held fasts and offered prayers for the success of their Garman brethren.

The first years of the residence of Puritans in America were years of great hardship and affliction; this short season of distress was promptly followed by abundance and happiness. The people struck root in the soil immediately. They were, from the first, industrious, enterprising, and frugal; and affluence followed of course. When persecution ceased in England, there were already in New England "thousands who would not change their place for any other in the world;" and they were tempted in vain with invitations to the Bahama Isles, to Ireland, to Jamaica, to Trinidad. The purity of morals completes the picture of colonial felicity. "As Ireland will not brook venomous beasts, so will not that land vile livers." One might dwell there "from year to year, and not see a drunkard, or hear an oath, or meet a beggar." As a consequence, the average duration of life in New England, compared with Europe of that day, was doubled; and, of all who were born into the world, more than two in ten, full four in nineteen, attained the age of seventy. Of those who lived beyond ninety, the proportion, as compared with European tables of longevity, was still more remarkable.

I have dwelt the longer on the character of the early Puritans of New England, for they were the parents of one-third the whole white population of the United States as it was in 1834. Within the first fifteen years,—and there was never afterwards any considerable increase from England,—we have seen that there came over twenty-one thousand two hundred persons, or four thousand families. Their descendants were in 1834 not far from four millions. Each family had multiplied on the average to one thousand souls. To New York and Ohio, where they then constituted half the population, they carried the Puritan system of free schools; and their example is spreading it through the civilized world.

Historians have loved to eulogize the manners and virtues, the glory and the benefits, of chivalry. Puritanism accomplished for mankind far more. If it had the sectarian crime of intolerance, chivalry had the vices of dissoluteness. The knights were brave from gallantry of spirit; the Puritans, from the fear of God. The knights obeyed the law of honor; the Puritans hearkened to the voice of duty. The knights were proud of loyalty; the Puritans, of liberty. The knights did homage to monarchs, in whose smile they beheld honor, whose rebuke was the wound of disgrace; the Puritans, disdaining ceremony, would not bow at the name of Jesus, nor bend the knee to the King of kings. Chivalry delighted in outward show, favored pleasure, multiplied amusements, and degraded the human race by an exclusive respect for the privileged classes; Puritanism bridled the passions, commanded the virtues of self-denial, and rescued the name of man from dishonor. The former valued courtesy; the latter, justice. The former adorned society by graceful refinements; the latter founded national grandeur on universal education. The institutions of chivalry were subverted by the gradually increasing weight and knowledge and opulence of the industrious classes; the Puritans, rallying upon those classes, planted in their hearts the undying principles of democratic liberty.

The golden age of Puritanism was passing away. Time was silently softening its asperities, and the revolutions of England prepared an era in its fortunes. Massachusetts never acknowledged Richard Cromwell; it read in the aspect of parties the impending restoration. The protector had left the benefits of self-government and the freedom of commerce to New England and to Virginia; and Maryland, by the act of her inhabitants, was just beginning to share in the same advantages. Would the dynasty of the Stuarts deal benevolently with the colonies? Would it imitate the magnanimity of Cromwell, and suffer the staple of the south still to seek its market freely throughout the world? Could the returning monarch forgive the friends of the Puritans in England? Would he show favor to the institutions that the outcasts had reared beyond the Atlantic?

Virginia after the Restoration

FOR more than eight years, from 1652 to 1660, "the people of Virginia" had governed themselves. Tranquillity and a rapid increase of population promised the extension of its borders; the colonial life was sweetened by the enjoyment of equal franchises. No trace of established privilege appeared in its code or its government; in its forms and in its legislation, Virginia was a representative democracy; so jealous of a landed aristocracy that it insisted on universality of suffrage; so hostile to the influence of commercial wealth that it would not tolerate the "mercenary" ministers of the law; so considerate for religious freedom that each parish was left to take care of itself. Every officer was, directly or indirectly, chosen by the people.

The power of the people naturally grew out of the character of the early settlers, who were, most of them, adventurers, bringing to the New World no wealth but enterprise, no rank but that of manhood, no privileges but those of Englishmen. The principle of the English law which grants real estate to the eldest born was respected; but generations of Virginians had hardly as yet succeeded each other; the rule had produced no effect upon society, and, from the beginning, had been modified in many counties by the custom of gavelkind. Virginia had no need to imitate those great legislative reforms of the Long Parliament, because her happier soil was free from the burdens of forest laws and military tenures, courts of wards, and star-chambers. The tendency towards a multiplication of religious sects began to be perceptible under the freedom of a popular government. In its care for a regular succession of representative assemblies, Viginia exceeded the jealous friends of republican liberty in England; there triennial parliaments had been established by law; the Virginians, imitating the "act of 1640 for preventing inconveniences happening by the long intermission of parliament," claimed the privilege of a biennial election of their legislators. In addition to the strength derived from the natural character of the emigrants, from the absence of feudal institutions, from the entire absence of the excessive refinements of legal erudition, and from the constitution, legislation, and elective franchises of the colonists, a new and undefined increase was gained by the universal prevalence of the spirit of personal independence. An instinctive aversion to too much government was always a trait of southern character, expressed in the solitary manner of settling the country, in the absence of municipal governments, in the indisposition of the scattered inhabitants to engage in commerce, to collect in towns, or to associate in townships under corporate powers. As a consequence, there was little commercial industry or accumulation of commercial wealth. The exchanges were made almost entirely—and it continued so for more than a century—by factors of foreign merchants. Thus the influence of wealth, under the modern form of stocks and dealings in money, was always inconsiderable; and men were so widely scattered that far the smallest number were within reach of the direct influence of the established church or of government. In Virginia, except in matters that related to foreign commerce, a man's own will went far towards being his law.

Yet the seeds of an aristocracy existed; and there was already a disposition to obtain for it the sanction of colonial legislation. Unlike Massachusetts, Virginia was a continuation of English society. Its history is the development of the genuine principle of English liberty under other conditions than in England. The first colonists were not fugitives from persecution; they came, rather, under the auspices of the nobility, the church, and the mercantile interests of England; they brought with them an attachment to monarchy, a reverence for the Anglican church, a love for England and English institutions. Their minds had never been disciplined into an antipathy to feudalism; their creed had never been shaken by the progress of skepticism; no new ideas of natural rights had as yet inclined them to "faction." The Anglican church was therefore, without repugnance, sanctioned as the religion of the state; and a religion established by law always favors an upper class; for it seeks support not in conviction only, but in vested rights. The rise of the plebeian sects, which swarmed in England, was, for the present at least, prevented; and unity of worship with few exceptions continued for about a century from the settlement of Jamestown. The aristocracy of Virginia was, from its origin, exclusively a landed aristocracy; its germ lay in the manner in which rights to the soil had been obtained. For every person whom a planter should, at his own charge, transport into Virginia, he could claim fifty acres of land; and thus a body of large proprietors had existed from the infancy of the settlement. These vast possessions were often an inheritance for the eldest born.

The power of the rising aristocracy was still further increased by the deplorable want of the means of popular education in Virginia. The great mass of the rising generation could receive little literary culture; its higher degrees were confined to a small number of favored emigrants. Many of the royalists who came over after the death of Charles I brought to the colony the breeding that belonged to the English gentry of that day; and the direction of affairs fell into their hands. The instinct of liberty may create popular institutions; they cannot be preserved except by the conscious intelligence of the people.

But the distinctions in society were rendered more marked by the character of the population of Virginia. Many had reached the shores of Virginia as servants; doomed, according to the severe laws of that age, to a temporary bondage. Some of them, even, were convicts; but it must be remembered the crimes of which they were convicted were chiefly political. The number transported to Virginia for social crimes was never considerable; scarcely enough to sustain the sentiment of pride in its scorn of the laboring population; certainly not enough to affect its character. Yet the division of society into two classes was marked in a degree unequalled in any northern colony, and unmitigated by public care for education. "The almost general want of schools for their children was of most sad consideration, most of all bewailed of the parents there." "Every man," said Sir William Berkeley in 1671, "instructs his children according to his ability;" a method which left the children of the ignorant to hopeless ignorance. "The ministers," continued Sir William, "should pray oftener and preach less. But, I thank God, there are no free schools nor printing; and I hope we shall not have, these hundred years; for learning has brought disobedience and heresy and sects into the world, and printing has divulged them, and libels against the best government. God keep us from both."

Servants were emancipated, when their years of servitude were ended; and the law was designed to secure and to hasten their enfranchisement. The insurrection, which was plotted by a number of servants in 1663, had its origin in impatience of servitude and oppression. A few bondmen, soldiers of Cromwell, and probably Roundheads, were excited by their own sufferings, and by the nature of life in the wilderness, to indulge once more in vague desires for a purer church and a happier condition. From the character of the times, their passions were sustained by political fanaticism; but the conspiracy did not extend beyond a scheme of indented servants to anticipate the period of their freedom. The effort was the work of ignorant men, and was easily suppressed. The facility of escape compelled humane treatment of white servants, who formed one fifth of the adult population.

In 1671, the number of blacks in a population of forty thousand was estimated at two thousand; not above two or three ships of negroes arrived in seven years. The statute of the previous year, which declares who are slaves, followed an idea, long prevalent through Christendom: "All servants, not being Christians, imported into this country by shipping, shall be slaves." In 1682 it was added: "Conversion to the Christian faith doth not make free." The early Anglo-Saxon rule, interpreting every doubtful question in favor of liberty, declared the children of freemen to be free. Doubts arose if the offspring of an Englishman by a negro woman should be bond or free; and the rule of the Roman law prevailed over the Anglo-Saxon.

The offspring followed the condition of its mother. In 1664, Maryland, by "the major vote" of its lower house, decided that "the issue of such marriages should serve thirty years." Enfranchisement of the colored population was not encouraged in Virginia; the female slave was not subject to taxation; the emancipated negress was "a tithable." "The death of a slave from extremity of correction was not accounted felony; since it cannot be presumed," such is the language of the statute, "that prepensed malice, which alone makes murther felony, should induce any man to destroy his own estate." Finally, it was made lawful for "persons pursuing fugitive colored slaves to wound, or even to kill them." The master was absolute lord over the negro. The slave, and the slave's posterity, were bondmen. As property in Virginia consisted mainly of land and laborers, the increase of negro slaves was grateful to the pride and to the interests of the large landed proprietors.

The aristocracy, which was thus confirmed in its influence by the extent of its domains, by its superior intelligence, and by the character of a large part of the laboring class, aspired to the government of the country; from among them the council was selected; many of them were returned as members of the legislature; and they held commissions in the militia. The entire absence of local municipal governments led to an anomalous extension of the power of the magistrates. The justices of the peace for each county fixed the amount of county taxes, assessed and collected them, and superintended their disbursement; so that military, judicial, legislative, and executive powers were deposited in their hands.

At the restoration, two elements were contending for the mastery in the political life of Virginia; on the one hand, there was in the Old Dominion a people; on the other, a rising aristocracy. The present decision of the contest would depend on the side to which the sovereign of the country would incline. During the few years of the interruption of monarchy in England, that sovereign had been the people of Virginia; and its mild and beneficent legislation had begun to loosen the cords of religious bigotry, to confirm equality of franchises, to foster colonial industry by freedom of traffic with the world. The restoration of monarchy took from the people of Virginia the power which was not to be recovered for more than a century, and gave to the superior class an ally in the royal government and its officers. The early history of Virginia not only illustrates the humane and ameliorating influences of popular freedom, but also presents a picture of the confusion, discontent, and carnage, which are the natural consequences of selfish legislation and a retrograde movement in the cause of liberty.

The emigrant royalists had hitherto not acted as a political party, but took advantage of peace to establish their fortunes. Their numbers were consantly increasing; their character and education procured them respect and influence; yet no collisions ensued. If one assembly had, what Massachusetts never did, submitted to Richard Cromwell; if another had elected Berkeley as governor, the power of the people still controlled legislative action. But, on the tidings of the restoration of Charles II, the fires of loyalty blazed up. Virginia shared the passionate joy of England. In the mother country, the spirit of popular liberty, contending with ancient institutions which it could not overthrow, had been productive of much calamity, and had overwhelmed the tenets of popular enfranchisement in disgust and abhorrence: in Virginia, where no such ancient abuses existed, the same spirit had been productive only of benefits. Yet to the colony England seemed a home; and the spirit of English loyalty pervaded the plantations along the Chesapeake. With the people it was a generous enthusiasm; to many of the leading men loyalty opened a career for ambition; and, with general consent, Sir William Berkeley, assuming such powers as his royal commission bestowed, issued writs for an assembly in the name of the king. The sovereignty over itself, which Virginia had exercised so well, had come to an end. . . .

The legislature was friendly to the power of the crown. In every colony where Puritanism prevailed there was a uniform disposition to refuse a fixed salary to the royal governor. Virginia, at a time when the chief magistrate was elected by its own citizens, had voted a fixed salary for that magistrate; but the measure, even then, was so little agreeable to the people that its next assembly repealed the law. The royalist legislature, for the purpose of well paying his majesty's officers, established a perpetual revenue by a permanent imposition on all exported tobacco; and the royal officers of Virginia, requiring no further action of an assembly for granting taxes, were placed above the influence of colonial legislation. They depended on the province neither for their appointment nor their salary; and the country was governed according to royal instructions, which did indeed recognise the existence of colonial assemblies, but offered no guarantee for their continuance. The permanent salary of the governor of Virginia, increased by a special grant from the colonial legislature, exceeded the whole annual expenditure of Connecticut; but Berkeley was dissatisfied. A thousand pounds a year would not, he used to say, "maintain the port of his place; no government of ten years' standing but has thrice as much allowed him. But I am supported by my hopes that his gracious majesty will one day consider me."

The governor and council were the highest ordinary tribunal; and these were all appointed, directly or indirectly, by the crown. Besides this, there were in each county eight unpaid justices of the peace, commissioned by the governor during his pleasure. These justices held monthly courts in their respective counties. Thus the administration of justice in the counties was in the hands of persons holding their offices at the good-will of the governor; while the governor himself and his executive council constituted the general court, and had cognizance of all sorts of causes. Was an appeal made to chancery, it was but for another hearing before the same men; and it was only for a few years longer that appeals were permitted from the general court to the assembly. The place of sheriff in each county was conferred in rotation on one of the justices for that county.

The county courts, thus independent of the people, possessed and exercised the arbitrary power of levying county taxes, which, in their amount, usually exceeded the public levy. This system proceeded so far that the commissioners of themselves levied taxes to meet their own expenses. In like manner, the self-perpetuating vestries made out their lists of tithables, and assessed taxes without regard to the consent of the parish. These private levies were unequal and oppressive; were seldom, it is said never, brought to audit, and were, in some cases at least, managed by men who combined to defraud the public.

For the organization of the courts, ancient usage could be pleaded; a series of innovations gradually effected a revolution in the system of representation. The duration of assemblies was limited by law to two years. By the members of the first assembly, elected after the restoration for a period of two years only, the law, which limited the duration of their legislative service, and secured the benefits of frequent elections and swift responsibility, was "utterly abrogated and repealed." The legislators, on whom the people had conferred a political existence of two years, assumed to themselves, by their own act, an indefinite continuance of their powers. The parliament of England, chosen on the restoration, was not dissolved for eighteen years; the legislature of Virginia retained its authority for almost as long a period, and yielded it only to an insurrection. Meantime, "the meeting of the people, at the usual places of election," had for their object, not to elect burgesses, but to present their grievances to the burgesses of the adjourned assembly.

The wages of the burgesses were paid by the respective counties; and their constituents had possessed influence to determine both thhe number of burgesses to be elected and the rate of their emoluments. This method of influence was taken away by a law, which, wisely but for its coincidence with other measures, fixed both the number and the charge of the burgesses. But the rate of wages was for that age enormously burdensome, far greater than is tolerated in the wealthiest states in these days of opulence; and it was fixed by an assembly for its own members, who had usurped, as it were, a perpetuity of office. The taxes for this purpose were paid with great reluctance, and, as they amounted to about two hundred and fifty pounds of tobacco or about nine dollars, for the daily emoluments of each member, became for a new country an intolerable grievance. Discontent was increased by the favoritism which exempted councillors from the levies.

The freedom of elections was further impaired by "frequent false returns" made by the sheriffs. Against these the people had no redress, for the sheriffs were responsible neither to them nor to officers of their appointment. And how could a more pregnant cause of discontent exist in a country where the elective franchise was cherished as the dearest civil privilege?

No direct taxes were levied in those days except on polls; lands escaped taxation. The method, less arbitrary in Virginia, where property consisted chiefly in a claim to the labor of servants and slaves, than in a commercial country, or where labor is free, was yet oppressive to the less wealthy classes. The burgesses, themselves great landholders, resisted the reform which Berkeley had urged, of "a levy upon lands, and not upon heads," and connected the burden of the tax with the privileges of citizenship. If lands should be taxed, none but landholders should elect the legislature; and then, it was added, "the other freemen, who are the more in number, may repine to be bound to those laws they have no representations to assent to the making of. And we are so well acquainted with the temper of the people that we have reason to believe they had rather pay their tax than lose that privilege."

The jealous love for liberty was remembered when it furnished an excuse for continuing an unjust method of taxation. But the system of universal suffrage could not permanently find favor with an assembly which had given to itself an indefinite existence, and which labored to reproduce in the New World the inequalities of English legislation. It was discovered that "the usual way of chusing burgesses by the votes of all freemen" produced "tumults and disturbance." The instinct of aristocratic bigotry denied that the electors would make "choyce of persons fitly qualified for so greate a trust." The restrictions adopted by the monarchical government of England were cited as a fit precedent for English colonies; and it was enacted that "none but freeholders and housekeepers shall hereafter have a voice in the election of any burgesses." The majority of the people of Virginia were disfranchised by the act of their own representatives.

The great result of modern civilization is the diffusion of intelligence among the masses, and a consequent increase of their political consideration. That the power of the people has everywhere increased, is the undisputed induction from the history of every nation of European origin. The restoration of Charles II was to Virginia a political revolution, opposed to the principles of popular liberty which she professed and the course of human legislation on which she had entered. An assembly continuing for an indefinite period at the pleasure of the governor, and decreeing to its members extravagant and burdensome emoluments; a royal governor, whose salary was established by a permanent system of taxation; a constituency restricted and diminished; religious liberty taken away almost as soon as it had been won; arbitrary taxation in the counties by irresponsible magistrates; a hostility to popular education and to the press,—these were the changes which, in a period of ten years, had been wrought by a usurping government.

Meantime, the beauty and richness of the province were becoming better known. Towards the end of May, 1670, the governor of Virginia sent out an exploring party of men to discover the country beyond the mountains, which, it was believed, would open a way to the South Sea. The Blue Ridge they found high and rocky, and thickly grown with wood. Early in June they were stopped by a river, which they guessed to be four hundred and fifty yards wide. It was very rapid and full of rocks, running, so far as they could see, due north between the hills, "with banks in most places," according to their computation, "one thousand yards high." Beyond the river they reported other hills, naked of wood, broken by white cliffs, which in the morning were covered with a thick fog. The report of the explorers did not destroy the confidence that those mountains contained silver or gold, nor that there were rivers "falling the other way into the ocean." In the autumn of the next year the exploration of the valley of Kanawha was continued.

AT CAREFULLY *chosen points in his* History *Bancroft paused to summarize the meanings of that portion of the narrative just concluded, and to indicate something of the significance of that which was to come. Choosing 1754—marked by the opening of the French and Indian War, as well as by the publication of Jonathan Edwards'* Freedom of the Will—*as such a point he inserted in Volume III a survey of the state of affairs in each of the thirteen colonies. The French and Indian War, he believed, marked the beginnings of the rift between colonies and mother country; he saw in the emergent society of the mid-eighteenth century the first manifestations of those trends which were to eventuate in revolution and independence; at the same time, he pointed out that the ideas of the Reformation, borne across the Atlantic by the stout Calvinists of New England, were about to bear fruit. "These British American colonies," Bancroft wrote, "were the last trophy of modern civilization; on them for the next forty years rests the chief interest in the history of man."*

The Old Thirteen Colonies (1754)

IN 1754, David Hume, who had discovered the hollowness of the prevailing systems of thought in Europe, yet without offering any better substitute in philosophy than a selfish ideal skepticism, or hoping for any other euthanasia to the British constitution than its absorption in monarchy, said of America, in words which he never need have erased, and in a spirit which he never disavowed: "The seeds of many a noble state have been sown in climates kept desolate by the wild manners of the ancient inhabitants, and an asylum is secured in that solitary world for liberty and science." The thirteen American colonies, of which the union was projected, contained, at that day, about one million one hundred and sixty-five thousand white inhabitants, and two hundred sixty-three thousand negroes: in all, one million four hundred and twenty-eight thousand souls.

Vol. III, Chap. VI.

The board of trade reckoned a few thousands more; and some, on revising their judgment, stated the amount at less.

Of persons of European ancestry, perhaps fifty thousand dwelt in New Hampshire, two hundred and seven thousand in Massachusetts, thirty-five thousand in Rhode Island, and one hundred and thirty-three thousand in Connecticut; in New England, therefore, four hundred and twenty-five thousand souls.

Of the middle colonies, New York may have had eighty-five thousand; New Jersey, seventy-three thousand; Pennsylvania, with Delaware, one hundred and ninety-five thousand; Maryland, one hundred and four thousand: in all, not far from four hundred and fifty-seven thousand.

For the southern provinces, where the mild climate invited emigrants into the interior,—where the crown lands were often occupied on mere warrants of surveys or even without warrants,—there was room for glaring mistakes in the enumerations. To Virginia may be assigned one hundred and sixty-eight thousand white inhabitants; to North Carolina, scarcely less than seventy thousand; to South Carolina, forty thousand; to Georgia, not more than five thousand; to the whole country south of the Potomac, two hundred and eighty-three thousand.

The white population of any one of five, or perhaps even of six, of the American provinces, was greater, singly, than that of all Canada; and the aggregate in America exceeded that in Canada fourteen-fold.

Of persons of African lineage the home was chiefly determined by climate. New Hampshire, Massachusetts, and Maine may have had six thousand negroes; Rhode Island, four thousand five hundred; Connecticut, three thousand five hundred: all New England, therefore, about fourteen thousand.

New York alone had not far from eleven thousand; New Jersey, about half that number; Pennsylvania, with Delaware, eleven thousand; Maryland, forty-four thousand: the central colonies, collectively, seventy-one thousand.

In Virginia, there were not less than one hundred and sixteen thousand; in North Carolina, perhaps more than twenty thousand; in South Carolina, full forty thousand; in Georgia, about two thousand: so that the country south of the Potomac may have had one hundred and seventy-eight thousand.

Of the southern group, Georgia, the asylum of misfortune, had been languishing under a corporation whose benefits had not equalled the benevolence of its designs. The council of its trustees had granted no legislative rights to those whom they assumed to protect, but, meeting at a London tavern, by their own power imposed taxes on its Indian trade. Industry was disheartened by the entail of freeholds; summer, extending through months not its own, engendered pestilent vapors from the lowlands, as they were opened to the sun; American silk, it is true, was admitted into London duty free, but the wants of the wilderness left no leisure to feed the silk-worm and reel its thread; nor had the cultivator learned to gather the down of the cotton plant; the indigent, for whom charity had proposed a refuge, murmured at an exile that had sorrows of its own; the few men of substance withdrew to Carolina. In December, 1751, the trustees unanimously desired to surrender their charter; and, with the approbation of Murray, all authority for two years emanated from the king alone. In 1754, when the first royal governor with a royal council entered upon office, a legislative assembly convened under the sanction of his commission. The crown instituted the courts, and appointed executive officers and judges, with fixed salaries paid by England; but the people, through its representative body, and the precedence of older colonies, gained vigor in its infancy to restrain every form of delegated authority.

The fiery people of South Carolina had increased their power by every method of encroachment on the executive; but they did not excite English jealousy by competing with English industry, or engaging largely in illicit trade; and British legislation was ever lenient to their interests. In favor of rice, the laws of navigation were mitigated; the planting of indigo, like the production of naval stores, was cherished by a bounty from the

British exchequer; and they thought it in return no hardship to receive through England even foreign manufactures, which, by the system of partial drawbacks, came to them burdened with a tax, yet at a less cost than to the consumer in the metropolis. They had desired, and had obtained, the presence of troops to intimidate the wild tribes on their frontiers and to overawe their slaves. The people were yeomen, owing the king small quit-rents, which could never be rigorously exacted; a title to portions of the royal domain was granted on easy terms; and who would disturb the adventurer that, at his own will, built his cabin and pastured his herds in savannas and forests which had never been owned in severalty? The slave-merchant supplied laborers on credit. Free from excessive taxation, protected by soldiers in British pay, the frugal planter enjoyed the undivided returns of his enterprise, and might double his capital in three or four years. The love for rural life prevailed universally; the thrifty mechanic abandoned his workship, the merchant the risks of the sea, to plant estates of their own.

North Carolina, with nearly twice as many white inhabitants as its southern neighbor, had not one considerable village. Its swamps near the sea produced rice; its alluvial lands teemed with maize; free labor, little aided by negroes, busily drew turpentine and tar from the pines of its white, sandy plains; a hardy and rapidly increasing people lay scattered among its fertile uplands. There, through the boundless wilderness, hardy emigrants, careless of the strifes of Europe, ignorant of deceit, free from tithes, answerable to no master, fearlessly occupied lands that seemed without an owner. Their swine had the range of the forest; the greenwood was the pasture of their untold herds. Their young men trolled along the brooks that abounded in fish, and took their sleep under the forest tree; or trapped the beaver; or, with gun and pouch, lay in wait for the deer, as it slaked its thirst at the running stream; or, in small parties, roved the spurs of the Alleghanies, in quest of marketable skins. When Arthur Dobbs, the royal governor, an author of some repute, insisted on introducing the king's prerogative, the legislature did not scruple to leave the government unprovided for. When he attempted to establish the Anglican church, they were ready to welcome the institution of public worship, if their own vestries might choose their ministers. When he sought to collect quit-rents from a people who were nearly all tenants of the king, they deferred indefinitely the adjustment of the rent-roll.

For the Carolinas and for Virginia, as well as other royal governments, the king, under his sign manual, appointed the governor and the council; these constituted a court of chancery; the provincial judges, selected by the king or the royal governor, held office at the royal pleasure; for the courts of vice-admiralty, the lords of the admiralty named a judge, register, and marshal; the commissioners of the customs appointed the comptrollers and the collectors, of whom one was stationed at each considerable harbor; the justices and the militia officers were named by the governor in council. The freeholders elected but one branch of the legislature; and here, as in every royal government, the council formed another. In Virginia, there was less strife than elsewhere between the executive and the assembly: partly because the king had a permanent revenue from quit-rents and perpetual grants; partly because the governor resided in England, and was careful that his deputy should not hazard his sinecure by controversy. In consequence, the council, by its weight of personal character, gained unusual influence. The church of England was supported by legislative authority, and the plebeian sects were as yet proscribed; but the great extent of the parishes prevented unity of public worship. Bedford, when in office, had favored the appointment of an Anglican bishop in America; but, as his decisive opinion and the importunities of Sherlock and Secker had not prevailed, the benefices were filled by priests ordained in England, and for the most part of English birth, too often ill-educated and licentious men. The province had not one large town; the scattered mode of life made free schools not easily practicable. Sometimes the sons of wealthy planters repaired to Europe; here and there a man of great learning, some Scottish loyalist, some exile around whom misfortune spread a mystery, sought safety and gave instruction in Virginia. The country within tide-water was divided among planters, who, in the culture of tobacco, were favored by British legislation. Insulated on their large estates, they were cordially hospitable. In the quiet of their solitary life, unaided by an active press, they learned from nature what others caught from philosophy,—to reason boldly, to bound their freedom of mind only by self-circumscribed limits. They were philosophers after the pattern of Montaigne, without having heard of him. The horse was their pride; the county courts, their holidays; the race-course, their delight. On permitting the increase of negro slavery, opinions were nearly equally divided; but England kept slave-marts open at every court-house, as far, at least, as the South-west Mountain: partly to enrich her slave-merchants; partly, by balancing the races, to weaken the power of colonial resistance. The industry of the Virginians did not compete with that of the mother country; they had few mariners, took no part in the fisheries, and built no ships for sale. British factors purchased their products and furnished their supplies. Their connection with the metropolis was more intimate than with the northern colonies. England was their market and their storehouse, and was still called their "home."

Yet the prerogative had little support in Virginia. Its assembly sent, when it would, its own special agent to England, elected the colonial treasurer, and conducted its deliberations with dignity. Among the inhabitants, the pride of individual freedom paralyzed royal influence. They were the more independent, because they were the oldest colony, the most numerous, the most opulent, and in territory by far the most extensive. The property of the crown in its unascertained domain was admitted, yet they easily framed theories that invested the rightful ownership in the colony itself. Its people spread more and more widely over the mild, productive, and enchanting interior. They ascended rivers to the uplands, and gathered in the valleys of its mountain ranges, where the productive red soil bore wheat luxuriantly, and gave to fruits the most delicate flavor.

Among the half-opened forests of Orange county, in a home of plenty, there sported on the lawn the child Madison, round whose gentle nature clustered the hopes of American union. Deeper in the wilderness, on the highlands of Albemarle, Thomas Jefferson, son of a surveyor, of whose ancestral descent memory preserved but one generation, dwelt on the skirt of forest life, with no intercepting ridge between his dwelling-place and the far distant ocean. Beyond the Blue Ridge, men came southward from the glades of Pennsylvania; of most various nations, Irish, Scottish, and German; ever in strife with the royal officers; occupying lands without allotment, or on mere warrants of survey, without patents or payment of quit-rents; baffling to the last the policy of England. Everywhere in Virginia the sentiment of individuality was the parent of its republicanism.

North of the Potomac, at the centre of America, were the proprietary governments of Maryland and of Pennsylvania, with Delaware. There the king had no officers but in the customs and the admiralty courts; his name was hardly known in the acts of government.

During the last war, Maryland enjoyed unbroken quiet; furnishing no levies of men for the army, and very small contributions of money. Its legislature hardly looked beyond its own internal affairs; and its growth in numbers proved its prosperity. The youthful Frederic, Lord Baltimore, sixth of that title, dissolute and riotous, fond of wine to madness and of women to folly, as a prince zealous for prerogative, though negligent of business, was the sole landlord of the province. To him seemed to belong the right of initiating all laws, though the popular branch of the legislature had assumed that power; yet leaving to the proprietary a triple veto, by his council, by his deputy, and by himself. He established courts and appointed all their officers; punished convicted offenders, or pardoned them; appointed at pleasure councillors, all officers of the colony, and all the considerable county officers; and possessed exclusively the unappropriated domain. Reserving choice lands for his own manors, he had the whole people for his tenants on quit-rents, which, in 1754, exceeded twenty-five thousand dollars a year, and were rapidly increasing. On every new grant from the wild domain he received caution money; his were all escheats, wardships, and fruits of the feudal tenures. Fines of alienation, though abolished in England, were paid for his benefit on every transfer; and fines upon devises were still exacted. He enjoyed a perpetual port duty of fourteen pence a ton, on vessels not owned in the province, yielding not far from five thousand dollars a year; and he exacted a tribute for licenses to hawkers and pedlers, and to ordinaries.

These were the private income of Lord Baltimore. For the public service he needed no annual grants. By an act of 1704, which was held to be permanent, an export tax of a shilling on every hogshead of tobacco gave an annually increasing income of already not much less than seven thousand dollars, more than enough for the salary of his lieutenant-governor; while other officers were paid by fees and perquisites. Thus the assembly scarcely had occasion to impose taxes, except for the wages of its own members.

Beside the power of appointing colonial officers, independent of the people, Lord Baltimore, as prince palatine, could raise his liege-men to defend his province. His was also the power to pass ordinances for the preservation of order; to erect towns and cities; to grant titles of honor; and his the advowson of every benefice. The colonial act of 1702 had divided Maryland into parishes, and established the Anglican church by an annual tax of forty pounds of tobacco on every poll. The parishes were about forty in number, increasing in value, some of them promising a thousand pounds sterling a year. Thus the lewd Lord Baltimore had more church patronage than any land-holder in England; and, as there was no bishop in America, ruffians, fugitives from justice, men stained by intemperance and lust (I write with caution, the distinct allegations being before me), nestled themselves, through his corrupt and easy nature, in the parishes of Maryland.

The king had reserved no right of revising the laws of Maryland; nor could he invalidate them, except as they should be found repugnant to those of England. Though the acts of trade were in force, the royal power was by charter restrained "from imposing, or causing to be imposed, any customs or other taxations, quotas, or contributions whatsoever, within the province, or upon any merchandise, whilst being laden or unladen in its ports." Of its people, about one twelfth were Roman Catholics; and these suffered the burden of double taxation.

In Pennsylvania, with the counties on Delaware, the people, whose numbers appeared to double in sixteen years, were already the masters; and to dispute their authority was but to introduce an apparent anarchy. Of the noble territory, the joint proprietors were Thomas and Richard Penn; the former holding three quarters of the whole. Inheritance might subdivide it indefinitely. The political power that had been bequeathed to them brought little personal dignity or benefit. The wilderness domain was theirs; though Connecticut, which claimed to extend to the Pacific, was already appropriating to itself a part of their territory, and, like the Penns, sought to confirm its claim by deeds from the Six Nations.

The lieutenant-governor had a negative on legislation; but he depended on the assembly for his annual support, and had often to choose between compliance and poverty. To the council, whom the proprietaries appointed, and to the proprietaries themselves, the right to revise legislative acts was denied; and long usage confirmed the denial. In the land of the Penns, the legislature had but one branch; and of that branch Benjamin Franklin was the soul. It had an existence of its own; could meet on its own adjournments, and no power could prorogue or dissolve it; but a swift responsibility brought its members annually before their constituents. The assembly would not allow the proprietaries in England to name judges; they were to be named by the lieutenant-governor on the spot, and, like him, depended for their salaries on the yearly vote of the assembly. All sheriffs and coroners were chosen by the people. Moneys were raised by an excise, and were kept and were disbursed by provincial commissioners. The land-office was under proprietary control; and, to balance its political influence, the assembly kept the loan-office of paper money under their own supervision. The laws established for Pennsylvania complete enfranchisement in the domain of thought. Its able press developed the principles of civil rights; its principal city cherished science; and, by private munificence, a ship, at the instance of Franklin, had attempted to discover the north-western passage. A library, too, was endowed, and an academy chartered. No oaths or tests barred the avenue to public posts. The church of England, unaided by law, competed with all forms of dissent. The Presbyterians, who were willing to fight for their liberties, began to balance the enthusiasts, who were ready to suffer for them. Yet the Quakers, humblest amongst plebeian sects, and boldest of them all,—disjoined from the middle age without even a shred or a mark of its bonds; abolishing not the aristocracy of the sword only, but all war; not prelacy and priestcraft only, but outward symbols and ordinances, external sacraments and forms,—pure spiritualists, and apostles of the power and the freedom of mind, still swayed legislation and public opinion. Ever restless of authority, they were jealous of the new generation of proprietaries who had fallen off from their society, regulated the government with a view to their own personal profit, shunned taxation of their colonial estates, and would not answer as equals to the plain, untitled names which alone the usages of the Society of Friends allowed.

New Jersey, now a royal government, enjoyed, with the aged Belcher, comparative tranquillity. The generality of the people he found to be "very rustical," and deficient in "learning." To the Calvinist governor, the Quakers of this province seemed to want "orthodoxy in the principles of religion;" but he parried for them the oppressive disposition of the board of trade, and the rapacity of the great claimants of lands, who held seats in the council. "I have to steer," he would say, "between Scylla and Charybdis; to please the king's ministers at home, and a

touchy people here; to luff for one, and bear away for another."
Sheltered by its position, New Jersey refused to share the expense of Indian alliances; often left its own annual expenses
unprovided for; and its gentle and most obstinate enthusiasts
trusted in the extension of the peaceable kingdom "from sea to
sea," and the completion of the prophecies that "nation shall
not lift up sword against nation, neither shall they learn war
any more."

There, too, on the banks of the Delaware, men that labored
for inward stillness, and to live in the spirit of truth, learned
to love God in all his manifestations in the visible world; and
they testified against cruelty towards the least creature in whom
his breath had kindled the flame of life. Conscious of an enlargement of gospel love, John Woolman, a tailor by trade,
"stood up like a trumpet, through which the Lord speaks to his
people," to make the negro masters sensible of the evil of holding the people of Africa in slavery; and, by his testimony at
the meetings of Friends, recommended that oppressed part of
the creation to the notice of each individual and of the society.
Having discerned by a bright and radiant light the certain
evidence of divine truth, and not fearing to offend man by its
simplicity, he travelled much on the continent of America, and
would say to the thoughtful, that "a people used to labor mod-
erately for their living, training up their children in frugality
and business, have a happier life than those who live on the
labor of slaves; that freemen find satisfaction in improving and
providing for their families; but negroes, laboring to support
others who claim them as their property, and expecting nothing
but slavery during life, have not the like inducement to be
industrious."

"Men having power," he continued, "too often misapply it;
though we make slaves of the negroes, and the Turks make
slaves of the Christians, liberty is the natural right of all men
equally." "The slaves look to me like a burdensome stone to
such who burden themselves with them. The burden will grow
heavier and heavier, till times change in a way disagreeable to

us." "It may be just," answered one of his hearers, "for the Almighty so to order it." And while he had fresh and heavenly openings in respect to the care and providence of the Almighty over man, as the most noble amongst his creatures which are visible, and was fully persuaded that, as the life of Christ comes to reign in the earth, all abuse and unnecessary oppression will draw towards an end, yet, under the sense of the overflowing stream of unrighteousness, his life was often a life of mourning; and it was a matter fixed in his mind, that this trade of importing slaves, and way of life in keeping them, were dark gloominess hanging over the land. "Though many willingly ran into it, yet the consequences would be grievous to posterity." Therefore he went about, environed with heavenly light and consolation, persuading men that "the practice of continuing slavery was not right;" and in calmest and most guarded words he endeavored, through the press, "to raise an idea of a general brotherhood, and a disposition easy to be touched with a feeling of each other's afflictions." The men whom he addressed on both banks of the Delaware were not agreed, in all the branches of the question, on the propriety of keeping negroes; yet their masters began the work of setting them free, "because they had no contract for their labor, and liberty was their right." A general epistle from the yearly meeting of Friends, in 1754, declared it to be the "concern" of their body to bear testimony against the iniquitous practice of slave-dealing, and to warn their members against making any purchase of slaves.

But New York was at this time the central point of political interest. Its position invited it to foster American union. Having the most convenient harbor on the Atlantic, with bays expanding on either hand, and a navigable river penetrating the interior, it held the keys of Canada and the lakes. Crown Point and Niagara, monuments of French ambition, were encroachments upon its limits. Its unsurveyed inland frontier, sweeping round on the north, disputed with New Hampshire the land between Lake Champlain and the Connecticut, and extended into unmeasured distances in the west. Within its bosom, at

Onondaga, burned the council-fire of the Six Nations, whose irregular bands had seated themselves near Montreal, on the northern shore of Ontario, and on the Ohio; whose hunters roamed over the northwest and the west; whose war-parties had for ages strolled to Carolina. Here were concentrated by far the most important Indian relations, round which the idea of a general union was shaping itself into a reality. It was to still the hereditary warfare of the Six Nations with the southern Indians that South Carolina and Massachusetts first met at Albany; it was to confirm friendship with them and their allies that New England, and all the central states but New Jersey, had assembled in congress. But a higher principle was needed to blend the several colonies under one sovereignty, and that principle existed on the banks of the Hudson.

England never possessed the affection of the country which it had acquired by conquest. British officials sent home complaints of "the Dutch republicans" as disloyal. The descendants of the Huguenot refugees were taunted with their origin, and invited to accept English liberties gratefully as a boon. Nowhere was the collision between the royal governor and the colonial assembly so violent or so inveterate; nowhere had the legislature, by its method of granting money, so nearly exhausted and appropriated to itself all executive authority; nowhere had the relations of the province to Great Britain been more sharply controverted. The board of trade esteemed the provincial legislature to be subordinate, resting for its existence on acts of the royal prerogative, the king's commissions and the king's instructions, and possessed of none of the attributes of sovereignty; while the people looked upon their representatives as a body participant in sovereignty, existing by an inherent right, and co-ordinate with the British house of commons.

Affairs of religion also involved political strife. In a province chiefly of Calvinists, the English church was favored, though not established by law; but an act of the prerogative, which limited the selection of the president of the provincial college to those in communion with the church of England, agitated the public mind, and united the Presbyterians in distrust of the royal authority.

The laws of trade excited still more resistance. Why should a people, of whom one half were of foreign ancestry, be cut off from all the world but England? Why must the children of Holland be debarred from the ports of the Netherlands? Why must their ships seek the produce of Europe, and, by a later law, the produce of Asia, in English harbors alone? Why were negro slaves the only considerable object of foreign commerce which England did not compel to be first landed on its shores? The British restrictive system was never acknowledged by New York as valid, and was trangressed by all America; but most of all by this province, to an extent that could not easily be imagined. Especially the British ministry had been invited, in 1752, to observe that, while the consumption of tea was annually increasing in America, the export from England was decreasing. During the next twenty years, England sought a remedy; and, meantime, the little island of St. Eustatius, a heap of rocks, but two leagues in length by one in breadth, without a rivulet or a spring, gathered in its storehouses the products of Holland, of the Orient, of the world; and its harbor was more and more filled with fleets of colonial trading-vessels, which, if need were, completed their cargoes by entering the French islands with Dutch papers. Under the British statutes, which made the commercial relations of America to England not a union, but a bondage, America bought of England hardly more than she would have done on the system of freedom; and this small advantage was dearly purchased by the ever increasing cost of cruisers, custom-house officers, and vice-admiralty courts, and the discontent of the merchants.

The large landholders, whose grants, originally prodigal, irregular, and ill-defined, promised opulence for generations, were equally jealous of British authority, which threatened to bound their pretensions, or question their titles, or, through parliament, to impose a land-tax. The lawyers of the colony, chiefly Presbyterians, and educated in Connecticut, joined heartily with the merchants and the great proprietors to resist every encroachment from England; meeting the political theories of colonial subordination at the threshold; teaching the method of increasing colonial power by the system of annual grants; demanding permanent commissions for their judicial officers; opposing the extension of the admiralty jurisdiction; and resisting the admission of bishops, as involving ecclesiastical courts and new prerogatives. In no province was the near approach of independence discerned so clearly, or so openly predicted.

New York had been settled under large patents of lands to individuals; New England, under grants to towns; and the institution of towns was its glory and its strength. The inhabited part of Massachusetts was recognised as divided into little territories, each of which, for its internal purposes, constituted a separate integral government, free from supervision; having power to choose annually its own officers; to hold meetings of all freemen at its pleasure; to discuss in those meetings any subject of public interest; to see that every able-bodied man within its precincts was enrolled in the militia and provided with arms, ready for immediate use; to elect and to instruct its representatives; to raise and appropriate money for the support of the ministry, of schools, of highways, of the poor, and for defraying other necessary expenses within the town. It was incessantly deplored, by royalists of later days, that the law which confirmed these liberties had received the unconscious sanction of William III, and the most extensive interpretation in practice. Boston even, on more than one occasion, ventured in town meeting to appoint its own agent to present a remonstrance to the board of trade. New Hampshire, Connecticut, Rhode Island, and Maine, which was a part of Massachusetts, had similar regulations; so that all New England was an aggregate of organized democracies. But the complete development of the institution was to be found in Connecticut and the Massachusetts Bay. There each township was also substantially a territorial parish; the town was the religious congregation; the independent church was established by law; the minister was elected by the people, who annually made grants for his support. There, too, the system of free schools was carried to such perfection that an adult born in New England and unable to write and read could not be found. He that will understand the political character of New England in the eighteenth century must study the constitution of its towns, its congregations, its schools, and its militia.

Yet in these democracies the hope of independence, as a near event, had not dawned. Driven from England by the persecution of the government, its inhabitants still clung with confidence and persevering affection to the land of their ancestry, the people of their kindred, and the nationality of their language. They were of homogeneous origin, nearly all tracing their descent to English emigrants of the reigns of Charles I and Charles II. They were a frugal and industrious race. Along the seaside, wherever there was a good harbor, fishermen, familiar with the ocean, gathered in hamlets; and each returning season saw them, with an ever increasing number of mariners and vessels, taking the cod and mackerel, and sometimes pursuing the whale into the icy labyrinths of the northern seas; yet loving home, and dearly attached to their modest freeholds. At Boston a society was formed for promoting domestic manufactures: on one of its anniversaries, three hundred young women appeared on the common, clad in homespun, seated in a triple row, each with a spinning-wheel, and each busily transferring the flax from the distaff to the spool. The town built "a manufacturing house," and there were bounties to encourage the workers in linen. How the board of trade were alarmed at the news! How they censured Shirley for not having frowned on the business! How committees of the house of commons examined witnesses, and made proposals for prohibitory laws, till the Boston manufacturing house, designed to foster home industry fell into decay!—a commentary on the provident care of England for her colonies. Of slavery there was not enough to affect the character of the people, except in the south-east of Rhode

Island, where Newport was conspicuous for engaging in the slave-trade; and where, in two or three towns, negroes composed even a third of the inhabitants.

In the settlements which grew up in the interior, on the margin of the greenwood, the plain meeting-house of the congregation for public worship was everywhere the central point; near it stood the public school, by the side of the very broad road, over which wheels enough did not pass to do more than mark the path by ribbons in the sward. The snug farm-houses, owned as freeholds, without quit-rents, were dotted along the way; and the village pastor among his people, enjoying the calm raptures of devotion, "appeared like such a little white flower as we see in the spring of the year, low and humble on the ground, standing peacefully and lovingly in the midst of the flowers round about; all, in like manner, opening their bosoms to drink in the light of the sun." In every hand was the Bible; every home was a house of prayer; in every village all had been taught, many had comprehended, a methodical theory of the divine purpose in creation, and of the destiny of man.

Child of the Reformation, closely connected with the past centuries and with the greatest intellectual struggles of mankind, New England had been planted by enthusiasts who feared no sovereign but God. In the universal degeneracy and ruin of the Roman world, when freedom, laws, imperial rule, municipal authority, social institutions, were swept away; when not a province, nor city, nor village, nor family was safe,—Augustine, the African bishop, with a burning heart, confident that, though Rome tottered, the hope of man would endure, rescued from the wreck of the Old World the truths that would renew humanity; and sheltered them in the cloister, among successive generations of men, insulated by their vows from decaying society, and bound to the state neither by ambition, nor by allegiance, nor by the sweet attractions of wife and child.

After the sighs and sorrows of centuries, in the dawn of serener days, an Augustine monk, having also a heart of flame, seized on the same great ideas; and he and his followers, with wives and children, restored them to the world. At his bidding, truth leaped over the cloister walls, and challenged every man to make her his guest; aroused every intelligence to acts of private judgment; changed a dependent, recipient people into a reflecting, inquiring people; lifted each human being out of the castes of the middle age, to endow him with individuality; and summoned man to stand forth as man. The world heaved with the fervent conflict of opinion. The people and their guides recognised the dignity of labor; the oppressed peasantry took up arms for liberty; men reverenced and exercised the freedom of the soul. The breath of the new spirit moved over the earth; it revived Poland, animated Germany, swayed the north; and the inquisition of Spain could not silence its whispers among the mountains of the peninsula. It invaded France; and, though bonfires of heretics, by way of warning, were lighted at the gates of Paris, it infused itself into the French mind, and led to unwonted free discussions. Exile could not quench it. On the banks of the Lake of Geneva, Calvin stood forth the boldest reformer of his day; not personally engaging in political intrigues, yet, by promulgating great ideas, forming the seed-plot of revolution; bowing only to the Invisible; acknowledging no sacrament of ordination but the choice of the laity, no patent of nobility but that of the elect of God, with its seals of eternity.

Luther's was still a Catholic religion: it sought to instruct all, to confirm all, to sanctify all; and so, under the shelter of princes, it gave established forms to Protestant Germany, and Sweden, and Denmark, and England. But Calvin taught an exclusive doctrine, which, though it addressed itself to all, rested only on the chosen. Lutheranism was, therefore, not a political party; it included prince and noble and peasant. Calvinism was revolutionary; wherever it came, it created division; its symbol, as set up on the "Institutes" of its teacher, was a flaming sword. By the side of the eternal mountains and perennial snows and arrowy rivers of Switzerland, it established a religion without a prelate, a government without a king. Fortified by its faith in fixed decrees, it kept possession of its homes among the Alps. It grew powerful in France, and invigorated, between the feudal nobility and the crown, the long contest, which did not end, till the subjection of the nobility, through the central despotism, prepared the ruin of that despotism, by promoting the equality of the commons. It entered Holland, inspiring an industrious nation with heroic enthusiasm; enfranchising and uniting provinces; and making burghers, and weavers, and artisans, victors over the highest orders of Spanish chivalry, the power of the inquisition, and the pretended majesty of kings. It penetrated Scotland, and, while its whirlwind bore along persuasion among glens and mountains, it shrunk from no danger, and hesitated at no ambition; it nerved its rugged but hearty envoy to resist the flatteries of the beautiful Queen Mary; it assumed the education of her only son; it divided the nobility; it penetrated the masses, overturned the ancient ecclesiastical establishment, planted the free parochial school, and gave a living energy to the principle of liberty in a people. It infused itself into England, and placed its plebeian sympathies in daring resistance to the courtly hierarchy; dissenting from dissent, longing to introduce the reign of righteousness, it invited every man to read the Bible, and made itself dear to the common mind, by teaching, as a divine revelation, the unity of the race and the natural equality of man; it claimed for itself freedom of utterance, and through the pulpit, in eloquence imbued with the authoritative words of prophets and apostles, spoke to the whole congregation; it sought new truth, denying the sanctity of the continuity of tradition; it stood up against the middle age and its forms in church and state, hating them with a fierce and unquenchable hatred.

Imprisoned, maimed, oppressed at home, its independent converts in Great Britain looked beyond the Atlantic for a better world. Their energetic passion was nurtured by trust in the divine protection, their power of will was safely intrenched in their own vigorous creed; and under the banner of the gospel, with the fervid and enduring love of the myriads who in Europe adopted the stern simplicity of the discipline of Calvin, they sailed for the wilderness, far away from "popery and prelacy," from the traditions of the church, from hereditary power, from the sovereignty of an earthly king,—from all dominion but the Bible, and "what arose from natural reason and the principles of equity."

The ideas which had borne the New England emigrants to this transatlantic world were polemic and republican in their origin and their tendency. And how had the centuries matured the contest for mankind! Against the authority of the church of the middle ages, Calvin arrayed the authority of the Bible; the time was come to connect religion and philosophy, and show the harmony between faith and reason. Against the feudal aristocracy, the plebeian reformer summoned the spotless nobility of the elect, foreordained from the beginning of the world; but New England, which had no hereditary caste to beat down, ceased to make predestination its ruling idea, and, maturing a character of its own, "Saw love attractive every system bind." The transition had taken place from the haughtiness of its self-assertion against the pride of feudalism, to the adoption of love as the benign spirit which was to animate its new teachings in politics and religion.

From God were derived its theories of ontology, of ethics, of science, of happiness, of human perfectibility, and of human liberty.

God himself, wrote Jonathan Edwards, is, "in effect, universal Being." Nature in its amplitude is but "an emanation of his own infinite fulness;" a flowing forth and expression of himself in objects of his benevolence. In every thing there is a calm, sweet cast of divine glory. He comprehends "all entity and all excellence in his own essence." Creation proceeded from a disposition in the fulness of Divinity to flow out and diffuse its existence. The infinite Being is Being in general. His existence, being infinite, comprehends universal existence. There are and there can be no beings distinct and independent. God is "All and alone."

The glory of God is the ultimate end of moral goodness,

which in the creature is love to the Creator. Virtue consists in
public affection or general benevolence. But as to the New
England mind God included universal being, so to love God
seemed to include love to all that exists; and was, therefore,
in opposition to selfishness, the sum of all morality, the universal benevolence comprehending all righteousness.

God is the fountain of light and knowledge, so that truth
in man is but a conformity to God; knowledge in man, but "the
image of God's own knowledge of himself." Nor is there a motive to repress speculative inquiry. "There is no need," said
Edwards, "that the strict philosophic truth should be at all concealed from men." "The more clearly and fully the true system
of the universe is known, the better." Nor can any outward
authority rule the mind; the revelations of God, being emana-
tions from the infinite fountain of knowledge, have certainty
and reality; they accord with reason and common sense; and
give direct, intuitive, and all-conquering evidence of their divinity.

God is the source of happiness. His angels minister to his
servants; the vast multitudes of his enemies are as great heaps
of light chaff before the whirlwind. Against his enemies the
bow of God's wrath is bent, and the arrow made ready on the
string; and justice bends the arrow at their heart, and strains
the bow. God includes all being and all holiness. Enmity with
him is enmity with all true life and power; an infinite evil,
fraught with infinite and endless woe. To exist in union with
him is the highest well-being, that shall increase in glory and
joy throughout eternity.

God is his own chief end in creation. But, as he includes all
being, his glory includes the glory and the perfecting of the
universe. The whole human race, throughout its entire career of
existence, hath oneness and identity, and "constitutes one complex person," "one moral whole." The glory of God includes
the redemption and glory of humanity. From the moment of
creation to the final judgment, it is all one work. Every event
which has swayed "the state of the world of mankind," "all its

revolutions," proceed, as it was determined, towards "the glorious time that shall be in the latter days," when the new shall be more excellent than the old.

God is the absolute sovereign, doing according to his will in the armies of heaven, and among the inhabitants on earth. Scorning the thought of free agency as breaking the universe of action into countless fragments, the greatest number in New England held that every volition, even of the humblest of the people, is obedient to the fixed decrees of Providence, and participates in eternity.

Yet, while the common mind of New England was inspired by the great thought of the sole sovereignty of God, it did not lose personality and human freedom in pantheistic fatalism. Like Augustine, who made war both on Manicheans and Pelagians; like the Stoics, whose morals it most nearly adopted,—it asserted by just dialectics, or, as some would say, by a sublime inconsistency, the power of the individual will. In every action it beheld the union of the motive and volition. The action, it saw, was according to the strongest motive; and it knew that what proves the strongest motive depends on the character of the will. Hence, the education of that faculty was, of all concerns, the most momentous. The Calvinist of New England, who longed to be "morally good and excellent," had no other object of moral effort than to make "the will truly lovely and right."

Action, therefore, as flowing from an energetic, right, and lovely will, was the ideal of New England. It rejected the asceticism of entire spiritualists, and fostered the whole man, seeking to perfect his intelligence and improve his outward condition. It saw in every one the divine and the human nature. It did not extirpate the inferior principles, but only subjected them. It placed no merit in vows of poverty or celibacy, and spurned the thought of non-resistance. In a good cause its people were ready to take up arms and fiight, cheered by the conviction that God was working in them both to will and to do.

BANCROFT *interpreted the French and Indian War as a conflict between the forces of the Reformation and the forces of medieval Catholicism for possession of the New World, as well as a struggle between France and England for imperial supremacy. "The successes of the Seven Years' War," he wrote, "were the triumphs of Protestantism," nor did he consider the French monarchy a suitable instrument either of political liberty or freedom of conscience—"a government which could devise the massacre of St. Bartholomew," he said, "was neither able nor worthy to found new states." Like Parkman, Bancroft believed France the agent of regression; it "thought only to transmit to its American empire the exhausted polity of the middle ages; the castes of feudal Europe; its monarchy, its nobility, its dependent peasantry," whereas England's colonies "retained what they called English privileges, but left behind in the parent country English inequalities, the monarch and nobility and prelacy." In seizing control of Canada, the English and colonial armies erased the last vestiges of medievalism from North America, and by removing the last barriers to colonial westward expansion, opened the continent to "the free people who were making for humanity a new existence in America." Since the outcome of the battle on the Plains of Abraham was a significant factor in "hastening American independence," Bancroft recognized its importance by making it a set piece occupying a separate chapter.*

The Conquest of Canada (1759)

AMERICA more and more drew the attention of statesmen; and Pitt, who through his under-secretaries continued to profit by Franklin's wisdom, resolved that the boundless north of that continent should be a conquest for his country. With astonishing unanimity, parliament voted for the year twelve millions sterling, and such forces, by sea and land, as till those days had been unimagined in England.

Vol. III, Chap. XIV.

In the arrangements for the campaign, the secretary disregarded seniority of rank. Stanwix was to complete the occupation of the posts at the west from Pittsburg to Lake Erie; Prideaux to reduce Fort Niagara; and Amherst, now commander in chief and the sinecure governor of Virginia, to advance with the main army to Lake Champlain. To command the fleet which was to support the attack on Quebec, Pitt selected the generous and kind-hearted Saunders, an officer who to unaffected modesty and steady courage joined the love of civil freedom. The command of the army in the river St. Lawrence was conferred on Wolfe. "I feel called upon," he had once written, on occasion of his early promotion, "to justify the notice taken of me by such exertions and exposure of myself as will probably lead to my fall." And the day before departing for his command, in the inspiring presence of Pitt, he forgot danger, glory, every thing but the overmastering purpose to devote himself for his country.

All the while, ships from every part of the world were bringing messages of the success of British arms. In the preceding April, a small English squadron made a conquest of Senegal; in December, negroes crowded on the heights of the Island of Goree to gaze on the strange spectacle of war, and to witness the surrender of its forts to Commodore Augustus Keppel. In the Indian seas, Pococke maintained the superiority of England. In the West Indies, in January, 1759, a fleet of ten line-of-battle ships, with six thousand effective troops, made a fruitless attack on Martinique; but, sailing for Guadaloupe, the best of the West India possessions of France, after the losses and daring deeds of more than three months, in May it gained, by capitulation, that delightful and well-watered island, whose harbor can screen whole navies from hurricanes, whose position gives the command of the neighboring seas.

From the continent of Europe came the assurance that a victory at Minden had protected Hanover. The French, having repulsed Prince Ferdinand of Brunswick at Frankfort, pursued their advantage, occupied Cassel, compelled Munster to capit-

ulate, and took Minden by assault; so that Hanover could be
saved only by a victory. Contades and Broglie, the French
generals, with their superior force were allured from their
strong position, and accepted battle on narrow and inconveni-
ent ground, on which their horse occupied the centre, their foot
the wings. The French cavalry charged, but, swept by artillery
and the rolling fire of the English and Hanoverian infantry,
they were repulsed. At this moment, Ferdinand, who had detached the hereditary prince of Brunswick with ten thousand
men to cut off the retreat, sent a message to the commander
of the British cavalry, Lord George Sackville, by a German
aide-de-camp. Lord George affected not to understand. Ligonier
came next, with express directions that he should bring up the
cavalry and attack the French, who were faltering. "See the
confusion he is in!" cried Sloper to Ligonier; "for God's sake,
repeat your orders!" Fitzroy arrived with a third order from
Ferdinand. "This cannot be so," said Lord George; "would he
have me break the line?" Fitzroy urged the command. "Do
not be in a hurry," said Lord George. "I am out of breath with
galloping," replied young Fitzroy, "which makes me speak
quick; but my orders are positive; the French are in confusion;
here is a glorious opportunity for the English to distinguish
themselves." "It is impossible," repeated Lord George, "that
the prince could mean to break the line." "I give you his orders," rejoined Fitzroy, "word for word." "Who will be the
guide to the cavalry?" asked Lord George. "I," said the brave
boy, and led the way. Lord George, pretending to be puzzled,
was reminded by Smith, one of his aids, of the necessity of
immediate obedience; on which he sent Smith to lead on the
British cavalry, while he himself rode to the prince for explanation. Ferdinand, in scorn, renewed his orders to the Marquis of Granby, the second in command, and was obeyed with
alacrity; but the decisive moment was lost. "Lord George's fall
was prodigious," said Horace Walpole; "nobody stood higher;
nobody had more ambition or more sense." Pitt softened his
misfortune with the offices of humanity, but condemned his

conduct. George II dismissed him from all his posts. A court-martial, the next year, found him guilty of disobeying orders, and unfit for employment in any military capacity; on which the king struck his name out of the council-book and forbade his appearance at court.

In America, every colony north of Maryland seconded this zeal of William Pitt. In New York and New England, there was not one village but grew familiar with war from the experience of its own inhabitants. Massachusetts sent into the service more than seven thousand men, or nearly one sixth part of all who were able to bear arms. Connecticut raised, as in the previous year, five thousand men. To meet the past expense, the little colony incurred heavy debts, and appointed taxes on property to discharge them. New Jersey had already lost one thousand men, and yet voted to raise one thousand more; and expended yearly for the war an amount equal to about five dollars for each inhabitant. Such was the free service of the loyal colonies under an administration which respected their liberty.

To encounter the preparations of England and America, Canada received scanty supplies of provisions from France. "The king," wrote the minister to Montcalm, "relies on your zeal and obstinacy of courage;" but Montcalm informed Belle-Isle plainly, that, without unexpected good fortune, or great fault in the enemy, Canada must be taken this campaign, or certainly the next. Its census showed but a population of about eighty-two thousand, of whom not more than seven thousand men could serve as soldiers; the eight French battalions counted but thirty-two hundred; while the English were thought to have almost fifty thousand men in arms. There was a dearth in the land; the fields were hardly cultivated; domestic animals were failing; the soldiers were unpaid; paper money had increased to thirty millions of livres, and would that year be increased twelve millions more; while the civil officers were making haste to enrich themselves before the surrender, which was to screen their frauds.

The western brigade, commanded by Prideaux, composed of two battalions from New York, a battalion of royal Americans, and two British regiments, with a detachment of royal artillery, and Indian auxiliaries under Sir William Johnson, was the first to engage actively. Fort Niagara stood, as its ruins yet stand, on the flat and narrow promontory round which the deep and rapid Niagara sweeps into the lower lake. There La Salle, first of Europeans, had driven a light palisade. There Denonville had constructed a fortress and left a garrison for a winter. It commanded the portage between Ontario and Erie, and gave the dominion of the western fur-trade. Leaving a detachment with Colonel Haldimand to construct a tenable post at the mouth of the Oswego, the united American, British, and Indian forces embarked, on the first day of July [1759], on Lake Ontario, and landed without opposition at one of its inlets, six miles east of the junction of the Niagara. The fortress on the peninsula was easily invested.

Aware of the importance of the station, D'Aubry collected from Detroit and Erie, Le Bœuf and Venango, an army of twelve hundred men, larger than that which defeated Braddock, and marched to the rescue. Prideaux made the best dispositions to frustrate the design; but, on the fifteenth of July, he was killed by the bursting of a cohorn, leaving his honors immature. Sir William Johnson, who succeeded to the command, commemorated his rare abilities and zeal, and carefully executed his plans. He posted the British army on the left, above the fort, so as to intercept the approach of the enemy and to support the guard in the trenches. On the morning of the twenty-fourth of July, the French made their appearance. The Mohawks gave a sign for a parley with the French Indians; but, as it was not returned, they raised the war-whoop. While the regulars advanced to meet the French in front, the English Indians gained their flanks and threw them into disorder on which the English rushed to the charge with irresistible fury. The French broke, retreated, and were pursued. The carnage continued till fatigue stayed its hand. The bodies of the dead lay uncounted among the forests. On the next day, the garrison, consisting of about six hundred men, capitulated. Thus did New York extend its limits to the Niagara River and Lake Erie. The victory was so decisive, that the officer and troops sent by Stanwix from Pittsburg took possession of the French posts as far as Erie without resistance.

The success of the English on Lake Ontario drew De Levi, the second in military command in New France, from before Quebec. He ascended beyond the Rapids, and endeavored to guard against a descent to Montreal by occupying the passes of the river near Ogdensburg. The number of men at his disposal was too few to accomplish the object; and Amherst directed Gage, whom he detached as successor to Prideaux, to take possession of the post. But Gage made excuses for neglecting the orders, and whiled away his harvest-time of honor.

Meantime, the commander in chief assembled the main army at Lake George. The temper of Amherst was never ruffled by collisions with the Americans; his displeasure, when excited, was concealed under apparent apathy or impenetrable self-command. His judgment was slow, but safe; his mind solid, but never inventive. Taciturn and stoical, he displayed respectable abilities as a commander, without fertility of resources, or daring enterprise. In five British regiments, with the royal Americans, he had fifty-seven hundred and forty-three regulars; of provincials and Gage's light infantry he had nearly as many more. On the longest day in June, he reached the lake, and the next day, with useless precaution, traced out the ground for a fort. On the twenty-first of July, the invincible flotilla moved in four columns down the water, with artillery and more than eleven thousand men. On the twenty-second, the army disembarked on the eastern shore, nearly opposite the landing-place of Abercrombie; and that night, after a skirmish of the advanced guard, they lay under arms at the saw-mills. The next day, the French army under Bourlamarque, leaving a garrison of but four hundred in Fort Carillon, deserted their lines, of which possession was immediately taken.

Conscious of their inability to resist the British artillery and army, the French, on the twenty-sixth, abandoned Ticonderoga; and, five days afterwards, retreated from Crown Point to Isle-aux-Noix. The whole mass of the people of Canada had been called to arms; the noblesse piqued themselves much on the antiquity of their families, their own military glory and that of their ancestors; nor had the world known greater courage and loyalty than they displayed. So general had been the levy that there were not men enough left to reap the fields round Montreal; and, to prevent starvation, women, old men, and children were ordered to gather in the harvest alike for rich and poor. Yet, as the chief force was with Montcalm near Quebec, as the Indians no longer thronged to the camp of the French, the army that opposed Amherst had but one fourth of his numbers, and could not be recruited. An immediate descent on Montreal was universally expected. In a fortnight, Crown Point was occupied, without opposition. Amherst must advance, or Wolfe may perish. But, after repairing Ticonderoga, he wasted labor in building fortifications at Crown Point, which the conquest of Canada would render useless. Thus he let all August, all September, and ten days of October go by, before boats were ready; and when at last he embarked, and victory, not without honor, might still have been within his grasp, he received messengers from Quebec, and turned back, having done nothing but occupy and repair deserted forts. Sending a detachment against the St. Francis Indians, he went into winter-quarters, leaving his unfinished work for another costly campaign. Amherst was a brave and faithful officer, but his intellect was dull. He gained a great name, because New France was occupied during his chief command; but, had Wolfe resembled him, Quebec would not have fallen.

As soon as the floating masses of ice permitted, the forces for the expedition against Quebec repaired to Louisburg; and Wolfe, by his activity and zeal, his good judgment and the clearness of his orders, inspired unbounded confidence. His army consisted of eight regiments, two battalions of royal Americans, three companies of rangers, artillery, and a brigade of engineers,—in all, about eight thousand men; the fleet under Saunders had two-and-twenty ships of the line, and as many frigates and armed vessels. On board of one of the ships was Jervis, afterwards Earl Saint-Vincent; another, which followed, bore as master James Cook, the navigator, who was destined to explore and reveal the paths and thousand isles of the Pacific. The brigades had for their commanders the brave, open-hearted, and liberal Robert Monckton, afterwards governor of New York and conqueror of Martinique; George Townshend, elder brother of Charles Townshend, soon to succeed his father in the peerage, and become known as a legislator for America, a man of quick perception, but unsafe judgment; and the rash and inconsiderate James Murray. For his adjutant-general, Wolfe selected Isaac Barré, an old associate at Louisburg. The grenadiers of the army were formed into a corps, commanded by Colonel Guy Carleton; a detachment of light infantry was to receive orders from Lieutenant-colonel, afterwards Sir William, Howe.

On the twenty-sixth of June, the whole armament arrived, without the least accident, off the Isle of Orleans, on which, the next day, they disembarked. A little south of west, the cliff of Quebec was seen distinctly, seemingly impregnable, rising precipitously in the midst of one of the grandest scenes in nature. To protect this guardian citadel of New France, Montcalm had of regular troops no more than six wasted battalions; of Indian warriors few appeared, the wary savages preferring the security of neutrals; the Canadian militia gave him the superiority in numbers; but he put his chief confidence in the natural strength of the country. Above Quebec, the high promontory on which the upper town is built expands into an elevated plain, having towards the river the steepest acclivities. For nine miles or more above the city, as far as Cape Rouge, every landing-place was intrenched and protected. The river St. Charles, after meandering through a fertile valley, sweeps the rocky base of the town, which it covers by expanding into sedgy marshes. Nine miles below Quebec, the impetuous Mont-morenci, after fretting itself a whirlpool route, and leaping for miles down the steps of a rocky bed, rushes with velocity towards the ledge, over which, falling two hundred and fifty feet, it pours its fleecy cataract into the chasm.

As Wolfe disembarked on the Isle of Orleans, the fleet with the numerous transports lay at anchor on his left; the tents of his army stretched across the island; the intrenched troops of France, having their centre at the village of Beauport, extended from the Montmorenci to the St. Charles; the city of Quebec, garrisoned by five battalions, bounded the horizon. At midnight, on the twenty-eighth, the short darkness was lighted up by a fleet of fire-ships, that, after a furious storm of wind, came down with the tide in the proper direction; but the British sailors grappled with them and towed them free of the shipping.

The river was Wolfe's: the men-of-war made it so; and, being master of the deep water, he also had the superiority on the south shore of the St. Lawrence. In the night of the twenty-ninth, Monckton, with four battalions, having crossed the south channel, occupied Point Levi; and where the mighty current, which below the town expands as a bay, narrows to a deep stream of but a mile in width, batteries of mortar and cannon were constructed. Early in July, the citizens of Quebec, fore-seeing the ruin of their houses, volunteered to pass over the river and destroy the works; but, at the trial, their courage failed them, and they retreated. The English, by the discharge of red-hot balls and shells, set on fire fifty houses in a night, demolished the lower town, and injured the upper; but the citadel was beyond their reach, and every avenue from the river to the cliff was too strongly intrenched for an assault.

As yet no real progress had been made. Wolfe was eager for battle, being willing to risk all his hopes on the issue. He saw that the eastern bank of the Montmorenci was higher than the ground occupied by Montcalm, and, on the ninth, he crossed the north channel and encamped there; but the armies and their chiefs were still divided by the river precipitating itself down its rocky way in impassable eddies and rapids. Three miles in the interior, a ford was found; but the opposite bank was steep, woody, and well intrenched. Not a spot on the line of the Montmorenci for miles into the interior, nor on the St. Lawrence to Quebec, was left unprotected by the vigilance of the inaccessible Montcalm.

The general proceeded to reconnoitre the shore above the town. In concert with Saunders, on the eighteenth he sailed along the well-fortified bank from Montmorenci to the St. Charles; he passed the deep and spacious harbor, which, at four hundred miles from the sea, can shelter a hundred ships of the line; he neared the high cliff of Cape Diamond, towering like a bastion over the waters and surmounted by the banner of the Bourbons; he coasted along the craggy wall of rock that extends beyond the citadel; he marked the outline of the precipitous hill that forms the north bank of the river: and everywhere he beheld a natural fastness, vigilantly defended; intrenchments, cannon, boats, and floating batteries guarding every access. Had a detachment landed between the city and Cape Rouge, it would have encountered the danger of being cut off before it could receive support. He would have risked a landing at St. Michael's Cove, three miles above the city, but the enemy prevented him by planting artillery and a mortar to play upon the shipping.

Meantime, at midnight, on the twenty-eighth, the French sent down a raft of fire-stages, consisting of nearly a hundred pieces; but these, like the fire-ships a month before, did but light up the river, without injuring the British fleet. Scarcely a day passed but there were skirmishes of the English with the Indians and Canadians, who trod stealthily in the footsteps of every exploring party.

Wolfe returned to Montmorenci. July was almost gone, and he had made no effective advances. He resolved on an engagement. The Montmorenci, after falling over a perpendicular rock, flows for three hundred yards, amidst clouds of spray and rainbow glories, in a gentle stream to the St. Lawrence. Near the junction, the river may, for a few hours of the tide, be passed on foot. It was planned that two brigades should ford the Montmorenci at the proper time of the tide, while Monckton's regiments should cross the St. Lawrence in boats from Point Levi. The signal was made, but some of the boats grounded on a ledge of rocks that runs out into the river. While the seamen were getting them off, and the enemy were firing a vast number of shot and shells, Wolfe, with some of the navy officers as companions, selected a landing-place; and his desperate courage thought it not yet too late to begin the attack. Thirteen companies of grenadiers, and two hundred of the second battalion of the royal Americans, who got first on shore, not waiting for support, ran hastily towards the intrenchments, and were repulsed in such disorder that they could not again come into line; though Monckton's regiments had arrived, and had formed with the coolness of invincible valor. But hours hurried by; night was near; the clouds of midsummer gathered heavily, as if for a storm; the tide rose; and Wolfe, wiser than Frederic at Colin, ordered a timely retreat. A strand of deep mud; a hillside, steep, and in many places impracticable; the heavy fire of a brave, numerous, and well-protected enemy,—were obstacles which intrepidity and discipline could not overcome. In general orders, Wolfe censured the impetuosity of the grenadiers; he praised the coolness of Monckton's regiments, as able alone to beat back the whole Canadian army.

This severe check, in which four hundred lives were lost, happened on the last day of July. Murray was next sent, with twelve hundred men, above the town, to destroy the French ships and open a communication with Amherst. Twice he attempted a landing on the north shore, without success; at Deschambault, a place of refuge for women and children, he won advantages over a guard of invalid soldiers, and learned that Niagara had surrendered, that the French had abandoned Ticonderoga and Crown Point. The eyes of Wolfe were strained to see Amherst approach. Vain hope! The commander in chief, though opposed by no more than three thousand men, was loitering at Crown Point; nor did even a messenger from him arrive. Wolfe was alone to struggle with difficulties which every hour made more appalling. The numerous body of armed men under Montcalm "could not," he said, "be called an army;" but the French had the strongest country, perhaps, in the world, on which to rest the defence of the town. Their boats were numerous, and weak points were guarded by floating batteries; the keen eye of the Indian prevented surprise; the vigilance and hardihood of the Canadians made intrenchments everywhere necessary. The peasantry were zealous to defend their homes, language, and religion; old men of seventy and boys of fifteen fired at the English detachments from the edges of the wood; every one able to bear arms was in the field. Little quarter was given on either side. Thus for two months the British fleet had ridden idly at anchor, the army had lain in their tents. The feeble frame of Wolfe sunk under the energy of his restless spirit, and the pain of anxious inactivity.

Yet, while disabled by fever, he laid before the brigadiers three several and equally desperate methods of attacking Montcalm in his intrenchments at Beauport. Meeting at Monckton's quarters, they wisely and unanimously gave their opinions against them all, and advised to convey four or five thousand men above the town, and thus draw Montcalm from his impregnable situation to an open action. Wolfe acquiesced in their proposal; and, with despair in his heart, yet as one conscious that he lived under the eye of Pitt and of his country, he prepared to carry it into effect. Attended by the admiral, he examined once more the citadel, with a view to a general assault. Although every one of the five passages from the lower to the upper town was carefully intrenched, Saunders was willing to join in any hazard for the public service; "but I could not propose to him," said Wolfe, "an undertaking of so dangerous a nature and promising so little success." He had the whole force of Canada to oppose, and, by the nature of the river, the fleet could render no assistance. "In this situation," wrote Wolfe to Pitt, on the second of September, "there is such a choice of difficulties, that I am myself at a loss how to determine. The affairs of Great Britain require most vigorous measures; but, then, the courage of a handful of brave men should be exerted only where there is some hope." England read the despatch with dismay, and feared to hear further tidings.

Securing the posts on the Isle of Orleans and opposite Quebec, he marched, with the army, on the fifth and sixth of September, from Point Levi, to which place he had transferred all the troops from Montmorenci, and embarked them in transports that had passed the town for the purpose. On the three following days, Admiral Holmes, with the ships, ascended the river to amuse De Bougainville, who had been sent up the north shore to watch the movements of the British army, and prevent a landing. New France began to feel joy, believing the worst dangers of the campaign over. De Levi, the second officer in command, was sent to protect Montreal, with a detachment, it was said, of three thousand men. Summer, which in that climate hurries through the sky, was over; and the British fleet must soon withdraw from the river. "My constitution," wrote the general to Holdernesse, on the ninth, just four days before his death, "is entirely ruined, without the consolation of having done any considerable service to the state, and without any prospect of it."

But, in the mean time, Wolfe applied himself intently to reconnoitring the north shore above Quebec. Nature had given him good eyes, as well as a warmth of temper to follow first impressions. He himself discovered the cove which now bears his name, where the bending promontories almost form a basin, with a very narrow margin, over which the hill rises precipitously. He saw the path that wound up the steep, though so narrow that two men could hardly march in it abreast; and he knew, by the number of tents which he counted on the summit, that the Canadian post which guarded it could not exceed a hundred. Here he resolved to land his army by surprise. To mislead the enemy, his troops were kept far above the town; while Saunders, as if an attack was intended at Beauport, set

Cook, the great mariner, with others, to sound the water and plant buoys along that shore.

The day and night of the twelfth were employed in preparations. The autumn evening was bright; and the general, under the clear starlight, visited his stations, to make his final inspection and utter his last words of encouragement. As he passed from ship to ship, he spoke to those in the boat with him of the poet Gray, and the "Elegy in a Country Churchyard." "I," said he, "would prefer being the author of that poem to the glory of beating the French to-morrow;" and, while the oars struck the river as it rippled in the silence of the night air under the flowing tide, he repeated:—

> The boast of heraldry, the pomp of power,
>   And all that beauty, all that wealth e'er gave,
> Await alike the inevitable hour.
>   The paths of glory lead but to the grave.

Every officer knew his appointed duty, when, at one o'clock in the morning of the thirteenth of September, Wolfe, Monckton, and Murray, and about half the forces, set off in boats, and, using neither sail nor oars, glided down with the tide. In three quarters of an hour the ships followed; and, though the night had become dark, aided by the rapid current, they reached the cove just in time to cover the landing. Wolfe and the troops with him leaped on shore; the light infantry, who found themselves borne by the current a little below the intrenched path, clambered up the steep hill, staying themselves by the roots and boughs of the maple and spruce and ash trees that covered the precipitous declivity, and, after a little firing, dispersed the picket which guarded the height; the rest ascended safely by the pathway. A battery of four guns on the left was abandoned to Colonel Howe. When Townshend's division disembarked, the English had already gained one of the roads to Quebec; and, advancing in front of the forest, Wolfe stood at daybreak with his invincible battalions on the Plains of Abraham, the battlefield of the Celtic and Saxon races.

"It can be but a small party, come to burn a few houses and retire," said Montcalm, in amazement, as the news reached him in his intrenchments the other side of the St. Charles; but, obtaining better information, "Then," he cried, "they have at last got to the weak side of this miserable garrison; we must give battle and crush them before mid-day." And, before ten, the two armies, equal in numbers, each being composed of less than five thousand men, were ranged in presence of one another for battle. The English, not easily accessible from intervening shallow ravines and rail-fences, were all regulars, perfect in discipline, terrible in their fearless enthusiasm, thrilling with pride at their morning's success, commanded by a man whom they obeyed with confidence and love. The doomed and devoted Montcalm had what Wolfe had called but "five weak French battalions," of less than two thousand men, "mingled with disorderly peasantry," formed on commanding ground. The French had three little pieces of artillery; the English, one or two. The two armies cannonaded each other for nearly an hour; when Montcalm, having summoned De Bougainville to his aid, and despatched messenger after messenger for De Vaudreuil, who had fifteen hundred men at the camp, to come up before he should be driven from the ground, endeavored to flank the British and crowd them down the high bank of the river. Wolfe counteracted the movement by detaching Townshend with Amherst's regiment, and afterwards a part of the royal Americans, who formed on the left with a double front.

Waiting no longer for more troops, Montcalm led the French army impetuously to the attack. The ill-disciplined companies broke by their precipitation and the unevenness of the ground; and fired by platoons, without unity. Their adversaries, especially the forty-third and the forty-seventh, where Monckton stood, of which three men out of four were Americans, received the shock with calmness; and after having, at Wolfe's command, reserved their fire till their enemy was within forty yards, their line began a regular, rapid, and exact discharge of musketry. Montcalm was present everywhere, braving danger, wounded, but cheering by his example. The second in command, De Sennezergues, an associate in glory at Ticonderoga, was killed. The brave but untried Canadians, flinching from a hot fire in the open field, began to waver; and, so soon as Wolfe, placing himself at the head of the twenty-eighth and the Louisburg grenadiers, charged with bayonets, they everywhere gave way. Of the English officers, Carleton was wounded; Barré, who fought near Wolfe, received in the head a ball which made him blind of one eye, and ultimately of both. Wolfe, also, as he led the charge, was wounded in the wrist; but, still pressing forward, he received a second ball; and, having decided the day, was struck a third time, and mortally, in the breast. "Support me," he cried to an officer near him; "let not my brave fellows see me drop." He was carried to the rear, and they brought him water to quench his thirst. "They run! they run!" spoke the officer on whom he leaned. "Who run?" asked Wolfe, as his life was fast ebbing. "The French," replied the officer, "give way everywhere." "What," cried the expiring hero, "do they run already? Go, one of you, to Colonel Burton; bid him march Webb's regiment with all speed to Charles River to cut off the fugitives." Four day before, he had looked forward to early death with dismay. "Now, God he praised, I die happy." These were his words as his spirit escaped in the blaze of his glory. Night, silence, the rushing tide, veteran discipline, the sure inspiration of genius, had been his allies; his battle-field, high over the ocean river, was the grandest theatre for illustrious deeds; his victory, one of the most momentous in the annals of mankind, gave to the English tongue and the institutions of the Germanic race the unexplored and seemingly infinite west and north. He crowded into a few hours actions that would have given lustre to length of life; and, filling his day with greatness, completed it before its noon.

Monckton, the first brigadier, after greatly distinguishing himself, was shot through the lungs. Townshend, the next in command, recalled the troops from the pursuit; and, when De Bougainville appeared in view, declined a contest with a fresh enemy. But already the hope of New France was gone. Born and educated in camps, Montcalm had been carefully instructed, and was skilled in the language of Homer as well as in the art of war. Laborious, just, disinterested, hopeful even to rashness, sagacious in council, swift in action, his mind was a well-spring of bold designs; his career in Canada, a wonderful struggle against inexorable destiny. Sustaining hunger and cold, vigils and incessant toil, anxious for his soldiers, unmindful of himself, he set, even to the forest-trained red men, an example of self-denial and endurance; and, in the midst of corruption, made the public good his aim. Struck by a musket-ball, as he fought opposite Monckton, he continued in the engagement till, in attempting to rally a body of fugitive Canadians in a copse near St. John's gate, he was mortally wounded.

On hearing from the surgeon that death was certain, "I am glad of it," he cried; "how long shall I survive?" "Ten or twelve hours, perhaps less." "So much the better; I shall not live to see the surrender of Quebec." To the council of war he showed that in twelve hours all the troops near at hand might be concentrated and renew the attack before the English were intrenched. When De Ramsay, who commanded the garrison, asked his advice about defending the city, "To your keeping," he replied, "I commend the honor of France. As for me, I shall pass the night with God, and prepare myself for death." Having written a letter recommending the French prisoners to the generosity of the English, his last hours were given to the offices of his religion, and at five the next morning he expired.

The day of the battle had not passed, when De Vaudreuil, who had no capacity for war, wrote to De Ramsay at Quebec not to wait for an assault, but, as soon as his provisions were exhausted, to raise the white flag of surrender. "We have cheerfully sacrificed our fortunes and our houses," said the citizens; "but we cannot expose our wives and children to a massacre." At a council of war, Fiedmont, a captain of artillery, was the only one who wished to hold out to the last extremity; and on the seventeenth of September, before the English had constructed batteries, De Ramsay capitulated.

America rung with exultation; the towns were bright with illuminations, the hills with bonfires; legislatures, the pulpit, the press, echoed the general joy; provinces and families gave thanks to God. England, too, which had shared the despondency of Wolfe, triumphed at his victory and wept for his death. Joy, grief, curiosity, amazement, were on every countenance. When the parliament assembled, Pitt modestly and gracefully put aside the praises that were showered on him. "The more a man is versed in business," said he, "the more he finds the hand of Providence everywhere." "I will own I have a zeal to serve my country beyond what the weakness of my frail body admits of;" and he foretold new successes at sea. November fulfilled his predictions. In that month, Sir Edward Hawke attacked the fleet of Constans off the northern coast of France; and, though it retired to the shelter of shoals and rocks, he gained the battle during a storm at night-fall.

ALTHOUGH *recent scholarship has found Pontiac's war much less of an organized "conspiracy" than Bancroft and the historians of his time believed, the siege of Detroit and the fall of Fort Michilimackinac provided him with an opportunity both for a dramatic battle piece and for a comment on the last despairing effort of the red man to regain his lost Great Lakes empire. Bancroft could write a swift-paced, stripped, and energetic narrative when he wished to do so, and his chapter on Pontiac shows his later prose style to its best advantage.*

Pontiac's War (1763)

THE western territory, of which England believed itself to have come into possession, was one continuous forest, interrupted only by rocks or prairies or waters, or an Indian cleared field for maize. The English came into the illimitable waste as conquerors; and here and there in the solitudes, all the way from Niagara to the Falls of the St. Mary and the banks of the St. Joseph's, a log fort with a picketed enclosure was the emblem of their pretensions. In their haste to supplant the French, they were blind to danger; and their posts were often left dependent on the Indians for supplies. The smaller garrisons consisted only of an ensign, a sergeant, and perhaps fourteen men; and were stationed at points so remote from one another that, lost in the boundless woods, they could no more be discerned than a fleet of canoes scattered over the Atlantic, too minute to be perceptible, and safe only during fair weather. Yet, feeble as they were, their presence alarmed the red man; for it implied the design to occupy the country which for ages had been his own. His canoe could no longer quiver on the bosom of the St. Mary's, or pass into the clear waters of Lake Huron, or paddle through the strait that connects Huron and Erie, or cross to the waters of the Ohio, without passing by the British flag. By what right was that banner unfurled in the west? What claim

to the red man's forest could the English derive from victories
over the French? The latter seemed no more to be masters, but
rather companions and friends. Enemies now appeared, arrogant in their pretensions, insolent toward those whom they
superseded, driving away their Catholic priests, and introducing the traffic in rum, which till then had been affectually prohibited. Since the French must go, no other nation should take
their place. The red men must vindicate their right to their
own heritage.

The conspiracy began with the lower nations, who were the
chief instigators of discontent. "The English mean to make
slaves of us, by occupying so many posts in our country. We
had better attempt something now, to recover our liberty, than
wait till they are better established." So spoke the Senecas to
the Delawares, and they to the Shawnees, and the Shawnees
to the Miamis and Wyandots, whose chiefs, slain in battle by
the English, were still unavenged, until, from the Niagara and
the Alleghanies to the Mississippi and Lake Superior, all the
nations concerted to rise and put the English to death.

The plot was discovered in March by the officer in command
at Miami; and, "after a long and troublesome" interview, the
bloody belt, which was then in the village and was to be sent
forward to the tribes on the Wabash, was obtained from the
Miami chiefs.

On receiving the news, Amherst prepared re-enforcements,
and threatened that the mischief should recoil on the Indians
themselves, and end in their destruction.

But Pontiac, "the king and lord of all the north-west,"—a
Catawba prisoner, as is said, adopted into the clan of the Ottawas, and elected their chief; respected, and in a manner
adored, by all the nations around him; a man "of integrity and
humanity," according to the morals of the wilderness; fertile
in resources, and of an undaunted nature,—persevered in the
design of recovering the land of the Senecas, and all west of it,
by a confederacy of Indian nations.

Of the remote north-western settlements, Detroit was the

largest and the most important. The deep, majestic river, more than a half mile broad, carrying its vast flood calmly and noiselessly between the strait and well-defined banks of its channel imparted grandeur to a country whose rising grounds and meadows, plains festooned with prolific wild vines, woodlands, brooks, and fountains, were so mingled together that nothing was left to desire. The climate was mild, and the air salubrious. Good land abounded, yielding maize, wheat, and every vegetable. The forests were a natural park, stocked with buffaloes, deer, quails, partridges, and wild turkeys. Water-fowl of delicious flavor hovered along its streams, which yielded to the angler an astonishing variety of fish, especially the white fish, the richest and most luscious of them all. Every luxury of the table might be enjoyed at the sole expense of labor. The cheerful region attracted settlers, alike white men and savages. About sixty French families occupied both banks of the river, on farms, which were about three or four acres wide upon the river, and eighty acres deep; indolent in the midst of plenty, graziers as well as tillers of the soil, and enriched by Indian traffic.

The English fort, of which Gladwin was the commander, was a large stockade, about twenty feet high and twelve hundred yards in circumference, enclosing, perhaps, eighty houses. It stood within the limits of the present city, on the river bank, commanding a wide prospect for nine miles above and below. The garrison was composed of the eightieth regiment, reduced to about one hundred and twenty men and eight officers. Two armed vessels lay in the river; of artillery, there were but two six-pounders, one three-pounder, and three mortars, so badly mounted as to be of no use except to inspire terror.

The nation of the Pottawatomies dwelt about a mile below the fort; the Wyandots, a little lower down, on the eastern side of the strait; and five miles higher up, but on the same eastern side, the Ottawas.

On the first day of May, Pontiac entered the fort with about fifty of his warriors, announcing his purpose in a few days to pay a more formal visit. He appeared on the seventh, with about three hundred warriors, armed with knives, tomahawks, and guns cut short and hid under their blankets. He was to sit down in council, and, when he should rise, was to speak with a belt white on one side and green on the other; and turning the belt was to be the signal for a general massacre. But Gladwin had the night before been informed of his coming, and took such precautions that the interview passed off without results.

On the morning of the same day, an English party who were sounding the entrance of Lake Huron were seized and murdered. On the eighth, Pontiac appeared once more with a pipe of peace, proposing to come the next day with the Ottawa nation to renew his friendship. But on the afternoon of the ninth he struck his tent, and strictly beleaguered the garrison, which had not on hand provisions enough for three weeks. "The first man that shall bring them provisions, or any thing else, shall suffer death:" such was Pontiac's proclamation. On the tenth, there was a parley, and the fort was summoned to capitulate. Not till after Gladwin had obtained the needed supplies did he break off the treaty, and bid the enemy defiance, yet leaving in their hands the unhappy officer who had conducted the parley. The garrison was in high spirits, though consisting of no more than one hundred and twenty men, against six or seven hundred besiegers.

The rovers of the wilderness, though unused to enterprises requiring time and assiduity, blockaded the place closely. The French inhabitants were divided in their sympathies. Pontiac made one of them his secretary, and supplied his wants by requisitions upon them all. Emissaries were sent even to Illinois to ask for an officer who should assume the conduct of the siege. The savages of the west took part in the general hatred of the English. "Be of good cheer, my father:" such were the words of one tribe after another to the commander at Fort Chartres; "do not desert thy children: the English shall never come here so long as a red man lives." "Our hearts," they repeated, "are with the French; we hate the English, and wish to kill them all.

We are all united: the war is our war, and we will continue it for seven years. The English shall never come into the west." But the French officers in Illinois desired to execute the treaty of Paris with loyalty.

On the sixteenth, a party of Indians appeared before the gate of Fort Sandusky. Ensign Paulli, the commander, ordered seven of them, four Hurons and three Ottawas, to be admitted as old acquaintances and friends. They sat smoking, till one of them raised his head as a signal, on which the two that were next Paulli seized and tied him fast without uttering a word. As they carried him out of the room, he saw the dead body of his sentry. The rest of the garrison lay one here and one there; the sergeant, in his garden, where he had been planting. The traders, also, were killed, and their stores plundered. Paulli was taken to Detroit.

An English ensign, a garrison of fourteen soldiers, and English traders, were stationed at the mouth of the St. Joseph's. On the morning of the twenty-fifth, a party of Pottawatomies from Detroit appeared near the fort. "We are come," said they, "to see our relatives and wish the garrison a good morning." A cry was suddenly heard in the barracks; "in about two minutes," Schlosser, the commanding officer, was seized, and all but three of his men were massacred.

Fort Pitt, where twenty boats had been launched to bear the English to the country of the Illinois, was the most important station west of the Alleghanies. Bands of Mingoes and Delawares were seen hovering round the place. On the twenty-seventh, these bitterest enemies of the English exchanged with English traders three hundred pounds' worth of skins for powder and lead, and then suddenly went away, as if to intercept any attempt to descend the river. On the same day, an hour before midnight, the chiefs of the Delawares, having received intelligence from the west, sent their message to Fort Pitt, recounting the attacks on the English posts. "We are sure," they added, giving their first summons, "a party is coming to cut you and your people off; make the best of your way to some place of safety, as we would not desire to see you killed in our town. What goods and other effects you have, we will keep safe."

The next day, Indians scalped a whole family, sparing neither woman nor child, and left a tomahawk in declaration of war. The passes to the eastward were so watched that it was very difficult to keep up any intercourse, while the woods resounded with the wild halloos which announced successive murders.

Near Fort Wayne, just where the great canal which unites the waters of Lake Erie and the Wabash leaves the waters of the Maumee, stood Fort Miami, garrisoned by an ensign and a few soldiers, deep in the forest, out of sight and hearing of civilized man. On the twenty-seventh, Holmes, its commander, was informed that the fort at Detroit had been attacked, and put his men on their guard; but an Indian woman came to him, saying that a squaw in a cabin, but three hundred yards off, was ill, and wished him to bleed her. He went on the errand of mercy, and two shots that were heard told how he fell. The sergeant who followed was taken prisoner; and the soldiers, nine in number, capitulated.

On the thirtieth, the besieged at Detroit saw a fleet of boats sweeping round the point. They flocked to the bastions to welcome friends; but the death-cry of the Indians announced that an English party from Niagara had, two nights previously, been attacked in their camp, on the beach near the mouth of Detroit River, and utterly defeated, a part turning back to Niagara, the larger part falling into the hands of the savages.

At eight o'clock in the night of the last day of May, the war-belt reached the Indian village near Fort Ouatanon, just below Lafayette, in Indiana; the next morning the commander was lured into an Indian cabin and bound, and his garrison surrendered. The French, moving the victors to clemency by gifts of wampum, received the prisoners into their houses.

At Michilimackinac, two acres on the main land, west of the strait, enclosed with pickets, gave room for the cabins of a few traders, and a fort with a garrison of about forty souls. Savages had arrived near it, as if to trade and beg for presents. On the second day of June, the Chippewas, who dwelt in a plain near the fort, assembled to play ball. This game is the most exciting sport of the red men. Each one has a bat curved like a crosier, and ending in a racket. Posts are planted apart on the open prairie. At the beginning of the game, the ball is placed midway between the goals. The eyes of the players flash; their cheeks glow. A blow is struck: all crowd with merry yells to renew it; the fleetest in advance now driving the ball home, now sending it sideways, with one unceasing passionate pursuit. On that day, the squaws entered the fort, and remained there. Etherington, the commander, with one of his lieutenants, stood outside of the gate, watching the game, fearing nothing. The Indians had played from morning till noon, when, throwing the ball close to the gate, they came behind the two officers, and seized and carried them into the woods; while the rest rushed into the fort, snatched their hatchets, which their squaws had kept hidden under their blankets, and in an instant killed an officer, a trader, and fifteen men. The rest of the garrison and all the English traders were made prisoners, and robbed of every thing they had; but the French traders were not harmed. Thus fell the old post of Mackinaw on the main.

On the eighteenth, the little fort of Le Bœuf was attacked. Its gallant officer kept off the enemy, till at midnight the Indians succeeded in setting the blockhouse on fire; but he escaped secretly, with his garrison, into the woods, while the enemy believed them all buried in the flames.

The fugitives, on their way to Fort Pitt, saw nothing but ruins at Venango. The fort at that place was consumed, never to be rebuilt; and not one of its garrison was left alive to tell the story of its destruction.

The fort at Presque Isle, now Erie, had a garrison of four-and-twenty men, and could most easily be relieved. On the twenty-second, after a two days' defence, the commander, out of his senses with terror, capitulated; giving up the sole chance of saving his men from the scalping-knife. He himself, with a few others, was carried in triumph by the Indians to Detroit.

Nor was it the garrisoned stockades only that encountered the fury of the savages. They struck down more than a hundred traders in the woods; scalping every one of them, quaffing their blood, horribly mutilating their bodies. They prowled round the cabins on the border; and their tomahawks fell alike on the laborer in the field and the child in the cradle. They menaced Fort Ligonier, the outpost of Fort Pitt; they passed the mountains, and spread death even to Bedford. The emigrant knew not if to brave danger, or to fly from his home. Nearly five hundred families, from the frontiers of Maryland and Virginia, fled to Winchester, bare of every comfort, and forced to scatter themselves among the woods.

In Virginia, nearly a thousand volunteers, at the call of the lieutenant-governor, hastened to Fort Cumberland and to the borders; and the lieutenant-governor of Maryland was able to offer aid.

The legislature of Pennsylvania was ready to arm and pay the farmers and reapers on the frontier, to the number of seven hundred, as a resident force for the protection of the country; but refused to place them under the orders of the British general. This policy, from which it would not swerve, incensed the officers of the army. Their invectives brought upon Pennsylvania once more the censure of the king for its "supine and neglectful conduct," and confirmed the ministry in the purpose of keeping up a regular army in America through taxes by parliament.

So the general, with little aid from Pennsylvania, took measures for the relief of the west. The fortifications of Fort Pitt had never been finished, and the floods had opened it on three sides; but the brave Ecuyer, its commander, without any engineer or any artificers but a few shipwrights, raised a rampart of logs round the fort, above the old one, palisaded the interior of the area, constructed a fire-engine, and, in short, took all precautions which art and judgment could suggest. The post had a garrison of three hundred and thirty men, and gave asylum to more than two hundred women and children.

On the twenty-first, a large party of Indians made a vigorous

though fruitless assault on Fort Ligonier; the next day, other
savages attacked Fort Pitt, on every side, killing one man and
wounding another. The night of the twenty-third, they recon-
noitred the fort, and after midnight sought a conference.

"Brother, the commanding officer," said Turtle's Heart, a
principal warrior of the Delawares, "all your posts and strong
places, from this backwards, are burnt and cut off. Your fort,
fifty miles down [meaning Ligonier], is likewise destroyed before now. This is the only one you have left in our country.
We have prevailed with six different nations of Indians, that
are ready to attack you, to forbear till we came and warned
you to go home. They have further agreed to permit you and
your people to pass safe to the inhabitants. Therefore, brother,
we desire that you may set off to-morrow, as great numbers of
Indians are coming here, and after two days we shall not be
able to do any thing with them for you."

In reply to this second summons, the commander warned the
Indians of their danger from three English armies, on their
march to the frontier of Virginia, to Fort Pitt, and to the north-
west.

A schooner, with a re-enforcement of sixty men, reached Detroit in June; at daybreak of the twenty-ninth of July, the
garrison was gladdened by the appearance of Dalyell, an aide-
de-camp to Amherst, with a detachment of two hundred and
sixty men. They had entered the river in the evening, and came
up under cover of the night. After but one day's rest, Dalyell
proposed a midnight sally. He was cautioned that they were
on their guard; but the express instructions of Amherst were
on his side. Gladwin reluctantly yielded; and, half an hour before three o'clock on the last morning of July, Dalyell marched
out with two hundred and forty-seven chosen men, while two
boats followed along shore to protect the party and bring off
the wounded and dead. They proceeded in double file, along
the great road by the river side, for a mile and a half, then,
forming into platoons, they advanced a half mile further, when
they suddenly received, from the breastworks of the Indians, a

destructive fire, which threw them into confusion. The party which made the sally could escape being surrounded only by an inglorious retreat. Twenty of the English were killed, and forty-two wounded; leaving to a peaceful rivulet the name of The Bloody Run. Dalyell himself fell while attempting to bring off the wounded; his scalp became one more ornament to the red man's wigwam.

This victory encouraged the confederates; two hundred recruits joined the forces of Pontiac, and the siege of Detroit was kept up by bands exceeding a thousand men.

Once more the Delawares gathered around Fort Pitt, accompanied by the Shawnees. The chiefs, in the name of their tribes and of the north-western Indians, for a third time summoned the garrison to retire. "Brothers," said they, "you have towns and places of your own. You know this is our country. All the nations over the lakes are soon to be on their way to the forks of the Ohio. Here is the wampum. If you return quietly home to your wise men, this is the furthest they will go. If not, see what will be the consequence; so we desire that you do remove off."

The next day, Ecuyer gave his answer: "You suffered the French to settle in the heart of your country; why would you turn us out of it now? I will not abandon this post; I have warriors, provisions, and ammunition in plenty to defend it three years against all the Indians in the woods. Go home to your towns, and take care of your women and children."

No sooner was this answer received than the united forces of the Delawares, Shawnees, Wyandots, and Mingoes beset and attacked the fort. With incredible boldness, they took post under the banks of both rivers, close to the fort, where, digging holes, they kept up an incessant discharge of musketry and threw fire arrows. Though the English were under cover, they killed one and wounded seven. Ecuyer himself was struck on the leg by an arrow. This continued through the last day of July, when they suddenly vanished.

Bouquet was at that time making his way to relieve Fort Pitt and re-enforce Detroit, with about five hundred men, chiefly Highlanders; driving a hundred beeves and twice that number of sheep, with powder, flour, and provisions on pack-horses and in wagons drawn by oxen. Between Carlisle and Bedford, they passed the ruins of mills, deserted cabins, fields ripe for the harvest, but without a reaper.

On the second day of August, the troops and convoy arrived at Ligonier, whose commander could give no intelligence of the enemy. All the expresses for the previous month had been killed or forced to return. Leaving the wagons at Ligonier, Bouquet, on the fourth, proceeded with the troops and about three hundred and fifty pack-horses. At one o'clock on the fifth, the savages, who had been at Fort Pitt, attacked the advance-guard; but two companies of Highlanders drove them from their ambuscade. When the pursuit ceased, the savages returned. Again the Highlanders charged with fixed bayonets; but as soon as the savages were driven from one post they appeared in another, and at last were in such numbers as to surround the English, who would have been utterly routed and cut to pieces but for the cool behavior of the troops and the excellent conduct of the officers. Night intervened, during which the English remained on Edge Hill, a ridge a mile to the east of Bushy Run, commodious for a camp except for the total want of water.

All that night hope cheered the red men. Morning dawned only to show the English party that they were beleaguered on every side. They could not advance to give battle, for then their convoy and their wounded men would have fallen a prey to the enemy; if they remained quiet, they would be picked off one by one. With happy sagacity, Bouquet feigned a retreat. The red men hurried to charge with the utmost daring, when two companies, that had lain hid, fell upon their flank; others turned and met them in front; and the Indians were routed and put to flight. But Bouquet in the two actions lost, in killed and wounded, about one fourth of his men, and almost all his horses, so that he was obliged to destroy his stores. At night, the English encamped at Bushy Run, and in four days more they arrived at Pittsburg.

Before news of this last conflict with the red men could reach New York, the wrath of Amherst against "the bloody villains" had burst all bounds; and he became himself a man of blood. "As to accommodation with the savages, I will have none," said he, "until they have felt our just revenge. I would have every measure that can be fallen upon for their destruction taken." "Whoever kills Pontiac, the chief ringleader of mischief, shall receive from me a reward of one hundred pounds;" and of this he bade the commander at Detroit make public proclamation. He deemed the Indians not only unfit to be allies and unworthy of being respected as enemies, "but as the vilest race of beings that ever infested the earth, and whose riddance from it must be esteemed a meritorious act, for the good of mankind. You will, therefore," such were his instructions to the officers engaged in the war, "take no prisoners, but put to death all that fall into your hands."

Had this spirit prevailed, the war would have been continued by an endless series of alternate murders, in which the more experienced Indian excelled the white man. The Senecas, against whom Amherst had specially directed unsparing hostilities, lay in ambush for one of his convoys about three miles below Niagara Falls; and, on its passing over the carrying-place, fell upon it with such suddenness and vigor that but eight wounded men escaped with their lives, while seventy-two were victims to the scalping-knife.

The first effective measures towards a general pacification proceeded from the French in Illinois. De Neyon, the French officer at Fort Chartres, sent belts and messages and peace-pipes to all parts of the continent, exhorting the many nations of savages to bury the hatchet, and take the English by the hand, for a representative of the king of France would be seen among them nevermore.

VOLUMES *IV, V (1852), and VI (1854) of the* History *were published as a unit (reduced to Volume III and part of IV in the Centenary Edition), carrying the narrative from 1748 to May, 1774. Bancroft constructed the unit about two themes: the gradual disintegration of the British colonial system combined with the estrangement of the colonies; and the corresponding emergence in the colonies themselves of a sense of common cause and a desire for independence. Believing that the American Revolution was part of a divine, worldwide design for human liberty, Bancroft carefully placed the growth of the American revolutionary spirit within the larger European context. He introduced his narrative of eighteenth-century colonial resistance to British policy with a chapter each on "The Continent of Europe, 1763," "France, 1763," and two chapters on "England and Its Dependencies, 1763," a survey of the state of British society and of the entire imperial system. The British empire, he wrote, "being founded on injustice, was at war with itself"; instead of recognizing the colonists' rights, the administration at London "chose the policy of exclusion and conquest." The colonies, meanwhile, in their resistance, found even greater unity of purpose and strength of will. The reader could follow the struggle between the British forces of repression and the American drive toward liberty in great detail, as Bancroft skillfully led the narrative through a maze of proclamations, taxes, orders-in-council, and statutes until, in the Stamp Act, "the harbinger of American independence," he located the central issue of the long conflict. This, he explained, lay in the imposition of taxation without representation, a principle which by implication and extension meant nothing less than the abject surrender of American liberty. Here, in the final phase of unified colonial resistance to King and Parliament, "dawned the day-star of the American union."*

The Day-Star of the American Union (April-May, 1765)

IF THE British parliament can tax America, it may tax Ireland and India, and hold the wealth of the east and of the west at the service of its own septennial oligarchy. As the relation of the government to its outlying dominions would become one of power and not of right, it could not but employ its accumulated resources to make itself the master of the ocean and the oppressor of mankind. "This system, if it is suffered to prevail," said Oxenbridge Thacher, of Boston, "will extinguish the flame of liberty all over the world."

On the discovery of the new hemisphere, the tradition was spread through the old that it conceals a fountain whose waters have power to restore age to its prime. The tradition was true; but the youth to be renewed was the youth of society; the life to bloom afresh was the life of the race.

> Freedom, thy brow,
> Glorious in beauty though it be, is scarred
> With tokens of old wars; they massive limbs
> Are strong with struggling. Power at thee has launched
> His bolts, and with his lightnings smitten thee;
> They could not quench the life thou hast from heaven.

Here, in the western world, the ancient warrior, "twin-born with man," counselled by the ripened wisdom of thousands of years, will renovate his being, and guide the people of every tongue through the self-direction of the individual mind to the harmonious exercise of the collective reason of the state.

Massachusetts had been led to rely on the inviolability of English freedom and on the equity of parliament; and, when the blow fell, which, though visibly foreshown, had not been certainly expected, "the people looked upon their liberties as gone." "Tears," said Otis, "relieve me a moment;" and, repelling the imputation "that the continent of America was about to become insurgent," "it is the duty of all," he added, "humbly and silently to acquiesce in all the decisions of the supreme legislature. Nine hundred and ninety-nine in a thousand of the colonists will never once entertain a thought but of submission to our sovereign, and to the authority of parliament in all possible contingencies." "They undoubtedly have the right to levy internal taxes on the colonies." "From my soul, I detest and abhor the thought of making a question of jurisdiction."

On learning the decision of parliament, Hutchinson made haste to say that "it could be to no purpose to claim a right of exemption, when the whole body of the people of England were against it." He was only "waiting to know what more parliament would do towards raising the sums which the colonies were to pay," and which as yet were not half provided for. As chief justice, he charged "the jurors and people" of the several counties to obey. Nor did the result seem doubtful. There could be no danger but from union; and "no two colonies," said he, "think alike; there is no uniformity of measures; the bundle of sticks thus separated will be easily broken." "The stamp act," he assured the ministry, five weeks after the news of its passage, "is received among us with as much decency as could be expected; it leaves no room for evasion, and will execute itself."

In Boston, the annual election of representatives in May excited the passions of the people. Men called to mind the noble sentiments which had been interwoven into the body of the remonstrances of New York. They were embittered at the thought that their legislature had been cajoled by Hutchinson into forbearing to claim exemption from taxation as a right; and that yet their prayer had been suppressed by the ministry with impartial disdain. While the patriots, on the one side, censured the fatal acquiescence of Otis, as a surrender of their liberties, the friends of government jeered at his strange moods, and called him a Massaniello and a madman. In the gloom that was thickening around him, he repelled the insult with scorn.

"The divine Brutus," said he, "once wore the cloak of a fool and a madman; the only cloak a man of true honor and spirit condescends to put on." And to merited reproaches he answered like one who could find no consolation: "Tell me, my once dear friends, what I have got by all this, besides the curse causeless of thousands, for whose welfare my heart has bled yearly, and is now ready to burst? Were it lawful to get at the cause of all your calamities, I would leap like the roe to purchase your ransom with my life or his."

The town of Boston remained faithful to the most genial of its patriots, and showed him honor, so long as he retained enough of the light of reason to be sensible of its support.

Opinion was fermenting at the north, but as yet without a declared purpose in action. Virginia received the stamp act with consternation. At first the planters foreboded universal ruin; but soon they resolved that the act should recoil on England: articles of luxury of English manufacture were banished; and thread-bare coats came into fashion. A large provincial debt enforced the policy of thrift. The legislature of Virginia was then assembled; and the electors of Louisa county had just filled a vacancy in their representation by making choice of Patrick Henry. He had resided among them scarcely a year, but his benignity of temper, pure life, and simple habits had already won their love. Devoted to their interest, he never flattered the people, and was never forsaken by them. As he took his place, not yet acquainted with the forms of business in the house or with its members, he saw the time for the enforcement of the stamp-tax drawing near, while all the other colonies, through timid hesitation or the want of opportunity, remained silent, and cautious loyalty hushed the experienced statesmen of his own. More than half the assembly had made the approaching close of the session an excuse for returning home; but Patrick Henry disdained submission. Alone, a burgess of but a few days, unadvised and unassisted, in an auspicious moment, of which the recollection cheered him to his latest day, he came forward in the committee of the whole house; and while Thomas Jefferson, a young collegian, from the mountain frontier, stood outside of the closed hall, eager to catch the first tidings of resistance, and George Washington, as is believed, was in his place as a member, he maintained by resolutions that the inhabitants of Virginia inherited from the first adventurers and settlers of that dominion equal franchises with the people of Great Britain; that royal charters had declared this equality; that taxation by themselves, or by persons chosen by themselves to represent them, was the distinguishing characteristic of British freedom and of the constitution; that the people of that most ancient colony had uninterruptedly enjoyed the right of being thus governed by their own laws respecting their internal polity and taxation; that this right had never been forfeited, nor in any other way given up, but had been constantly recognised by the king and people of Great Britain.

It followed from these resolutions, and Patrick Henry so expressed it in a fifth supplementary one, that the general assembly of the whole colony have the sole right and power to lay taxes on the inhabitants of the colony, and that any attempt to vest such power in any other persons whatever tended to destroy British as well as American freedom. It was still further set forth, yet not by Henry, in two resolutions, which, though they were not officially produced, equally imbodied the mind of the younger part of the assembly, that the inhabitants of Virginia were not bound to yield obedience to any law designed to impose taxation upon them other than the laws of their own general assembly; and that any one who should, either by speaking or writing, maintain the contrary, should be deemed an enemy to the colony.

A stormy debate arose, and many threats were uttered. Robinson, the speaker, already a defaulter, Peyton Randolph, the king's attorney, and the frank, honest, and independent George Wythe, a lover of classic learning, accustomed to guide the house by his strong understanding and single-minded integrity, exerted all their powers to moderate the tone of "the hot and virulent resolutions;" while John Randolph, the best lawyer in the colony, "singly" resisted the whole proceeding. But, on the other side, George Johnston, of Fairfax, reasoned with solidity and firmness; and Henry flamed with impassioned zeal. Lifted beyond himself, "Tarquin," he cried, "and Cæsar, had each his Brutus; Charles I, his Cromwell; and George III"— "Treason!" shouted the speaker; "treason! treason!" was echoed round the house; while Henry, fixing his eye on the first interrupter, continued without faltering, "may profit by their example!"

Swayed by his words, the committee of the whole showed its good-will to the spirit of all the resolutions enumerated; but the five offered by Patrick Henry were alone reported to the house; and on Thursday, the thirtieth of May, having been adopted by small majorities, the fifth by a vote of twenty to nineteen, they became a part of the public record. "I would have given five hundred guineas for a single vote," exclaimed the attorney-general aloud, as he came out past Jefferson. But Henry "carried all the young members with him." That night, thinking his work done, he rode home; but the next day, in his absence, an attempt was made to strike all the resolutions off the journals, and the fifth, and the fifth only, was blotted out. The lieutenant-governor, though he did not believe new elections would fall on what he esteemed cool, reasonable men, dissolved the assembly; but the four resolutions which remained on the journals, and the two others on which no vote had been taken, were published in the newspapers throughout America, as the avowed sentiment of the Old Dominion.

This is the "way the fire began." "Virginia rang the alarum bell for the continent."

At the opening of the legislature of Massachusetts, Oliver, who had been appointed stamp distributor, was, on the joint ballot of both branches, re-elected councillor by a majority of but three out of about one hundred and twenty votes. More than half the representatives voted against him.

On the day on which the resolves of Virginia were adopted, and just as the speech of Barré acquainted all the people that within parliament itself they had been hailed as the "Sons of Liberty," a message from Governor Bernard informed the new legislature of Massachusetts that "the general settlement of the American provinces, though it might necessarily produce some regulations disagreeable from their novelty, had been long ago proposed, and would now be prosecuted to its utmost completion; that submission to the decrees of the supreme legislature, to which all other powers in the British empire were subordinate, was the duty and the interest of the colonies; that this supreme legislature, the parliament of Great Britain, was happily the sanctuary of liberty and justice; and that the prince who presided over it realized the idea of a patriot king."

Contrary to usage, the house made no reply; but, on the sixth of June, James Otis, of Boston, advised the calling of an American congress, which should consist of committees from each of the thirteen colonies, to be appointed respectively by the delegates of the people, without regard to the other branches of the legislature. Such an assembly had never existed; and the purpose of deliberating upon the acts of parliament was equally novel. The tories sneered at the proposal as visionary and impracticable; Grenville himself had circulated through the colonies the opinion that, "from jealousy of neighborhood and clashing interests, they could never form a dangerous alliance among themselves;" but the representatives of Massachusetts shared the creative instinct of Otis. Avoiding every expression of a final judgment, and insuring unanimity by even refusing to consider the question of their exclusive right to originate measures of internal taxation, they sent letters to every assembly on the continent, proposing that committees of the several assemblies should meet at New York, on the first Tuesday of the following October, "to consult together," and "consider of a united representation to implore relief." They also elected Otis and two others of their own members to repair to New York accordingly.

At the same time, the province increased its strength by perseverance in appropriating annually fifty thousand pounds towards discharging its debt; and so good was its credit, and so affluent its people, that the interest on the remaining debt was reduced from six to five per cent by a public subscription among themselves.

Before the proceedings in Virginia and Massachusetts were known in New York, where the reprint of the stamp act was hawked about the streets as the "folly of England and the ruin of America," a freeman of that town, discussing the policy of Grenville, and the arguments on which it rested, demonstrated that they were leading alike to the reform of the British parliament and the independence of America.

"It is not the tax," said he, "it is the unconstitutional manner of imposing it, that is the great subject of uneasiness to the colonies. The minister admitted in parliament that they had in the fullest sense the right to be taxed only by their own consent, given by their representatives; and grounds his pretence of the right to tax them entirely upon this, that they are virtually represented in parliament.

"It is said that they are in the same situation as the inhabitants of Leeds, Halifax, Birmingham, Manchester, and several other corporate towns; and that the right of electing does not comprehend above one tenth part of the people of England.

"And in this land of liberty, for so it was our glory to call it, are there really men so insensible to shame as before the awful tribunal of reason to mention the hardships which, through their practices, some places in England are obliged to bear without redress, as precedents for imposing still greater hardships and wrongs upon America?

"It has long been the complaint of the most judicious in England, as the greatest misfortune to the nation, that its people are so unequally represented. Time and change of circumstances have occasioned defects in the rules or forms of choosing representatives for parliament. Some large towns send none to represent them; while several insignificant places, of only a few indigent persons, whose chief support is the sale of their votes, send many members. Seats are purchased with the nation's money; and a corrupt administration, by bribing others with places and pensions, can command a majority in the house of commons that will pass what laws they please. These evils are too notorious to escape general observation, and too atrocious to be palliated. Why are not these crying grievances redressed? Only because they afford the greatest opportunities for bribery and corruption.

"The fundamental principle of the English constitution is reason and natural right. It has within itself the principle of self-preservation, correction, and improvement. That there are several towns, corporations, and bodies of people in England in similar circumstances as the colonies, shows that some of the people in England, as well as those in America, are injured and oppressed, but shows no sort of right for the oppression. Those places ought to join with the Americans in remonstrances to obtain redress of grievances.

"The absurdity of our being represented in parliament is so glaring that it is almost an affront to common sense to use arguments to expose it; and yet it has been so much insisted upon that it seems as if the free use of common sense was to be prohibited as well as our other common rights.

"But the cases in England, cited to justify the taxation of America, are in no way similar. The taxation of America is arbitrary and tyrannical, and what the parliament of England have no right to impose. The colonies are not only unconnected in interest with any members of parliament, but, in many respects, entirely opposite; indeed, I believe, in all respects where their affairs would come before that house; for when has it meddled with any matter relating to them, except to lay some imposition upon them?

"As to the towns in England which send no members to parliament, there are many persons in parliament deeply interested in them; all the counties where they stand do send members; and many of their inhabitants are voters for the county members. As to the moneyed interest, there are in the house a sufficient number of those who have considerable property in money to take due care of that interest. Those persons who have no votes have yet the opportunity of influence in elections. Nor is it difficult for any man of fortune to procure a right of voting. So that the mention of these cases, as parallel with that of the colonies, is wonderfully trifling and impertinent.

"Our adherence to the English constitution is on account of its real excellence. It is not the mere name of English rights that can satisfy us. It is the reality that we claim as our inheritance, and would defend with our lives. Can any man be represented without his own consent? Where is the advantage of it, if persons are appointed to represent us without our choice? Would not our greatest enemies be the most likely to endeavor to be chosen for that office? Could such a right of representation be ever desired by any reasonable man? Is English liberty such a chimera as this?

"The great fundamental principles of a government should be common to all its parts and members, else the whole will be endangered. If, then, the interest of the mother country and her colonies cannot be made to coincide, if the same constitution may not take place in both, if the welfare of the mother country necessarily requires a sacrifice of the most valuable natural rights of the colonies,—their right of making their own laws, and disposing of their own property by representatives of their own choosing,—if such is really the case between Great Britain and her colonies, then the connection between them ought to cease; and sooner or later it must inevitably cease. The English government cannot long act towards a part of its dominions upon principles diametrically opposed to its own, without losing itself in the slavery it would impose upon the colonies, or learning them to throw it off and assert their freedom.

"There never can be a disposition in the colonies to break off their connection with the mother country, so long as they are permitted to have the full enjoyment of those rights to which the English constitution entitles them. They desire no more; nor can they be satisfied with less."

These words imbodied the sober judgment of New York. They were caught up by the impatient colonies; were reprinted in nearly all their newspapers; were approved of by their most learned and judicious statesmen; and even formed part of the instructions of South Carolina to its agent in England.

Thus revolution proceeded. Virginia marshalled resistance, Massachusetts entreated union, New York pointed to independence.

South Carolina Founds the American Union (June-July, 1765)

THE summons for the congress had gone forth from Massachusetts, when the resolves of Virginia were published to the world. "They have spoken treason," said the royalists. "Is it treason," retorted others, "for the deputies of the people to assert their rights, or to give them away?" "Oh! those Virginians," cried Oxenbridge Thacher, from his death-bed, where, overplied by public exertions, he was wasting away with a hectic, "those Virginians are men; they are noble spirits. I long to speak in court against tyranny words that shall be read after my death." "Why," said one of his friends, "are not our rights and liberties as boldly asserted by every government in America as by Virginia?" "Behold," cried another, "a whole continent awakened, alarmed, restless, and disaffected." Everywhere, from north to south, through the press, in letters, or as they met in private for counsel or in groups in the street the "Sons of Liberty" told their griefs to one another, and planned retaliation or redress.

"No good reason can be given," observed the more calm among them, "why the colonies should not modestly and soberly inquire what right the parliament of Great Britain has to tax them." "We were not sent out to be slaves," they continued, citing the example of ancient Greece and the words of Thucydides; "we are the equals of those who remained behind. Americans hold equal rights with those in Britain, not as conceded privileges, but inherent and indefeasible." "We have the rights of Englishmen," was the common voice, "and as such we are to be ruled by laws of our own making, and tried by men of our own condition."

"If we are Englishmen," said one, "on what footing is our property?" "The great Mr. Locke," said another, "lays it down that no man has a right to that which another may take from him;" and a third, proud of his respect for the law, sheltered himself under the words of the far-famed Coke: "The lord may tax his villein, high or low; but it is against the franchises of the land for freemen to be taxed but by their own consent in parliament." "If the people in America are to be taxed by the representatives of the people in England, their malady," said Hopkins, of Rhode Island, "is an increasing evil, that must always grow greater by time." "When the parliament once begins," such was the discourse at Boston, "there is no drawing a line." "And it is only the first step," repeated the New York owners of large estates; "a land-tax for all America will be thought of next."

"It is plain," said even the calmest, "Englishmen do not regard Americans as members of the same family, brothers, and equals, but as subordinates, bound to submit to oppression at their pleasure." "A bill was even prepared," thus men warned each other against new dangers, "that authorized quartering British soldiers upon American private families." "And is not our property seized," they further exclaimed, "by men who cry, 'give, give,' and never say, 'enough,' and thrown into a prerogative court to be forfeited without a jury?"

"There is not silver enough in the colonies to pay for the stamps," computed patriot financiers, "and the trade by which we could get more is prohibited." "And yet," declared the merchants of New York, "we have a natural right to every freedom of trade of the English." "To tax us, and bind our commerce and restrain manufactures," reasoned even the most patient, "is to bid us make brick without straw." "The northern colonies will be absolutely restricted from using any articles of clothing of their own fabric," predicted one colony to another. And men laughed as they added: "Catching a mouse within his majesty's colonies with a trap of our own making will be deemed, in the ministerial cant, an infamous, atrocious, and nefarious crime." "A colonist," murmured a Boston man, who had dipped into Grenville's pamphlet, "a colonist cannot make a horseshoe or a hobnail but some ironmonger of Britain shall bawl that he is robbed by the 'American republican.' " "Yes, they are even stupid enough," it was said in the town of Providence, "to judge it criminal for us to become our own manufacturers."

"We will eat no lamb," promised the multitude, seeking to retaliate; "we will wear no mourning at funerals." "We will none of us import British goods," said the traders in the towns. The inhabitants of North Carolina set up looms for weaving their own clothes, and South Carolina was ready to follow the example. "The people," wrote Lieutenant-governor Sharpe, of Maryland, "will go on upon manufactures." "We will have homespun markets of linens and woollens," passed from mouth to mouth, till it found its way across the Atlantic, and alarmed the king in council; "the ladies of the first fortune shall set the example of wearing homespun." "It will be accounted a virtue in them to wear a garment of their own spinning." "A little attention to manufactures will make us ample amends for the distresses of the present day, and render us a great, rich, and happy people."

When the churchmen of New York preached loyalty to the king as the Lord's anointed, "The people," retorted William Livingston, "are the Lord's anointed. Though named 'mob' and 'rabble,' the people are the darling of Providence." Was the Bible quoted as demanding deference to all in authority? "This," it was insisted, "is to add dulness to impiety." For "tyranny," they cried, "is no government; the gospel promises liberty, glorious liberty." "The gospel," so preached Mayhew, of Boston, "the gospel permits resistance."

And then patriots would become maddened with remembering that "some high or low American had had a hand in procuring every grievance." "England," it was said, "is deceived and deluded by place-men and office-seekers." "Yes," exclaimed the multitude; "it all comes of the horse-leeches." When "the friends to government" sought to hush opposition by terror of parliament, "You are cowards," was the answer; "you are fools, parasites, or, rather, parricides."

"Power is a sad thing," wrote the Presbyterians of Philadelphia: "our mother should remember we are children, and
not slaves." "When all Israel saw that the king hearkened not
unto them," responded the Calvinists of the north, "the people
answered the king, saying: 'What portion have we in David?
what inheritance in the son of Jesse? To your tents, O Israel!
Now see to thine own house, David!' " "Who cares," reasoned
the more hardy, "whether George or Louis is the sovereign, if
both are alike?" "The beast of burden," continued others, "asks
not whose pack it carries." "I would bear allegiance to King
George," said one who called himself a lover of truth, "but not
be a slave to his British subjects."

"But the members of parliament," argued the royalists, "are
men of wisdom and integrity, and incapable of dealing un-
justly." "One who is bound to obey the will of another," retorted
Hopkins, "is as really a slave, though he may have a good master, as if he had a bad one; and this is stronger in politic bodies
than in natural ones."

"It is an insult on the most common understanding," thought
James Habersham, of Georgia, and every American from the
Savannah to Maine, "to talk of our being virtually represented
in parliament." "It is an insult on common sense to say it,"
repeated the Presbyterian ministers of the middle states. "Are
persons chosen for the representatives of London and Bristol
in like manner chosen to be the representatives of Philadelphia
or Boston? Have two men chosen to represent a poor English
borough that has sold its votes to the highest bidder any pretence to say that they represent Virginia or Pennsylvania? And
have four hundred such fellows a right to take our liberties?"

But it was argued again and again: "Manchester, Birmingham, and Sheffield, like America, return no members." "Why,"
rejoined Otis, and his answer won applause in England, "why
ring everlasting changes to the colonists on them? If they are
not represented, they ought to be." "Every man of a sound
mind," he continued, "should have his vote." "Ah, but," replied the royalists, holding Otis to his repeated concessions,

"you own that parliament is the supreme legislature; will you question its jurisdiction?" And his answer was on the lips of all patriots, learned and unlearned: "Lord Coke declares that it is against Magna Charta and against the franchises of the land for freemen to be taxed but by their own consent; Lord Coke rules that an act of parliament against common law is void."

Thus opinion was echoed from mind to mind, as the sun's rays beam from many clouds, all differing in tints, but every one taking its hue from the same fire. In the midst of the gloom, light broke forth from the excitement of a whole people. Associations were formed in Virginia, as well as in New England, to resist the stamp act by all lawful means. Hope began to rise that American rights and liberties might safely be trusted "to the watchfulness of a united continent."

The insolence of the royal officers provoked to insulated acts of resistance. The people of Rhode Island, angry with the commander of a ship-of-war, who had boarded their vessels and impressed their seamen, seized his boat, and burned it on Newport common. Men of New England, "of a superior sort," had obtained of the government of New Hampshire a warrant for land down the western slope of the Green Mountains, on a branch of the Hoosic, twenty miles east of the Hudson River. They formed already a community of sixty-seven families, in as many houses, with an ordained minister, their own municipal officers, three several public schools, their meeting-house among the primeval forests of beech and maple; in a word, they enjoyed the flourishing state which springs from rural industry, intelligence, and piety. They called their village Bennington. The royal officers at New York disposed anew of that town, as well as of others near it, so that the king was known to the settlers near the Green Mountains chiefly by his agents, who had knowingly sold his lands twice over. In this way, the soil of Bennington became a fit battle-ground for independence.

Events like these sowed the seeds of discontent; but there was no present relief for America, unless union could be perfected. Union was the hope of Otis; union that "should knit

and work into the very blood and bones of the original system
every region, as fast as settled." Yet how comprehensive and
how daring the idea! The traditions of the board of trade
branded it as "mutinous." Massachusetts had proceeded tim-
idly, naming for its delegates to the proposed congress, with
the patriot Otis, two others who were "friends to government."

Virginia was ready to convince the world that her people
were firm and unanimous in the cause of liberty, but its newly
elected assembly was not suffered by Fauquier to come together.
New Jersey received the circular letter of Massachusetts on
the twentieth of June, the last day of the session of its legislature. The speaker, a friend to the British government, at first
inclined to urge sending delegates to the proposed congress;
but, on some "advice" from the governor, changed his mind,
and the house, in the hurry preceding the adjournment, rather
from uncertainty than the want of good-will, unanimously declined the invitation. The assembly of New Hampshire seémed
to approve, but did not adopt it. "Nothing will be done in consequence of this intended congress," wrote Bernard, in July;
and he seized the opportunity to press "more and more" upon
the government at home "the necessity of taking into their
hands the appointment of the American civil list," as well as
changing the council of the province. Even the liberal governor
of Maryland reported "that the resentment of the colonists
would probably die out; and that, in spite of the violent outcries of the lawyers, the stamp act would be carried into execution."

But, far away towards the lands of the sun, the assembly
of South Carolina was in session; and, on the twenty-fifth of
July, debated the circular from Massachusetts. Many objections were made to the legality, the expediency, and most of
all to the efficiency of the proposed measure; and many eloquent
words were uttered, especially by the youthful John Rutledge,
when the subject, on the deliberate resolve of a small majority,
was referred to a committee, of which Gadsden was the chair-
man. He was a man of deep and clear convictions; thoroughly

sincere; of an unbending will and a sturdy, impetuous integrity, which drove those about him, like a mountain torrent dashing on an over-shot wheel, though sometimes clogging with back water from its own violence. He possessed not only that courage which defies danger, but that persistence which neither peril nor imprisonment nor the threat of death can shake. Full of religious faith, and at the same time inquisitive and tolerant, methodical, yet lavish of his fortune for public ends, he had in his nature nothing vacillating or low, and knew not how to hesitate or feign. After two legislatures had held back, South Carolina, by "his achievement," pronounced for union. "Our state," he used to say, particularly attentive to the interest and feelings of America, was the first, though at the extreme end, and one of the weakest, as well internally as externally, to listen to the call of our northern brethren in their distresses. Massachusetts sounded the trumpet, but to Carolina is it owing that it was attended to. Had it not been for South Carolina, no congress would then have happened."

As the united American people spread through the vast expanse over which their jurisdiction now extends, be it remembered that the blessing of union is due to the warm-heartedness of South Carolina. "She was all alive, and felt at every pore." And when we count up those who, above others, contributed to the great result, we are to name the inspired "badman," James Otis, and the magnanimous, unwavering lover of his country, Christopher Gadsden.

Otis now seemed to himself to hear the prophetic song of the "Sibyls," chanting the spring-time of a "new empire."

BANCROFT'S *narrative up to May, 1774, the date he chose for the opening of "The American Revolution: Epoch Third," told of increased bitterness and misunderstanding between colonists and mother country, and of confused and wrong-headed policy in London versus American protest and resistance. He introduced his cast of characters—the "imbecilic" Newcastle, firebrand Sam Adams, George III ("an innate love of authority"), "chief incendiary" James Otis, Patrick Henry ("child of the forest, his serene mind ripening for duty"), weak and vacillating Hutchinson, and many more. As tensions grew and arguments waxed hotter, Bancroft divided his dramatis personae into fainthearts and heroes, tyrants and crusaders, until the breakdown of British-American relations in early 1774, he thought, wholly "dissolved the moral connections between the two countries." Then, with his keen sense of the dramatic, Bancroft set the scene for the last act, the Revolution itself: "The knell of the ages of servitude and inequality was rung; those of equality and brotherhood were come into life. As the fleets and armies of England went forth to consolidate arbitrary power, the sounds of war elsewhere on earth died away. Kings sat still in awe, and nations turned to watch the issue."*

America, Britain, and France in May, 1774

THE hour of the American revolution was come. The people of the continent obeyed one general impulse, as the earth in spring listens to the command of nature, and without the appearance of effort bursts forth to life. The change which Divine Wisdom ordained, and which no human policy or force could hold back, proceeded as majestically as the laws of being. The movement was quickened, even when it was most resisted; and its fiercest adversaries worked together for its fulfilment. The indestructible elements of freedom in the colonies asked room for expansion and growth. Standing in manifold relations with the governments, the culture, and the experience of the past, the Americans seized as their peculiar inheritance the traditions of liberty. Beyond any other nation, they had made trial of the possible forms of popular representation, and respected the activity of individual conscience and thought. The resources of the country in agriculture and commerce, forests and fisheries, mines and materials for manufactures, were so diversified and complete that their development could neither be guided nor circumscribed by a government beyond the ocean. The numbers, purity, culture, industry, and daring of its inhabitants proclaimed the existence of a people rich in creative energy, and ripe for institutions of their own.

They were rushing towards revolution, and they knew it not. They refused to acknowledge even to themselves the hope that was swelling within them; and yet they were possessed by the truth that man holds inherent and indefeasible rights; and as their religion had its witness coeval and coextensive with intelligence, so in their political aspirations they deduced from universal principles a bill of rights, as old as creation and as wide as humanity. The idea of freedom had always revealed itself at least to a few of the wise, whose prophetic instincts were quickened by love of their kind; its light flashed joy across the darkest centuries; and its growth can be traced in the tendency of the ages. In America, it was the breath of life to the people. For the first time, it found a region and a race where it could be professed with the earnestness of an indwelling conviction, and be defended with the enthusiasm that heretofore had marked no wars but those for religion. When all Europe slumbered over questions of liberty, a band of exiles, keeping watch by night, heard the glad tidings which promised the political regeneration of the world. A revolution, unexpected in the moment of its coming, but prepared by glorious forerunners, grew naturally and necessarily out of the series of past events by the formative principle of a living belief. And why should man organize resistance to the grand design of Providence? Why

should not the consent of the ancestral land and the gratula-
tions of every other call the young nation to its place among
the powers of the earth? Britain was the mighty mother who
bred and formed men capable of laying the foundation of so
noble an empire; and she alone could have formed them. She
had excelled all the world as the planter of colonies. The condition which entitled them to independence was now more than
fulfilled. Their vigorous vitality refused conformity to foreign
laws and external rule. They could take no other way to perfection than by the unconstrained development of that which
was within them. They were not only able to govern themselves,
they alone were able to do so; subordination visibly repressed
their energies. It was only by self-direction that they could at
all times and in entireness freely employ in action their collective and individual faculties to the fullest extent of their
ever increasing intelligence. Could not the illustrious nation,
which had gained no distinction in war, in literature, ór in
science, comparable to that of having wisely founded distant
settlements on a system of liberty, willingly perfect its beneficent work, now when no more was required than the acknowledgment that its offspring was come of age, and its own duty
accomplished? Why must the ripening of lineal virtue be struck
at, as rebellion in the lawful sons? Why is their unwavering
attachment to the essential principle of their existence to be
persecuted as treason, rather than viewed with delight as the
crowning glory of the country from which they sprung? If the
institutions of Britain were so deeply fixed in the usages and
opinions of its people that their deviations from justice could
not as yet be rectified; if the old continent was pining under
systems of authority which were not fit to be borne, and which
as yet no way opened to amend, why should not a people be
heartened to build a commonwealth in the wilderness, where
alone it was offered a home?

So reasoned a few in Britain, who were jeered at "as visionary
enthusiasts," deserving no weight in public affairs. Parliament
had asserted an absolute lordship over the colonies in all cases

whatsoever; and, fretting itself into a frenzy at the denial of its unlimited dominion, was destroying all its recognised authority by the intensity of its zeal for more. The majority of the ministers, including the most active and determined, were bent on the immediate employment of force. Lord North, who recoiled from civil war, exercised no control over his colleagues, leaving the government to be conducted by the several departments. As a consequence, the king became the only point of administrative union, and ruled as well as reigned. In him an approving conscience had no misgiving as to his duty. His heart knew no relenting; his will never wavered. Though America were to be drenched in blood and its towns reduced to ashes, though its people were to be driven to struggle for total independence, though he himself should find it necessary to bid high for hosts of mercenaries from the Scheldt to Moscow, and in quest of savage allies go tapping at every wigwam from Lake Huron to the Gulf of Mexico, he was resolved to coerce the thirteen colonies into submission. The people of Great Britain identified themselves, though but for the moment, with their king, and talked of their subjects beyond the Atlantic. Of their ability to crush resistance they refused to doubt; nor did they, nor the ministers, nor George III, apprehend interference, except from that great neighboring realm whose colonial system Britain had just overthrown.

All Europe, though at peace, was languishing under exhaustion from wars of ambition or vices of government, and crying out for relief from abuses which threatened to dissolve the old social order. In France, enduring life belonged to two elements only in the state, the people and monarchical power; and every successive event increased the importance of the one and the other. It was its common people which saved that country from perishing of unbelief, and made it the most powerful state of continental Europe. The peasants, it is true, were poor and oppressed and ignorant; but all Frenchmen, alike townspeople and villagers, were free. There was no protecting philanthropy on the part of the nobility; no hierarchy of mutually dependent ranks; no softening of contrasts by the blending of colors and harmonizing of shades: the poor, though gay by temperament, lived sad and apart; bereft of intercourse with superior culture; never mirthful but in mockery of misery; not cared for in their want, nor solaced in hospitals, nor visited in prisons; but the bonds had been struck alike from the mechanic in the workshop and the hind in the fields. The laborer at the forge was no longer a serf; the lord of the manor exercised jurisdiction no more over vassals; in all of old France the peasants were freemen, and in the happiest provinces had been so for half a thousand years. Only a few of them, as of the nobles in the middle ages, could read; but a vast number owned the acres which they tilled. By lineage, language, universality of personal freedom, and diffusion of landed property, the common people of France formed one compact and indivisible nation.

Two circumstances which aggravated the wretchedness of the third estate increased their importance. The feudal aristocracy had been called into being for the protection of the kingdom; but, in the progress of ages, they escaped from the obligation to military service. In this manner they abdicated their dignity as the peers of their sovereign; and, though they still scorned every profession but that of arms, they received their commissions from the king's favor, and drew from his exchequer their pay as hirelings. Thus the organization of the army ceased to circumscribe royal power, which now raised soldiers directly from the humbler classes. The defence of the country had passed from the king and his peers with their vassals to the king in direct connection with those vassals who were thus become a people.

Again, the nobility, carefully securing the exemption of their own estates, had, in their struggles with the central power, betrayed the commons, by allowing the monarch to tax them at will. Proving false to their trust as the privileged guardians of liberty, and renouncing the military service that had formed the motive to their creation, they made themselves an insulated caste. All that was beneficent in feudalism had died out. Soulless relics of the past, the nobles threw up their hereditary rustic independence to fasten themselves as courtiers upon the treasury. They hung like a burden on the state, which they no longer guided, nor sustained, nor defended, nor consoled. Some few among them, superior to their rank, helped to bear society onwards to its regeneration; but, as a class, their life was morally at an end. They had renounced their political importance, which passed to the people. The imposts which they refused to share, and which in two centuries had increased tenfold, fell almost exclusively on the lowly, who toiled and suffered, having no redress against those employed by the government; regarding the monarch with touching reverence and love, though they knew him mostly as the power that harried them; ruled as though joy were no fit companion for labor; as though want were the necessary goad to industry, and sorrow the only guarantee of quiet. They were the strength of the kingdom, the untiring producers of its wealth; the repairer of its armies; the sole and exhaustless source of its revenue; and yet, in their forlornness, they cherished scarcely a dim vision of a happier futurity on earth.

Meantime, monarchy was concentrating a mass of power, which a strong arm could wield with irresistible effect, which an effeminate squanderer could not exhaust. Instead of a sovereign restrained by his equals, and depending on free grants from the states, one will commanded a standing army, and imposed taxes on the unprivileged classes. These taxes, moreover, it collected by its own officers; so that throughout all the provinces of France an administration of plebeians, accountable to the king alone, superseded in substance, though not always in form, the methods of feudalism.

Nor had the established religion wholly escaped dependence on the crown. The Catholic Church assumes to represent the Divine Wisdom itself, and, as a logical consequence, its decisions, though pronounced by an alien, should be supreme. The Gallican church had at least a name of its own; and when it was observed that Jesuits had inculcated the subordination of the temporal sovereign to a superior rule under which the wicked tyrant might be arraigned, dethroned, or even slain, Louis XV uprooted by his word and exiled the best organized religious society in Christendom; not perceiving that the sudden closing of their schools of learning left the rising generation more easy converts to unbelief in royalty itself. The clergy were tainted with the general skepticism; they stooped before the temporal power to win its protection, and did not scruple to enforce by persecution a semblance of homage to the symbols of religion, of which the life was put to sleep.

The magistrates, with graver manners than the clergy or the nobility, did not so much hate administrative despotism as grasp at its direction; they themselves had so scanty means of self-defence against its arm that, when they hesitated to register the king's decrees, even the word of Louis XV could make an end of parliaments which were almost as old as the French monarchy itself.

For the benefit of the king's treasury, free charters, granted or confirmed in the middle ages to towns and cities, had over and over again been confiscated, to be ransomed by the citizens or sold to an oligarchy; so that municipal liberties were no longer independent of the royal caprice.

France was the most lettered nation of the world, and its authors loved to be politicians. Of these, the conservative class, whose fanatical partisanship included in their system of order the continuance of every established abuse, had no support but in the king. Scoffers also abounded; but they did not care to restrain arbitrary power, or remove the abuses which they satirized. One universal skepticism questioned the creed of churches and the code of feudal law, the authority of the hierarchy and the sanctity of monarchy; but unbelief had neither the capacity nor the wish to organize a new civilization. The philosophy of the day could not guide a revolution, for it professed to receive no truth but through the senses, denied the moral government of the world, and derided the possibility of disinterested goodness. As there was no practical school of politics in which experience might train statesmen to test new projects, the passion for elementary theories had no moderating counterpoise; and the authors of ameliorating plans favored the unity of administration, that one indisputable word might substitute a uniform and rational system for the complicated usages and laws which had been the deposits of many conquests and ages.

At this time, the central power, in the hands of a monarch infamous by his enslavement to pleasure, had become hideously selfish and immoral, palsied and depraved; swallowing up all other authority, and yet unconscious of the attendant radical change in the feudal constitution; dreaming itself absolute, yet wanting personal respectability; confessing the necessity of administrative reforms, which it was yet unable to direct. For great ends it was helpless, though it was able to torture and distress the feeble; to fill the criminal code with the barbarisms of arrogant cruelty; to evoke before exceptional courts every accusation against even the humblest of its agents; to judge by special tribunals questions involving life and fortune; to issue arbitrary warrants of imprisonment; to punish without information or sentence; making itself the more hateful the less it was restrained.

The duty and honor of the kingdom were sacrificed in its foreign policy. Louis XV courted the friendship of George III of England, not to efface the false notion of international enmity which was a brand on the civilization of that age, but to gain a new support for monarchical power. For this end, the humiliations of the last war would have been forgiven by the monarch, had not the heart of the nation still palpitated with resentment. Under the supremacy of the king's mistress, sensual pleasure ruled the court; dictated the appointment of ministers; confused the administration; multiplied the griefs of the overburdened peasantry; and would have irretrievably degraded France, but for its third estate, who were ready to lift their head and assert their power, whenever in any part of the world a happier people should give them an example.

The heir to the throne of France was not admitted to the royal council, and grew up ignorant of business and inert. The dauphiness Marie Antoinette, in the splendor of supreme rank, preserved the gay cheerfulness of youth. Soon after her arrival in France, her mother had written to her: "God has crowned you with so much grace and sweetness and docility that all the world must love you." She was conscious of being lovely, and was willing to be admired; but she knew how to temper graceful condescension with august severity. Impatient of stately etiquette, which controlled her choice of companions even more than the disposition of her hours, she broke away from wearisome formalities with the eager vivacity of self-will, and was happiest when she could forget that she was a princess and be herself. From the same quickness of nature, she readily took part in any prevailing public excitement, regardless of reasons of state or the decorum of the palace. In music, her taste was exquisite; and she merited the graceful flattery of Glück. Unless her pride was incensed, she was merciful; and she delighted in bestowing gifts; but her benevolence was chiefly the indulgence of a capricious humor, which never attracted the affection of the poor. Faithful in her devotedness to the nobles, she knew not the utter decay of their order; and had no other thought than that they were bound by the traditions of centuries to defend her life and name. But the rugged days of feudalism were gone by; and its frivolous descendants were more ready to draw their swords for precedence in a dance at court than to protect the honor of their future queen. From her arrival in France, Marie Antoinette was hated by the opponents of the Austrian alliance; and, in her first years at Versailles, a faction in the highest ranks began to calumniate her artless impulsiveness as the evidence of crime.

On this scene of a degenerate nobility and popular distress; of administrative corruptness and ruined finances; of a brave but luxurious army and a slothful navy; of royal authority, unbounded, unquestioned, and yet despised; of rising deference to public opinion in a nation thoroughly united and true to its nationality, Louis XVI, the "desired one" of the people, while not yet twenty years old, entered as king. When on the tenth of May, 1774, he and the still younger Marie Antoinette were told that his grandfather was no more, "I feel," said he, "as if the universe were about to crush me;" and the two threw themselves on their knees, crying, "We are too young to reign," and praying God to direct their inexperience. The city of Paris was delirious with joy at their accession. "It is our paramount wish to make our people happy," was the language of the first edict of the new absolute prince. "He excels in writing prose," said Voltaire, on reading the words of promise; "he seems inspired by Marcus Aurelius; he desires what is good, and does it. Happy they, who, like him, are but twenty years old, and will long enjoy the sweets of his reign." Caron de Beaumarchais, the sparkling dramatist and restless plebeian adventurer, made haste to recommend to the royal patronage his genius for intrigue. "Is there," said he through De Sartine, the head of the police, "any thing which the king wishes to know alone and at once, any thing which he wishes done quickly and secretly, here am I, who have at his service a head, a heart, arms, and no tongue."

The young monarch, with all his zeal for administrative improvements, had no revolutionary tendencies, and held, like his predecessor, that the king alone should reign; yet his state papers were soon to cite reverently the law of nature and the rights of man; and the will of the people was to walk its rounds in the palace, invisible yet supreme.

The sovereign of Spain, on wishing his kinsman joy of his accession, reminded him, as the head of the Bourbons, of their double relationship by his mother's side, as well as his father's; and expressed the wish for "their closest union and most perfect harmony;" for, said he, "the family compact guarantees the prosperity and glory of our house." At that time, the Catholic king was fully employed in personally regulating his finances, and in preparations to chastise the pirates of Algiers, as well as to extort from Portugal a renunciation of its claims to extend the boundaries of Brazil. The sovereign of France was engrossed by the pressing anxieties attending the dismissal of an odious ministry, and the inauguration of domestic reform; so that neither of the princes seemed at leisure to foment troubles in North America.

Yet, next to Du Barry and her party, there was no such sincere mourner for Louis XV as George III. The continuance of the cordial understanding between the two crowns would depend upon the persons in whom the young king should place his confidence. The "London Court Gazette" announced him as "king of France," though English official language had heretofore spoken only of "the French king," and the Herald's Office still knew no other king of France than the head of the house of Hanover.

At the same time, the British ministers, always jealous of the Bourbons, kept spies to guess at their secrets; to hearken after the significant whispers of their ministers; to bribe workmen in their navy yards for a report of every keel that was laid, every new armament or re-enforcement to the usual fleets. Doubting the French assurances of a wish to see the troubles in America quieted, they resolved to force the American struggle to an immediate issue, hoping not only to insulate Massachusetts, but even to confine the contest to its capital.

On the day of the accession of Louis XVI, the act closing the port of Boston, transferring the board of customs to Marblehead, and the seat of government to Salem, reached the devoted town. The king was confident that the slow torture which was to be applied would constrain its inhabitants to cry out for mercy and promise unconditional obedience. Success in resistance could come only from an American union, which was not to be hoped for, unless Boston should offer herself as a willing sacrifice. The mechanics and merchants and laborers, altogether scarcely so many as thirty-five hundred able-bodied men, knew that they were acting not for the liberty of a province or of America, but for freedom itself. They were inspired by the thought that the Providence which rules the world demanded of them heroic self-denial, as the champions of humanity. The country never doubted their perseverance, and they trusted the fellow-feeling of the continent.

As soon as the act was received, the Boston committee of correspondence, by the hand of Joseph Warren, invited eight neighboring towns to a conference "on the critical state of public affairs." On the twelfth at noon, Metcalf Bowler, the speaker of the assembly of Rhode Island, came before them with the cheering news that, in answer to a recent circular letter from the body over which he presided, all the thirteen governments were pledged to union. Punctually, at the hour of three in the afternoon of that day, the committees of Dorchester, Roxbury, Brookline, Newton, Cambridge, Charlestown, Lynn, and Lexington, joined them in Faneuil Hall, the cradle of American liberty, where for ten years the freemen of the town had debated the great question of justifiable resistance. The lowly men who now met there were most of them accustomed to feed their own cattle; to fold their own sheep; to guide their own ploughs; all trained to public life in the little democracies of their towns; some of them captains in the militia and officers of the church according to the discipline of Congregationalists; nearly all of them communicants, under a public covenant with God. They grew in greatness as their sphere enlarged. Their virtues burst the confines of village life. They felt themselves to be citizens not of little municipalities, but of the whole world of mankind. In their dark hour, light broke upon them from their own truth and courage. Placing Samuel Adams at their head, and guided by a report prepared by Joseph Warren of Boston, Gardner of Cambridge, and others, they agreed unanimously on the injustice and cruelty of the act, by which parliament, without competent jurisdiction, and contrary as well to natural right as to the laws of all civilized states, had, without a hearing, set apart, accused, tried, and condemned the town of Boston. The delegates from the eight villages were reminded by those of Boston that that port could recover its trade by paying for the tea which had been thrown overboard; but they held it unworthy even to notice the humiliating offer, promising on their part to join "their suffering brethren in every measure of relief."

To make a general union possible, self-restraint must regulate courage. The meeting knew that a declaration of independence would have alienated their sister colonies, and thus far they had not found out that independence was really the desire of their own hearts. To suggest nothing till a congress could be convened, would have seemed to them like abandoning the town to bleed away its life. The king had expected to starve its people into submission; in their circular letter to the committees of the other colonies, they proposed as a counter action a general cessation of trade with Britain. "Now," they added, "is the time when all should be united in opposition to this violation of the liberties of all. The single question is, whether you consider Boston as suffering in the common cause, and sensibly feel and resent the injury and affront offered to her? We cannot believe otherwise; assuring you that, not in the least intimidated by this inhuman treatment, we are still determined to maintain to the utmost of our abilities the rights of America."

The next day, while Gage was sailing into the harbor with the vice-regal powers of commander in chief for the continent, as well as the civil authority of governor in the province, Samuel Adams presided over a very numerous town-meeting, which was attended by many that had hitherto kept aloof. The thought of republican Rome, in its purest age, animated their consultations. The port act was read, and in bold debate was pronounced repugnant to law, religion, and common sense. At the same time, those who, from loss of employment, were to be the first to encounter want, were remembered with tender compassion, and measures were put in train to comfort them. Then the inhabitants, by the hand of Samuel Adams, made their appeal "to all the sister colonies, inviting a universal suspension of exports and imports, promising to suffer for America with a becoming fortitude, confessing that singly they might find their trial too severe, and entreating not to be left to struggle alone, when the very being of every colony, considered as a free people, depended upon the event."

On the seventeenth of May, Gage, who had remained four days with Hutchinson at Castle William, landed at Long Wharf, amidst salutes from ships and batteries. Received by the council and civil officers, he was escorted by the Boston cadets, under Hancock, to the state house, where the council presented a loyal address, and his commission was proclaimed with three volleys of musketry and as many cheers. He then partook of a public dinner in Faneuil Hall, at which he proposed "the prosperity of the town of Boston." His toast in honor of Hutchinson "was received with a general hiss." Yet many favored a compromise, and put forward a subscription to pay for the tea; and on the eighteenth Jonathan Amory very strongly urged that measure in town-meeting, but it was rejected by the common voice. There still lingered a hope of relief through the intercession of Gage; but he was fit neither to reconcile nor to subdue. By his mild temper and love of society, he gained the good-will of his boon companions, and escaped personal enmities; but in earnest business he inspired neither confidence nor fear. Though his disposition was far from being malignant, he was so poor in spirit and so weak of will, so dull in his perceptions and so unsettled in his opinions, that he was sure to follow the worst advice, and vacillate between words of concession and merciless severity. He had promised the king that with four regiments he would play the "lion," and troops beyond his requisition were hourly expected. His instructions enjoined upon him the seizure and condign punishment of Samuel Adams, Hancock, Joseph Warren, and other leading patriots; but he stood too much in dread of them to attempt their arrest.

The people of Massachusetts were almost exclusively of English origin; beyond any other colony, they loved the land of their ancestors; but their fond attachment made them only the more sensitive to its tyranny. To subject them to taxation without their consent was robbing them of their birthright; they scorned the British parliament as "a junto of the servants of the crown, rather than the representatives of England." Not disguising to themselves their danger, but confident of victory, they were resolved to stand together as brothers for a life of liberty.

The merchants of Newburyport were the first who agreed to suspend all commerce with Britain and Ireland. Salem, also, the place marked out as the new seat of government, in a very full town-meeting, and after unimpassioned debates, decided almost unanimously to stop trade not with Britain only, but even with the West Indies. If in Boston a few cravens still proposed to purchase a relaxation of the blockade by "a subscription to pay for the tea," the majority were beset by no temptation so strong as that of routing at once the insignificant number of troops who had come to overawe them. But Samuel Adams, while he compared their spirit to that of Sparta or Rome, inculcated "patience as the characteristic of a patriot;" and the people, having sent forth their cry to the continent, waited self-possessed for voices of consolation.

THE *Reverend Aaron Bancroft, George Bancroft's father, was supposed to have been one of a group of young men who shouldered muskets and marched from Harvard College toward Lexington at the news of the fighting there; young Bancroft, growing up in Worcester, heard stories of the Revolution from veterans who had looked at plenty of the king's soldiers through gun sights. Above the mantel in many Worcester homes were muskets last fired at Breed's Hill or Saratoga, and Bancroft himself walked in green country lanes where redcoats and militia clashed not many years before. To young men born in New England before 1820 the Revolution was very close; the phrase "life, liberty, and the pursuit of happiness" had a contemporary ring in the years of Bancroft's youth, and the air of Massachusetts, when he wrote history, still quivered with the sound of the shots at Lexington and Concord. Such things made a difference in the way Bancroft wrote about the Revolutionary War, and his chapters on Lexington and Concord are unmatched anywhere else in his writing.*

Bancroft had at his disposal full accounts of both engagements, including the testimony of men who fought in them. It was then, and still is, impossible to determine who fired first at Lexington, but Bancroft unhesitatingly fixed responsibility on British Major Pitcairn, since it would have been impossible to do otherwise and still maintain the logic of the controlling design in his History.

Lexington and Concord, April 19, 1775

ON THE afternoon of the day on which the provincial congress of Massachusetts adjourned, Gage took the light infantry and grenadiers off duty, and secretly prepared an expedition to destroy the colony's stores at Concord. But the attempt had for several weeks been expected; a strict watch was kept; and signals were concerted to announce the first movement of troops for the country. Samuel Adams and Hancock, who had

Vol. IV, Chaps. XXVII and XXVIII.

not yet left Lexington for Philadelphia, received a timely message from Warren, and in consequence the committee of safety removed a part of the public stores and secreted the cannon.

On Tuesday the eighteenth of April, ten or more sergeants in disguise dispersed themselves through Cambridge and further west, to intercept all communication. In the following night, the grenadiers and light infantry, not less than eight hundred in number, the flower of the army at Boston, commanded by the incompetent Lieutenant-colonel Smith, crossed in the boats of the transport ships from the foot of the common to East Cambridge. There they received a day's provisions; and near midnight, after wading through wet marshes, that are now covered by a stately town, they took the road through West Cambridge to Concord.

"They will miss their aim," said one of a party who observed their departure. "What aim?" asked Lord Percy, who overheard the remark. "The cannon at Concord," was the answer. Percy hastened to Gage, who instantly directed that no one should be suffered to leave the town. But Warren had already, at ten o'clock, despatched William Dawes through Roxbury, and Paul Revere by way of Charlestown to Lexington.

Revere stopped only to engage a friend to raise the concerted signals, and two friends rowed him across Charles River five minutes before the sentinels received the order to prevent it. All was still, as suited the hour. The "Somerset" man-of-war was winding with the young flood; the waning moon just peered above a clear horizon; while, from a couple of lanterns in the tower of the North church, the beacon streamed to the neighboring towns, as fast as light could travel.

A little beyond Charlestown Neck, Revere was intercepted by two British officers on horseback; but, being well mounted, he turned suddenly, and leading one of them into a clay pond escaped from the other by the road to Medford. Of that town, he waked the captain of the minute men, and continued to rouse almost every house on the way to Lexington.

The troops had not advanced far, when the firing of guns

and ringing of bells announced that their expedition had been heralded before them; and Smith sent back for a re-enforcement.

On the nineteenth of April, just after midnight, the message from Warren reached Adams and Hancock, who at once divined the object of the expedition. Revere, therefore, and Dawes, joined by Samuel Prescott, "a high Son of Liberty" from Concord, rode forward, calling up the inhabitants as they passed along, till in Lincoln they fell upon a party of British officers. Revere and Dawes were seized and taken back to Lexington, where they were released; but Prescott leaped over a low stone wall, and galloped on for Concord.

There, at about two in the morning, a peal from the belfry of the meeting-house brought together the inhabitants of the place, young and old, with their firelocks, ready to make good the resolute words of their town debates. Among the most alert was William Emerson the minister, with gun in hand, his powder-horn and pouch of balls slung over his shoulder. By his sermons and his prayers, he had so hallowed the enthusiasm of his flock that they held the defence of their liberties a part of their covenant with God; his presence with arms strengthened their sense of duty.

From daybreak to sunrise, the summons ran from house to house through Acton. Express messengers and the call of minute men spread widely the alarm. How children trembled as they were scared out of sleep by the cries! how women, with heaving breasts, bravely seconded their husbands! how the countrymen, forced suddenly to arm, without guides or counsellors, took instant counsel of their courage! The mighty chorus of voices rose from the scattered farm-houses, and, as it were, from the very ashes of the dead. Come forth, champions of liberty; now free your country; protect your sons and daughters, your wives and homesteads; rescue the houses of the God of your fathers, the franchises handed down from your ancestors. Now all is at stake; the battle is for all.

Lexington, in 1775, may have had seven hundred inhabitants;

forming one parish, and having for their minister the learned and fervent Jonas Clark, the bold inditer of patriotic state papers, that may yet be read on their town records. In December, 1772, they had instructed their representative to demand "a radical and lasting redress of their grievances, for not through their neglect should the people be enslaved." A year later, they spurned the use of tea. In 1774, at various town-meetings, they voted "to increase their stock of ammunition," "to encourage military discipline, and to put themselves in a posture of defence against their enemies." In December, they distributed to "the train-band and alarm list" arms and ammunition, and resolved to "supply the training soldiers with bayonets."

At two in the morning, under the eye of the minister, and of Hancock and Adams, Lexington common was alive with the minute men; and not with them only, but with the old men also, who were exempts, except in case of immediate danger to the town. The roll was called, and, of militia and alarm men, about one hundred and thirty answered to their names. The captain, John Parker, ordered every one to load with powder and ball, but to take care not to be the first to fire. Messengers, sent to look for the British regulars, reported that there were no signs of their approach. A watch was therefore set, and the company dismissed with orders to come together at beat of drum. Some went to their own homes; some to the tavern, near the south-east corner of the common. Adams and Hancock, whose proscription had already been divulged, and whose seizure was believed to be intended, were persuaded to retire towards Woburn.

The last stars were vanishing from night, when the foremost party, led by Pitcairn, a major of marines, was discovered, advancing quickly and in silence. Alarm guns were fired, and the drums beat, not a call to village husbandmen only, but the reveille to humanity. Less than seventy, perhaps less than sixty, obeyed the summons, and, in sight of half as many boys and unarmed men, were paraded in two ranks, a few rods north of the meeting-house.

How often in that building had they, with renewed professions of their faith, looked up to God as the stay of their fathers
and the protector of their privileges! How often on that village
green, hard by the burial-place of their forefathers, had they
pledged themselves to each other to combat manfully for their
birthright inheritance of liberty! There they now stood side by
side, under the provincial banner, with arms in their hands,
silent and fearless, willing to fight for their privileges, scrupulous not to begin civil war, and unsuspicious of immediate
danger. The ground on which they trod was the altar of freedom, and they were to furnish the victims.

The British van, hearing the drum and the alarm guns, halted
to load; the remaining companies came up; and, at half an
hour before sunrise, the advance party hurried forward at
double quick time, almost upon a run, closely followed by the
grenadiers. Pitcairn rode in front, and, when within five or six
rods of the minute men, cried out: "Disperse, ye villains! ye
rebels, disperse! lay down your arms! why don't you lay down
your arms and disperse?" The main part of the countrymen
stood motionless in the ranks, witnesses against aggression; too
few to resist, too brave to fly. At this, Pitcairn discharged a
pistol, and with a loud voice cried, "Fire!" The order was followed first by a few guns, which did no execution, and then
by a close and deadly discharge of musketry.

In the disparity of numbers, Parker ordered his men to disperse. Then, and not till then, did a few of them, on their own
impulse, return the British fire. These random shots of fugitives or dying men did no harm, except that Pitcairn's horse
was perhaps grazed, and a private of the tenth light infantry
was touched slightly in the leg.

Jonas Parker, the strongest and best wrestler in Lexington,
had promised never to run from British troops; and he kept his
vow. A wound brought him on his knees. Having discharged
his gun, he was preparing to load it again, when as sound a
heart as ever throbbed for freedom was stilled by a bayonet,
and he lay on the post which he took at the morning's drum-

beat. So fell Isaac Muzzey, and so died the aged Robert Munroe, the same who in 1758 had been an ensign at Louisburg. Jonathan Harrington, Jr., was struck in front of his own house on the north of the common. His wife was at the window as he fell. With blood gushing from his breast, he rose in her sight, tottered, fell again, then crawled on hands and knees towards his dwelling; she ran to meet him, but only reached him as he expired on their threshold. Caleb Harrington, who had gone into the meeting-house for powder, was shot as he came out. Samuel Hadley and John Brown were pursued, and killed after they had left the green. Asahel Porter, of Woburn, who had been taken prisoner by the British on the march, endeavoring to escape, was shot within a few rods of the common.

Day came in all the beauty of an early spring. The trees were budding; the grass growing rankly a full month before its time; the blue bird and the robin gladdening the genial season, and calling forth the beams of the sun which on that morning shone with the warmth of summer; but distress and horror gathered over the inhabitants of the peaceful town. There on the green lay in death the gray-haired and the young; the grassy field was red "with the innocent blood of their brethren slain," crying unto God for vengeance from the ground.

Seven of the men of Lexington were killed, nine wounded; a quarter part of all who stood in arms on the green. These are the village heroes, who were more than of noble blood, proving by their spirit that they were of a race divine. They gave their lives in testimony to the rights of mankind, bequeathing to their country an assurance of success in the mighty struggle which they began. Their names are had in grateful remembrance, and the expanding millions of their countrymen renew and multiply their praise from generation to generation. They fulfilled their duty not from the accidental impulse of the moment; their action was the slowly ripened fruit of Providence and of time. The light that led them on was combined of rays from the whole history of the race; from the traditions of the Hebrews in the gray of the world's morning; from the heroes and sages of republican Greece and Rome; from the examples of Him who died on the cross for the life of humanity; from the religious creed which proclaimed the divine presence in man, and on this truth, as in a life-boat, floated the liberties of nations over the dark flood of the middle ages; from the customs of the Germans transmitted out of their forests to the councils of Saxon England; from the burning faith and courage of Martin Luther; from trust in the inevitable universality of God's sovereignty as taught by Paul of Tarsus and Augustine, through Calvin and the divines of New England; from the avenging fierceness of the Puritans, who dashed the mitre on the ruins of the throne; from the bold dissent and creative self-assertion of the earliest emigrants to Massachusetts; from the statesmen who made, and the philosophers who expounded, the revolution of England; from the liberal spirit and analyzing inquisitiveness of the eighteenth century; from the cloud of witnesses of all the ages to the reality and the rightfulness of human freedom. All the centuries bowed themselves from the recesses of the past to cheer in their sacrifice the lowly men who proved themselves worthy of their forerunners, and whose children rise up and call them blessed.

Heedless of his own danger, Samuel Adams, with the voice of a prophet, exclaimed: "Oh, what a glorious morning is this!" for he saw his country's independence hastening on, and, like Columbus in the tempest, knew that the storm did but bear him the more swiftly towards the undiscovered world.

The British troops drew up on the village green, fired a volley, huzzaed thrice by way of triumph, and, after a halt of less than thirty minutes, marched on for Concord. There, in the morning hours, children and women fled for shelter to the hills and the woods, and men were hiding what was left of cannon and military stores.

The minute companies and militia formed on the usual parade, over which the congregation of the town, for near a century and a half, had passed to public worship, the freemen to every town-meeting, and lately the patriot members of the provincial congress twice a day to their little senate house. Near that spot Winthrop, the father of Massachusetts, had given counsel; and Eliot, the apostle of the Indians, had spoken words of benignity and wisdom. The people of Concord, of whom about two hundred appeared in arms on that day, were unpretending men, content in their humility; their energy was derived from their sense of the divine power. This looking to God as their sovereign brought the fathers to their pleasant valley; this controlled the loyalty of the sons; and this has made the name of Concord venerable throughout the world.

The alarm company of the place rallied near the liberty pole on the hill, to the right of the Lexington road, in the front of the meeting-house. They went to the perilous duties of the day "with seriousness and acknowledgment of God," as though they were to engage in acts of worship. The minute company of Lincoln, and a few from Acton, pressed in at an early hour; but the British, as they approached, were seen to be four times as numerous as the Americans. The latter therefore retreated, first to an eminence eighty rods further north, then across Concord River by the North Bridge, till just beyond it, by a back road, they gained high ground, about a mile from the centre of the town. There they waited for aid.

About seven o'clock, under brilliant sunshine, the British marched with rapid step into Concord; the light infantry along the hills, and the grenadiers in the lower road. Left in undisputed possession of the hamlet, they made search for stores. To this end, one small party was sent to the South Bridge over Concord River; and, of six companies under Captain Laurie, three, comprising a hundred soldiers or more, were stationed as a guard at the North Bridge, while there others advanced two miles further, to the residence of Barrett, the highest military officer of the neighborhood, where arms were thought to have been concealed. But they found there nothing to destroy except some carriages for cannon. His wife at their demand gave them refreshment, but refused pay, saying: "We are commanded to feed our enemy, if he hunger."

At daybreak, the minute men of Acton crowded at the drumbeat to the house of Isaac Davis, their captain, who "made haste to be ready." Just thirty years old, the father of four little ones, stately in his person, a man of few words, earnest even to solemnity, he parted from his wife, saying: "Take good care of the children," as though he had foreseen that his own death was near; and, while she gazed after him with resignation, he led off his company to the scene of danger.

Between nine and ten, the number of Americans on the rising ground above Concord bridge had increased to more than four hundred. Of these, there were twenty-five minute men from Bedford, with Jonathan Wilson for their captain; others were from Westford, among them Thaxter, a preacher; others from Littleton, from Carlisle, and from Chelmsford. The Acton company came last, and formed on the right. The whole was a gathering not so much of officers and soldiers as of brothers and equals; of whom every one was a man well known in his village, observed in the meeting-house on Sundays, familiar at town-meetings, and respected as a freeholder or a freeholder's son.

Near the base of the hill, Concord River flows languidly in a winding channel, and was approached by a causeway over the wet ground of its left bank. The by-road from the hill on which the Americans had rallied ran southerly till it met the causeway at right angles. The Americans saw before them within gunshot British troops holding possession of their bridge; and in the distance a still larger number occupying their town, which, from the rising smoke, seemed to have been set on fire.

In Concord itself, Pitcairn had fretted and fumed with oaths and curses at the tavern-keeper for shutting against him the doors of the inn, and exulted over the discovery of two twenty-four pounders in the tavern yard, as though they reimbursed the expedition. These were spiked; sixty barrels of flour were broken in pieces, but so imperfectly that afterwards half the flour was saved; five hundred pounds of ball were thrown into a mill-pond. The liberty pole and several carriages for artillery were burnt; and the court-house took fire, though the fire was put out. Private dwellings were rifled; but their slight waste of public stores was all the advantage for which Gage precipitated a civil war.

The Americans had as yet received only uncertain rumors of the morning's events at Lexington. At the sight of fire in the village, the impulse seized them "to march into the town for its defence." But were they not subjects of the British king? Had not the troops come out in obedience to acknowledged authorities? Was resistance practicable? Was it justifiable? By whom could it be authorized? No union had been formed; no independence proclaimed; no war declared. The husbandmen and mechanics who then stood on the hillock by Concord River were called on to act, and their action would be war or peace, submission or independence. Had they doubted, they must have despaired.

But duty is bolder than theory, more confident than the understanding, older and more imperative than speculative science; existing from eternity. Prudent statesmanship would have asked for time to ponder. Wise philosophy would have lost from hesitation the glory of opening a new era on mankind. The train-bands at Concord acted, and God was with them.

"I never heard from any person the least expression of a wish for a separation," Franklin, not long before, had said to Chatham. In October, 1774, Washington wrote: "No such thing as independence is desired by any thinking man in America." "Before the nineteenth of April, 1775," relates Jefferson, "I never heard a whisper of a disposition to separate from Great Britain." Just thirty-seven days had passed since John Adams in Boston published to the world: "That there are any who pant after independence, is the greatest slander on the province."

The American revolution did not proceed from precarious intentions. It grew out of the soul of the people, and was an inevitable result of a living affection for freedom, which actuated harmonious effort as certainly as the beating of the heart sends warmth and color and beauty through the system. The rustic heroes of that hour obeyed the simplest, the highest, and the surest instincts, of which the seminal principle existed in all their countrymen. From necessity they were impelled by a strong endeavor towards independence and self-direction; this day revealed the plastic will which was to attract the elements of a nation to a centre, and by an innate force to shape its constitution.

The officers, meeting in front of their men, spoke a few words with one another, and went back to their places. Barrett, the colonel, on horseback in the rear, then gave the order to advance, but not to fire unless attacked. The calm features of Isaac Davis, of Acton, became changed; the town schoolmaster, who was present, could never afterwards find words strong enough to express how deeply his face reddened at the word of command. "I have not a man that is afraid to go," said Davis, looking at the men of Acton; and, drawing his sword, he cried: "March!" His company, being on the right, led the way towards the bridge, he himself at their head, and by his side Major John Buttrick of Concord, with John Robinson of Westford, lieutenant-colonel in Prescott's regiment, but on this day a volunteer without command.

Thus these three men walked together in front, followed by minute men and militia, in double file, trailing arms. They went down the hillock, entered the byroad, came to its angle with the main road, and there turned into the causeway that led straight to the bridge. The British began to take up the planks; to prevent it, the Americans quickened their step. At this, the British fired one or two shots up the river; then another, by which Luther Blanchard and Jonas Brown were wounded. A volley followed, and Isaac Davis and Abner Hosmer, the latter a son of the deacon of the Acton church, fell dead. Three hours before, Davis had bid his wife and children farewell. That afternoon, he was carried home and laid in her bedroom. His countenance was little altered and pleasant in death. The bodies of two others of his company, who were slain that day, were brought also to her house, and the three were followed to the village graveyard by a concourse of the neighbors from miles around. Heaven gave her length of days in the land which his generous self-devotion assisted to redeem. She lived to see her country touch the Gulf of Mexico and the Pacific; and when it was grown great in numbers, wealth, and power, the United States in congress paid honors to her husband's martyrdom, and comforted her under the double burden of sorrow and more than ninety years.

As the British fired, Emerson, who was looking on from his chamber window near the bridge, was for one moment uneasy lest the fire should not be returned. It was only for a moment; Buttrick, leaping into the air, and at the same time partially turning round, cried aloud, as if with his country's voice: "Fire, fellow-soldiers! for God's sake, fire!" and the cry, "fire, fire, fire," ran from lip to lip. Two of the British fell; several were wounded. In two minutes, all was hushed. The British retreated in disorder towards their main body; the countrymen were left in possession of the bridge. This is the world renowned battle of Concord; more eventful than Agincourt or Blenheim.

The Americans had acted from impulse, and stood astonished at what they had done. They made no pursuit and did no further harm, except that one wounded soldier, attempting to rise as if to escape, was struck on the head by a young man with a hatchet. The party at Barrett's might have been cut off, but was not molested. As the Sudbury company, commanded by the brave Nixon, passed near the South Bridge, Josiah Haynes, then eighty years of age, deacon of the Sudbury church, urged an attack on the British party stationed there; his advice was rejected by his fellow-soldiers as premature, but the company in which he served proved among the most alert during the rest of the day.

In the town of Concord, Smith, for half an hour, showed by marches and countermarches his uncertainty of purpose. At last, about noon, he left the town, to retreat the way he came, along the hilly road that wound through forests and thickets. The minute men and militia, who had taken part in the fight,

ran over the hills opposite the battle-field into the east quarter
of town, crossed the pasture known as the "Great Fields," and
placed themselves in ambush a little to the eastward of the
village, near the junction of the Bedford road. There they were
re-enforced by men from all around, and at that point the chase
of the English began.

Among the foremost were the minute men of Reading, led
by John Brooks, and accompanied by Foster, the minister of
Littleton, as a volunteer. The company of Billerica, whose inhabitants, in their just indignation at Nesbit and his soldiers,
had openly resolved to "use a different style from that of petition and complaint," came down from the north, while the
East Sudbury company appeared on the south. A little below
the Bedford road at Merriam's corner, the British faced about;
but after a sharp encounter, in which several of them were
killed, they resumed their retreat.

At the high land in Lincoln, the old road bent towards the
north, just where great trees on the west, and thickets on the
east, and stone walls in every direction, offered cover to the
pursuers. The men from Woburn came up in great numbers,
and well armed. Along these defiles, eight of the British were
left. Here Pitcairn was forced to quit his horse, which was taken
with his pistols in their holsters. A little further on, Jonathan
Wilson, captain of the Bedford minute men, too zealous to keep
on his guard, was killed by a flanking party. At another defile
in Lincoln, the minute men of Lexington, commanded by John
Parker, renewed the fight. Every piece of wood, every rock by
the wayside, served as a lurking-place. Scarce ten of the Americans were at any time seen together; yet the hills on each side
seemed to the British to swarm with "rebels," as if they had
dropped from the clouds, and "the road was lined" by an un-
intermitted fire from behind stone walls and trees.

At first the invaders moved in order; as they drew near
Lexington, their flanking parties became ineffective from
weariness; the wounded were scarce able to get forward. In the
west of Lexington, as the British were rising Fiske's hill, a

sharp contest ensued. It was at the eastern foot of the same hill that James Hayward, son of the deacon of Acton church, encountered a regular, and both at the same moment fired; the regular dropped dead, James Hayward was mortally wounded. A little further on fell the octogenarian Josiah Haynes, of Sudbury, who had kept pace with the swiftest in the pursuit.

The British troops, "greatly exhausted and fatigued, and having expended almost all their ammunition," began to run rather than retreat in order. The officers vainly attempted to stop their flight. "They were driven before the Americans like sheep." At last, about two in the afternoon, after they had hurried through the middle of the town, about a mile below the field of the morning's bloodshed, the officers made their way to the front, and by menaces of death began to form them under a very heavy fire.

At that moment, Lord Percy came in sight with the first brigade, consisting of Welsh fusileers, the fourth, the forty-seventh, and the thirty-eighth regiments, in all about twelve hundred men, with two field-pieces. Insolent as usual, they marched out of Boston to the tune of Yankee Doodle but they grew alarmed at finding every house on the road deserted. They met not one person to give them tidings of the party whom they were sent to rescue; and, now that they had made the junction, they could think only of their own safety.

While the cannon kept the Americans at bay, Percy formed his detachment into a square, enclosing the fugitives, who lay down for rest on the ground, "their tongues hanging out of their mouths like those of dogs after a chase."

From this time, the Americans had to contend against nearly the whole of the British army in Boston. Its best troops, fully two thirds of its whole number, and more than that proportion of its strength, were now with Percy. And yet delay was sure to prove ruinous. The British must fly speedily and fleetly, or be overwhelmed. Two wagons, sent out to them with supplies, were waylaid and captured by Payson, the minister of Chelsea. From far and wide minute men were gathering. The men of Dedham, even the old men, received their minister's blessing and went forth, in such numbers that scarce one man between sixteen and seventy was left at home. That morning William Prescott mustered his regiment; and, though Pepperell was so remote that he could not be in season for the pursuit, he hastened down with five companies of guards. Before noon, a messenger rode at full speed into Worcester, crying, "To arms!" A fresh horse was brought, and the tidings went on; while the minute men of that town, after joining hurriedly on the common in a fervent prayer from their minister, kept on the march till they reached Cambridge.

Aware of his perilous position, Percy, resting but half an hour, renewed his retreat. The light infantry marched in front, the grenadiers next, while the first brigade, which now furnished the very strong flanking parties, brought up the rear. They were exposed to a fire on each side, in front, and from behind. The Americans, who were good marksmen, would lie down concealed to load their guns at one place, and discharge them at another, running from front to flank, and from flank to rear. Rage and revenge and shame at their flight led the regulars to plunder houses by the wayside, to destroy in wantonness windows and furniture, to set fire to barns and houses.

Beyond Lexington, the troops were attacked by men chiefly from Essex and the lower towns. The fire from the rebels slackened, till they approached West Cambridge, where Joseph Warren and William Heath, both of the committee of safety, the latter a provincial general officer, gave for a moment some little appearance of organization, and the fight grew sharper and more determined. Here the company from Danvers, which made a breastwork of a pile of shingles, lost eight men, caught between the enemy's flank guard and main body. Here, too, a musketball grazed the hair of Warren, whose heart beat to arms, so that he was ever in the place of greatest danger. The British became more and more "exasperated," and indulged themselves in savage cruelty. In one house they found two aged, helpless, unarmed men, and butchered them both without mercy, stabbing them, breaking their skulls, and dashing out their brains. Hannah Adams, wife of Deacon Joseph Adams of Cambridge, lay in child-bed with a babe of a week old, but was forced to crawl with her infant in her arms and almost naked to a corn-shed, while the soldiers set her house on fire. At Cambridge, an idiot, perched on a fence to gaze at the regular army, was wantonly shot at and killed. Of the Americans, there were never more than four hundred together at any one time but, as some grew tired or used up their ammunition, others took their places, and, though there was not much concert or discipline, and no attack with masses, the pursuit never flagged.

Below West Cambridge, the militia from Dorchester, Roxbury, and Brookline came up. Of these, Isaac Gardner of the latter place, one on whom the colony rested many hopes, fell about a mile west of Harvard College. The fieldpieces began to lose their terror, so that the Americans pressed upon the rear of the fugitives, whose retreat could not become more precipitate. Had it been delayed a half hour longer, or had Pickering, with his fine regiment from Salem, Danvers, and Marblehead, been alert enough to have intercepted them in front, it was thought that, worn down as they were by fatigue and exhausted of ammunition, they must have surrendered. But, a little after sunset, the survivors escaped across Charlestown Neck.

The troops of Percy had marched thirty miles in ten hours; the party of Smith, in six hours, had retreated twenty miles; the guns of the ships-of-war and a menace to burn the town of Charlestown saved them from annoyance during their rest on Bunker Hill, and while they were ferried across Charles River.

On that day, forty-nine Americans were killed, thirty-four wounded, and five missing. The loss of the British in killed, wounded, and missing, was two hundred and seventy-three; greater than in the battle before Quebec where Wolfe fell. Among the wounded were many officers; Smith was hurt severely. Many more were disabled by fatigue.

All the following night, the men of Massachusetts streamed in from scores of miles around, old men as well as young. They had scarce a semblance of artillery or war-like stores, no powder, nor organization, nor provisions; but there they were, thousands with brave hearts, determined to rescue the liberties of their country. "The night preceding the outrages at Lexington, there were not fifty people in the whole colony that ever expected any blood would be shed in the contest;" the night after, the king's governor and the king's army found themselves closely beleaguered in Boston.

"The next news from England must be conciliatory, or the connection between us ends," said Warren. "This month," so William Emerson, of Concord, late chaplain to the provincial congress, chronicled in a blank leaf of his almanac, "is remarkable for the greatest events of the present age." "From the nineteenth of April, 1775," said Clark, of Lexington, on its first anniversary, "will be dated the liberty of the American world."

THE *study of history, Bancroft believed, offered ample evidence that a great people produced great men to lead them in times of crisis. Among the leaders of colonial and revolutionary America he identified John Winthrop, Roger Williams, William Penn, Franklin, Samuel Adams, Jefferson, and the greatest of all, "America's Lycurgus and Augustus," George Washington. Born only a year after Washington's death, Bancroft grew to manhood with the Washington legend. His father published one of the best early biographies,* The Life of Washington *(1807), and as a twelve-year-old Exeter student the boy served as a private in the school's cadet company, the "Washington Whites," founded in 1800 to commemorate the late President's memory. For the Virginian, Bancroft held a lifelong admiration, from his early essay in 1838 for the* Eclectic Review *on "Washington's Place in History," to his final eulogy in the constitutional history almost forty years later. What impressed Bancroft most in Washington was the classic balance of his character, the "faultless proportion" of his qualities, "all order, all proportion, all completeness . . . , a golden mean of excellencies." To Bancroft Washington represented whole, harmonious man, as well as a great and wise military and political leader.*

Washington as Commander in Chief

ON THE fifteenth of June [1775, Congress] voted to appoint a general. Thomas Johnson, of Maryland, nominated George Washington; and, as he had been brought forward "at the particular request of the people in New England," he was elected by ballot unanimously.

Washington was then forty-three years of age. In stature he a little exceeded six feet; his limbs were sinewy and well proportioned; his chest broad; his figure stately, blending dignity of presence with ease. His robust constitution had been tried and invigorated by his early life in the wilderness, the habit of occupation out of doors, and rigid temperance; so that few equalled him in strength of arm, or power of endurance, or noble horsemanship. His complexion was florid; his hair dark brown; his head in its shape perfectly round. His broad nostrils seemed formed to give expression and escape to scornful anger. His eyebrows were rayed and finely arched. His dark blue eyes, which were deeply set, had an expression of resignation, and an earnestness that was almost pensiveness. His forehead was sometimes marked with thought, but never with inquietude; his countenance was mild and pleasing and full of benignity.

At eleven years old left an orphan to the care of an excellent but unlettered mother, he grew up without learning. Of arithmetic and geometry he acquired just knowledge enough to be able to practice measuring land; but all his instruction at school taught him not so much as the orthography or rules of grammar of his own tongue. His culture was altogether his own work, and he was in the strictest sense a self-made man; yet from his early life he never seemed uneducated. At sixteen, he went into the wilderness as a surveyor, and for three years continued the pursuit, where the forests trained him, in meditative solitude, to freedom and largeness of mind; and nature revealed to him her obedience to serene and silent laws. In his intervals from toil, he seemed always to be attracted to the best men, and to be cherished by them. Fairfax, his employer, an Oxford scholar, already aged, became his fast friend. He read little, but with close attention. Whatever he took in hand, he applied himself to with care; and his papers, which have been preserved, show how he almost imperceptibly gained the power of writing correctly; always expressing himself with clearness and directness, often with felicity of language and grace.

When the frontiers on the west became disturbed, he at nineteen was commissioned an adjutant-general with the rank of major. At twenty-one, he went as the envoy of Virginia to the council of Indian chiefs on the Ohio and to the French officers near Lake Erie. Fame waited upon him from his youth; and no one of his colony was so much spoken of. He conducted the first military expedition from Virginia that crossed the Alleghanies. Braddock selected him as an aid, and he was the only man who came out of the disastrous defeat near the Monongahela, with increased reputation, which extended to England. The next year, when he was four-and-twenty, "the great esteem" in which he was held in Virginia, and his "real merit," led the lieutenant-governor of Maryland to request that he might be "commissioned and appointed second in command" of the army designed to march to the Ohio; and Shirley, the commander in chief, heard the proposal "with great satisfaction and pleasure," for "he knew no provincial officer upon the continent to whom he would so readily give that rank as to Washington." In 1758 he acted under Forbes as a brigadier, and but for him that general would never have crossed the mountains.

Courage was so natural to him that it was hardly spoken of to his praise; no one ever at any moment of his life discovered in him the least shrinking in danger; and he had a hardihood of daring which escaped notice, because it was so enveloped by superior calmness and wisdom.

His address was most easy and agreeable; his step firm and graceful; his air neither grave nor familiar. He was as cheerful as he was spirited, frank and communicative in the society of friends, fond of the fox-chase and the dance, often sportive in his letters, and liked a hearty laugh. "His smile," writes Chastellux, "was always the smile of benevolence." This joyousness of disposition remained to the last, though the vastness of his responsibilities was soon to take from him the right of displaying the impulsive qualities of his nature, and the weight which he was to bear up was to overlay and repress his gayety and openness.

His hand was liberal; giving quietly and without observation, as though he was ashamed of nothing but being discovered in doing good. He was kindly and compassionate, and of lively sensibility to the sorrows of others; so that, if his country had only needed a victim for its relief, he would have willingly offered himself as a sacrifice. But while he was prodigal of himself, he was considerate for others; even parsimonious of the blood of his countrymen.

He was prudent in the management of his private affairs, purchased rich lands from the Mohawk valley to the flats of the Kanawha, and improved his fortune by the correctness of his judgment; but, as a public man, he knew no other aim than the good of his country, and in the hour of his country's poverty he refused personal emolument for his service.

His faculties were so well balanced and combined that his constitution, free from excess, was tempered evenly with all the elements of activity, and his mind resembled a well-ordered commonwealth; his passions, which had the intensest vigor, owned allegiance to reason; and, with all the fiery quickness of his spirit, his impetuous and massive will was held in check by consummate judgment. He had in his composition a calm, which gave him in moments of highest excitement the power of self-control, and enabled him to excel in patience, even when he had most cause for disgust. Washington was offered a command when there was little to bring out the unorganized resources of the continent but his own influence, and authority was connected with the people by the most frail, most attenuated, scarcely discernible threads; yet, vehement as was his nature, impassioned as was his courage, he so restrained his ardor that he never failed continuously to exert the attracting power of that influence, and never exerted it so sharply as to break its force.

In secrecy he was unsurpassed; but his secrecy had the character of prudent reserve, not of cunning or concealment. His great natural power of vigilance had been developed by his life in the wilderness.

His understanding was lucid, and his judgment accurate; so that his conduct never betrayed hurry or confusion. No detail was too minute for his personal inquiry and continued supervision; and at the same time he comprehended events in their wildest aspects and relations. He never seemed above the object that engaged his attention, and he was always equal, without an effort, to the solution of the highest questions, even when there existed no precedents to guide his decision. In the perfection of the reflective powers, which he used habitually, he had no peer.

In this way he never drew to himself admiration for the possession of any one quality in excess, never made in council any one suggestion that was sublime but impracticable, never in action took to himself the praise or the blame of undertakings astonishing in conception, but beyond his means of execution. It was the most wonderful accomplishment of this man that, placed upon the largest theatre of events, at the head of the greatest revolution in human affairs, he never failed to observe all that was possible, and at the same time to bound his aspirations by that which was possible.

A slight tinge in his character, perceptible only to the close observer, revealed the region from which he sprung, and he might be described as the best specimen of manhood as developed in the south; but his qualities were so faultlessly proportioned that his whole country rather claimed him as its choicest representative, the most complete expression of all its attainments and aspirations. He studied his country and conformed to it. His countrymen felt that he was the best type of American, and rejoiced in it, and were proud of it. They lived in his life, and made his success and his praise their own.

Profoundly impressed with confidence in God's providence, and exemplary in his respect for the forms of public worship, no philosopher of the eighteenth century was more firm in the support of freedom of religious opinion, none more remote from bigotry; but belief in God, and trust in his overruling power, formed the essence of his character. Divine wisdom not only illumines the spirit, it inspires the will. Washington was a man of action, and not of theory or words; his creed appears in his life, not in his professions, which burst from him very rarely, and only at those great moments of crisis in the fortunes of his country, when earth and heaven seemed actually to meet, and his emotions became too intense for suppression; but his whole being was one continued act of faith in the eternal, intelligent, moral order of the universe. Integrity was so completely the law of his nature, that a planet would sooner have shot from its sphere than he have departed from his uprightness, which was so constant that it often seemed to be almost impersonal. "His integrity was the most pure, his justice the most inflexible I have ever known," writes Jefferson; "no motives of interest or consanguinity, of friendship or hatred, being able to bias his decision."

They say of Giotto that he introduced goodness into the art of painting; Washington carried it with him to the camp and the cabinet, and established a new criterion of human greatness. The purity of his will confirmed his fortitude; and, as he never faltered in his faith in virtue, he stood fast by that which he knew to be just; free from illusions; never dejected by the apprehension of the difficulties and perils that went before him, and drawing the promise of success from the justice of his cause. Hence he was persevering, leaving nothing unfinished; devoid of all taint of obstinacy in his firmness; seeking, and gladly receiving advice, but immovable in his devotedness to right.

Of a "retiring modesty and habitual reserve," his ambition was no more than the consciousness of his power, and was subordinate to his sense of duty; he took the foremost place, for he knew from inborn magnanimity that it belonged to him, and he dared not withhold the service required of him; so that, with all his humility, he was by necessity the first, though never for himself or for private ends. He loved fame, the approval of coming generations, the good opinion of his fellow-men of his own time, and he desired to make his conduct coincide with their wishes; but not fear of censure, not the prospect of applause, could tempt him to swerve from rectitude, and the praise which he coveted was the sympathy of that moral sentiment which exists in every human breast, and goes forth only to the welcome of virtue.

There have been soldiers who have achieved mightier victories in the field, and made conquests more nearly corresponding to the boundlessness of selfish ambition; statesmen who have been connected with more startling upheavals of society; but it is the greatness of Washington that in public trusts he used power solely for the public good; that he was the life and moderator and stay of the most momentous revolution in human affairs, its moving impulse and its restraining power. Combining the centripetal and the centrifugal forces in their utmost strength and in perfect relations, with creative grandeur of instinct he held ruin in check, and renewed and perfected the institutions of his country. Finding the colonies disconnected and dependent, he left them such a united and well-ordered commonwealth as no visionary had believed to be possible. So that it has been truly said: "He was as fortunate as great and good."

This also is the praise of Washington: that never in the tide of time has any man lived who had in so great a degree the almost divine faculty to command the confidence of his fellowmen and rule the willing. Wherever he became known, in his family, his neighborhood, his country, his native state, the continent, the camp, civil life, among the common people, in foreign courts, throughout the civilized world, and even among the savages, he beyond all other men had the confidence of his kind.

Washington saw at a glance the difficulties of the position to which he had been chosen. He was appointed by a government which, in its form, was one of the worst of all possible governments in time of peace, and was sure to reveal its defects still more plainly in time of war. It was inchoate and without an executive head; the several branches of administration, if to be conducted at all, were to be conducted by separate, ever changing, and irresponsible communities; and all questions of legislation and of action ultimately decided by the one ill-organized body of men, who, in respect of granted powers, were

too feeble even to originate advice. They were not the representatives of a union; they alone constituted the union of
which as yet, there was no other bond. One whole department
of government, the judicial, was entirely wanting. So was, in
truth, the executive. The congress had no ability whatever to
enforce a decree of their own; they had no revenue, and no
authority to collect a revenue; they had none of the materials
of war; they did not own a cannon, nor a pound of powder, nor
a tent, nor a musket; they had no regularly enlisted army, and
had even a jealousy of forming an army, and depended on the
zeal of volunteers, or of men to be enlisted for less than seven
months. There were no experienced officers, and no methods
projected for obtaining them. Washington saw it all. He was in
the enjoyment of fame; he wished not to forfeit the esteem of
his fellow-men; and his eye glistened with a tear, as he said
in confidence to Patrick Henry on occasion of his appointment:
"This day will be the commencement of the decline of my
reputation."

But this consideration did not make him waver. On the sixteenth of June, he appeared in his place in congress, and, after
refusing all pay beyond his expenses, he spoke with unfeigned
modesty: "As the congress desire it, I will enter upon the momentous duty, and exert every power I possess in their service,
and for the support of the glorious cause. But I beg it may be
remembered by every gentleman in the room, that I this day
declare, with the utmost sincerity, I do not think myself equal
to the command I am honored with."

The next day, the delegates of all the colonies resolved unanimously in congress "to maintain and assist him, and adhere
to him, the said George Washington, Esquire, with their lives
and fortunes in the same cause."

By his commission, he was invested with the command
over all forces raised or to be raised by the United Colonies, and
with full power and authority to order the army as he should
think for the good and welfare of the service, "in unforseen

emergencies using his best circumspection, and advising with his council of war;" and he was instructed to take "special care that the liberties of America receive no detriment."

Washington knew that he must depend for success on a steady continuance of purpose in an imperfectly united continent, and on his personal influence over separate and half-formed governments, with most of which he was wholly unacquainted. He foresaw a long and arduous struggle; but a secret consciousness of his power bade him not to fear; and, whatever might be the backwardness of others, he never admitted the thought of sheathing his sword or resigning his command, till the work of vindicating American liberty should be done. To his wife he unbosomed his inmost mind: "I hope my undertaking this service is designed to answer some good purpose. I rely confidently on that Providence which has heretofore preserved and been bountiful to me."

His acceptance changed the aspect of affairs. John Adams, looking with complacency upon "the modest and virtuous, the amiable, generous, and brave general," as the choice of Massachusetts, said: "This appointment will have a great effect in cementing the union of these colonies." "The general is one of the most important characters of the world; upon him depend the liberties of America." All hearts turned with affection towards Washington. This is he who was raised up to be, not the head of a party, but the father of his country.

BANCROFT *occasionally suspended his narrative to discuss with his reader such broad issues as the nature and uses of the past, the meanings of experience, the relationships between God's plans and human actions, and kindred problems of philosophy, theology, and historical theory. As he drew closer to the decisive act of American independence, he paused to speak of such things as historical objectivity, providential rules of right and justice, the unity of human nature, distinguishing characteristics of the American mind, and the moral questions at issue in the colonial-English conflict. As he makes abundantly clear in this chapter, Bancroft believed in all sincerity that his position, as he considered "The Question between Britain and America," was one of absolute impartiality—but Britain was proud, perverse, and wrong; the colonists were duty- and destiny-bound to maintain both "the rights of mankind" and those "liberties of the English people" won in 1688 and now endangered by King and Parliament. The issue, in Bancroft's view, finally reduced itself simply to a contest between "a principle of freedom" and "an instrument of tyranny." Here the Americans had no choice.*

The Question between Britain and America (August, 1775)

THE chronicler of manners and events can alone measure his own fairness, for no one else knows so well what he throws aside. The greatest poet of action has brought upon the stage the panorama of mortal being, without once finding occasion to delineate a faultless hero. No man that lives has not sinned. Indiscriminate praise neither paints to the life, nor teaches by example, nor advances social science; history is no mosaic of funeral eulogies and family epitaphs, nor can the hand of truth sketch character without shadows as well as light. The crimes and the follies which stand in the line of causes of revolution, or modify the development of a state, or color the morals of an age, must be brought up for judgment; and yet the humane student of his race, in his searches into the past, contemplates more willingly those inspirations of the beautiful and the good, which lift the soul above the interests of the moment, illustrate our affinity with something higher than ourselves, point the way to principles that are eternal, and constitute the vital element of progress.

From immeasurable distances in the material universe, the observer of the stars brings back word that the physical forces which rule our neighborhood maintain an all-pervading energy; and the records imbedded in the rocks, teaching how countless myriads of seasons have watched the sun go forth daily from his chamber, and the earth turn on its axis, and the sea ebb and flow, demonstrate that the same physical forces have exerted their power without change for unnumbered periods of bygone years. The twin sciences of the stars and of the earth establish the cosmical unity of the material universe in all that we can know of time and space. But the conception of the perfect order and unity of creation does not unfold itself in its beauty and grandeur, so long as the guiding presence of intelligence is not apprehended. From the depths of man's consciousness, which envelops sublimer truths than the firmament over his head can reveal to his senses, rises the idea of right; and history, testing that idea by observation, traces the vestiges of moral law through the practice of the nations in every age, proves experimentally the reality of justice, and confirms by induction the intuitions of reason.

The historian, even more than philosophers and naturalists, must bring to his pursuit the freedom of an unbiased mind; in his case, the submission of reason to prejudice would have a deeper criminality; for he cannot neglect to be impartial without at once falsifying nature and denying providence. The exercise of candor is possible; for the world of action has its organization, and is obedient to law. The forces that constitute is antagonisms are very few, and are always and everywhere present, and are always and everywhere the same, though they make their appearance under many shapes. Human nature is for ever identical with itself; and the state ever contains in its own composition all the opposite tendencies which constitute parties. The problems of politics cannot be solved without passing behind transient forms to efficient causes; the old theories, founded on the distinction of monarchy, aristocracy, and democracy, must give place to an analysis of the faculties in man, and the unvarying conditions, principles, and inherent wants out of which the forms of government have been evolved; and it will be found that as every class of vertebrate animals has the forms of the same organs, so an exact generalization establishes the existence of every element of civil policy, and of the rudiments of all its possible varieties and divisions in every stage of human being.

Society is many and is one; and the organic unity of the state is to be reconciled with the separate existence of each of its members. Law which restrains all, and freedom which inheres in each individual, and the mediation which adjusts and connects these two conflicting powers, are ever present as constituent ingredients; each of which, in its due proportion, is essential to the well-being of a state, and is ruinous when it passes its bounds. It has been said that the world is governed too much; no statesman has ever said that there should be no government at all. Anarchy is at one extreme; and the pantheistic despotism, which is the absorption of the people into one man as the sovereign, at the other. All governments contain the two opposite tendencies; and were either attraction or repulsion, central power or individuality, to disappear, civil order would be crushed or dissolved.

The state has always for its life-giving principle the idea of right; the condition of facts can never perfectly represent that idea; and, unless this antagonism also is recommended, no durable constitution can be formed, and government totters of itself to its fall, or is easily overthrown. Here, then, is another cause of division; one party clings to tradition, and another

demands reform; the fanatics for conservatism are met by enthusiasts for ideal freedom, while there is always an effort
to bring the established order into a nearer harmony with the
eternal law of justice. These principles have manifested their
power in every country at every stage of its existence, and must
be respected, or society will perish in chaotic confusion or a
stagnant calm.

The duty of impartiality in accounting for political conflicts
is then made easy, if behind every party there lies what an
English poet has called "an eternal thought," and if the gen-
erating cause of every party, past or present or hereafter possible, is a force which never disappears, which in its proper
proportion is essential to the well-being of society, and which
turns into a poison only in its excess. It may take a diversity
of names as it comes into flower respectively among savages or
the civilized, in kingdoms, in empires, or in republics; yet every
party has its origin in human nature and the necessities of life
in a community.

To fail in impartiality with regard to men, is not merely at
variance with right; it is also sure to defeat itself. The fame
which shines only in an eclipse of that of others is necessarily
transistory; the eclipse soon passes away and the brighter light
recovers its lustre. The biographer, who constructs the road
to the monument of his idol over the graves of the reputation
of great men, will find the best part of his race refusing to travel
it. Besides, superior merit, to be discerned, must be surrounded
by the meritorious; the glory of the noblest genius of his age
would be sacrificed by detracting from the ability of his antagonists, his competitors, and his associates. Real worth de-
lights to be environed by the worthy; it is serene, and can be
duly estimated only by the serene.

The idea of humanity, which, by its ever increasing clearness, furnishes the best evidence of the steady melioration of
the race, teaches to judge with equity the reciprocal relations
of states. The free development of all inherent powers is the
common aim, and the acknowledgment of the universal right

to that free development is the bond of unity. Between Britain
and the new empire which she founded, the duty of impartiality
belongs equally to the men of the two countries; but experience
has shown that it is practised with most difficulty by those of
the parent land. The moral world knows only rule of right; but
men in their pride create differences among themselves. The
ray from the eternal source of justice suffers a deflection, as it
falls from absolute princes on their subjects, from an established church on heretics, from masters of slaves on men in
bondage, from hereditary nobles on citizens and peasants, from
a privileged caste on an oppressed one. Something of this per-
verseness of pride has prevailed in the metropolitan state
towards its colonies; it is stamped indelibly on the statute-book
of Great Britain, where all may observe and measure its intensity. That same pride rule dwithout check in the palace,
and was little restrained in the house of lords; it broke forth in
the conduct of the administration and its subordinates; it
tinged the British colonial state papers of the last century so
thoroughly that historians who should follow them implicitly
as guides would be as erroneous in their facts as the ministers
of that day were in their policy. This haughty feeling has so
survived the period of revolutionary strife that to this day it
sometimes hangs as a heavy bias on the judgment even of
Englishmen professing liberal opinions. The Americans more
easily recovered their equanimity. They intended resistance
to a trifling tax and a preamble, and they won peace with liberty; the vastness of the acquisition effaced the remembrance
of a transient attempt at oppression, and left no rankling discontent behind. The tone of our writers has often been deferen-
tially forbearing; those of our countrymen who have written
most fully of the war of our revolution brought to their task no
prejudices against England, and, while they gladly recall the
relations of kindred, no one of them has written a line with gall.

Nor are citizens of a republic most tempted to evil speaking
of kings and nobles; it takes men of the privileged class to scan-
dalize their peers and princes without stint. The shameless

slanders which outrage nature in the exaggeration of the pro-
fligacy of courts have usually originated with palaces, and been
repeated by men of rank; American writers have no motive to
take them up; the land of equality recognises sovereigns and
aristocrats as men, and places them under the protection of the
tribunal of humanity.

The Americans, entering most reluctantly on a war with
Britain, preserved an instinctive feeling that the relations of
affinity were suspended rather than destroyed; they held themselves called to maintain "the rights of mankind," the liberties of the English people, as well as their own; they never
looked upon the transient ministers who were their oppressors
as the type of the parent country. The moment approaches
when the king proclaimed his irrevocable decision; to understand that decision, it is necessary to state precisely the question at issue.

The administration of numerous colonies, each of which had
a representative government of its own, was conducted with
inconvenience from a want of unity; in war, experience showed
a difficulty in obtaining proportionate aid from them all; in
peace, the crown officers were impatient of owing their support
to the periodical votes of colonial legislatures. To remedy this
seeming evil by a concentration of power, James II usurped all
authority over the country north of the Potomac, and designed
to consolidate and govern it by his own despotic will.

The Revolution of 1688 restored to the colonies their representative governments, and the collision between the crown
officers and the colonial legislatures was renewed; threats of
parliamentary intervention were sometimes heard; but for
nearly three quarters of a century no minister had been willing to gratify the pertinacious entreaties of placemen by dis-
turbing America in the enjoyment of her liberties.

Soon after the accession of George III, the king, averse to
governing so many prosperous and free and loyal colonies by
consent, resolved, through the paramount power of parliament,
to introduce a new colonial system, with Halifax, Bedford,

and especially Charles Townshend, had matured, and which
was to have sufficient vigor to control the unwilling. First, the
charter governments were to be reduced to one uniform direct
dependence on the king, by the abolition of the jurisdiction
of the proprietaries in Maryland and Pennsylvania, and by the
alteration or repeal of the charters of Massachusetts, Connecticut, and Rhode Island. Secondly for the pay of the crown
officers, the British parliament was to establish in each colony
a permanent civil list, independent of the assemblies, so that
every branch of the judicial and executive government should
be wholly of the king's appointment and at the king's will.
Thirdly, the British parliament was, by its own act of taxation,
to levy on the colonies a revenue towards maintaining their
military establishment. Townshend, as the head of the board
of trade, was unfolding the plan in the house of commons just
before Bute retired.

The execution of the design fell to George Grenville. Now
Grenville conceived himself to be a whig of the straitest sect,
for he believed implicitly in the absolute power of parliament,
and this belief he regarded as the great principle of the Revolution of 1688. He was pleased with the thought of moulding
the whole empire into closer unity by means of parliamentary
taxation; but his regard for vested rights forbade him to consent to a wilful abrogation of charters. The Americans complained to him that a civil list raised by the British parliament
would reduce the colonial assemblies to a nullity; Grenville
saw the justice of the objection, disclaimed the purpose,
dropped that part of the plan, and proposed to confine the use
of the parliamentary revenue to the expenses of the military
establishment. The colonists again interposed with the argument that, by the theory of the British constitution, taxation
and representation are inseparable correlatives; to this Grenville listened, and answered that in parliament, as the common
council, the whole empire was represented collectively, though
not distributively; but that as in Britain some reform by an increase of the number of voters was desirable, so taxation of

the colonies ought to be followed by a special colonial representation; and, with this theory of constitutional law, he passed the stamp act.

When a difference at court drove Grenville from office, his theory lost its importance; for no party in England or America undertook its support. The new ministers by whom his colonial policy was to be changed had the option between repealing the tax as an act of justice to the colonies, or repealing it as a measure of expediency to Britain. The first was the choice of Pitt, and its adoption would have ended the controversy; the second was that of Rockingham. He abolished the tax, and sent over assurances of his friendship; but his declaratory act established, as the rule for the judiciary and the law of the empire, that the legislative power of parliament reached to the colonies in all cases whatsoever. The declaration opened the whole question of the nature of representation, and foreshadowed a revolution or peaceful reform in America and in England. In 1688, the assertion of the paramount power of parliament against a king who would have sequestered all legislative liberty was a principle of freedom; but, in the eighteenth century, the assertion of the absolute power of a parliament acting in concert with the king was to frame an instrument of tyranny. The colonies denied the unqualified authority of a legislature in which they were not represented; and when they were told that they were as much represented as nine-tenths of the people of Britain, the British people, enlightened by the discussion, from that day complained unceasingly of the inadequateness of a parliament in whose election nine-tenths of them had no voice whatever.

The reform for England was long deferred; the issue was precipitated upon America. In the very next year, Charles Townshend, resuming the system which he had advocated in the administration of Bute, proposed a parliamentary tax to be collected in America on tea, glass, paper, and painters' colors, and introduced the tax by a preamble, asserting that "it

is expedient that a revenue should be raised in his majesty's
dominions in America for defraying the charge of the administration of justice and support of civil government, and towards
further defraying the expenses of defending the said dominions." Grenville had proposed taxes for the defence of the colonies; Townshend's preamble promised an ever increasing
American civil list, independent of American assemblies, to be
disposed of by ministers at their discretion for salaries, gifts,
or pensions. Here lay the seeds of a grievance indefinite in its
extent, taking from the colonies all control over public officers,
and introducing a government to be administered for the benefit of office-holders, without regard to the rights and liberties
and welfare of the people.

Just as Townshend had intrenched the system in the
statute-book, he died, and left behind him no great English
statesman for its steadfast upholder; while the colonies were
unanimous in resisting the innovation, and avoided the taxes
by stopping imports from Britain. The government gave way,
and repealed all Townshend's taxes except on tea. Of that duty
Lord North maintained that it was no innovation, but a reduc-
tion of the ancient duty of a shilling a pound to one of three-
pence only; and that the change of the place where the duty
was to be collected was no more than a regulation of trade to
prevent smuggling tea from Holland. The statement, so far as
the tax was concerned, was unanswerable; but the sting of the
tax act lay in its preamble; Rockingham's declaratory act affirmed the power of parliament in all cases whatsoever; Townshend's preamble declared the expediency of using that power
to raise a very large colonial revenue. Still, collision was prac-
tically averted; for the Americans, in their desire for peace,
gave up the importation of tea.

At this, the king, against the opinion of Lord North and of
the East India company, directed that company itself to export
tea to America, and there to pay the duty, hoping that a low
price would tempt Americans to buy. But the colonists would

not suffer the tea to be exposed for sale; the crown officers yielded to their unanimous resistance everywhere except at Boston, and there the tea was thrown overboard.

To close the port of Boston and require an indemnity for the East India company's loss, was the advice of Hutchinson, and neither New York, nor Pennsylvania, nor Virginia would have supported a refusal to such a requisition; but the king and the Bedford party seized the occasion to carry into effect part of their cherished system, and changed by act of parliament the charter granted by William and Mary to Massachusetts. The object of the change was the compression of popular power in favor of the prerogative. The measure could bring no advantage to Britain, and really had nothing to recommend it; to the people of Massachusetts and to the people of all the colonies, submission to the change seemed an acknowledgment of the absolute power of parliament over liberty and property in America. The people of Massachusetts resisted; the king answered: "Blows must decide." A congress of the colonies approved the conduct of Massachusetts; parliament pledged itself to the king. In 1773, a truce was possible; after the alteration of the charter of Massachusetts, in 1774, America would have been pacified by a simple repeal of obnoxious acts; in 1775, after blood had been shed at Lexington, some security for the future was needed.

British statesmen of all schools but Chatham's affirmed the power of parliament to tax America; America denied that it could be rightfully taxed by a body in which it was not represented, for taxation and representation were inseparable. British politicians rejoined that taxation was but an act of legislation; that, therefore, to deny to parliament the right of taxation was to deny parliament all right of legislation for colonies, even for the regulation of trade. To this America made answer that, in reason and truth, representation and legislation are inseparable; that the colonies being entitled to English freedom, were not bound by any act of a body to which they did not send members; that in theory the colonies were independent of the

British parliament; but, as they honestly desired to avoid a conflict, they proposed as a fundamental or an organic act their voluntary submission to every parliamentary diminution of their liberty which time had sanctioned, including the navigation acts and taxes for regulating trade, on condition of being relieved from every part of the new system of administration, and being secured against future attempts for its introduction. Richard Penn, the agent of congress, was in London with its petition to the king, to entreat his concurrence in this endeavor to restore peace and union.

SINCE *the Declaration of Independence marked a decisive turning point in human history, Bancroft allotted seven chapters of Volumes VII and IX of the* History *(reduced only slightly in the Centenary revision) to the consideration of its preparation, execution, and the impact on the world. Chapter LXVIII, "The People of the Colonies Demand Independence," treated events in June, 1776; Chapters LXIX and LXX covered July 1–4, 1776; and the first three chapters of the next book, "Epoch Fourth," described the reception of the Declaration in each of the original thirteen states and in Europe. In what Bancroft perceived as the grand design of American history, what happened during June and July, 1776, in Philadelphia stood forth as the culmination of God's plan for the advancement of the human race. The men who met there, Bancroft explained, acting as surrogates for humanity at large, "avowed for their object the welfare of mankind, and believed that they were in the service of their own and all future generations." The document which they produced and approved, deeply rooted in principles of "eternal justice," represented "the highest creative powers of which man is capable" and "the assertion of right for the entire world of mankind." It was the tone of this and similar sections of the* History *which led Francis Bowen of the* North American Review *to chide Bancroft for a "love of country too exalted to be discriminating"; yet the ideas and attitudes he expressed in these chapters were fundamental to his view of America's history.*

The Resolution of Independence, July 1 and 2, 1776

ON THE morning of the first of July, the day set apart for considering the resolution of independence, John Adams, confident as if the vote had been taken, invoked the blessing of Heaven to make the new-born republic more glorious than any

Vol. V, Chap. LXIX.

which had gone before. His heart melted with sorrow at the sufferings of the army that had been in Canada; he knew that England, having recovered that province, commanded the upper lakes and the Mississippi; that she had a free communication with all the tribes of Indians along the frontiers of all the colonies, and would induce them by bloodshed and fire to drive in the inhabitants upon the middle settlements, at a time when the coasts might be ravaged by the British navy, and a single day might bring the army before New York. Independence could be obtained only by a great expense of life; but the greater danger, the stronger was his determination; for a free constitution of civil government could not be purchased at too dear a rate. He called to mind the fixed rule of the Romans, never to send or receive ambassadors to treat of peace with their enemies while their affairs were in a disastrous situation; and he was cheered by the belief that his countrymen were of the same temper and principle.

At the appointed hour, the members, probably on that day fifty in number, appeared in their places; among them, the delegates lately chosen in New Jersey. The great occasion had brought forth superior statesmen; men who joined the power of moderation to energy. After they had all passed away, their longevity was remarked as a proof of their calm and temperate nature; full two-thirds of the New England representatives lived beyond seventy years; some of them to be eighty or ninety. Every colony was found to be represented, and the delegates of all but one had received full power of action. Comprehensive instructions, reaching the question of independence without explicitly using the word, had been given by Massachusetts in January, by South Carolina in March, by Georgia on the fifth of April. North Carolina, in the words of Cornelius Harnett, on the twelfth of April, was the first to direct expressly its representatives in congress to concur in a declaration of independence. On the first of May, Massachusetts expunged the regal style from all public proceedings, and substituted the name of her "government and people;" on the fourth Rhode

Island more explicitly renounced allegiance, and made its delegates the representatives of an independent republic; Virginia on the fifteenth, the very day on which John Adams in congress carried his measure for instituting governments by the sole authority of the people, ordered her delegates at Philadelphia to propose independence and by a circular letter communicated her resolve to all her sister colonies. The movement of Virginia was seconded almost in her words by Connecticut on the fourteenth of June, New Hampshire on the fifteenth, New Jersey on the twenty-first, the conference of committees of Pennsylvania on the twenty-fourth, Maryland on the twenty-eighth. Delaware on the twenty-second of March had still hoped for conciliation; but on the fifteenth of June she instructed her delegates to concur in forming further compacts between the united colonies, concluding treaties with foreign powers, and adopting such other measures as should be deemed necessary for promoting the liberty, safety, and interests of America. The vote of the eleventh of June showed the purpose of New York; but, under the accumulation of dangers, her statesmen waited a few days longer, that her voice for independence might have the full authority of her people.

The business of the day began with reading various letters, among others one from Washington, who returned the whole number of his men, present and fit for duty, including one regiment of artillery, at seven thousand seven hundred and fifty-four. Of near fourteen hundred, the firelocks were bad; more than eight hundred had none at all; three thousand eight hundred and twenty-seven, more than half the whole number of infantry, had no bayonets. Of the militia who had been called for, only about a thousand had joined the camp; and with this force the general was to defend extensive lines against an army, near at hand, of thirty thousand veterans. An express from Lee made known that fifty-three ships, with Clinton, had arrived before Charleston, of which the safety was involved in doubt.

A more cheering letter, which Chase had forwarded by express from Annapolis, brought the first news of the unanimity of the Maryland convention, whose vote for independence was produced and read.

The order of the day came next, and congress resolved itself "into a committee of the whole to take into consideration the resolution respecting independency." For a few minutes, silence prevailed. In the absence of the mover of the resolution, the eyes of every one turned towards its seconder, John Adams; and the new members from New Jersey requested that the arrangements used in former debates might be recapitulated. He had made no preparation for that morning; but for many months independence had been the chief object of his thoughts and his discourse, and the strongest arguments ranged themselves before his mind in their natural order. Of his sudden, impetuous, unpremeditated speech, no minutes ever existed, and no report was made. It is only remembered that he set forth the justice and the necessity, the seasonableness and the advantages of a separation from Great Britain; he dwelt on the neglect and insult with which their petitions had been treated by the king; and on the vindictive spirit manifested in the employment of German troops whose arrival was hourly expected. He concluded by urging the present time as the most suitable for resolving on independence, inasmuch as it had become the first wish and the last instruction of the communities they represented.

Dickinson of Pennsylvania rose, not so much to reply as to justify himself before congress. He took pride in being the ardent assertor of freedom, and was conscious that his writings had won him a great name. Accustomed to lead, he loved to be recognised as the guide. Now for the first time in his life his excessively sensitive nature was writhing under the agonies of wounded self-love. For one year he had been at variance with John Adams, and during all that time had till recently triumphed over him or kept him at bay; congress had loved to employ his pen and to follow his counsel; at last he had been baffled even in his own province. He had seen the proprietary government go to its long sleep in the house of its friends; he had seen a delegate from Delaware bring before congress from the Pennsylvania conference instructions in favor of independence, which he did not mean to regard; and he had prepared himself with the utmost care to vindicate his opinions, which he would have held it guilt to suppress. It is from the report made by himself that I abridge his elaborate discourse, using no words but his own.

"I value the love of my country as I ought, but I value my country more, and I desire this illustrious assembly to witness the integrity, if not the policy, of my conduct. The first campaign will be decisive of the controversy. The declaration will not strengthen us by one man, or by the least supply, while it may expose our soldiers to additional cruelties and outrages. Without some prelusory trials of our strength, we ought not to commit our country upon an alternative, where to recede would be infamy, and to persist might be destruction.

"No instance is recollected of a people, without a battle fought or an ally gained, abrogating for ever their connection with a warlike commercial empire. It might unite the different parties in Great Britain against us, and it might create disunion among ourselves.

"With other powers it would rather injure than avail us. Foreign aid will not be obtained but by our actions in the field, which are the only evidences of our union and vigor that will be respected. In the war between the united provinces and Spain, France and England assisted the provinces before they declared themselves independent; if it is the interest of any European kingdom to aid us, we shall be aided without such a declaration; if it is not, we shall not be aided with it. Before such an irrevocable step shall be taken, we ought to know the disposition of the great powers, and how far they will permit any one or more of them to interfere. The erection of an independent empire on this continent is a phenomenon in the world; its effects will be immense, and may vibrate round the globe. How they may affect, or be supposed to affect, old estab-

lishments, is not ascertained. It is singularly disrespectful to
France to make a declaration before her sense is known, as we
have sent an agent expressly to inquire whether such a declaration would be acceptable to her, and we have reason to believe
he is now arrived at the court of Versailles. The measure ought
to be delayed, till the common interests shall in the best manner be consulted by common consent. Besides, the door to accommodation with Great Britain ought not to be shut, until we
know what terms can be obtained from some competent power.
Thus to break with her before we have compacted with another is to make experiments on the lives and liberties of my
countrymen, which I would sooner die than agree to make; at
best, it is to throw us into the hands of some other power, and
to lie at mercy, for we shall have passed the river that is never
to be repassed. We ought to retain the declaration, and remain
masters of our own fame and fate. We ought to inform that
power that we are filled with a just destination of our oppressors; that we are determined to cast off for ever all subjection
to them, to declare ourselves independent, and to support that
declaration with our lives and fortunes, provided that power
will approve the proceeding, acknowledge our independence,
and enter into a treaty with us upon equitable and advantageous conditions.

"Other objections to the declaration at this time are suggested by our internal circumstances. The formation of our
governments, and an agreement upon the terms of our confederation, ought to precede the assumption of our station
among sovereigns. A sovereignty composed of several distinct
bodies of men, not subject to established constitutions, and
not combined together by confirmed articles of union, is such
a sovereignty as has never appeared. These particulars would
not be unobserved by foreign kingdoms and states, and they
will wait for other proofs of political energy before they will
treat us with the desired attention.

"With respect to ourselves, the consideration is still more
serious. The forming of our governments is a new and difficult

work. When this is done, and the people perceive that they and their posterity are to live under well-regulated constitutions, they will be encouraged to look forward to independence, as completing the noble system of their political happiness. The objects nearest to them are now enveloped in clouds, and those more distant appear confused; the relation one citizen is to bear to another, and the connection one state is to have with another they do not, cannot, know. Mankind are naturally attached to plans of government that promise quiet and security. General satisfaction with them, when formed, would indeed be a great point attained; but persons of reflection will perhaps think it absolutely necessary that congress should institute some mode for preserving them from future discords.

"The confederation ought to be settled before the declaration of independence. Foreigners will think it most regular; the weaker states will not be in so much danger of having disadvantageous terms imposed upon them by the stronger. If the declaration is first made, political necessities may urge on the acceptance of conditions, highly disagreeable to parts of the union. The present comparative circumstances of the colonies are now tolerably well understood; but some have very extraordinary claims to territory, that, if admitted, as they might be in a future confederation, the terms of it not being yet adjusted, all idea of the present comparison between them would be confounded. Those whose boundaries are acknowledged would sink in proportion to the elevation of their neighbors. Besides, the unlocated lands, not comprehended within acknowledged boundaries, are deemed a fund sufficient to defray a vast part, if not the whole, of the expenses of the war. These ought to be considered as the property of all, acquired by the arms of all. For these reasons the boundaries of the colonies ought to be fixed before the declaration, and their respective rights mutually guaranteed; and the unlocated lands ought also, previous to that declaration, to be solemnly appropriated to the benefit of all; for it may be extremely difficult, if not impracticable, to obtain these decisions afterwards. Upon the whole, when things shall be thus deliberately rendered firm at home and favorable abroad, then let America, *Attollens humeris famam et fata nepotum,* bearing up her glory and the destiny of her descendants, advance with majestic steps and assume her station among the sovereigns of the world."

Wilson of Pennsylvania could no longer agree with his colleague. He had at an early day foreseen independence as the probable though not the intended result of the contest; he had uniformly declared in his place that he never would vote for it contrary to his instructions, nay, that he regarded it as something more than presumption to take a step of such importance without express instructions and authority. "For," said he, "ought this act to be the act of four or five individuals, or should it be the the the act of the people of Pennsylvania?" But now that their authority was communicated by the conference of committees, he stood on very different ground.

A little before the end of the debate rose Witherspoon, of New Jersey. In a short speech, he remarked that though he had not heard all the discussions in that body, yet he had not wanted ample sources of information, and that in his judgment the country was not only ripe for independence, but was in danger of becoming rotten for want of it, if its declaration were longer delayed. Others spoke; among them probably Paca of Maryland, Mackean of Delaware, and undoubtedly Edward Rutledge of South Carolina; but I have not met with any authentic record of their remarks. Richard Henry Lee and Wythe were both on that day attendants on the Virginia convention in Williamsburg. Before the vote was taken, the delegates from New York, of whom all but Alsop were personally ready to vote for independence and were confident of the adhesion of their constituents, read to the committee a letter which they had received from the provincial congress, explaining why their formal concurrence must, for a few days longer, be withheld. The resolution for independence was then sustained by nine colonies; two-thirds of the whole number; the vote of South Carolina, unanimously it would seem, was in the negative; so was that of Pennsylvania, by the vote of Dickinson, Morris, Humphreys, and Willing, against Franklin, Morton, and Wilson; owing to the absence of Rodney, Delaware was divided, each member voting under the new instruction according to his former known opinions, Mackean for independence and Read against it.

The committee rose, and Harrison reported the resolution; but at the request of Edward Rutledge, on behalf of South Carolina, the determination upon it was put off till the next day.

A letter from Washington, of the twenty-ninth of June, was then read, from which it appeared that Howe and forty-five ships or more, laden with troops, had arrived at Sandy Hook, and that the whole fleet was expected in a day or two. "I am hopeful," wrote the general, "that I shall get some re-enforcements before they are prepared to attack; be that as it may, I shall make the best disposition I can of our troops." Not all who were round him had firmness like his own; Reed, the new adjutant-general, quailed before the inequality of the British and American force, and thus on the fourth described the state of the American camp: "With an army of force before, and a secret one behind, we stand upon a point of land, with six thousand old troops, if a year's service of about half can entitle them to the name, and about fifteen hundred new levies of this province, many disaffected and more doubtful; every man, from the general to the private, acquainted with our true situation, is exceedingly discouraged; had I known the true posture of the affairs, no consideration would have tempted me to have taken an active part in this scene; and this sentiment is universal." No one knew better than the commander in chief the exceedingly discouraging aspect of military affairs; but his serene and unfaltering courage in this hour was a support to congress. His letter was referred to the board of war, which they had recently established, and of which John Adams was the president; the faculties of the members were too intensely strained by their enthusiasm to be much agitated by reports of danger. Especially John Adams, revolving the incidents of the day at its close, not disguising to his own mind the approaching conflict of which America could not ward off the calamities, not even flattering himself with halcyon days among the colonies after their separation from Great Britain, was content with what he had done; for freedom was in his eyes a counterbalance to poverty, discord, and war.

On the second of July there were present in congress probably forty-nine members. Rodney had arrived from Delaware, and, joining Mackean, secured that colony. Dickinson and Morris stayed away, which enabled Franklin, Wilson, and Morton, of Pennsylvania, to outvote Willing and Humphreys. The South Carolina members, still uncertain if Charleston had not fallen, for the sake of unanimity, came round; so, though New York was still unable to vote, twelve colonies, with no dissenting one, resolved: "That these united colonies are, and of right ought to be, free and independent states; that they are absolved from all allegiance to the British crown, and that all political connection between them and the state of Great Britain is, and ought to be, totally dissolved."

At the end of this great day, the mind of John Adams heaved like the ocean after a storm. "The greatest question," he wrote, "was decided which ever was debated in America, and a greater, perhaps, never was nor will be decided among men. When I look back to 1761, and run through the series of political events, the chain of causes and effects, I am surprised at the suddenness as well as greatness of this revolution. Britain has been filled with folly, and America with wisdom. It is the will of Heaven that the two countries should be sundered for ever; it may be the will of Heaven that America shall suffer calamities still more wasting and distresses yet more dreadful. If this is to be the case, the furnace of affliction produces refinement in states as well as individuals; but I submit all my hopes and fears to an overruling Providence, in which, unfashionable as the faith may be, I firmly believe.

"Had a declaration of independence been made seven months

ago, we might before this hour have formed alliances with foreign states; we should have mastered Quebec, and been in possession of Canada; but, on the other hand, the delay has many great advantages attending it. The hopes of reconciliation which were fondly entertained by multitudes of the honest and well-meaning, through weak and mistaken, have been gradually and at last totally extinguished. Time has been given for the whole people maturely to consider the great question of independence, so that in every colony of the thirteen they have now adopted it as their own act.

"But the day is passed. The second day of July, 1776, will be the most memorable epocha in the history of America; to be celebrated by succeeding generations as the great anniversary festival, commemorated as the day of deliverance, by solemn acts of devotion to God Almighty, from one end of the continent to the other, from this time forward for evermore.

"You will think me transported with enthusiasm, but I am not. I am well aware of the toil and blood and treasure that it will cost us to maintain this declaration, and support and defend these states; yet, through all the gloom, I can see the rays of light and glory; that the end is worth all the means; that posterity will triumph in that day's transaction, even though we should rue it, which I trust in God we shall not."

The Declaration of the United States, July 2-4, 1776

THE resolution of congress changed the old thirteen British colonies into free and independent states. It remained to set forth the reason for this act, and the principles which the new people would own as their guides. Of the committee appointed for that duty, Thomas Jefferson of Virginia had received the largest number of votes, and was in that manner singled out to draft the confession of faith of the rising empire. He owed this distinction to respect for the colony which he represented, to the consummate ability of the state papers which he had already written, and to that general favor which follows merit, modesty, and a sweet disposition; but the quality which specially fitted him for the task was the sympathetic character of his nature, by which he was able with instinctive perception to read the soul of the nation, and, having collected its best thoughts and noblest feelings, to give them out in clear and bold words, mixed with so little of himself, that his country, as it went along with him, found nothing but what it recognised as its own. No man of his century had more trust in the collective reason and conscience of his fellow-men, or better knew how to take their counsel; and in return he came to be a ruler over the willing in the world of opinion. Born to an independent fortune, he had from his youth been an indefatigable student. "The glow of one warm thought was worth more to him than money." Of a hopeful temperament and a tranquil, philosophic cast of mind, always temperate in his mode of life and decorous in his manners, he was a perfect master of his passions. He was of a delicate organization, and fond of elegance; his tastes were refined; laborious in his application to business or the pursuit of knowledge, music, the most spiritual of all pleasures of the senses, was his favorite recreation; and he took a never-failing delight in the varied beauty of rural life, building himself a home in the loveliest region of his native state. He was a skilful horseman, and with elastic step would roam the mountains on foot. The range of his studies was very wide; he was not unfamiliar with the literature of Greece and Rome; had an aptitude for mathematics and mechanics, and loved especially the natural sciences; scorning nothing but metaphysics. British governors and officials had introduced into Williamsburg the prevalent free-thinking of Englishmen of that century, and Jefferson had grown up in its atmosphere; he was not only a hater of priestcraft and superstition and bigotry and intolerance, he was thought to be indifferent to religion; yet his instincts all inclined him to trace every fact to a general law, and to put faith in ideal truth; the world of the senses did not bound his aspirations, and he believed more than he himself was aware of. He was an idealist in his habits of thought and life, as indeed is every one who has an abiding and thorough confidence in the people; and he was kept so in spite of circumstances by the irresistible bent of his character. He had great power in mastering details as well as in searching for general principles. His profession was that of the law, in which he was methodical, painstaking, and successful; at the same time, he pursued it as a science, and was well read in the law of nature and of nations. Whatever he had to do, it was his custom to prepare himself for it carefully; and in public life, when others were at fault, they often found that he had already hewed out the way; so that in council men willingly gave him the lead, which he never appeared to claim, and was always able to undertake. But he rarely spoke in public, and was less fit to engage in the war of debate than calmly to sum up its conclusions. It was a beautiful trait in his character that he was free from envy; had he kept silence, there would have been wanting to John Adams the best witness to his greatness as the ablest advocate and defender of independence. A common object now riveted the two statesmen together in close bonds. I cannot find that at that period Jefferson had an enemy; by the general consent of Virginia, he stood first among her civilians. Just thirty-three years old, married, and happy in his family, affluent, with a bright career before him, he was no rash innovator by his character or his position; if his convictions drove him to demand independence, it was only because he could no longer live with honor under the British "constitution, which he still acknowledged to be better than all that had preceded it." His enunciation of general principles was fearless; but he was no visionary devotee of abstract theories, which, like disembodied souls, escape from every embrace; the nursling of his country, the offspring of his time, he set about the work of a practical statesman, and his measures grew so naturally out of previous law and the facts of the past that they struck deep root and have endured.

From the fulness of his own mind, without consulting one single book, yet having in his memory the example of the Swiss and of the United Provinces of the Netherlands, Jefferson drafted the declaration, in which, after citing the primal principles of government, he presented the complaints of the United States against England in the three classes of the iniquitous use of the royal prerogative, the usurpation of legislative power over America by the king in parliament, and the measures for enforcing the pretended acts of legislation. He submitted the paper separately to Franklin and to John Adams, accepted from each of them one or two verbal, unimportant corrections, and on the twenty-eighth of June reported it to congress, which now on the second of July, immediately after adopting the resolution of independence, entered upon its consideration. During the remainder of that day, and the next two, the language, the statements, and the principles of the paper were closely scanned.

In the indictment against George III, Jefferson had written:

"He has waged cruel war against human nature itself, violating its most sacred rights of life and liberty in the persons of a distant people who never offended him, captivating and carrying them into slavery in another hemisphere, or to incur miserable death in their transportation thither. This piratical warfare, the opprobrium of infidel powers, is the warfare of the

Christian king of Great Britain. Determined to keep open a market where men should be bought and sold, he has prostituted his negative for suppressing every legislative attempt to prohibit or to restrain this execrable commerce. And, that this assemblage of horrors might want no fact of distinguished dye, he is now exciting those very people to rise in arms among us, and to purchase that liberty of which he has deprived them, by murdering the people on whom he also obtruded them; thus paying off former crimes committed against the liberties of one people with crimes which he urges them to commit against the lives of another."

These words expressed with precision what had happened in Virginia; she, as well as other colonies, had perseveringly attempted to repress the slave-trade; the king had perseveringly used his veto to protect it; the governor, clothed with the king's authority, had invited slaves to rise against their masters; but it could not be truly said that all the colonies had been always without blame in regard to the commerce, or that in America it had been exclusively the guilt of the king of Great Britain; and therefore the severe strictures on the use of the king's negative, so Jefferson wrote for the guidance of history, "were disapproved by some southern gentlemen, whose reflections were not yet matured to the full abhorrence of that traffic; and the offensive expressions were immediately yielded. Congress had already manifested its own sentiments by the absolute prohibition of the slave-trade; and that prohibition was then respected in every one of the thirteen states, including South Carolina and Georgia. This is the occasion when the slave-trade was first branded as a piracy. Many statesmen, among them Edmund Pendleton, president of the Virginia convention, always regretted that the passage had been stricken out; and the earnestness of the denunciation lost its author no friends.

All other changes and omissions in Jefferson's paper were either insignificant or much for the better, rendering its language more terse, more dispassionate, and more exact; and in the evening of the fourth day of July, New York still abstaining from the vote, twelve states, without one negative, agreed to the "Declaration by the Representatives of the United States of America in Congress assembled. . . .

This immortal state paper was "the genuine effusion of the soul of the country at that time," the revelation of its mind, when, in its youth, its enthusiasm, its sublime confronting of danger, it rose to the highest creative powers of which man is capable. The bill of rights which it promulgates is of rights that are older than human institutions, and spring from the eternal justice. Two political theories divided the world: one founded the commonwealth on the advantage of the state, the policy of expediency, the other on the immutable principles of morals; the new republic, as it took its place among the powers of the world, proclaimed its faith in the truth and reality and unchangeableness of freedom, virtue, and right. The heart of Jefferson in writing the declaration, and of congress in adopting it, beat for all humanity; the assertion of right was made for the entire world of mankind and all coming generations, without any exception whatever; for the proposition which admits of exceptions can never be self-evident. As it was put forth in the name of the ascendent people of that time, it was sure to make the circuit of the world, passing everywhere through the despotic countries of Europe; and the astonished nations, as they read that all men are created equal, started out of their lethargy, like those who have been exiles from childhood, when they suddenly hear the dimly remembered accents of their mother tongue.

In the next place, the declaration, avoiding specious and vague generalities, grounds itself with anxious care upon the past, and reconciles right and fact. Of universal principles, enough is repeated to prove that America chose for her own that system of politics which recognises the rule of eternal justice; and independence is vindicated by the application of that rule to the grievous instructions, laws, and acts, proceeding from the king, in the exercise of his prerogative, or in con-

currence with the lords and commons of Great Britain. The
colonies professed to drive back innovations; and not with roving zeal, to overturn all traditional inequalities; they were no
rebels against the past, of which they knew the present to be the
child; with all the glad anticipations of greatness that broke
forth from the prophetic soul of the youthful nation, they took
their point of departure from the world as it was. They did not
even declare against monarchy itself; they sought no general
overthrow of all kings, no universal system of republics; nor did
they cherish in their hearts a lurking hatred against princes.
Till within a few years or months, loyalty to the house of Hanover had been to them another name for the love of civil and religious liberty; the British constitution, the best system that
had ever been devised for the security of liberty and property
by a representative government. Neither Franklin, nor Washington, nor John Adams, nor Jefferson, nor Jay, had ever expressed a preference for a republic. The voices that rose for independence spoke also for alliances with kings. The sovereignty of George III was renounced, not because he was a
king, but because he was deemed to be "a tyrant."

The insurgents, as they took up self-government, manifested
no impatience at the recollection of having been ruled by a
royal line, no eagerness to blot out memorials of their former
state; they sent forth no Hugh Peter to recommend to the
mother country the abolition of monarchy, which no one seems
to have proposed or to have wished; in the moment of revolution in America, they did not counsel the English to undertake
a revolution. The republic was to America a godsend; it came,
though unsought, because society contained the elements of no
other organization. Here, and, in that century, here only, was
a people, which, by its education and large and long experience,
was prepared to act as the depositary and carrier of all political
power. America developed her choice from within herself; and
therefore it is that, conscious of following an inner law, she
never made herself a propagandist of her system, where the conditions of success were wanting.

Finally, the declaration was not only the announcement of the birth of a people, but the establishment of a national government; a most imperfect one, it is true, but still a government in conformity with the limited constituent powers which each colony had conferred upon its delegates in congress. The war was no longer a civil war; Britain was become to the United States a foreign country. Every former subject of the British king in the thirteen colonies now owned primary allegiance to the dynasty of the people, and became a citizen of the new republic; except in this, every thing remained as before; every man retained his rights; the colonies did not dissolve into a state of nature; nor did the new people undertake a social revolution. The management of the internal police and government was carefully reserved to the separate states, which could, each for itself, enter upon the career of domestic reforms. But the states which were henceforth independent of Britain were not independent of one another: the United States of America, presenting themselves to mankind as one people, assumed powers over war, peace, foreign alliances, and commerce.

The declaration was not signed by the members of congress on the day on which it was agreed to, but it was duly authenticated by the president and secretary, and published to the world. The nation, when it made the choice of its great anniversary, selected not the day of the resolution of independence, when it closed the past, but that of the declaration of the principles on which it opened its new career.

THE *famous crossing of the Delaware at Christmas-time, 1776, and the subsequent American victory at the Battle of Trenton provided Bancroft with an opportunity for a tense, dramatic chapter featuring Washington holding his tattered army together by sheer force of will and dedication while fainthearted subordinates drifted away and Congress temporized. The account as originally published in Volume IX in 1866 stirred up a sharp controversy, for in it Bancroft virtually accused Joseph Reed of Pennsylvania, Washington's adjutant general, of treason. William Reed of Philadelphia, the state's attorney general and ex-minister to China, sprang to his family's defense, and Bancroft was soon involved in a lively argument over his sources. At the same time the grandsons of Generals Greene, Sullivan, and Schuyler made heated response to certain other remarks made by Bancroft in the course of his descriptions of the campaigns of 1776 and 1777. The "War of the Grandsons," as Bancroft called it, ceased only with President Andrew Johnson's appointment of him as minister to Prussia in 1867 and his departure for Berlin. Somewhat anticlimactically, he discovered in 1876 that he had confused Joseph Reed with a Colonel Charles Reed who actually had deserted to the British during the Trenton-Princeton campaign, and corrected the error in the Centenary Edition.*

Trenton (December 11-26, 1776)

THE British posts on the eastern side of the Delaware drew near to Philadelphia; rumor reported ships-of-war in the bay; the wives and children of the inhabitants were escaping with their papers and property; and the contagion of panic broke out in congress. On the eleventh of December they called on the states to appoint, each for itself a day of fasting and humiliation; and, with a feverish pretension to courage, they resolved that "Washington should contradict, in general orders, the false and malicious report that they were about to disperse, or adjourn from Philadelphia, unless the last necessity should direct it." He declined publishing the vote, and wisely; for, on the twelfth, after advice from Putnam and Mifflin, they voted to adjourn to Baltimore, throwing upon the commander in chief the responsibility of directing all things relative to the operations of war. It is on record that Samuel Adams, whom Jefferson has described as "exceeded by no man in congress for depth of purpose, zeal and sagacity," mastered by enthusiasm and excitement, which grew with adversity, resisted the proposition of removal. His speech has not been preserved, but its purport may be read in his letters of the time: "I do not regret the part I have taken in a cause so just and interesting to mankind. The people of Pennsylvania and the Jerseys seem determined to give it up, but I trust that my dear New England will maintain it at the expense of every thing dear to them in this life; they know how to prize their liberties. May Heaven bless them. If this city should be surrendered, I should by no means despair." "Britain will strain every nerve to subjugate America next year; she will call wicked men and devils to her aid. Our affairs abroad wear a promising aspect; but I conjure you not to depend too much upon foreign aid. Let America exert her own strength. Let her depend on God's blessing, and he who cannot be indifferent to her righteous cause will even work miracles, if necessary, to carry her through this glorious conflict, and establish her feet upon a rock."

As a military precaution, Putnam ordered "the inhabitants of the city not to appear in the streets after ten o'clock at night." He promised in no event to burn the city which he was charged to defend to the last extremity, and would not allow any one to remain an idle spectator of the contest, "persons under conscientious scruples alone excepted." But the Quakers did not remain neutral. Indirectly disfranchised by the new form of government, they yearned for their old connection with England; at their meeting held at Philadelphia for Pennsylvania and New Jersey, they refused "in person or by other assistance to join in carrying on the war;" and with fond regret they recalled to mind "the happy constitution" under which "they and others had long enjoyed peace." The needless fight of congress, which took place amidst the jeers of tories and the maledictions of patriots, gave a stab to public credit, and fostered a general disposition to refuse continental money. At his home near the sea, John Adams was as stout of heart as ever. The conflict thus far had been less severe than he from the first had expected; though greater disappointments should be met, though France should hold back, though Philadelphia should fall, "I," said he, "do not doubt of ultimate success."

Confident that the American troops would melt away at the approaching expiration of their engagements, Howe on the thirteenth prepared to return to his winter quarters in New York, leaving Donop as acting brigadier, with two Hessian brigades, the yagers, and the forty-second Highlanders, to hold the line from Trenton to Burlington. At Princeton, he refused to see Lee, who was held as a deserter from the British army, and was taken under a close guard to Brunswick and afterwards to New York. Cornwallis left Grant in command in New Jersey, and was hastening to embark for England. By orders committed to Donop, the inhabitants who in bands or separately should fire upon any of the army were to be hanged upon the nearest tree without further process. All provisions which exceeded the wants of an ordinary family were to be seized alike from whig or tory. Life and property were at the mercy of foreign hirelings. There were examples where English soldiers forced women to suffer what was worse than death, and on one occasion pursued girls, still children in years, who had fled to the woods. The attempts to restrain the Hessians were given up, under the apology that the habit of plunder prevented desertions. A British officer reports officially: "They were led to believe, before they left Hesse-Cassel, that they were to come to America to establish their private fortunes, and hitherto they have certainly acted with that principle."

It was the opinion of Donop that Trenton should be protected on the flanks by garrisoned redoubts; but Rall, who, as a reward for his brilliant services, through the interposition of Grant obtained the separate command of that post, with fifty yagers, twenty dragoons, and the whole of his own brigade, would not heed the suggestion. Renewing his advice at parting, on the morning of the fourteenth, Donop marched out with his brigade to find quarters chiefly at Bordentown, and Blackhorse, till Burlington, which lies low should be protected from the American row-galleys by heavy cannon. On the sixteenth, it was rumored that Washington with a large force hovered on the right flank of Rall; but, in answer to Donop's reports of that day and the next, Grant wrote: "I am certain the rebels no longer have any strong corps on this side of the river; the story of Washington's crossing the Delaware at this season of the year is not to be believed." "Let them come," said Rall; "what need of intrenchments? We will at them with the bayonet." At all alarms he set troops in motion, but not from apprehension; for he laughed the mouldering army of the rebels to scorn. His delight was in martial music; and for him the hautboys at the main guard could never play too long. He was constant at parade; and, on the relief of the sentries and of the pickets, all officers and under-officers were obliged to appear at his quarters, to give an aspect of great importance to his command. Cannon, which should have been in position for defence, stood in front of his door, and every day were escorted for show through the town. He was not seen in the morning until nine, or even ten or eleven; for every night he indulged himself in late carousals. So passed his twelve days of command at Trenton; and they were the proudest and happiest of his life.

"No man was ever overwhelmed by greater difficulties, or had less means to extricate himself from them," than Washington; but the sharp tribulation which assayed his fortitude carried with it a divine and animating virtue. Hope and zeal illuminated his grief. His emotions come to us across the country like strains from that eternity which repairs all losses and rights all wrongs; in his untold sorrows, his trust in Providence kept up in his heart an undersong of wonderful sweetness. The spirit of the Most High dwells among the afflicted, rather than the prosperous; and he who has never broken his bread in tears knows not the heavenly powers. We know from Washington himself that in all this period of trials and darkness, as he wrought out his country's salvation, the light of hope which was within never went out.

On the fourteenth of December, believing that Howe was on his way to New York, he resolved "to attempt a stroke upon the forces of the enemy, who lay a good deal scattered, and to all appearance in a state of security," as soon as he could be joined by the troops under Lee.[1] Meantime, he obtained exact

[1] When any thing in the campaign went ill, there were never wanting persons to cast the blame on Washington; and there was always some pretender to the merit of what he did well. Washington, on his retreat from Princeton, formed the fixed design to turn upon the British as soon as he should be joined by Lee's division. "I shall face about and govern myself by the movements of General Lee," wrote Washington, Dec. 5, to congress (Sparks's *Washington*, iv. 202). Dec. 12, to Trumbull (Force, iii. 1186): "to turn upon the enemy and recover most of the ground they had gained." He shadowed out his purpose more definitely as soon as it was known that Howe had left Trenton. Dec. 14, to Trumbull (*Washington*, iv. 220): "a stroke upon the forces of the enemy, who lie a good deal scattered." The like to Gates, Dec. 14, in Force, iii. 1216. On the twenty-sixth, Robert Morris wrote of the attack on Trenton: "This manœuvre of the general had been determined on some days ago, but he kept it secret as the nature of the service would admit." How many days he does not specify; but, Dec. 18, Marshall, a leading and well-informed patriot in Philadelphia, enters in his accurate diary, p. 122: "Our army intend to cross at Trenton into the Jerseys." A letter of the nineteenth, in Force, iii. 1295, says: "before one week." On the same nineteenth, Greene writes of Washington's purpose "to give the enemy a stroke in a few days" (Force, iii. 1342). On the twentieth, Washington writes: "The present exigency will not admit of delay in the field." On the twenty-first, Robert Morris writes to Washington: "I have been told to-day that you are preparing to cross into the Jerseys. I hope it may be true; . . . nothing would give me greater pleasure than to hear of such occurrences as your exalted merit deserves" (Force, iii. 1331). On the same twenty-first, Robert Morris, by letter, communicated the design to the American commissioners in France, as a matter certainly resolved upon (Force, iii. 1333). The Donop journal, in reporting the information which was furnished by General Grant's spy, appears to me to have reported nothing but what happened before any letter of the twenty-second could have been considered. The elaborate letter of Reed to Washington, Dec. 22, 1776, proves that Reed was not in the secret. As adjutant-general, his place was at Washington's side, if he was eager for action. Lord Bacon says: "Letters are good, when it may serve afterwards for a man's justification to produce his own letter." In 1782 Reed wished to

accounts of New Jersey and its best military positions, from opposite Philadelphia to the hills at Morristown. Every boat was secured far up the little streams that flow to the Delaware; and his forces, increased by fifteen hundred volunteers from Philadelphia, guarded the crossing-places from the falls at Trenton to below Bristol. He made every exertion to threaten the Hessians on both flanks by militia, at Morristown on the north, and on the south at Mount Holly.

The days of waiting he employed in presenting congress with a plan for an additional number of battalions, to be raised and officered directly by the United States without the intervention of the several states; thus taking the first great step towards a real unity of government. On the twelfth he had written: "Perhaps congress have some hope and prospect of re-enforcements. I have no intelligence of the sort, and wish to be informed on the subject. Our little handful is daily decreasing by sickness and other causes; and, without considerable exertions on the part of the people, what can we reasonably look for? The subject is disagreeable; but yet it is true." On the sixteenth he continued: "I am more and more convinced of the necessity of raising more battalions for the new army than what have been voted. The enemy will leave nothing unessayed in the next campaign; and fatal experience has given its sanction to the truth, that the militia are not to be depended upon but in cases of the most pressing emergency. Let us have an army competent to every exigency." On the twentieth he grew more urgent: "I have waited with much impatience to know the determination of congress on the propositions made in October last for augmenting our corps of artillery. The time is come when it cannot be delayed without the greatest injury to the safety of these states; and therefore, under the resolution of congress bearing date the twelfth instant, by the pressing advice of all

produce this letter for his justification; and somehow or other garbled extracts from it found their way into Gordon, ii. 391, and into Wilkinson, i. 124, with a letter from Washington to Reed. Washington nowhere gives Reed credit for aid in the plan or execution of the affair at Trenton; nor does any one else who was concerned in the preparations for that action.

the general officers now here, I have ventured to order three battalions of artillery to be immediately recruited. This may appear to congress premature and unwarrantable; but the present exigency of our affairs will not admit of delay, either in the council or the field. Ten days more will put an end to the existence of this army. If, therefore, in the short interval in which we have to make these arduous preparations, every matter that in its nature is self-evident is to be referred to congress, at the distance of a hundred and thirty or forty miles, so much time must elapse as to defeat the end in view.

"It may be said that this is an application for powers too dangerous to be intrusted; I can only say, that desperate diseases require desperate remedies. I have no lust after power; I wish with as much fervency as any man upon this wide extended continent for an opportunity of turning the sword into the ploughshare; but my feelings as an officer and as a man have been such as to force me to say, that no person ever hád a greater choice of difficulties to contend with than I have. It is needless to add, that short enlistments, and a mistaken dependence upon militia, have been the origin of all our misfortunes, and of the great accumulation of our debt. The enemy are daily gathering strength from the disaffected. This strength will increase, unless means can be devised to check effectually the progress of his arms. Militia may possibly do it for a little while; but in a little while, also, the militia of those states which have been frequently called upon will not turn out at all; or, if they do, it will be with so much reluctance and sloth as to amount to the same thing. Instance New Jersey! Witness Pennsylvania! The militia come in, you cannot tell how; go, you cannot tell when; and act, you cannot tell where; consume your provisions, exhaust your stores, and leave you at last at a critical moment.

"These are the men I am to depend upon ten days hence; this is the basis on which your cause must for ever depend, till you get a standing army, sufficient of itself to oppose the enemy. This is not a time to stand upon expense. If any good officers will offer to raise men upon continental pay and establishment in this quarter, I shall encourage them to do so, and regiment them, when they have done it. If congress disapprove of this proceeding, they will please to signify it, as I mean it for the best. It may be thought I am going a good deal out of the line of my duty, to adopt these measures, or to advise thus freely. A character to lose, an estate to forfeit, the inestimable blessings of liberty at stake, and a life devoted, must be my excuse."

On the twenty-fourth he resumed his warnings: "Very few have enlisted again, not more from an aversion to the service than from the non-appointment of officers in some instances, the turning out of good and appointing of bad in others; the last of this month I shall be left with from fourteen to fifteen hundred effective men in the whole. This handful, and such militia as may choose to join me, will then compose our army. When I reflect upon these things, they fill me with concern. To guard against General Howe's designs, and the execution of them, shall employ my every exertion; but how is this to be done?

"The obstacles which have arisen to the raising of the new army from the mode of appointing officers induce me to hope that, if congress resolve on an additional number of battalions to those already voted, they will devise some other rule by which the officers, especially the field-officers, should be appointed. Many of the best have been neglected, and those of little worth and less experience put in their places or promoted over their heads."

On the same day, Greene wrote, in support of the new policy: "I am far from thinking the American cause desperate, yet I conceive it to be in a critical situation. To remedy evils, the general should have power to appoint officers to enlist at large. The present existence of the civil depends upon the military power. I am no advocate for the extension of military power; neither would I advise it at present but from the fullest conviction of its being absolutely necessary. There never was a man that might be more safely trusted, nor a time when there was a louder call." Here was the proposed beginning of a new era in the war. Hitherto, congress had raised troops by requisitions on the states; and, as their requisitions had failed, leave was now asked for Washington himself to recruit and organize two-and-twenty battalions for the general service under the authority of the union.

On the twentieth, the very day on which Franklin reached Paris, Gates and Sullivan arrived at headquarters, at Newtown. The former was followed by five hundred effective men, who were all that remained of four New England regiments; but these few were sure to be well led, for Stark of New Hampshire was their oldest officer. Sullivan brought Lee's division, with which he had crossed the Delaware at Easton.

No time was lost in preparing for the surprise of Trenton. Counting all the troops from head-quarters to Bristol, including the detachments which came with Gates and Sullivan and the militia of Pennsylvania, the army was reported at no more than six thousand two hundred men, and there were in fact not so many by twelve or fourteen hundred. "Our numbers," said Washington, "are less than I had any conception of; but necessity, dire necessity will, nay must, justify an attack." On the twenty-third, he wrote for the watchword: "Victory or death." The like devoted spirit animates the words which were penned by Jay, and which the representatives of New York on that same day addressed to its people.

The general officers, especially Stirling, Mercer, Sullivan, and, above all, Greene, rendered the greatest aid in preparing the expedition; but the men who had been with Lee were so cast down and in want of every thing that the plan could not be ripened before Christmas night. Washington approved the detention at Morristown of six hundred New England men from the northern army; and sent Maxwell, of New Jersey, to take command of them and the militia collected at the same place, with orders to distress the enemy, to harass them in their quarters, to cut off their convoys, and, if a detachment should move towards Trenton or the Delaware, to fall upon their rear and annoy them on their march. Griffin, with all the force he could concentre at Mount Holly, was to engage the attention of the Hessians under Donop. Ewing, with more than five hundred men, who lay opposite Trenton, was to cross near the town. Putnam, to whom Washington took care to send orders, was at the last moment to lead over a force from Philadelphia. The most important subsidiary movement was to be made with about two thousand troops from Bristol, and of this party Gates was requested to take the lead. "If you could only stay there two or three days, I should be glad," said Washington, using the language of entreaty. . . .

The day arrived for the concerted attack on the British posts along the Delaware; and complete success could come only from the exact co-operation of every part. With wilful disobedience Gates turned his back on danger, duty, and honor. He disapproved of Washington's station above Trenton: the British would secretly construct boats, pass the Delaware in his rear, and take Philadelphia; so that he ought to retire to the south of the Susquehannah. Eager to intrigue with congress at Baltimore, Gates, with Wilkinson, rode away from Bristol; and, as they entered Philadelphia after dark on Christmas eve, the tread of their horses resounded in all directions through the silent wilderness of streets. Griffin, flying before Donop, had already abandoned New Jersey; Putnam would not think of conducting an expedition across the river.

At nightfall, General John Cadwalader, who was left in sole command at Bristol, with honest zeal marched to Dunk's ferry; it was the time of the full moon, but the clouds were thick and dark. For about an hour that remained of the ebb-tide the river was passable in boats, and Reed, who just then arrived from a visit to Philadelphia, was able to cross on horseback; but the tide beginning to rise, threw back the ice in such heaps on the Jersey shore that, though men on foot still got over, neither horses nor artillery could reach the land. Sending word that it was impossible to carry out their share in Washington's plan, and leaving the party who had crossed the river to get back as they could, Reed found for himself covert within the enemy's lines at Burlington. Meanwhile, during one of the worst nights of December, the men waited with arms in their hands for the floating ice to open a passage; and only after vainly suffering for many hours, they returned to their camp, to shake the snow from their garments, and creep into their tents, without fire or light. Cadwalader, and the best men about him, were confident that Washington, like themselves, must have given up the expedition. Ewing did not even make an effort to cross at Trenton; and Moylan, who set off on horseback to overtake Washington and share the honors of the day, became persuaded that no attempt could be made in such a storm and stopped on the road for shelter.

Superior impulses acted upon Washington and his devoted soldiers. From his wasted troops he could muster but twenty-four hundred men strong enough to be his companions; but they were veterans and patriots, chiefly of New England, Pennsylvania, and Virginia. Among his general officers were Greene and Mercer and Stirling and Sullivan; of field-officers and others, Stark of New Hampshire, Hand of Pennsylvania, Glover and Knox of Massachusetts, Webb of Connecticut, Scott and William Washington and James Monroe of Virginia, and Alexander Hamilton of New York. At three in the afternoon they began their march, each man carrying three days' provisions and forty rounds; and with eighteen field-pieces they reached Mackonkey's ferry just as twilight began. The current was swift and strong, hurling along masses of ice. At the water's edge, Washington asked aloud: "Who will lead us on?" and the mariners of Marblehead stepped forward to man the boats. Just then a letter came from Reed, announcing that no help was to be expected from Putnam or the troops at Bristol; and Washington, at six o'clock, wrote this note to Cadwalader: "Notwithstanding the discouraging accounts I have received from Colonel Reed of what might be expected from the operations below, I am determined, as the night is favorable, to cross the river, and make the attack on Trenton in the morning. If you can do nothing real, at least create as great a diversion as possible." Hardly had these words been sent when Wilkinson joined the troops, "whose route he had easily traced by the blood on the snow from the feet of the men who wore broken shoes." He delivered a letter from General Gates. "From General Gates!" said Washington; "Where is he?" "On his way to congress," replied Wilkinson. "On his way to congress!" repeated Washington, who had only given him a reluctant consent to go as far as Philadelphia.

At that hour an American patrol of twenty or thirty men, led by Captain Anderson to reconnoitre Trenton, made a sudden attack upon the post of a Hessian subaltern, and wounded five or six men. The alarm was sounded, the Hessian brigade put under arms, and a part of Rall's regiment sent in pursuit. On their return, they reported that they could discover nothing; the attack was like those which had been made repeatedly before, and was held to be of no importance. The post was strengthened; additional patrols were sent out; but every apprehension was put to rest; and Rall, till late into the night, sat by his warm fire, in his usual revels, while Washington was crossing the Delaware.

"The night," writes Thomas Rodney "was as severe a night as ever I saw;" the frost was sharp, the current difficult to stem. the ice increasing, the wind high, and at eleven it began to snow. It was three in the morning of the twenty-sixth before the troops and cannon were all over; and another hour passed before they could be formed on the Jersey side. A violent northeast storm of wind and sleet and hail set in as they began their nine miles' march to Trenton, against an enemy in the best condition to fight. The weather was terrible for men clad as the Americans were, and the ground slipped under their feet. For a mile and a half they had to climb a steep hill, from which they descended to the road, that ran for about three miles between hills and through forests of hickory, ash, and black oak. At Birmingham the army was divided; Sullivan continued near the river, and Washington passed up into the Pennington road.

While Sullivan, who had the shortest route, halted to give time
for the others to arrive, he reported to Washington by one of
his aids, that the arms of his party were wet. "Then tell your
general," answered Washington, "to use the bayonet, and
penetrate into the town; for the town must be taken and I am
resolved to take it." The return of the aide-de-camp was
watched by the soldiers, who raised their heads to listen; and
hardly had he spoken, when those who had bayonets fixed them
without waiting for a command.

It was now broad day. The slumber of the Hessians had
been undisturbed; their patrols reported that all was quiet; and
the night-watch of yagers had turned in, leaving the sentries at
their seven advanced posts, to keep up the communication between their right and left wings. The storm beat violently in
the faces of the Americans; the men were stiff with cold and a
continuous march of fifteen miles; but now when the time for
the attack was come, they thought of nothing but victory. The
battle was begun by Washington's party with an attack on the
outermost picket on the Pennington road; the men with Stark,
who led the van of Sullivan's party, gave three heartening
cheers, and with the bayonet rushed upon the enemy's picket
near the river. A company came out of the barracks to protect
the patrol; but, surprised and astonished at the fury of the
charge, they all, including the yagers, fled in confusion, escaping across the Assanpink, followed by the dragoons and the
party which was posted near the river bank. Washington entered the town by King and Queen Streets, now named after
Warren and Greene; Sullivan moved by the river-road into
Second Street, cutting off the way to the Assanpink bridge; and
both divisions pushed forward with such equal ardor, as never
to suffer the Hessians to form completely. The two cannon
which stood in front of Rall's quarters were from the first separated from the regiment to which they belonged and were not
brought into the action. The Americans were coming into line
of battle, when Rall made his appearance, received a report,
rode up in front of his regiment, and, without presence of mind,

cried out to them: "Forward, march; advance, advance," reeling in the saddle like one not yet recovered from a night's dabauch. Before his own regiment could form in the street, a party pushed on rapidly and dismounted its two cannon, with no injury but slight wounds to Captain William Washington and James Monroe. Forest's American battery of six guns was opened upon two regiments at a distance of less than three hundred yards, under Washington's own direction. His position was near the front, a little to the right, a conspicuous mark for musketry; but he remained unhurt, though his horse was wounded under him. The moment for breaking through the Americans was lost by Rall, who drew back the Lossberg regiment and his own, but without artillery, into an orchard east of the town, as if intending to reach the road to Princeton by turning Washington's left. To check this movement Hand's regiment was thrown in his front. By a quick resolve, the passage might still have been forced; but the Hessians had been plundering ever since they landed in the country; and, loath to leave behind the wealth which they had amassed, they urged Rall to recover the town. In the attempt to do so, his force was driven by the impetuous charge of the Americans further back than before; he was himself struck by a musket-ball; and the two regiments were mixed confusedly, and almost surrounded. Riding up to Washington, Baylor could now report: "Sir, the Hessians have surrendered." Silent joy thrilled through the breast of him whose strong will had been strained for seventeen hours, and with clasped hands he raised his eyes in thankfulness to heaven. The Knyphausen regiment, which had been ordered to cover the flank, strove to reach the Assanpink bridge through the fields on the south-east of the town; but, losing time in extricating their two cannon from the morass, they found the bridge guarded on each side; and, after a vain attempt to ford the rivulet, they surrendered to Lord Stirling on condition of retaining their swords and their private baggage. The action, in which the Americans lost not one man, lasted thirty-five minutes. One hundred and sixty-two of the Hessians who at sunrise were in Trenton escaped, about fifty to Princeton, the rest to Bordentown; one hundred and thirty were absent on command; seventeen were killed. All the rest of Rall's command, nine hundred and forty-six in number, were taken prisoners, of whom seventy-eight were wounded. The Americans gained twelve hundred small-arms, six brass field-pieces, of which two were twelve-pounders, and all the standards of the brigade.

Until that hour, the life of the United States flickered like a dying flame. "But the Lord of hosts heard the cries of the distressed, and sent an angel for their deliverance," wrote the *præses* of the Pennsylvania Lutherans. "All our hopes," said Lord George Germain, "were blasted by the unhappy affair at Trenton." That victory turned the shadow of death into the morning.

Since *the theme of his study of the colonial period was the inexorable march of the American colonies toward freedom and union, Bancroft was well aware that although the Declaration of Independence accomplished one of those aims, it also introduced a number of complications affecting the achievement of the other. At the close of his chapters on the Declaration he referred briefly to the "imperfections" of the now "confederated" government, leaving the topic for an extended consideration in that portion of the* History *to deal with the constitutional period. Many of the internal political issues raised by the act of independence, Bancroft noted, were confronted within the states, whose constitutions were the first practical embodiments of American revolutionary theory. He was among the earliest American historians to show how these constitutions grew out of colonial experience, the immediate political needs of independence, and the general principles of the Declaration itself. As he explains in this chapter, the gains of the Revolution were first consolidated in the states, whose frames of government, though differing among themselves in particulars, later provided a stable base for federal union in their unanimous acceptance of the Declaration and its implications.*

The Constitutions of the Several States of America (1776-83)

Had the decision of the war hung on armies alone, America might not have gained the victory; but the contest involved the introduction into political life of ideas which had long been hovering in the atmosphere of humanity, and which the civilized world assisted to call into action. The spirit of the age moved the young nation to own justice as older and higher than the state, and to found the rights of the citizen on the rights of man. And yet, in regenerating its institutions, it was not guided by any speculative theory or metaphysical distinctions.

Vol. V, Chap. XV.

Its form of government grew naturally out of its traditions by the simple rejection of all personal hereditary authority, which in America had never had much more than a representative existence. Its people were industrious and frugal; accustomed to the cry of liberty and property, they harbored no dream of a community of goods; and their love of equality never degenerated into envy of the rich. No successors of the fifth-monarchy men proposed to substitute an unwritten higher law, interpreted by individual conscience, for the law of the land and the decrees of human tribunals. The people proceeded with self-possession and moderation, after the manner of their ancestors. Their large inheritance of English liberties saved them from the necessity and from the wish to uproot their old political institutions; and, as happily the scaffold was not wet with the blood of their statesmen, there arose no desperate hatred of England, such as the Netherlands kept up for centuries against Spain. The wrongs inflicted or attempted by the British king were felt to have been avenged by independence; respect and affection remained behind for the parent land, from which the United States had derived trial by jury, the writ for personal liberty, the practice of representative government, and the separation of the three great co-ordinated powers in the state. From an essentially aristocratic model America took just what suited her condition, and rejected the rest. Thus the transition of the colonies into self-existent commonwealths was free from vindictive bitterness, and attended by no violent or wide departure from the past.

In all the states it was held that sovereignty resides in the people; that the majesty of supreme command belongs of right to its collective intelligence; that government is to be originated by its impulse, organized by its consent, and conducted by its imbodied will; that it alone possesses the living energy out of which all powers flow forth, and to which they all return; that it is the sole legitimate master to name, directly or indirectly, every one of the officers of the state, and bind them as its servants to toil only for its good.

The American people went to their great work of building up the home of humanity without misgiving. They were confident that the judgment of the sum of the individual members of the community was the safest criterion of truth in public affairs. They harbored no fear that the voice even of a wayward majority would be more capricious or more fallible that the good pleasure of an hereditary monarch; and, unappalled by the skepticism of European kings, they proceeded to extend self-government over regions which, in all previous ages, had been esteemed too vast for republican rule. They were conscious of long and varied experience in representative forms; and of all the nations on earth they were foremost in the principles and exercise of popular power. The giant forms of monarchies on their way to ruin cast over the world their fearful shadows; it was time to construct states in the light of truth and freedom, on the basis of inherent, inalienable right.

England was "a land of liberty;" this is her glory among the nations. It is because she nurtured her colonies in freedom, that, even in the midst of civil war, they cherished her name with affection; it is because her example proved that the imperishable principles of mental and civil freedom can form the life of government that she has endeared herself for ever to the human race.

Of the American statesmen who assisted to frame the new government, not one had been originally a republican. They had been as it were seized by the godlike spirit of freedom, and compelled to advance its banner. But, if the necessity of constructing purely popular institutions came upon them unexpectedly, the ages had prepared for them their plans and the materials with which they were to build.

The recommendations to form governments proceeded from the general congress; the work was done by the several states, in the full enjoyment of self-direction. South Carolina and Massachusetts each claimed to be of right a free, sovereign, and independent state; each bound its officers by oath to bear to it true allegiance, and to maintain its freedom and independence.

Massachusetts, which was the first state to conduct a government independent of the king, following the resolution of congress, deviated as little as possible from the letter of its charter; and, assuming that the place of the governor was vacant from the nineteenth of July, 1775, it recognised the council as the legal successor to executive power. On the first day of May, 1776, in all commissions and legal processes, it substituted the name of its "government and people" for that of the king. In June, 1777, its legislature thought itself warranted by instructions to prepare a constitution; but, on a reference to the people, the act was disavowed. In September, 1779, a convention which the people had authorized framed a constitution. It was in a good measure the compilation of John Adams, who was guided by the English constitution, by the bill of rights of Virginia, and by the experience of Massachusetts herself; and this constitution, having been approved by the people, went into effect in 1780.

On the fifth of January, 1776, New Hampshire formed a government with the fewest possible changes from its colonial forms like Massachusetts merging the executive power in the council. Not till June, 1783, did its convention form a more perfect instrument, which was approved by the people, and established on the thirty-first of the following October.

The provisional constitution of South Carolina dates from the twenty-sixth of March, 1776. In March, 1778, a permanent constitution was introduced by a simple act of the legislature, without any consultation of the people.

Rhode Island enjoyed under its charter a form of government so thoroughly republican that independence of monarchy in May, 1776, required no change beyond a renunciation of the king's name in the style of its public acts. A disfranchisement of Catholics had stolen into the book of laws; but, so soon as it was noticed, the clause was expunged.

In a like manner, Connecticut had only to substitute the people of the colony for the name of the king; this was done provisionally on the fourteenth of June, 1776, and made perpetual on the tenth of the following October. In this state and in Rhode Island the assembly was chosen annually.

Before the end of June of the same year, Virginia, sixth in in the series, first in the completeness of her work came forth with her bill or rights, her declaration of independence, and her constitution, adopted at once by her legislative convention without any further consultation of the people.

On the second of July, 1776, New Jersey perfected its new, self-created charter.

Delaware next proclaimed its bill of rights, and on the twentieth of September, 1776, finished its constitution, the representatives in convention having been chosen by the freemen of the state for that very purpose.

The Pennsylvania convention adopted its constitution on the twenty-eighth of September, 1776; but the opposition which it received, alike from the Quakers, whom it indirectly disfranchised, and from a large body of patriots, delayed its thorough organization for more than five months.

The delegates of Maryland, meeting on the fourteenth of August, 1776, framed its constitution with great deliberation; and it was established on the ninth of the following November.

On the eighteenth of December 1776, the constitution of North Carolina was openly ratified in the congress by which it had been framed.

On the fifth of February, 1777, Georgia, the twelfth state, perfected its organic law by the unanimous agreement of its convention.

Last of the thirteenth came New York, whose empowered convention, on the twentieth of April, 1777, established a constitution that, in the largeness of its humane liberality, excelled them all.

In elective governments which sprung from the recognition of the freedom of the individual, every man might consistently claim the right of contributing by his own reason his proportionate share of influence in forming the collective reason which was to rule the state. Such was the theory; in practice, no jealous inquiry was raised respecting those who should actually participate in this sovereignty. The privilege of the suffrage had been far more widely extended in the colonies than in England; in most of the thirteen states, no discontent broke out at existing restrictions, and no disposition was manifested to depart from them abruptly by an immediate equalization of the primary political functions. The principle of the revolution involved an indefinite enlargement of the number of the electors, which could have no other term than universal suffrage; but, by general consent the consideration of the subject was postponed. The age of twenty-one was universally required as a qualification. So, too, was residence, except that in Virginia and South Carolina it was enough to own in the district or town a certain freehold or "lot." South Carolina required of the electors to "acknowledge the being of a God, and to believe in a future state of rewards and punishments." White men alone could claim the franchise in Virginia, in South Carolina, and in Georgia; but in South Carolina a benign interpretation of the law classed the free octaroon as a white, even though descended through an unbroken line of mothers from an imported African slave; the other ten states raised no question of color. In Pennsylvania, in New Hampshire, and partially in North Carolina, the right to vote belonged to every resident tax-payer; in Georgia to any white inhabitant "being of any mechanic trade;" with this exception, Georgia and all the other colonies required the possession of a freehold, or of property variously valued, in Massachusetts at about two hundred dollars, in Georgia at ten pounds. Similar conditions had always existed, with the concurrence or by the act of the colonists themselves.

Maryland prescribed as its rule that votes should be given by word of mouth; Virginia and New Jersey made no change in their former usage; Rhode Island had a way of its own, analogous to its charter: each freeman was in theory expected to be present in the general court; he therefore gave his proxy to the representative by writing his name on the back of his vote; all others adopted the ballot, New York at the end of the war, the other eight without delay.

The first great want common to all was a house of representatives, so near the people as to be the image of their thoughts and wishes, so numerous as to appear to every individual voter as his direct counterpart, so frequently renewed as to insure swift responsibility. Such a body every one of the British colonies had enjoyed. They now gained certainty as to the times of meeting of the assemblies, an unalterable precision in the periods of election, and in some states a juster distribution of representation. In theory, the houses of legislation should everywhere have been in proportion to population; and for this end a census was to be taken at fixed times in Pennsylvania and New York; but in most of the states old inequalities were continued, and even new ones introduced. In New England, the several towns had from the first enjoyed the privilege of representation, and from a love of equality this custom was retained; in Virginia, the counties and boroughs in the low country, where the aristocracy founded in land and slaves had its seat, secured an undue share of the members of the assembly; the planters of Maryland, jealous of the growing weight of Baltimore, set an arbitrary and most unequal limit to the representation of that city; in South Carolina, for seven years Charleston was allowed to send thirty members, and the parishes near the sea took almost a monopoly of political power; after that period, representatives were to be proportioned according to the number of white inhabitants and to the taxable property in the several districts. In South Carolina the assembly was chosen for two years, everywhere else for but one. To the assembly was reserved the power of originating taxes. In Georgia, the delegates to the continental congress had a right to sit, debate, and vote in its house of assembly, of which they were deemed to be a part.

Franklin would have one legislative body, and no more; he approved the decision of the framers of the constitution of Pennsylvania to repose all legislative powers in an uncontrolled assembly. This precedent was followed in Georgia. From all the experience of former republics, John Adams argued for a legislature with two branches. But the Americans of that day neither

listened to the theories of Franklin, nor to the lessons from
history of John Adams; finding themselves accustomed almost
from the beginning to a double legislative body, eleven of the
thirteen states adhered to the ancient usage. In constructing
the co-ordinate branch of the legislature, they sought to impart
greater weight to their system and to secure its conservation.
This branch, whether called a senate, or legislative council, or
board of assistants, was less numerous than the house of representatives. In the permanent constitutions of Massachusetts
and New Hampshire, the proportion of public taxes paid by a
district was regarded in the assignment of its senatorial number; in New York and North Carolina, the senate was elected
by a narrower constituency than the assembly. In six of the
eleven states the senate was chosen annually; but the period of
service in South Carolina embraced two years, in Delaware
three, in New York and Virginia four, in Maryland five. To increase the dignity and fixedness of the body, Virginia, New
York and Delaware gave it permanence by renewing, the first
two one fourth, Delaware one third, of its members annually.
Maryland, which of all the states showed the strongest desire
to preserve political importance to the large proprietors of
land, prescribed a double election for its senate. Once in five
years the several counties, the city of Annapolis, and Baltimore towns, chose *viva voce*, their respective delegates to an
electoral body, each member of which was "to have in the state
real or personal property above the value of five hundred pounds
current money." These electors were to elect by ballot "six out
of the gentlemen residents of the eastern shore," and "nine out
of the gentlemen residents of the western shore," of the Chesapeake Bay; the fifteen "gentlemen" thus chosen constituted
the quinquennial senate of Maryland, and themselves filled up
any vacancy that might occur in their number during their term
of five years. This is the strongest measure which was devised
to curb or balance popular power, and marks the reluctance
with which its authors parted from their institutions under the
crown of England.

Each state had its governor or president, as in the days of monarchy; but the source of his appointment was changed, and his powers abridged. In the four New England states he was chosen directly by all the primary electors, which is the safest way in a republic; in New York by the freeholders who possessed freeholds of the value of two hundred and fifty dollars; in Georgia, by the representatives of the people; in Pennsylvania, by the joint vote of the council and assembly, who were confined in their selection to the members of the council; in the other six states, by the joint ballot of the two branches of the legislature.

Except in Pennsylvania, a small property qualification was usually required of a representative; more, of a senator; most, of a governor. New York required only that its governor should be a freeholder; Massachusetts, that his freehold should be of the value of about thirty-three hundred dollars; New Hampshire required but half as much; South Carolina, that his plantation or freehold, counting the slaves "settled" upon it, should be of the value of forty-two thousand eight hundred dollars in currency.

In New York and Delaware, the governor was chosen for three years; in South Carolina, for two; in all the rest, for only one. South of New Jersey, the capacity of re-election was jealously restricted; in those states which were most republican there was no such restriction; in Massachusetts, Connecticut, and Rhode Island, a governor was often re-elected for a long succession of years.

In the declaration of independence, the king was complained of for having refused his assent to wholesome laws: the jealousy fostered by long conflicts with the crown led to the general refusal of a negative power to the governor. The thoughtful men who devised the constitution of New York established the principle of a conditional veto; a law might be negatived, and the veto was final, unless it should be passed again by a majority of two thirds of each of the two branches; but they unwisely confided the negative power to a council, of which the governor formed but one; Massachusetts in 1779 improved upon the precedent, and placed the conditional veto in the hands of the governor alone. In her provisional form, South Carolina clothed her executive chief with a veto power; but in the constitution of 1778 it was abrogated. In all the other colonies, the governor either had no share in making the laws, or had only a casting vote, or at most a double vote in the least numerous of the two branches.

Nowhere had the governor power to dissolve the legislature, or either branch of it, and so appeal directly to the people; and, on the other hand, the governor, once elected could not be removed during his term of office except by impeachment.

In most of the states, all important civil and military officers were elected by the legislature. The power intrusted to a governor, wherever it was more than a shadow, was still further restrained by an executive council, formed partly after the model of the British privy council, and partly after colonial precedents. In the few states in which the governor had the nomination of officers, particularly in Massachusetts and New Hampshire, they could be commissioned only with the consent of council. In New York, the appointing power, when the constitution did not direct otherwise, was confided to the governor and a council of four senators, elected by the assembly from the four great districts of the state; and in this body the governor had "a casting vote, but no other vote." This worst arrangement of all, so sure to promote faction and intrigue, was the fruit of the deliberate judgment of wise and disinterested patriots, in their zeal for administrative purity. Whatever sprung readily from the condition and intelligence of the people had enduring life; while artificial arrangements, like this of the council of appointment in New York, and like the senate of Maryland, though devised by earnest statesmen of careful education and great endowments, pined from their birth, and soon died away.

The third great branch of government was in theory kept distinct from the other two. In Connecticut and Rhode Island, some judicial powers were exercised by the governor and assistants; the other courts were constituted by the two branches of the legislature. In Massachusetts and New Hampshire, the governor, with the consent of council, selected the judges; in New York, the council of appointment; but for the most part they were chosen by the legislature. In South Carolina, Massachusetts, and New Hampshire, a judge might be removed, as in England, upon the address of both houses of the legislature, and this proved the wisest practical rule; in New York, he must at the age of sixty; in New Jersey and Pennsylvania, the supreme court was chosen for seven years, in Connecticut and Rhode Island, for but one; in Delaware, Maryland, Virginia, and North Carolina, the tenure of the judicial office was good behavior; in Maryland, even a conviction in a court of law was required before removal. Powers of chancery belonged to the legislature in Connecticut and Rhode Island; in South Carolina, to the lieutenant-governor and the privy council; in New Jersey, the governor and council were the court of appeals in the last resort. The courts were open to all, without regard to creed or race.

The constitution of Massachusetts required a system of universal public education as a vital element in the state. The measure was a bequest from their fathers, endeared by a long experience of its benefits, and supported by the reflective judgment of the people. As yet, the system was established nowhere else except in Connecticut. Pennsylvania aimed at no more than "to instruct youth at low prices." The difference between the two systems was infinite. The first provided instruction at the cost of the state for every child within its borders, and bound up its schools in its public life; while the other only proposed to dole out a bounty to the poor.

How to secure discreet nominations of candidates for high office was cared for only in Connecticut. There, twenty men were first selected by the vote of the people; and, out of these twenty, the people at a second election set apart twelve to be the governor and assistants. This method was warmly recommended by Jay to the constituent convention of New York.

Thus far the American constitutions bore a close analogy to

that of England. The English system was an aristocracy, partly hereditary, partly open, partly elective, with a permanent executive head; the American system was in idea an elective government of the best. Some of the constitutions required the choice of persons "best qualified," or "persons of wisdom, experience, and virtue." These clauses were advisory; the suffrage was free, and it was certain from the first that water will not rise higher than its fountain, that untrammelled elections will give a representation of the people no better than they are; that the adoption of republican institutions, though it creates and quickens the love of country, does not change the nature of man, or quell the fierceness of selfish passion. Timid statesmen were anxious to introduce some palpable element of permanence by the manner of constructing a council or a senate; but there was no permanence except of the people. The people, with all its greatness and all its imperfections, was immortal, or at least had perpetual succession; its waves of thought, following eternal laws, were never still, flowing now with gentle vibrations, now a sweeping flood; and upon that mighty water the fortunes of the state were cast.

That nothing might be wanting to the seeming hazard of the experiment, or to the certainty of its success, full force was given to one principle which was the supreme object of universal desire. That which lay nearest the heart of the American people, that which they above all demanded, from love for freedom of inquiry, and from the earnestness of their convictions, was not the abolition of hereditary monarchy and hereditary aristocracy, not universal suffrage, not the immediate emancipation of slaves; for more than two centuries the humbler Protestant sects had set up the cry to heaven for freedom to worship God. To the panting for this freedom half the American states owed their existence, and all but one or two their increase in free population. The immense majority of the inhabitants of the thirteen colonies were Protestant dissenters; and from end to end of their continent, from the rivers of Maine and the hills of New Hampshire to the mountain val-

leys of Tennessee and the borders of Georgia, one voice called
to the other, that there should be no connection of the church
with the state, that there should be no establishment of any one
form of religion by the civil power, that "all men have a natural and unalienable right to worship God according to the
dictates of their own consciences and understandings." With
this great idea the colonies had travailed for a century and a
half; and now, not as revolutionary, not as destructive, but
simply as giving utterance to the thought of the nation, the
states stood up in succession, in the presence of one another,
and before God and the world, to bear their witness in favor
of restoring independence to conscience and the mind. Henceforward, worship was known to the law only as a purely individual act, a question removed from civil jurisdiction, and reserved for the conscience of every man.

In this first grand promulgation by states of the "creation
right" of mental freedom, some shreds of the old system clung
round the new; but the victory was gained for the collective
American people. The declaration of independence rested on
"the laws of nature and of nature's God;" in the separate American constitutions, New York, the happy daughter of the ancient
Netherlands, true to her lineage, did, "in the name of" her
"good people, ordain, determine, and declare the free exercise
of religious profession and worship, without discrimination or
preference, to all mankind;" for the men of this new commonwealth felt themselves "required, by the benevolent principles
of national liberty, not only to expel civil tyranny, but also to
guard against that spiritual oppression and intolerance where-
with the bigotry and ambition of weak and wicked princes have
scourged mankind." Independent New York with even justice
secured to the Catholic equal liberty of worship and equal civil
franchises, and almost alone had no religious test for office. Her
liberality was wide as the world and as the human race. Henceforth, no man on her soil was to suffer political disfranchisement
for creed or lineage or color; the conscious memory of her people confirms, what honest history must ever declare, that at the

moment of her assertion of liberty she placed no constitutional disqualification on the free black. Even the emancipated slave gained instantly with his freedom equality before the constitution and the law. New York placed restrictions on the suffrage and on eligibility to office; but those restrictions applied alike to all. The alien before naturalization was required to renounce allegiance to foreign powers, alike ecclesiastical or civil.

The establishment of freedom of conscience, which brought with it absolute freedom of mind, of inquiry, of speech, and of the press, was, in the several states, the fruit not of philosophy, but of Protestant sects and the natural love of freedom. Had the Americans been skeptics, had they wanted faith, they could have founded nothing. Let not the philosopher hear with scorn that their constitutions were so completely the offspring of the past, and not the phantasms of theories, that at least seven of them required some sort of religious test as a qualification for office. In Maryland and Massachusetts, it was enough to declare "belief in the Christian religion;" in South Carolina and Georgia, in "the Protestant religion;" in North Carolina, "in God, the Protestant religion, and the divine authority of the Old and of the New Testament;" in Pennsylvania, the test was "a belief in God, the creator and governor of the universe, the rewarder of the good and punisher of the wicked," with a further acknowledging "the scriptures of the Old and New Testament to be given by divine inspiration." Beside this last acknowledgment, Delaware required the officer to "profess faith in God the Father, Jesus Christ his only Son, and the Holy Ghost, one God, blessed for evermore."

These restrictions were but incidental reminiscences of ancient usages and dearly cherished creeds, not vital elements of the constitutions; and they were opposed to the bent of the American mind. In the states where they were established, they created discussions, chiefly on the full enfranchisement of the Catholic and of the Jew; and they were eliminated, almost as soon as their inconvenience arrested attention. At first, the Jew was eligible to office only in Rhode Island, New York, New Jersey, and Virginia; the Catholic, in those states, and in

Massachusetts, Pennsylvania, Delaware, Maryland, and perhaps in Connecticut. But from the beginning the church no longer formed a part of the state; and religion, ceasing to be a servant of the government or an instrument of dominion, asserted its independence, and became a life in the soul. Public worship was voluntarily sustained. The church, no longer subordinate to a temporal power, regained its unity by having no visible head, and becoming the affair of the conscience of each individual. Nowhere was persecution for religious opinion so nearly at an end as in America, and nowhere was there so religious a people. In this universal freedom of conscience and of worship, and of the use of reason publicly in all things, America, composed as it was of emigrants from many countries, found its nationality.

There were not wanting those who cast a lingering look on the care of the state for public worship. The conservative convention of Maryland declared that "the legislature may in their discretion lay a general and equal tax for the support of the Christian religion, leaving to each individual the appointing the money collected from him to the support of any particular place of public worship or minister;" but the power granted was never exercised. For a time Massachusetts required of towns or religious societies "the support of public Protestant teachers of piety, religion, and morality," of their own election; but as each man chose his own religious society, the requisition had no effect in large towns. In Connecticut, the Puritan worship was still closely interwoven with the state, and had moulded the manners, habits, and faith of the people; but the complete disentanglement was gradually brought about by inevitable processes of legislation.

Where particular churches had received gifts or inheritances, their right to them was respected. In Maryland and South Carolina, the churches, lands, and property that had belonged to the church of England, were secured to that church in its new form; in Virginia, where the church of England had been established as a public institution, the disposition of its glebes was assumed by the legislature; and, as all denominations had contributed to their acquisition, they came to be considered as the property of the state. Tithes were nowhere continued; and the rule prevailed that "no man could be compelled to maintain any ministry contrary to his own free will and consent." South Carolina, in her legislation on religion, attempted to separate herself from the system of the other states; she alone appointed a test for the voter, and made this declaration; "The Christian Protestant religion is hereby constituted and declared to be the established religion of this state." But the condition of society was stronger than the constitution, and this declaration proved but the shadow of a system that was vanishing away. In 1778, the administering of the test oath and the partaking of the communion according to the forms of the Episcopal Church ceased to be required as conditions for holding office.

The separation of the church and the state by the establishment of religious equality was followed by the wonderful result, that it was approved of everywhere, always, and by all. The old Anglican church, which became known as the Protestant Episcopal, wished to preserve its endowments, and might complain of their impairment; but it preferred ever after to take care of itself, and was glad to share in that equality which dispelled the dread of episcopal tyranny, and left it free to perfect its organization according to its own desires. The Roman Catholic eagerly accepted in America his place as an equal with Protestants, and found contentment and hope in his new relations. The rigid Presbyterians in America supported religious freedom; true to the spirit of the great English dissenter who hated all laws

> To stretch the conscience, and to bind
> The native freedom of the mind.

In Virginia, where alone there was an arduous struggle in the legislature, the presbytery of Hanover demanded the disestablishment of the Anglican church and the civil equality of every denomination; it was supported by the voices of Baptists and Quakers and all the sects that had sprung from the people; and, after a contest of eight weeks, the measure was carried, by the activity of Jefferson, in an assembly of which the majority were Protestant Episcopalians. Nor was this demand by Presbyterians for equality confined to Virginia, where they were in a minority; it was from Witherspoon of New Jersey that Madison imbibed the lesson of perfect freedom in matters of conscience. When the constitution of that state was framed by a convention composed chiefly of Presbyterians, they established perfect liberty of conscience, without the blemish of a test. Free-thinkers might have been content with toleration, but religious conviction would accept nothing less than equality. The more profound was faith, the more it scorned to admit a connection with the state; for, such a connection being inherently vicious, the state might more readily form an alliance with error than with truth, with despotism over mind than with freedom. The determination to leave truth to her own strength, and religious worship to the conscience and voluntary act of the worshipper, was the natural out-flow of religious feeling.

The constitution of Georgia declared that "estates shall not be entailed, and, when a person dies intestate, his or her estate shall be divided equally among the children." The same principle prevailed essentially in other states, in conformity to their laws and their manners. But, in Virginia, a system of entails, enforced with a rigor unknown in the old country, had tended to make the possession of great estates, especially to the east of the Blue Ridge, the privilege of the first-born. In England, the courts of law permitted entails to be docked by fine and recovery; in 1705 Virginia prohibited all such innovations, and the tenure could be changed by nothing less than a special statute. In 1727 it was further enacted, that slaves might be attached to the soil, and be entailed with it. These measures riveted an hereditary aristocracy, founded not on learning or talent or moral worth or public service, but on the possession of land and slaves. It was to perfect the republican institutions of Virginia by breaking down this aristocracy, that Jefferson was summoned from the national congress to a seat in the assembly of his native state. On the twelfth of October, 1776, he obtained leave to bring in a bill for the abolishment of entails; and against the opposition of Edmund Pendleton, who was no friend to innovations, all donees in tail, by the act of this first republican legislature of Virginia, were vested with the absolute dominion of the property entailed.

To complete the reform, it was necessary to change the rules of descent, so that the lands of an intestate might be divided equally among his representatives; and this was effected through a committee, of which Jefferson, Pendleton, and Wythe were the active members, and which was charged with the revision of the common law, the British statutes still valid in the state, and the criminal statutes of Virginia. The new law of descent was the work of Jefferson; and the candid historian of Virginia approves the graceful symmetry of the act which abolished primogeniture, and directed property into "the channels which the head and heart of every sane man would be prone to choose."

In the low country of Virginia, and of the states next south of it, the majority of the inhabitants were bondmen of another race, except where modified by mixture. The course of legislation on their condition will be narrated elsewhere.

Provision was made for reforming the constitutions which were now established. The greatest obstacles were thrown in the way of change in Pennsylvania, where the attempt could be made only once in seven years by the election of a council of censors; the fewest in South Carolina, where the majority of a legislature which was no adequate representative of the people expressly assumed to itself and its successors original, independent, and final constituent power.

The British parliament, in its bill of rights, had only summed up the liberties that Englishmen in the lapse of centuries had acquired, or had wrested from their kings; the Americans opened their career of independence by a declaration of the self-evident rights of man; and this, begun by Virginia, was repeated, with variations, in every constitution formed after independence, except that of South Carolina. In that state, the amended constitution breathed not one word for universal freedom, made no assertion of human rights, and no longer affirmed that the people is the source of power. Pennsylvania, Massachusetts, and New Hampshire proclaimed that all men are born free; Georgia recognised rights derived to Americans from "the laws of nature and reason;" at the bar of humanity and the bar of the people, South Carolina alone remained silent.

Here, then, we have the prevailing idea of political life in the United States. On the one hand, they continued the institutions received from England with as little immediate change as possible; and, on the other, they desired for their constitutions a healthy, continuous growth. They accepted the actual state of society as the natural one resulting from the antecedents of the nation; at the same time, they recognised the right of man to make unceasing advances towards realizing political justice, and the public conscience yearned for a nearer approach to ideal perfection. Civil power remained, under slight modifications, with those who had held it before; but, for their inviolable rule in its exercise, they were enjoined to take the general principles derived from the nature of man and the eternal reason. No one thought it possible to introduce by a decree the reign of absolute right. To have attempted to strike down all evil at one blow would have been to attempt to strike down human society itself; for, from the nature of man, imperfection clings to all the works of his hands. The American statesmen were not misled by this attractive but delusive hope, even while they held that their codes of law and their constitutions should reflect ever more and more clearly the equality and brotherhood of man.

America neither separated abruptly from the past, nor adhered to its decaying forms. The principles that gave life to the new institutions pervaded history like a prophecy. They did not compel a sudden change of social or of internal political relations; but they were as a light shining more and more into the darkness. In a country which enjoyed freedom of conscience, of inquiry, of speech, of the press, and of government, the universal institution of truth promised a never-ending career of reform and progress.

IN BANCROFT'S *view, the history of the United States was so much a part of the history of the world that it must constantly be considered within a universal context. What happened in America, beginning with Columbus' first landfall, was of such importance to the rest of humanity that it must always be related to the history of the world at large. Frequently, therefore, Bancroft paused in his narrative to survey the state of the world at decisive points in American history and to analyze the impact of American events on Europe's political and social progress. So far as the Revolution was concerned, he was convinced that the diplomatic aspects of the conflict were equally as important as the military, particularly in regard to the Americans' exploitation of the French alliance, whose role in the success of the war he was among the first to emphasize.*

Bancroft's political and academic connections in Europe provided him with unprecedented opportunities for access to its historical resources. The State Department, through its embassies, assisted him in locating and copying materials; he hired professional copyists in major European libraries and collections out of his own pocket; and he spent large sums for books and documents abroad for his library, which became one of the finest historical collections in the country. When he came to write Volume IX in 1866, he could say with quiet pride and considerable accuracy, "With regard to the diplomatic relations of the several European powers interested in our struggle, my collections leave nothing to be desired." Without leaving his own study, he wrote in his preface, he could state with certainty "the relations of the English and French and Spanish ministers and kings towards our revolution, as well as the other powers, especially the German powers, Holland, and Russia, even to the shades of difference in opinion and the varying counsels and policy of the sovereigns and their cabinets," referring in each case to original documents.

The United States and France (1778)

THE twentieth of March was the day appointed for the presentation of the American commissioners to the king of France in the palace built by Louis XIV at Versailles. The world thought only of Franklin; but he was accompanied by his two colleagues and by the unreceived ministers to Prussia and Tuscany. These four glittered in lace and powder; the patriarch was dressed in the plain gala coat of Manchester velvet which he had used at the levee of George III,—the same which, according to the custom of that age, he had worn, as it proved for the last time in England, when as agent of Massachusetts he had appeared before the privy council,— with white stockings, as was the use in England, spectacles on his nose, a round white hat under his arm, and his thin gray hair in its natural state. The crowd through which they passed received them with long-continued applause. The king, without any unusual courtesy, said to them: "I wish congress to be assured of my friendship." After the ceremony, they paid a visit to the young wife of Lafayette, and dined with the secretary for foreign affairs. Two days later, they were introduced to the still youthful Marie Antoinette, who yielded willingly to generous impulses in behalf of republicans, and by her sympathy made the cause of America a fashion at the French court. The king felt all the while as if he were wronging the cause of monarchy by his acknowledgment of rebels, and engaging in the American revolution against his own will, in obedience to the advice of Maurepas and the opinion of some members of his cabinet on his duty to France. Personally he was irritated, and did not disguise his vexation. The praises lavished on Franklin by those around the queen fretted him to peevishness, and he mocked what seemed to him the pretentious enthusiasm of the Countess Diana de Polignac by the coarsest jest.

The pique of the king was not due to any defect in Franklin. He was a man of the soundest understanding, never disturbed by recollections or fears, with none of the capricious anxieties of diseased minds or the susceptibilities of disturbed self-love. Free from the illusions of poetic natures he loved truth for its own sake, and looked upon things just as they were. As a consequence, he had no eloquence but that of clearness. He computed that the inheritor of a noble title in the ninth generation represents at most but the five hundred and twelfth part of the ancestor; nor was he awed by a crosier or dazzled by a crown. He knew the moral world to be subjected to laws like the natural world; in conducting affairs, he remembered the necessary relation of cause to effect, aiming only at what was possible; and with a tranquil mind he signed the treaty with France; just as with calm observation he had contemplated the dangers of his country. In regard to money he was frugal, that he might be independent, and that he might be generous. He owed good health to his exemplary temperance. Habitually gay, employment was his resource against weariness and sorrow, and contentment came from his superiority to ambition, interest, or vanity. There was about him more of moral greatness than appeared on the surface; and, while he made no boast of unselfish benevolence, there never lived a man who would have more surely met martyrdom in the course of duty.

The official conduct of Franklin and his intercourse with persons of highest rank were marked by the most delicate propriety as well as by perfect self-respect. His charm was simplicity, which gave grace to his style and ease to his manners. No life-long courtier could have been more free from vulgarity; no diplomat more true to his position as minister of a republic; no laborer more consistent with his former life as a workingman; and thus he won respect and love from all. When a celebrated cause was to be heard before the parliament of Paris, the throng which filled the house and its approaches opened a way on his appearance, and he passed to the seat reserved for him amidst the acclamations of the people. At the opera, at the theatres, similar honors were paid him. It is John Adams who said: "Not Leibnitz or Newton, not Frederic or Voltaire, had a more universal reputation; and his character was more beloved and esteemed than that of them all." Throughout Europe, there was scarcely a citizen or a peasant of any culture who was not familiar with his name, and who did not consider him as a friend to all men. At the academy, D'Alembert addressed him as the man who had wrenched the thunderbolt from the cloud, the sceptre from tyrants; and both these ideas were of a nature to pass easily into the common mind. From the part which he had taken in the emancipation of America, imagination transfigured him as the man who had separated the colonies from Great Britain, had framed their best constitutions of government, and by counsel and example would show how to abolish all political evil throughout the world. Malesherbes spoke of the excellence of the institutions that permitted a printer, the son of a tallow-chandler, to act a great part in public affairs; and, if Malesherbes reasoned so, how much more the workmen of Paris and the people. Thus Franklin was the venerable impersonation of democracy, yet so calmly decorous, so free from a disposition to quarrel with the convictions of others, that, while he was the delight of free-thinking philosophers, he escaped the hatred of the clergy, and his presence excited no jealousy in the old nobility, though sometimes a woman of rank might find fault with his hands and skin, which toil had embrowned. Yet he understood the movement of the French of his day. He remarked to those in Paris who learned of him the secret of statesmanship: "He who shall introduce into public affairs the principles of primitive Christianity will change the face of the world;" and we know from Condorcet that while in France he said in a public company: "You perceive liberty eastablish herself and flourish almost under your eyes; I dare to predict that by and by you will be anxious to taste her blessings." In this way he conciliated the most opposite natures, yet not for himself. Whatever favor he met in society, whatever honor he received from the academy, whatever authority he gained as a man of science, whatever distinction came to him through the good-will of the people, whatever fame he acquired through-

out Europe, he turned all to account for the good of his country. Surrounded by colleagues, some of whom were jealous
of his superiority, and for no service whatever were greedy
of the public money, he threw their angry demands into
the fire. Arthur Lee intrigued to supplant him with persevering
malignity; the weak and incompetent Izard brought against
him charges which bear the strangeness of frenzy; but he met
their hostility by patient indifference. Never detracting from
the merit of any one, he did not disdain glory, and he knew
how to pardon envy. Great as were the injuries which he
received in England, he used towards that power undeviating
frankness and fairness, and never from resentment lost an opportunity of promoting peace.

In England, Rockingham, Richmond, Burke Fox, Conway,
respected Franklin, and desired to meet his offers. So, too, did
Lord North, though he had not courage to be true to his convictions. On the other side stood foremost and firmest the king,
and Chatham arrayed himself against American independence.
Richmond, as a friend to liberty, made frank advances to Chatham, sending him the draft of an address which he was to
move in the house of lords, and entreating of him reunion,
mutual confidence, and support. Chatham rejected his over-
ture, and avowed the purpose of opposing his motion. Accordingly, on Tuesday the seventh of April, against earnest requests,
Lord Chatham, wrapped up in flannel to the knees, pale and
wasted away, his eyes still retaining their fire, came into the
house of lords, leaning upon his son William Pitt and his son-
in-law Lord Mahon. The peers stood up out of respect as he
hobbled to his bench. The Duke of Richmond proposed and
spoke elaborately in favor of an address to the king, which in
substance recommended the recognition of the independent
sovereignty of the thirteen revolted provinces and a change
of administration. Chatham, who alone of British statesmen
had a right to invite America to resume her old connection,
rose from his seat with slowness and difficulty, leaning on his
crutches and supported under each arm by a friend. His figure

was marked with dignity, and he seemed a being superior to those around him. Raising one hand from his crutch, and casting his eyes towards heaven, he said: "I thank God that, old and infirm, and with more than one foot in the grave, I have been able to come this day to stand up in the cause of my country, perhaps never again to enter the walls of this house." Stillness prevailed. His voice, at first low and feeble, rose and became harmonious; but his speech faltered, his sentences were broken, his words no more than flashes through darkness, shreds of sublime but unconnected eloquence. He recalled his prophecies of the evils which were to follow such American measures as had been adopted, adding at the end of each: "and so it proved." He could not act with Lord Rockingham and his friends, because they persisted in unretracted error. With the loftiest pride he laughed to scorn the idea of an invasion of England by Spain or by France or by both. "If peace cannot be preserved with honor, why is not war declared without hesitation? This kingdom has still resources to maintain its just rights. Any state is better than despair. My lords, I rejoice that the grave has not closed upon me, that I am still alive to lift up my voice against the dismemberment of this ancient and most noble monarchy." The Duke of Richmond answered with respect for the name of Chatham, so dear to Englishmen; but he resolutely maintained the wisdom of avoiding a war in which France and Spain would have America for their ally. Lord Chatham would have replied; but, after two or three unsuccessful efforts to rise, he fell backwards, and seemed in the agonies of death. Every one of the peers pressed round him, save only the Earl of Mansfield, who sat unmoved. The senseless sufferer was borne from the house with tender solicitude to the bed from which he never was to rise.

The king wrote at once to Lord North: "May not the political exit of Lord Chatham incline you to continue at the head of my affairs?" The world was saddened by the loss of so great a man. The elder Pitt never seemed more thoroughly the spokesman of the commoners of England than in these last months of his public career. He came to parliament with an all-impassioned love of liberty, the proudest sentiment of nationality, and his old disdain of the house of Bourbon; and the sorrows of his country were as massive clouds about his brilliant pathway to the grave. His eloquence in the early part of the session seemed to some of his hearers to surpass all that they had ever heard of the orators of Greece or Rome. In his last days, he was still dreaming of an ideal England with a parliament of the people; and, with a haughtiness all the more marvellous from his age, decrepitude, and insulation, he confronted alone all branches of the nobility, who had lost a continent in the vain hope of saving themselves a shilling in the pound of the land-tax, and declared that there could be no good government but under an administration that should crush to atoms the political influence of all parties of the aristocracy, and interpret law in favor of liberty. He died like a hero struck down on the field of battle after the day was lost, still in heart, though not in place, the great commoner. With logical consistency, the house of lords refused to attend his funeral.

By this time the news of the French alliance with the United States had spread through Europe. It was received at St. Petersburg with lively satisfaction. In England, the king, the ministry, parliament, the British nation, all were unwilling to speak the word independence, wishing at least to retain some preference by compact. France in her treaty of commerce asked no favor, considering equality as the only basis for a permanent friendship. Custom, mutual confidence, sameness of language and of civil law, the habit of using English manufactures, their cheapness and merit, of themselves secured to England almost a monopoly of American commerce for a generation, and yet she stickled for the formal concession of some special commercial advantages. Deluded by the long usage of monopoly, she would not see that equality was all she needed. Once more Hartley, as an informal agent from Lord North, repaired to Paris to seek of Franklin an offer of some alliance or at least of some favor in trade. Franklin answered him as he answered other emissaries, that as to independence the Americans enjoyed it already; its acknowledgment would secure to Britain equal but not superior advantages in commerce. Fox was satisfied with this offer; and on the tenth, when it was moved in the house of commons to enlarge the powers of the commissioners, he held up to view that greater benefits to trade would follow from friendly relations with independent America than from nominal dependence.

Fox was in the right, but was not heeded. Had Chatham lived and obtained power, the course of events would not have been changed. Jackson, the former colleague of Franklin and secretary of Grenville, refused to be of the commission for peace, because he saw that it was a delusion accorded by the king to quiet Lord North, and to unite the nation against the Americans. Long before the commissioners arrived, the United States had taken its part. On the twenty-first of April, Washington gave his opinion to a member of congress: "Nothing short of independence can possibly do. A peace on any other terms would be a peace of war. The injuries we have received from the British nation were so unprovoked, and have been so great and so many, that they can never be forgotten. Our fidelity as people, our character as men, are opposed to a coalition with them as subjects." Upon the twenty-second, a day of general public fasting and humiliation, with prayers to Almighty God to strengthen and perpetuate the union, in their house of worship congress resolved "to hold no conference or treaty with any commissioners on the part of Great Britain, unless they shall, as a preliminary thereto, either withdraw their fleets and armies, or in positive and express terms acknowledge the independence of the states." "Lord North is two years too late with his political manœuvre," responded George Clinton, then governor of New York. Jay met not a single American "willing to accept peace under Lord North's terms." "No offers," wrote Robert Morris, "ought to have a hearing of one moment, unless preceded by acknowledgment of our independence, because we can never be a happy people under their domination. Great

Britain would still enjoy the greatest share and most valuable parts of our trade."

Since Britain would grant no peace, on the tenth the French king despatched from Toulon a fleet, bearing Gerard as his minister to the congress of the United States, that the alliance between France and America might be riveted. On the twenty-ninth, when, in the presence of Franklin and his newly arrived colleague John Adams, Voltaire was solemnly received by the French academy, philosophic France gave the right hand of fellowship to America as its child by adoption. The numerous assembly demanded a visible sign of the union of the intellect of the two continents; and, in the presence of all that was most distinguished in letters and philosophy, Franklin and Voltaire kissed one another, in recognition that the war for American independence was a war for freedom of mind.

Many causes combined to procure the alliance of France and the American republic; but the force which brought all influences harmoniously together, overruling the timorous levity of Maurepas and the dull reluctance of Louis XVI, was the movement of intellectual freedom. We are arrived at the largest generalization thus far in the history of America.

The spirit of free inquiry penetrated the Catholic world as it penetrated the Protestant world. Each of their methods of reform recognised that every man shares in the eternal reason, and in each the renovation proceeded from within the soul. Luther, as he climbed on his knees the marble steps of a church at Rome, heard a voice within him cry out, "Justification is by faith alone;" and to all the people he vindicated man's individuality from the point of view of religion. The most stupendous thought that was ever conceived by man, such as had never been dared by Socrates or the academy, by Aristotle or the stoics, took possession of Descartes on a November night in his meditations on the banks of the Danube. His mind separated itself from every thing beside, and in the consciousness of its freedom stood over against all tradition, all received opinion, all knowledge, all existence except itself, thus asserting the principle of individuality as the key-note of all coming philosophy and political institutions. Nothing was to be received by a man as truth which did not convince his own reason. Luther opened a new world in which every man was his own priest, his own intercessor; Descartes opened a new world in which every man was his own philosopher, his own judge of truth.

A practical difference marked the kindred systems: the one was the method of continuity and gradual reform; the other of an instantaneous, complete, and thoroughly radical revolution. The principle of Luther waked up a superstitious world, "asleep in lap of legends old," but did not renounce all external authority. It used drags and anchors to check too rapid a progress, and to secure its moorings. So it escaped premature conflicts. By the principle of Descartes, the individual man at once and altogether stood aloof from king, church, universities, public opinion, traditional science, all external authority and all other beings, and, turning every intruder out of the inner temple of the mind, kept guard at its portal to bar the entry to every belief that had not first obtained a passport from himself. No one ever applied the theory of Descartes with rigid inflexibility; a man can as little move without the weight of the superincumbent atmosphere as escape altogether the opinions of the age in which he sees the light; but the theory was there, and it rescued philosophy from bondage to monkish theology, forbade to the church all inquisition into private opinion, and gave to reason, and not to civil magistrates, the maintenance of truth. The nations that learned their lessons of liberty from Luther and Calvin went forward in their natural development, and suffered their institutions to grow and to shape themselves according to the increasing public intelligence. The nations that learned their lessons of liberty from Descartes were led to question every thing, and by creative power renew society through the destruction of the past. The spirit of liberty in all Protestant countries was marked by moderation. The German Lessing, the antitype of Luther, said to his countrymen: "Don't put out the candles till day breaks." Out of Calvinistic Protestantism rose in that day four great teachers of four great nationalities, America, Great Britain, Germany, and France. Edwards, Reid, Kant, and Rousseau were all imbued with religiosity, and all except the last, who spoiled his doctrine by dreamy indolence, were expositors of the active powers of man. All these in political science, Kant most exactly of all, were the counterpart of America, which was conducting a revolution on the highest principles of freedom with such circumspection that it seemed to be only a war against innovation. On the other hand, free thought in France, as pure in its source as free thought in America, became speculative and skeptical and impassioned. The modern Prometheus, as it broke its chains, started up with a sentiment of revenge against the ecclesiastical terrorism which for centuries had sequestered the rights of mind. Inquiry took up with zeal every question in science, politics, and morals. Free thought paid homage to the "majesty of nature;" investigated the origin of species; analyzed the air we breathe; pursued the discoveries of Columbus and Copernicus; mapped the skies; explored the oceans and measured the earth; revived ancient learning; revelled in the philosophy of Greece, which, untrammelled by national theology, went forth to seek the reason of things; nursed the republican sentiment by study of the history of Athens and Rome; spoke words for liberty on the stage; and adapted the round of learning to the common understanding. Now it translated and scattered abroad the writings of Americans and the new American constitutions; and the proud intellect of France was in a maze. Turgot and Condorcet melted with admiration and sympathy as they read the organic laws in which the unpretending husbandmen of a new continent had introduced into the world of real life the ideas that for them dwelt only in hope. All influences that favored freedom of mind conspired together. Antiprelatical Puritanism was embraced by anti-prelatical skepticism. The exile Calvin was welcomed home as he returned by way of New England and the states where Huguenots and Presbyterians prevailed. The lineage of Calvin and the lineage of Descartes met together. One great current of vigorous living opinion, which there was no power in France capable of resisting, swept through society, driving all the clouds in the sky in one direction. Ministers and king and nation were hurried along together.

The wave of free thought broke as it rolled against the Pyrenees. The Bourbon of France was compelled into an alliance with America; the Bourbon of Spain, disturbed only by the remonstrances of De Aranda, his ambassador in Paris, was left to pursue a strictly national policy. The Spanish people did not share the passion and enthusiasm of the French, for they had not had the training of the French. In France, there was no inquisition; in Spain, the king would have submitted his own son to its tribunal. For the French soldier Descartes, the emancipator of thought, Spain had the soldier Loyola to organize repression; for the proud Corneille, so full of republican fire, Spain had the monkish Calderón. There no poet like Molière unfrocked hypocrisy. Not only had Spain no Calvin, no Voltaire, no Rousseau; she had no Pascal to mock at casuistry; no prelate to instruct her princes in the rights of the people like Fénelon, or defend her church against Rome, or teach the equality of all men before God like Bossuet; no controversies through the press like those with the Huguenots; no edict of toleration like that of Nantes. A richly endowed church always leans to Arminianism and justification by works; and it was so in Spain, where the spiritual instincts of man, which are the life of freedom, had been trodden under foot, and almsgiving to professed mendicants usurped the place of charity. Natural science in its progress gently strips from religion the follies of superstition, and purifies and spiritualizes faith; in Spain it was dreaded as of kin to the Islam; and, as the material world was driven from its rightful place among the objects of study, it avenged itself by overlaying religion. The idea was lost in the symbol; to the wooden or metal cross was imputed the worth of inward piety; religious feeling was cherished by magnificent ceremonies to delight the senses; penitence in this world made atonement by using the hair shirt, the scourge, and masceration; the immoral soul was thought to be purged by material flames; the merciless inquisition kept spies over opinion in every house by the confessional, and quelled unbelief by the dungeon, the torture, and the stake. Free thought was rooted out in the struggle for homogeneousness. Nothing was left in Spain that could tolerate Protestantism, least of all the stern Protestantism of America; nothing congenial to free thought, lease of all to free thought as it was in France.

France was alive with the restless spirit of inquiry; the country beyond the Pyrenees was still benumbed by superstition and priestcraft and tyranny over mind, and the church through its organization maintained a stagnant calm. As there was no union between the French mind and the Spanish mind, between the French people and the Spanish people, the union of the governments was simply the result of the family compact, which the engagement between France and the United States without the assent of Spain violated and annulled. Moreover, the self-love of the Catholic king was touched, that his nephew should have formed a treaty with America without waiting for his advice. Besides, the independence of colonies wasan example that might divest his crown of its possessions in both parts of America; and the danger was greatly enhanced by the establishment of republicanism on the borders of his transatlantic provinces, where he dreaded it as more surely fatal than all the power of Great Britain.

The king of France, while he declared his wish to make no conquest whatever in the war, held out to the king of Spain, with the consent of the United States, the acquisition of Florida; but Florida had not power to allure Charles III, or his ministry, which was a truly Spanish ministry and wished to pursue a truly Spanish policy. There was indeed one word which, if pronounced, would be a spell potent enough to alter their decision; a word that calls the blood into the cheek of a Spaniard as a brand of inferiority on his nation. That word was

Gibraltar. Meantime, the king of Spain declared that he would not then, nor in the future, enter into the quarrel of France and England; that he wished to close his life in tranquillity, and valued peace too highly to sacrifice it to the interests or opinions of another.

So the flags of France and the United States went together into the field against Great Britain, unsupported by any other government, yet with the good wishes of all the peoples of Europe. The benefit then conferred on the United States was priceless. In return, the revolution in America came opportunely for France. During the last years of Louis XIV and the reign of Louis XV, she lost her creative power and stumbled about in the regions of skepticism. She aspired to deny, and knew only how to deny; yet that France which its own clergy calumniated as a nation of atheists was the lineal successor of the France which raised cathedrals on each side of the channel, the France which took up the banner of the very God indwelling in man against paganized Christianity and against Islam, the France which maintained Gallican liberties against papal Rome, the France which after its fashion delivered thought from bondage to the church. To that same France, America brought new life and hope; she superseded skepticism by a wise and prudent enthusiasm in action, and bade the nation that became her ally lift up its heart from the barrenness of doubt to the highest affirmation of God and liberty, to freedom in union with the good, the beautiful, and the true.

Europe and American Independence (1778)

THE alliance of France with the United States brought the American question into the heart of Europe, where it called new political aspirations into activity, waked the hope of free trade between all the continents, and arraigned the British ministry at the judgment-seat of the civilized world. England could recover influence in the direction of external affairs only by a peace with her colonies. American independence was to be decided not by arms alone, but equally by the policy and the sympathies of foreign princes and nations.

Both the great belligerents were involved in contradictions at home. The government of England, in seeking to suppress in her dependencies English rights by English arms, made war on the life of her own life. Inasmuch as the party of freedom and justice, which is, indeed, one for all mankind, was at least seen to be one and the same for the whole English race, it appeared more and more clearly that the total subjugation of America would be the prelude to the repression of liberty in the British isles.

In point of commercial wealth, industry, and adventurous enterprise, England at the time had no equal; in pride of nationality, no rival but France: yet her movements were marked by languor. There was no man in the cabinet who could speak words of power to call out her moral resources, and harmonize the various branches of the public service. The country, which in the seven years' war had been wrought by the elder Pitt to deeds of magnanimity, found in the ministry no representative. Public spirit had been quelled, and a disposition fostered to value personal interest above the general good. Even impending foreign war could not hush the turbulence of partisans. The administration, having no guiding principle, held its majority in the house of commons only on sufferance, its own officials

only by its control of patronage. Insubordination showed itself
in the fleet and in the army, and most among the officers. England had not known so bad a government since the reign of
James II. It was neither beloved nor respected, and truly stood
neither for the people nor for any party of the aristocracy;
neither for the spirit of the time, nor for the past age, nor for
that which was coming. It was a conglomerate of inferior and
heterogeneous materials, totally unfit to conduct the policy of
a mighty empire, endured only during an interim.

The period in British history was one of great and increasing
intellectual vigor. It was distinguished in philosophy by Hume
and Reid and Price and Adam Smith; in painting by Reynolds;
in poetry and various learning by Gray and Goldsmith, Johnson and Cowper; in legislative eloquence by Chatham, Burke,
and Fox; in history by Gibbon; in the useful arts by Brindley,
Watt, and Arkwright. That the nation, in a state of high and advancing culture, should have been governed by a sordid ministry, so inferior to itself as that of Lord North, was not due to
the corruption of parliament alone; for there was always in the
house of commons an independent fraction. It cannot be fully
explained without considering the chaotic state of political
parties.

The conflict between England and her American colonies
sprang necessarily out of the development of British institutions. The supreme right of parliament as the representative
of English nationality, and bound to resist and overthrow the
personal government of the Stuarts, was the watch-word of the
Revolution of 1688, which had been dear to America as the
death-blow to monarchical absolutism throughout the English
dominions, and as the harbinger of constitutional liberty for the
civilized world. Parliament again asserted its paramount authority over the crown, when by its own enactment it transferred
the succession to the house of Hanover. These revolutions could
not have been achieved except through a categorical principle
that would endure no questioning of its rightfulness. Such a
principle could not submit to modifications, until it had ac-

complished its work; and, as it was imbedded with the love of liberty in the mass of the English nation, it had moved and acted with the strength and majesty of a national conviction.

In the process of years, the assertion of the supreme power of parliament soon assumed an exaggerated form, and was claimed to extend, without limit, over Ireland and over the colonies; so that the theory which had first been used to rescue and secure the liberties of England became an instrument of despotism. Meantime, both branches of parliament were but representatives of the same favored class; and the kings awakened no counterpoising sentiment of loyalty so long as the house of Hanover, the creature of parliament, was represented by princes of foreign birth, ignorant of the laws and the language of the land.

In this manner the government was conducted for a half-century by the aristocracy, which, keeping in memory the days of Cromwell and of James II, were led into the persuasion that the party of liberty, to use the words of Rockingham, was that which "fought up against the king and against the people."

But by the side of the theory of absolute power concentrated in parliament, which had twice been the sheet-anchor of the English constitution, there existed the older respect for the rights of the individual and the liberties of organized communities. These two elements of British political life were brought into collision by the American revolution, which had its provocation in the theory of the omnipotence of parliament, and its justification in the eyes of Englishmen in the principle of vital liberty diffused through all the parts of the commonwealth. The two ideas struggled for the ascendency in the mind of the British nation and in its legislature. They both are so embalmed in the undying eloquence of Burke as to have led to the most opposite estimates of his political character. They both appear in startling distinctness in the speeches and conduct of Fox, who put all at hazard on the omnipotence of parliament, and yet excelled in the clear statement of the attitude of America. Both lay in irreconciled confusion in the politics of Rockingham, whose administration signalized itself by enacting the right of the king, lords, and commons of Britain to bind America in all cases whatsoever, and humanely refused to enforse the pretension. The aristocratic party of liberty, organized on the principle of the absolute power of parliament, in order to defeat effectually and for all time the designs of the king against parliamentary usages and rights, had done its work and outlived its usefulness. In opposition to the continued rule of an aristocratic connection with the device of omnipotence over king and people, there rose up around the pure and venerable form of Chatham a new liberal party, willing to use the prerogative of the king to moderate the rule of the aristocracy in favor of the people.

The new party aimed at a double modification of the unrestricted sovereignty of parliament. The elder Pitt ever insisted, and his friends continued to maintain, that the commons of Great Britain had no right to impose taxes on unrepresented colonies. This was the first step in the renovation of English liberty. The next was to recognise that parliament, as then composed, did not adequately represent the nation; and statesmen of the connection of Rockingham desperately resisted both these cardinal principles of reform. This unyielding division among the opponents of Lord North prolonged his administration.

Besides, many men of honest intentions, neither wishing to see English liberties impaired, nor yet to consent to the independence of the colonies, kept their minds in a state of suspense; and this reluctance to decide led them to bear a little longer the ministry which alone professed ability to suppress the insurrection: for better men would not consent to take their places coupled with the condition of continuing their policy. Once in a moment of petulance, Lord George Germain resigned; and the king, who wished to be rid of him, regarded his defection as a most favorable event. But he was from necessity continued in his office, because no one else could be found willing to accept it.

In the great kingdom on the other side of the channel, antagonistic forces were likewise in action. As the representative of popular power, France had in reserve one great advantage over England in her numerous independent peasantry. Brought up in ignorance and seclusion, they knew not how to question any thing that was taught by the church or commanded by the monarch; but, however they might for the present suffer from grievous and unredressed oppression, they constituted the safeguard of order as well as of nationality.

It was in the capital and among the cultivated classes of society, in coffee-houses and saloons, that the cry rose for reform or revolution. The French king was absolute; yet the teachings of Montesquieu and the example of England raised in men of generous natures an uncontrollable desire for free institutions; while speculative fault-finders, knowing nothing of the self-restraint which is taught by responsibility in the exercise of office, indulged in ideal anticipations, which were colored by an exasperating remembrance of griefs and wrongs. France was the eldest daughter of the Roman church, with a king who was sincere though not a bigoted Roman Catholic; and its philosophers carried their impassioned war against the church to the utmost verge of skepticism and unbelief, while a suspicion that forms of religion were used as a mere instrument of government began to find its way into the minds of the discontented laboring class in the cities. But, apart from all inferior influences, the power of generalization, in which the French nation excels all others, imparts from time to time an idealistic character to its policy. The Parisians felt the reverses of the Americans as if they had been their own; and in November, 1776, an approaching rupture with England was the subject of all conversations.

The American struggle was avowedly a war in defence of the common rights of mankind. The Prince de Montbarey, who owed his place as minister of war to the favor of Maurepas and female influence, and who cherished the prejudices of his order without being aware of his own mediocrity, professed to despise

the people of the United States as formed from emigrants for
the most part without character and without fortune, ambitious
and fanatical, and likely to attract to their support "all the
rogues and the worthless from the four parts of the globe." He
had warned Lafayette against leaving his wife and wasting his
fortune to play the part of Don Quixote in their behalf, and
had raised in the council his feeble voice against the alliance
of France with the insurgents. He regarded a victory over England as of no advantage commensurate with the dangerous example of sustaining a revolt against established authority. Besides, war would accumulate disorder in the public finances,
retard useful works for the happiness of France, and justify
reprisals by Great Britain on the colonies of the Bourbon
princes.

It was against the interior sentiment of the king, the doubts
of Maurepas, and the vivid remonstrances of the minister of
war, that the lingering influence of the policy of the balance of
power, the mercantile aspirations of France, its spirit of philosophic freedom, its traditional antagonism to England as aiming at the universal monarchy of commerce and the seas,
quickened by an eagerness to forestall a seemingly imminent
reconciliation with the colonies, forced the French alliance with
America.

Just thirty-eight years before, when Maurepas was in the
vigor of manhood, he had been famed for his aversion to
England and for founding his glory on the restoration of the
French navy. In the administration of Cardinal Fleury; he was
thought to have had the mind of the widest range; and it was in
those days predicted of him that he would lead France to accomplish great results, if he should ever become the director of
the government. At length he was raised to be first minister by
a king who looked up to him with simple-minded deference
and implicit trust. The tenor of his mind was unchanged;
but he was so enfeebled by long exclusion from public affairs
and the heavy burden of years and infirmities that no daring
design could lure him from the love of quiet. By habit he put

aside all business which admitted of delay, and shunned every effort of heroic enterprise. When the question of the alliance with America became urgent, he shrunk from proposing new taxes, which the lately restored parliaments might refuse to register; and he gladly accepted the guarantee of Necker, that all war expenditures could be met by the use of credit, varied financial operations, and reforms. It was only after the assurance of a sufficient supply of money from loans, of which the repayment would not disturb the remnant of his life, that he no longer attempted to stem the prevailing opinion of Paris in favor of America. The same fondness for ease, after hostilities were begun, led him to protect Necker from the many enemies who, from hatred of his reforms, joined the clamor against him as a foreigner and a Calvinist.

The strength of the cabinet lay in Vergennes, whose superior statesmanship was yet not in itself sufficient to raise him above the care of maintaining himself in favor. He secured the unfailing good-will of his sovereign by his political principles, recognising no authority of either clergy, or nobility, or third estate, but only a monarch to give the word, and all, as one people, to obey. Nor did he ever for a moment forget the respect due to Maurepas as his superior, so that he never excited a jealousy of rivalship. He had no prejudice about calling republics into being, whether in Europe or beyond the Atlantic, if the welfare of France seemed to require it; he had, however, in his earliest approaches to the insurgent colonies, acted in conjunction with Spain, which he continued to believe would follow France into the war with England; and in his eyes the interests of that branch of the house of Bourbon took precedence over those of the United States, except where the latter were precisely guaranteed by treaty.

Not one of the chiefs of the executive government, not even the director-general of the finances, was primarily a hearty friend to the new republic: the opinion of Necker was in favor of neutrality; and his liberalism, though he was a Swiss by birth, and valued the praises of the philosophic world, did not go beyond admiration of the political institutions of England.

The statesmen of the nation had not yet deduced from experience and the intuitions of reason a system of civil liberty to supersede worn-out traditional forms; and the lighter literature of the hour, skeptical rather than hopeful, mocked at the contradiction between institutions and rights. "Gentlemen of America," wrote Parny, at Paris, just before the alliance between France and the United States, "what right have you, more than we, to this cherished liberty? Inexorable tyranny crushes Europe; and you, lawless and mutinous people, without kings and without queens, will you dance to the clank of the chains which weigh down the human race? And, deranging the beautiful equipoise, will you beard the whole world, and be free?" Mirabeau wrote a fiery invective against despotism, from a prison of which his passionate imploring for leave to serve in America could not open the doors.

Until chastened by affliction, Marie Antoinette wanted earnestness of character, and suffered herself to be swayed by generous caprices, or family ties, or the selfish solicitations of her female companions. She had an ascendency over the mind of the king, but never aspired to control his foreign policy, except in relation to Austria; and she could not always conceal her contempt for his understanding. It was only in the pursuit of offices and benefits for her friends that she would suffer no denial. She did not spare words of angry petulance to a minister who dared thwart her requests; and Necker retained her favor by never refusing them. To find an embassy for the aged, inexperienced, and incompetent father-in-law of the woman whom she appeared to love the most, she did not scruple to derange the diplomatic service of the kingdom. For the moment her emotions ran with the prevailing enthusiasm for the new republic; but they were only superficial and occasional, and could form no support for a steady conduct of the war.

It was the age of personal government in France. Its navy, its army, its credit, its administration, rested absolutely in the hands of a young man of four-and-twenty, whom his Austrian brother-in-law described as a child. He felt for the Americans neither as insurgents against wrongs nor as a self-governing people; and never understood how it came about that, contrary to his own faith in unlimited monarchical power and in the Catholic Church, his kingdom had plunged into a war to introduce to the potentates of the civilized world a revolutionary Protestant republic.

France was rich in resources; but its finances had not recovered from their exhaustion in the seven years' war. Their restoration became hopeless, when Necker promised to employ the fame of his severer administration only to add new weight to debts which were already too heavy to be borne. The king of Prussia, whose poverty made him a sharp observer of the revenues of wealthier powers, repeatedly foretold the bankruptcy of the royal treasury, if the young king should break the peace.

All this while Paris was the centre of the gay society and intelligence of Europe. The best artists of the day, the masters of the rival schools of music, crowded round the court. The splendor of the Bourbon monarchy was kept up at the Tuileries and Versailles with prodigal magnificence; and invention was ever devising new methods of refined social enjoyment. The queen was happy in the dazzling scenes of which she was the life; the king pleased with the supreme power which he held it his right to exercise. To France, the years which followed are the most glorious in her history; for they were those in which she most consistently and disinterestedly fought for the liberties of mankind, and so prepared the way for her own regeneration and the overthrow of feudalism throughout Europe; but Louis XVI and Marie Antoinette, when they embarked for the liberation of America, pleasure on the prow, and the uncertain hand of youth at the helm, might have cried out to the young republic which they fostered: *Morituri te salutant*, "The doomed to die salute thee."

The Catholic king might love to avenge himself on England by worrying her with chicanes and weakening her by promoting dissensions in her dominions; but he had learned from experience to recoil from war, and longed for tranquillity in his old age. A very costly and most unsuccessful expedition against Algiers, and a protracted strife with Portugal respecting the extension of Brazil to the La Plata, where Pombal by active forethought long counterbalanced superior power, had wasted the resources of his world-wide monarchy. Its revenue amounted to not much more than twenty millions of dollars, and a large annual deficit rapidly increased the public debt. Every consideration of sound policy enjoined upon the ruler of Spain to husband for his land the blessings of peaceful times; and above all, as the great possessor of colonies, to avoid a war which was leading to the complete and irretrievable ruin of the old colonial system.

The management of its foreign dependencies—colonies they could not properly be called, nor could Spain be named their mother country—was to that kingdom an object of anxiety and never-sleeping suspicion, heightened by a perpetual consciousness that the task of governing them was beyond its ability. The total number of their inhabitants greatly exceeded its own. By their very extent, embracing, at least in theory, all the Pacific coast of America; and north of the Gulf of Mexico the land eastward to the Mississippi or even to the Alleghanies, it could have no feeling of their subordination. The remoteness of the provinces on the Pacific still more weakened the tie of supremacy, which was nowhere confirmed by a common language, inherited traditions, or affinities of race. There was no bond of patriotism, or sense of the joint possession of political rights, or inbred loyalty. The connection between rulers and ruled was one of force alone; and the force was in itself so very weak that it availed only from the dull sluggishness of the governed. Distrust marked the policy of the home government, even toward those of its officials who were natives of Spain; still more toward the Creoles, as the offspring of Spaniards in America were called. No attempt had been made to bind the mind of the old races, except through the Roman religion, which was introduced by the sword and maintained by methods of super-

stition. There was, perhaps, never a time when the war-cry of
the semi-barbarous nations who formed the bulk of the population was not heard somewhere on their border. The restraints
on commerce were mishievous and vexatious, prompted by fear
and provoking murmurs and frauds.

Moreover, all the world was becoming impatient that so large
a portion of the globe should be monopolized by an incapable
and decrepit dynasty. The Dutch and the British and the
French sought opportunities of illicit trade. The British cut
down forest trees, useful in the workshop and the dye-house,
and carried them off as unappropriated products of nature. The
Russian flag waved on the American shore of the North Pacific.

To all these dangers from abroad, Charles III had added another, by making war on the so-called company of Jesus of the
prelates of Spain, seven archbishops and twenty-eight bishops,
two-thirds of them all, not only approved the exile of the order
from his dominions, but recommended its total dissolution;
while only one bishop desired to preserve it without reform.
With their concurrence, and the support of France and Portugal, he finally extorted the assent of the pope to its abolition.
But before the formal act of the see of Rome, on the second of
April, 1767, at one and the same hour in Spain, in the north and
south of Africa, in Asia, in America, in all the islands of the
monarchy, the royal decree was opened by officials of the crown,
enjoining them immediately to take possession of its houses,
to chase its members from their convents, and within twenty-
four hours to transport them as prisoners to some appointed harbor. These commands were followed with precision in Spain,
where the Jesuit priests, without regard to their birth, education, or age, were sent on board ships to land where they could.
They were executed less perfectly in Mexico and California,
and still less so along the South Pacific coast and the waters of
the La Plata.

But the power of Spain in her colonies had been promoted
by the unwearied activity of the Jesuits. Their banishment
weakened her authority over Spanish emigrants, and still more

confused the minds of the rude progeny of the aborigines. In Paraguay, where Spanish supremacy had rested on Jesuits alone, who had held in their hands all the attributes of Cæsar and pope, of state and church, the revolution which divided these powers between a civil chief and Dominicans, Franciscans, and monks of the Lady of Mercy, made a fracture that never could be healed. It was as colonial insurgents that Spain dreaded the Americans, not as a new Protestant power. The antipathy of the king to the United States arose from political motives: by the recognition of their independence, he was threatened with a new, unexpected, and very real danger in all his boundless vice-royalties. There could be no fear of a popular rising in any of them to avenge a breach of political privileges; but as they had been won by adventurous leaders, so a priest, an aboriginal chief, a descendant of an Inca, might waken a common feeling in the native population, and defy the Spanish monarch. Jesuits might find shelter among their neophytes, and reappear as the guides of rebellion. One of their fathers has written: "When Spain tore evangelical laborers away from the colonies, the breath of independence agitated the New World, and God permitted it to detach itself from the Old."

The example of the United States did not merely threaten to disturb the valley of the Mississippi; but, as epidemic disease leaps mysteriously over mountains and crosses oceans, spores of dicontent might be unaccountably borne, to germinate among the many-tongued peoples of South America. All alluring promises of lowering the strength of England could soothe Florida Blanca no more. His well-grounded sensitiveness was inflamed, till it became a continual state of morbid irritability; and, from the time when the court of France resolved to treat with the Americans, his prophetic fears could never for a moment be lulled to rest.

Portugal, which in the seven years' war, with the aid of England, escaped absorption by Spain, seemed necessarily about to become an ally of the British king. Its harbors, during the last year of the ministry of Pombal, were shut against the vessels of the United States; and congress, on the thirtieth of December, 1776, resenting the insult, was willing to incur its enmity, as the price of the active friendship of Spain. But when, two months later, on the twenty-fourth of February, 1777, the weak-minded, superstitious Maria I succeeded to the throne, Pombal retired before reactionary imbecility. Portugal, in exchange for a tract of land conterminous to Brazil, withdrew from the La Plata, and was scarcely heard of again during the war.

In the south-east of Europe, the chief political interest for the United States centred in the joint rulers of the Austrian empire. The Danube, first of rivers of the Old World, rolled through their dominions between valleys of exuberant fertility towards the great inland sea which drains a larger surface of Europe than the Mediterranean. Yet the culture and commerce of the eastern lands of the crown, by which alone their house could become great, were set aside as secondary objects, so that the mighty stream flowed almost in silence towards the Euxine.

In August, 1755, when Kaunitz was about to take in his hand the helm of the Austrian empire, and hold it for a third of a century, his first words in explanation of his policy were: "Prussia must be utterly thrown down from its very foundations, if the house of Austria is to stand upright." In the year in which the United States declared their independence, as Joseph II visited France to draw closer his relations with that power, Kaunitz thus counselled the young emperor: "Move against Prussia with all moderation and regard for good appearances. Never fully trust its court. Direct against it the sum total of political strength, and let our whole system of state rest on this principle."

Successive popes of Rome had wished an alliance of the two great Catholic powers of Central Europe against the smaller states, by which the Reformation had been rescued; and it was the chief boast of Kaunitz that he had effected that alliance. Twenty years after it was framed, his language was still: "Aus-

tria and Bourbon are natural allies, and have to regard the
Protestant powers as their common rivals and enemies."

Further the Austrian court in the time of Kaunitz desired,
above all, increased power and possessions in Germany, and
planned the absorption of Bavaria. And, as the dynastic interests of the imperial family claimed parity with those of the
state, the same minister knew how to find thrones at Parma, at
Paris, at Naples, for the three youngest of the six daughters of
Maria Theresa.

The arch-house looked upon itself as alone privileged to produce the chiefs of the holy Roman empire, the continuers of
Augustus, of Constantine, of Charlemagne, of Otho. In this idea
lay its fiction of a claim to universal monarchy, sanctified by the
church; so that any new acquisition could easily be regarded
but as a recovery of a rightful part of its dominions. For the
same reason it asserted precedence over every royal house, and
would not own an equal, even in the empress of Russia.

Since Austria, deserting its old connection with England, had
allied itself with France, and the two powers had faithfully
fought together in the seven years' war, it would have seemed at
least that the imperial court was bound to favor its Bourbon
ally in the great contest for American independence; but we
have seen an American agent rebuffed alike from the foreign
office in Vienna and from the saloons of Kaunitz. The emperor,
Joseph II, no less than his mother, from first to last condemned
the rising of the American people as a wrong done to the principle of superior power; and his sympathy as a monarch was
constant to England.

Such was the policy of the arch-house and its famous minister at this period of American history. But Prussia proved the
depth and vigor of its roots by the manner of its wrestling with
the storm; the Hapsburg alliance with Bourbon brought no advantage, and passed away, like every thing else that is hollow
and insincere. Bavaria still stands, clad in prouder honors than
before. Of the thrones on which the Austrian princesses were

placed, all three have crumbled; and their families are extinct or in exile. The fiction of the holy Roman empire has passed away, and its meaningless shadow figures only in misplaced arms and devices. The attitude of Austria to the United States will appear as our narrative proceeds. Kaunitz and the imperial house of his day sowed seed that had no life; and their policy bore no fruit, delaying for their generation the development of the great Austrian state.

In Italy, which by being broken into fragments was reft of its strength though not of its beauty, The United States had hoped to find support from the rulers of Florence, to whom they had commissioned an envoy: the world had been full of the praises of his code and of his government. But the hope was altogether vain. The south of Italy followed Spain. The pope took no thought of colonies which were soon to form a republic, with a people far more thoroughly Protestant than any nation in Europe. But the genius of the Italians has always revered the struggles of patriotism; and, while the Americans fought for their liberties, Filangieri was preparing the work, in which, with the applause of the best minds, he claimed for reason its rights in the governments of men. During the war, the king of Naples, as one of the Spanish Bourbons, conformed his commercial policy to that of Spain.

The Turkish empire affected the course of American affairs both during the war and at its close. The embroilment of the western maritime kingdoms seemed to leave its border provinces at the mercy of their neighbors; and there were statesmen in England who wished peace, in order that their country might speak with authority on the Bosphorus and within the Euxine.

Of the three northern powers, Russia was for the United States the most important; for Great Britain with ceaseless importunity sought its alliance: but its empress put aside every request to take an active part in the American contest, and repeatedly advised the restoration of peace by the concession of independence. In 1777, she desired to shut the cruisers of the

United States out of the Baltic, but confidentially assured the Bourbon family that she would not interfere in their quarrel, and would even be pleased to see them throw off the yoke of England. Her heart was all in the Orient. She longed to establish a Christian empire on the Bosphorus, and wondered why Christians of the west should prefer to maintain Mussulmans at Constantinople. Of England, she loved and venerated the people; but she had contempt for its king and for his ministry, of which she noticed the many blunders and foretold the fall. On the other hand, she esteemed Vergennes as a wise and able minister, but did not love the French nation.

In Gustavus III of Sweden, the nephew of Frederic of Prussia, France might expect a friend. The revolution of 1771, in favor of the royal prerogative, had been aided by French subsidies and the counsels of Vergennes, who was selected for the occasion to be the French minister at Stockholm. The oldest colonizers of the Delaware were Swedes, and a natural affection bound their descendants to the mother country. The adventurous king had the ambition to possess a colony, and France inclined to gratify his wish. His people, as builders and owners of ships, favored the largest interpretation of the maritime rights of neutrals; and we shall see their king, who had dashing courage, though not perseverance, now and then show himself as the boldest champion of the liberty of the seas.

Denmark, the remaining northern kingdom, was itself a colonial power, possessing small West India islands and a foothold in the east. Its king, as Duke of Holstein, had a voice in the German diet at Ratisbon. Its people were of a noble race; it is the land which, first of European states, forbade the slave-trade, and which, before the end of the century, abolished the remains of serfdom.

In 1778, a half-witted king, every day growing feebler in mind, yet in name preserving the functions of royalty; a crown prince of but ten years old, whose mother, divorced for adultery, had died in her youth an exile; a council of state, having the

brother of the king for a member, and divided into two nearly
equal factions; a queen-dowager, benevolent beyond her means,
and fond of meddling in public affairs,—gave no promise of
fixedness in the administration. Count Bernstorf, minister of
foreign affairs, a Hanoverian by birth, professed to believe that
the repose, the strength, and the happiness of civil society depend upon the principle that a people can never be justified in
renouncing fidelity, obedience, and subjection to its lawful government, and declaring itself independent. He watched, therefore, that the Danish government should not favor, or even
seem to favor, any step which promised help to the Americans.
Complying with the suggestion of the English court, Danish
subjects were forbidden to send, even to Danish West India
islands, munitions of war, lest they should find their way to the
United States. The Danish and Norwegian ports were closed
against prizes taken by American privateers. Yet, from its commercial interests, Denmark was forced to observe and to claim
the rights of a neutral.

Freedom has its favorite home on the mountains or by the
sea. Of the two European republics of the last century, the one
had established itself among the head-springs of the Rhine, the
other at its mouth. In Switzerland, which its mountains kept
apart alike from Italy and the north, the free people preserved
their ancient character, and, being content within themselves,
constituted a confederated republic, which rivalled in age the
oldest monarchies, and, by its good order and industry, morals
and laws, proved the stability of self-government, alike for the
Romanic and for the Germanic race. Of the compatibility of
extensive popular confederacies with modern civilization, it
removed every doubt; and America sheltered herself under its
example. Haldemand, a much-trusted brigadier in the British
service, belonged to it by birth; but England was never able to
enlist his countrymen in the rank and file of her armies. The
United States gratefully venerated their forerunner, but sought
from it no direct assistance. Had their cause been lost, Alex-

ander Hamilton would have retreated with his bride "o Geneva, where nature and society were in their greatest perfection."

The deepest and the saddest interest hovers over the republic of the Netherlands, for the war between England and the United States prepared its grave. Of all the branches of the Germanic family, that nation, which rescued from the choked and shallowed sea the unstable silt and sands brought down by the Rhine, has endured the most and wrought the most in favor of liberty of conscience, liberty of commerce, and liberty in the state. The republic which it founded was the child of the Reformation. For three generations the best interests of mankind were abandoned to its keeping; and, to uphold the highest objects of spiritual life, its merchants, landholders, and traders so abounded in heroes and martyrs that they tired out brute force, and tyranny, and death itself, and from war educed life and hope for coming ages. Their existence was an unceasing struggle with the ocean which beat against their dikes; with the rivers which cut away their soil; with neighbors that coveted their territory; with England, their ungenerous rival in trade. In proportion to numbers, they were the first in agriculture and in commerce; first in establishing credit by punctuality and probity; first in seeing clearly that great material interests are fostered best by liberty. Their land remained the storehouse of renovating political ideas for Europe, and the asylum of all who were persecuted for their thoughts. In freedom of conscience they were the light of the world. Out of the heart of a taciturn, phlegmatic, serious people, inclined to solitude and reflection, rose the men who constructed the code of international law in the spirit of justice.

In 1674, after England for about a quarter of a century had aimed by acts of legislation and by wars to ruin the navigation of the Netherlands, the two powers consolidated peace by a treaty of commerce, in which the rights of neutrals were guaranteed in language the most precise and the most intelligible.

Not only was the principle recognised that free ships make free goods; but, both positively and negatively, ship-timber and other naval stores were excluded from the list of contraband.

In 1688 England contracted to the Netherlands the highest debt that one nation can owe to another. Herself not knowing how to recover her liberties, they were restored by men of the united provinces; and Locke brought back from his exile in that country the theory on government which had been formed by the Calvinists of the continent, and which made his chief political work the text-book of the friends of free institutions for a century.

During the long wars for the security of the new English dynasty, and for the Spanish succession, in all which the republic had little interest of its own, it remained the faithful ally of Great Britain. Gibraltar was taken by ships and troops of the Dutch not less than by those of England; yet its appropriation by the stronger state brought them no corresponding advantage; on the contrary, their exhausted finances and disproportionate public debt crippled their power of self-defence.

For these faithful, unexampled, and unrequited services, the republic might, at least, expect to find in England a wall of protection. But during the seven years' war, in disregard of treaty obligations, its ships were seized on the ground that they had broken the arbitrary British rules of contraband and blockade. In the year 1758 the losses of its merchants on these pretences were estimated at more than twelve million guilders. In 1762, four of its ships, convoyed by a frigate, were taken, after an engagement; and, though the frigate was released, George Grenville, then secretary of state, announced by letter to its envoy that the right of stopping Dutch ships with naval stores must be and would be sustained.

These violences began to wean the Dutch people from their attachment to England. Could the prizes, which her courts wrongfully condemned, compensate for the affections of an ally of a hundred years? But this was not the worst: she took advantage of the imperfections in the constitution of the Netherlands to divide their government, and by influence and corruption she won the party of the stadholder to her own uses.

The republic was in many ways dear to the United States. It had given a resting-place to their emigrant pilgrims, and dismissed them to the New World with lessons of religious toleration. It had planted the valley of the Hudson; and in New York and New Jersey its sons still cherished the language, church rule, and customs of their parent nation. The Dutch saw in the American struggle a repetition of their own history; and the Americans looked to them for the evidence that a small but resolute state can triumph over the utmost efforts of the mightiest and wealthiest empire.

WASHINGTON'S *victories at Trenton and Princeton
(January, 1777), while important for morale, did not
alter British plans. In 1777 General Howe defeated
the Continental Army at Brandywine and occupied
Philadelphia, the American capital; at the same time,
General Burgoyne began a drive down the Hudson
Valley, only to be defeated by Gates and Arnold at
Saratoga later that year. Burgoyne's surrender undoubtedly encouraged the French to commit themselves to a military alliance with the new United
States in early 1778. They supplied the troops and
naval power that Washington badly needed, and their
example similarly encouraged Spain and Holland to
join the American cause. After the hard winter of
1777–78, spent by the Continentals at Valley Forge,
General Clinton, who had replaced Howe, shifted his
army to New York while Washington's troops waited
for his next move.*

*After 1778 most of the military action took place in
the South, where Loyalist feeling was strong and
American forces weak. The British captured Savannah that year and then in 1780 took Charleston;
in August, when Cornwallis defeated Gates' army at
Camden and took five thousand prisoners, the South
seemed lost. However, the destruction of Ferguson's
Loyalists at King's Mountain checked the British
advance and, coupled with the brilliant victory of
Daniel Morgan's frontiersmen at Cowpens in January, 1781, reversed the tide of British success.*

*The reading public of the earlier nineteenth cen-
tury expected history to be dramatic, a conflict of opposing forces personified in heroes and antagonists,
presented as a playwright might with due attention
to scenery, stagecraft, and extras. The historian, the
age assumed, imposed form and meaning on the flow
of events, finding dramatic tension, climax, and resolution in episodes he selected from the past. Bancroft wrote this kind of history extremely well, and
the British campaigns in the South in 1780 gave him
exactly the kind of materials and characters he needed
to write it—proud, cruel Cornwallis and his troops,
harried and confused by Marion and his sturdy frontier yeomen, defeated at King's Mountain, the Tories
disheartened, the invader finally forced to withdraw.*

Bancroft explains the episode's place in the larger strategy of the war, skilfully arranges and clarifies the details of this rather complex campaign, and analyzes the results, all the while without interrupting the swift current of his narrative.

Cornwallis and the Men of the South and West (1780)

FROM the moment of his victory near Camden, Cornwallis became the principal figure in the British service in America,— the pride and delight of Germain, the desired commander in chief, the one man on whom rested the hopes of the ministry for the successful termination of the war. His friends disparaged the ability of Sir Henry Clinton, accused him of hating his younger and more enterprising compeer, and censured him for leaving at the south forces disproportioned to the service for which they were required.

We are come to the series of events which closed the American contest and restored peace to the world. In Europe, the sovereigns of Prussia, of Austria, of Russia, were offering their mediation; the united Netherlands were struggling to preserve their neutrality; France was straining every nerve to cope with her rival in the four quarters of the globe; Spain was exhausting her resources for the conquest of Gibraltar; but the incidents which overthrew the ministry of North, and reconciled Great Britain to America, had their springs in South Carolina.

Cornwallis, elated with success and hope, prepared for the northward march, which was to conduct him from victory to victory, till he should restore all America south of Delaware to its allegiance. He was made to believe that North Carolina would rise to welcome him; and, in the train of his flatterers, he carried Martin, its former governor, who was to re-enter on his office. He requested Clinton to detach three thousand men to establish a post on the Chesapeake Bay; and Clinton knew too well the wishes of the British government to venture to refuse.

In carrying out his plan, the first measure of Cornwallis was a reign of terror. Professing to regard South Carolina as restored to the dominion of George III, he accepted the suggestions of Martin and Tarleton, and the like, that severity was the true mode to hold the recovered province. He therefore addressed the most stringent orders to the commandants at Ninety-Six and other posts, to imprison all who would not take up arms for the king, and to seize or destroy their whole property. He most positively enjoined that every militia-man who had borne arms with the British and had afterwards joined the Americans should be hanged immediately. He set up the gallows at Camden for the indiscriminate execution of those among his prisoners who had formerly given their parole, even when it had been kept till it was cancelled by the proclamation of Clinton. To bring these men to the gibbet was an act of military murder.

The destruction of property and life assumed still more hideous forms, when the peremptory orders and example of Cornwallis were followed by subordinates in remote districts away from supervision. Cruel measures seek and are sure to find cruel executive agents; officers whose delight was in blood patrolled the country, burned houses, ravaged estates, and put to death whom they would. The wives and daughters of the opulent were left with no fit clothing, no shelter but a hovel too mean to attract the destroyer. Of a sudden, the woodman in his cabin would find his house surrounded, and he himself or his guest might be shot, because he was not in arms for the king. There was no question of proofs and no trial. For two years, cold-blooded assassinations, often in the house of the victim and in the presence of his wife and little children, were perpetrated by men holding the king's commission; and they obtained not indemnity merely, but reward for their zeal. The enemy were determined to break every man's spirit, or to ruin him. No engagement by proclamation or by capitulation was respected.

The ruthless administration of Cornwallis met the hearty and repeated applause of Lord George Germain, who declared himself convinced that "to punish rebellion would have the best consequences." As to the rebels, his orders to Clinton and Cornwallis were: "No good faith or justice is to be expected from them, and we ought in all our transactions with them to act upon that supposition." In this manner, the minister released his generals from their pledges to those on whom they made war.

In violation of agreements, the continental soldiers who capitulated at Charleston, nineteen hundred in number, were transferred from buildings in the town to prison-ships, where they were joined by several hundred prisoners from Camden. In thirteen months, one-third of the whole number perished by malignant fevers; others were impressed into the British service as mariners; several hundred young men were taken by violence on board transports, and forced to serve in a British regiment in Jamaica, leaving wives and young children to want. Of more than three thousand confined in prison-ships, all but about seven hundred were made away with.

On the capitulation of Charleston, eminent patriots remained prisoners on parole. Foremost among these stood the aged Christopher Gadsden, whose unselfish love of country was a constant encouragement to his countrymen never to yield. Their silent example restrained the timid from exchanging their paroles for the protection of British subjects. To overcome this influence, eleven days after the victory at Camden, he, and thirty-six of his most resolute associates, in flagrant disregard of the conditions on which they had surrendered, were early in the morning taken from their houses and beds and transported to St. Augustine. Gadsden and others, refusing to give a new parole, were immured in the castle of St. Mark. After some weeks, a like cargo was shipped to the same place.

The system of slaveholding kept away from defensive service not only more than half the population, whom the planters would not suffer to be armed, but the numerous whites, needed to watch the black men, if they were to be kept in bondage while war was raging. Moreover, the moral force of their owners was

apt to become enervated. Men deriving their livelihood from
the labor of slaves ceased to respect labor, and shunned it as a
disgrace. Some had not the courage to face the idea of poverty
for themselves, still less for their wives and children. Many
fainted at the hard option between submission and ruin. Charles
Pinckney, lately president of the South Carolina senate, class-
ing himself among those who from the hurry and confusion of
the times had been misled, desired to show every mark of allegiance. Rawlins Lowndes, who but a few months before had
been president of the state of South Carolina, excused himself
for having reluctantly given way to necessity, and accepted
any test that might be required to prove that, with the unre-
strained dictates of his own mind, he now attached himself to
the royal government. Henry Middleton, president of the first
American congress, though still "partial to a cause for which
he had been so long engaged," promised to do nothing to keep
up the spirit of independence, and to demean himself as a faithful subject.

But the people of South Carolina were never conquered. From
the moment of the fall of Charleston, Colonel James Williams,
of the district of Ninety-Six, did not rest in gathering the armed
friends of the union. From the region above Camden, Sumter
and his band hovered over all British movements. "Sumter certainly has been our greatest plague in this country," writes
Corwallis.

In the swamps between the Pedee and the Santee, Marion and
his men kept watch. Of a delicate organization, sensitive to
truth and honor and right, humane, averse to bloodshed, never
wreaking vengeance nor suffering those around him to do so,
scrupulously respecting private property, he had the love and
confidence of all people in that part of the country. Tarleton's legion had laid it waste to inspire terror; and volunteer
partisans gathered round Marion to redeem their land.

A body of three hundred royalist militia and two hundred
regular troops had established a post at Musgrove's Mills on
the Enoree River. On the eighteenth of August, they were at-

tacked by inferior numbers under Williams of Ninety-Six, and routed, with sixty killed and more than that number wounded. Williams lost but eleven.

At dawn of the twentieth, a party, convoying a hundred and fifty prisoners of the Maryland line, were crossing the great savanna near Nelson's ferry over the Santee, upon the route from Camden to Charleston, when Marion and his men sprang upon the guard, liberated the prisoners, and captured twenty-six of the escort.

"Colonel Marion," wrote Cornwallis, "so wrought on the minds of the people that there was scarcely an inhabitant between the Pedee and the Santee that was not in arms against us. Some parties even crossed the Santee and carried terror to the gates of Charleston." Balfour, the commandant of Charleston, wrote home: "In vain we expected loyalty and attachment from the inhabitants; they are the same stuff as compose all Americans." The British historian of the war, who was then in South Carolina, relates that "almost the whole country seemed upon the eve of a revolt."

In the second week of September, when the heats of summer had abated, the earlier cereal grains had been harvested, and the maize was nearly ripe, Cornwallis began his projected march. He relied on the loyalists of North Carolina to recruit his army. On his left, Major Patrick Ferguson, the ablest British partisan, was sent with two hundred of the best troops to the uplands of South Carolina, where he enlisted young men of that country, loyalists who had fled to the mountains for security, and fugitives of the worst character who sought his standard for safety and the chances of plundering with impunity.

The Cherokees had been encouraged during the summer to join insurgent loyalists in ravaging the American settlements west of the mountains as far as Chiswell's lead mines. Against this danger, Jefferson organized, in the south-western counties of the state of which he was the governor, a regiment of four hundred backwoodsmen under the command of Colonel William Campbell, brother-in-law of Patrick Henry; and in an interview with William Preston, the lieutenant of Washington county, as the south-west of Virginia was then called, he dwelt on the resources of the country, the spirit of congress, and the character of the people; and for himself and for his state would admit no doubt that, in spite of all disasters, a continued vigorous resistance would bring the war to a happy issue.

At Waxhaw, Cornwallis halted for a few days, and, that he might eradicate the spirit of patriotism from South Carolina before he passed beyond its borders, he, on the sixteenth day of September, sequestered by proclamation all estates belonging to the friends of America, and appointed a commissioner for the seizure of such estates both real and personal. The concealment, removal, or injury of property doomed to confiscation, was punishable as an abetting of rebellion. The sequestration extended to debts due to the person whose possessions were confiscated; and, to prevent collusive practices, a great reward was offered to those who should make discovery of the concealment of negroes, horses, cattle, plate, household furniture, books, bonds, deeds, and other property. To patriots, no alternative was left but to fight against their country and their consciences, or to encounter exile and poverty.

The custom of military executions of Carolinians taken in arms was vigorously maintained, and the chiefs of the Cherokees were at that very time on their way to Augusta to receive the presents which were to stimulate their activity. Aware of their coming, Clark, a fugitive from Georgia, forced his way back with one hundred riflemen; having joined to them a body of woodsmen, he defeated the British garrison under Colonel Brown at Augusta, and captured the costly presents designed for the Cherokees. The moment was critical; for Cornwallis, in his eagerness to draw strength to his own army, had not left a post or a soldier between Augusta and Savannah, and the alienated people had returned most reluctantly to a state of obedience. With a corps of one hundred provincials and one hundred Cherokees, Brown maintained a position on Garden Hill for nearly a week, when he was rescued by Cruger from

Ninety-Six. At his approach, the Americans retired. On the pursuit, some of them were scalped and some taken prisoners. Of the latter, Captain Ashby and twelve others were hanged under the eyes of Brown; thirteen who were delivered to the Cherokees were killed by tortures, or by the tomahawk, or were thrown into fires. Thirty in all were put to death by the orders of Brown.

Cruger desired to waylay and capture the retreating party, and Ferguson eagerly accepted his invitation to join in the enterprise. Cruger moved with circumspection, taking care not to be led too far from the fortress of Ninety-Six; Ferguson was more adventurous, having always the army of Cornwallis on his right. Near the Broad River, his party encountered Macdowell with one hundred and sixty militia from Burk and Rutherford counties in North Carolina, pursued them to the foot of the mountains, and left them no chance of safety but by fleeing beyond the Alleghanies.

During these events, Cornwallis encountered no serious impediment till he approached Charlotte. There his van was driven back by the fire of a small body of mounted men, commanded by Colonel William Richardson Davie of North Carolina. The general rode up in person, and the American party was dislodged by Webster's brigade; but not till the mounted Americans, scarcely forty in number, had for several minutes kept the British army at bay.

From Charlotte, Cornwallis pursued his course towards Salisbury. Meantime, the fugitives under Macdowell recounted the sorrows of their families to the emigrant freemen on the Watauga, among whom slavery was scarcely known. The backwoodsmen, though remote from the world, love their fellowmen. In the pure air and life of the mountain and the forest, they join serenity with courage. They felt for those who had fled to them; with one heart, they resolved to restore the suppliants to their homes, and for that purpose formed themselves into regiments under Isaac Shelby and John Sevier. Shelby despatched a messenger to William Campbell on the forks of

Holston; and the field-officers of South-western Virginia unanimously resolved that he, with four hundred men, should join in the expedition. An express was sent to Colonel Cleaveland of North Carolina; and all were to meet at Burk county courthouse, on the waters of the Catawba. The three regiments from the west of the Alleghanies under Campbell, Shelby, and Sevier, and the North Carolina fugitives under Macdowell, assembled on the twenty-fifth of September at Watauga. On the next day, each man mounted on his own horse, armed with his own rifle, and carrying his own store of provisions, they began the ride over the mountains, where the passes through the Alleghanies are the highest. Not even a bridle-path led through the forest, nor was there a house for forty miles between the Watauga and the Catawba. The men left their families in secluded valleys, distant one from the other, exposed not only to parties of royalists, but of Indians. In the evening of the thirtieth, they formed a junction with the regiment of Colonel Benjamin Cleaveland, consisting of three hundred and fifty men from the North Carolina counties of Wilkes and Surry. The next day, Macdowell was despatched to request Gates to send them a general officer; "till he should arrive, Campbell was chosen to act as commandant."

Ferguson, who had pursued the party of Macdowell to the foot of the Alleghanies, and had spread the terror of invasion beyond them, moved eastwardly towards Cornwallis by a road from Buffalo ford to King's Mountain, which offered ground for a strong encampment. Of the parties against him, he thus wrote to Cornwallis: "They are become an object of consequence. I should hope for success against them myself; but, numbers compared, that must be doubtful. Three or four hundred good soldiers, part dragoons, would finish the business. Something must be done soon. This is their last push in this quarter."

On receiving this letter, Cornwallis ordered Tarleton to march with the light infantry, the British legion, and a three-pounder to his assistance.

At that time, Colonel James Williams was about seventy

miles from Salisbury, in the forks of the Catawba, with nearly four hundred and fifty horsemen, in pursuit of Ferguson. Wise and vigilant, he kept out scouts on every side; and, on the second of October, one of them "rejoiced his heart," by bringing him the news that one half of the whole population beyond the mountains were drawing near.

Following a path between King's Mountain and the main ridge of the Alleghanies, "the western army," so they called themselves, under Campbell, already more than thirteen hundred strong, marched on to the Cowpens on Broad River, where, on the evening of the sixth, they were joined by Williams with four hundred men. From Williams, they learned nearly where Ferguson's party was encamped; and a council of the principal officers decided to go that very night to strike them by surprise. For this end, they picked out nine hundred of their best horsemen; at eight o'clock on that same evening, they began their march. Riding all night, with the moon two days past its first quarter, on the afternoon of the seventh they were at the foot of King's Mountain.

The little brook that ripples through the narrow valley flows in an easterly direction. The mountain, which rises a mile and a half south of the line of North Carolina, is the termination of a ridge that branches from the north-west to the south-east from a spur of the Alleghanies. The British, in number eleven hundred and twenty-five, of whom one hundred and twenty-five were regulars, were posted on its summit, "confident that they could not be forced from so advantageous a post," to which the approach was precipitously steep, the slaty rock cropping out in craggy cliffs and forming natural breastworks along its sides and on its heights.

The Americans dismounted, and, though inferior in numbers, formed themselves into four columns. A part of Cleaveland's regiment, headed by Major Winston, and Colonel Sevier's regiment, formed a large column on the right wing. The other part of Cleaveland's regiment, headed by Cleaveland himself, and the regiment of Williams, composed the left wing. The post of extreme danger was assigned to the column formed by Campbell's regiment on the right centre, and Shelby's regiment on the left centre; so that Sevier's right nearly adjoined Shelby's left. The right and left wings were to pass the position of Ferguson, and from opposite sides climb the ridge in his rear; while the two central columns were to attack in front. In this order, "the western army" advanced to within a quarter of a mile of the enemy before they were discovered.

The two centre columns, headed by Campbell and Shelby, climbing the mountain, began the attack. Shelby, a man of the hardiest make, stiff as iron, among the dauntless singled out for dauntlessness, went right onward and upward like a man who had but one thing to do, and but one thought,—to do it. The British regulars with fixed bayonets charged Campbell; and his riflemen, who had no bayonets, were obliged to give way for a short distance; but "they were soon rallied by their gallant commander and some of his active officers," and "returned to the attack with additional ardor."

The two centre columns, with no aid but from a part of Sevier's regiment, kept up a furious and bloody battle with the British for ten minutes, when the right and left wings of the Americans, advancing upon their flank and rear, "the fire became general all around." For fifty-five minutes longer the fire on both sides was heavy and almost incessant. The regulars with bayonets could only make a momentary impression. At last, the right wing gained the summit of the eminence, and the position of the British was no longer tenable. Ferguson having been killed, the enemy attempted to retreat along the top of the ridge; but, finding themselves held in check by the brave men of Williams and Cleaveland, Captain Depeyster, the commanding officer of the British, hoisted a flag. The firing immediately ceased; the enemy laid down their arms and surrendered themselves prisoners at discretion.

The loss of the British on that day was at least eleven hundred and four. Four hundred and fifty-six of them were either killed, or too severely wounded to leave the ground; the number of prisoners was six hundred and forty-eight. On the Ameri-

can side, the regiment of Campbell suffered more than any
other in the action; the total loss was twenty-eight killed and
sixty wounded. Among those who fell was Colonel James Williams of Ninety-Six, a man of an exalted character, of a career
brief but glorious. An ungenerous enemy revenged themselves
for his virtues by nearly extirpating his family; they could not
take away his right to be remembered by his country with
honor and affection to the latest time.

Among the captives there were house-burners and assassins.
Private soldiers—who had witnessed the sorrows of children
and women, robbed and wronged, shelterless, stripped of all
clothes but those they wore, nestling about fires kindled on the
ground, and mourning for their fathers and husbands—executed
nine or ten in retaliation for the frequent and barbarous use of
the gallows at Camden, Ninety-Six, and Augusta; but Campbell at once intervened, and in general orders, by threatening
the delinquents with certain and effectual punishment, secured
protection to the prisoners.

Just below the forks of the Catawba, the tidings of the defeat reached Tarleton; his party in all haste rejoined Cornwallis.
The victory at King's Mountain, which in the spirit of the
American soldiers was like the rising at Concord, in its effects
like the successes at Bennington, changed the aspect of the
war. The loyalists of North Carolina no longer dared rise. It
fired the patriots of the two Carolinas with fresh zeal. It encouraged the fragments of the defeated and scattered American
army to seek each other and organize themselves anew. It
quickened the North Carolina legislature to earnest efforts. It
encouraged Virginia to devote her resources to the country
south of her border. The appearance on the frontiers of a numerous enemy from settlements beyond the mountains, whose
very names had been unknown to the British, took Cornwallis
by surprise, and their success was fatal to his intended expedition. He had hoped to step with ease from one Carolina to
the other, and from these to the conquest of Virginia; and he
had now no choice but to retreat.

On the evening of the fourteenth, his troops began their

march back form Charlotte to the Catawba ford. The men of Mecklenburg and Rowan counties had disputed his advance; they now harassed his foraging parties, intercepted his despatches, and cut off his communications. Soldiers of the militia hung on his rear. Twenty wagons were captured, laden with stores and the knapsacks of the light infantry legion. Single men would ride within gunshot of the retreating army, discharge their rifles, and escape.

The Catawba ford was crossed with difficulty on account of a great fall of rain. For two days, the royal forces remained in the Catawba settlement, Cornwallis suffering from fever, the army from want of forage and provisions. The command on the retreat fell to Rawdon. The soldiers had no tents. For several days, it rained incessantly. Waters and deep mud choked the roads. At night, the army bivouacked in the woods in unwholesome air. Sometimes, it was without meat; at others, without bread. For five days it lived upon Indian corn gathered from the fields, five ears being the day's allowance for two soldiers. But for the personal exertions of the militia, most of whom were mounted, the army would not have been supported in the field; and yet, in return for their exertions, they were treated with derision and even beaten by insolent British officers. After a march of fifteen days, the army encamped at Winnsborough, an intermediate station between Camden and Ninety-Six.

All the while Marion had been on the alert. Two hundred tories had been sent in September to surprise him; and with but fifty-three men he first surprised a part of his pursuers, and then drove the main body to flight.

At Black Mingo, on the twenty-eighth, he made a successful attack on a guard of sixty militia, and took prisoners those who were under its escort. The British were burning houses on Little Pedee, and he permitted his men of that district to return to protect their wives and families; but he would not suffer retaliation, and wrote with truth: "There is not one house burned by my orders or by any of my people. It is what I detest, to distress poor women and children."

"I most sincerely hope you will get at Mr. Marion," wrote Cornwallis on the fifth of November, as he despatched Tarleton in pursuit of him. This officer and his corps set fire to all the houses, and destroyed all the corn from Camden down to Nelson's ferry; beat the widow of a general officer because she could not tell where Marion was encamped, burned her dwelling, laid waste every thing about it, and did not leave her a change of raiment. The line of his march could be traced by groups of houseless women and children, once of ample fortune, sitting round fires in the open air.

As for Marion, after having kept his movements secret, and varied his encampment every night, his numbers increased; then selecting a strong post "within the dark morass," he defied an attack. But just at that moment new dangers impended from another quarter.

Sumter had rallied the patriots in the country above Camden, and in frequent skirmishes kept the field. Mounting his partisans, he intercepted British supplies of all sorts, and sent parties within fourteen miles of Winnsborough. Having ascertained the number and position of his troops, Cornwallis despatched a party under Major Wemyss against him. After a march of twenty-four miles with mounted infantry, Wemyss reached Fishdam on Broad River, the camp of General Sumter, and at the head of his corps charged the picket. The attack was repelled; he himself was wounded and taken prisoner. A memorandum was found upon him of houses burned by his command. He had hanged Adam Cusack, a Carolinian, who had neither given his parole nor accepted protection nor served in the patriot army; yet his captors would not harm a man who was their prisoner.

The position of the British in the upper country became precarious. Tarleton was suddenly recalled from the pursuit of Marion, and ordered to take the nearest path against Sumter, who had passed the Broad River, formed a junction with Clark and Brennan, and threatened Ninety-Six. One regiment was sent forward to join him on his march; another followed for his support. Apprised of Tarleton's approach, Sumter posted himself strongly on the plantation of Blackstock. At five in the afternoon of the twentieth of November, Tarleton drew near in advance of his light infantry; and with two hundred and fifty mounted men he made a precipitate attack on Sumter's superior force. The hillside in front of the Americans was steep; their rear was protected by the rapid river Tyger; their left was covered by a large barn of logs, between which the riflemen coul fire with security. The sixty-third British regiment having lost its commanding officer, two lieutenants, and one third of its privates, Tarleton retreated, leaving his wounded to the mercy of the victor. The loss of Sumter was very small; but, being himself disabled by a severe wound, he crossed the Tyger, taking his wounded men with him.

By the lavish distribution of presents, the Indian agents obtained promises from the chiefs of twenty-five hundred Cherokees, and a numerous body of Creeks, to lay waste the settlements on the Watauga, Holston, Kentucky, and Nolichucky, and even to extend their ravages to the Cumberland and Green Rivers, that the attention of the mountaineers might be diverted to their own immediate concerns. Moreover, Cornwallis gave orders to the re-enforcement of three thousand sent by Clinton into the Chesapeake to embark for Cape Fear River. So ended the first attempt of Cornwallis to penetrate to Virginia. He was driven back by the spontaneous risings of the southern and south-western people; and the unwholesome exhalations of autumn swept men from every garrison in the low country faster than Great Britain could replace them.

BANCROFT *decided quite early that the institution of slavery was dangerous to stable, republican government, and before he began writing the* History, *he published two essays ascribing the decline of Athens and Rome in large part to slavery's effects. In writing the* History, *however, he faced the difficult problem of explaining how slavery had developed within a society predicated on human freedom and how that institution had survived and prospered within a political system designed to secure each individual's natural rights. In Volume I he placed the responsibility for planting slavery in the colonies on England, explaining that the colonists, following "the customs and morals of the age,", accepted it as a solution to severe labor shortages rather than as a permanent part of colonial life. Public sentiment in most colonies, he wrote in Volume III, was opposed to slavery in principle but recognized it as a means of controlling social situations involving races at widely different cultural levels: "Every colony favored freedom as such. The real question at issue was from the first, not one of slavery and freedom generally, but of the relation to each other of the Ethiopian and Anglo-Saxon races." Later, Bancroft wrote, when economic reasons for slaveholding were less urgent, the colonies were prevented from abolishing the system "by the government of the mother country, under the influence of mercantile avarice, with the further purpose of weakening the rising colonies." By 1874, when he began work on the tenth and final volume of the* History, *Bancroft had developed an explanation which he believed would not only explain the relationship between slavery and states' rights (and the late war) but also fit plausibly into the grand design of his historical thesis. As the North and South developed along with different economic and social lines, coming "to represent different classes of culture and ideas and interests," he wrote, slavery became more and more important to the South. To protect and maintain the institution, the South seized upon the states' rights doctrine, latent in American political life since the beginnings, and made it, like slavery, a vital element in southern thought. "I have been able from new materials to trace the division between the*

North and South, arising from slavery," he said in
the preface to Volume X, "further back than had as
yet been done. As to separatism, or the exaggerated
expression of what we call States' Rights, it did not
grow out of the existence of slavery, but out of an
element in human nature." Although Bancroft's
narrative did not reach the nineteenth century, his
readers could, from his explanation of slavery and
states' rights, project for themselves his version of
the historical background of the Civil War.

The Rise of Free Commonwealths (1780)

FREEDOM is of all races and of all nationalities. It is older than
bondage, and ever rises from the enslavements laid on by the
hand of violence or custom or abuse of power; for the rights of
man spring from eternal law, are kept alive by the persistent
energy of constant nature, and by their own indestructibility
prove their lineage as the children of omnipotence.

In an edict of the eighth of August, 1779, Louis XVI announced "his regret that many of his subjects were still without personal liberty and the prerogatives of property, attached
to the glebe, and, so to say, confounded with it." To all serfs
on the estates of the crown he therefore gave back their freedom. It was his wish to do away, as with torture, so with every
vestige of a rigorous feudalism; but he was restrained by his
respect for the laws of property, which he held to be the ground-
work of order and justice. The delivering up of a runaway serf
was in all cases forbidden; for emancipation outside of his own
domains, he did no more than give leave to other proprietors to
follow his example, to which, from mistaken selfishness, even
the clergy would not conform. But the words of the king spoken
to all France deeply branded the wrong of keeping Frenchmen
in bondage to Frenchmen.

Vol. VI, Chap. XLVI.

In Overyssel, a province of the Netherlands, Baron van der Capellen tot den Pol, the friend of America, had seen with the deepest sorrow the survival of the ancient system of villeinage; and, in spite of the resistance and sworn hatred of almost all the nobles, he, in 1782, brought about its complete abolition.

Here the movement for emancipation during the American revolution ceased for the Old World. "He that says slavery is opposed to Christianity is a liar," wrote Luther in the sixteenth century. "The laws of all nations sanction slavery; to condemn it is to condemn the Holy Ghost," were the words of Bossuet near the end of the seventeenth. In the last quarter of the eighteenth, the ownership of white men by white men still blighted more than the half of Europe. The evil shielded itself under a new plea, where a difference of skin set a visible mark on the victims of commercial avarice, and strengthened the ties of selfishness by the pride of race. In 1780, Edmund Burke tasked himself to find out what laws could check the new form of servitude which wrapt all quarters of the globe in its baleful influences; yet he did not see a glimmering of hope even for an abolition of the trade in slaves, and only aimed at establishing regulations for their safe and comfortable transportation. He was certain that no one of them was ever so beneficial to the master as a freeman who deals with him on equal footing by convention, that the consumer in the end is always the dupe of his own tyranny and injustice; yet for slave plantations he suggested nothing more than some supervision by the state, and some mitigation of the power of the master to divide families by partial sales. For himself, he inclined to a gradual emancipation; yet his code for the negroes was founded on the conviction that slavery was "an incurable evil." He sought no more than to make that evil as small as possible, and to draw out of it some collateral good.

George III was the firm friend of the slave-trade; and Thurlow, one of his chancellors, so late as 1799 insisted that the proposal to terminate it was "altogether miserable and contemptible." Yet the quality of our kind is such that a government cannot degrade a race without marring the nobleness of our nature.

So long as the legislation of the several English colonies in America remained subject to the veto of the king, all hope of forbidding or even limiting the importation of negro slaves was made vain by the mother country. Now that they were independent the end of slavery might come either from the central government or from the several states.

We have seen that the first congress formed an association "wholly to discontinue the slave-trade," and that the denunciation of the slave-trade and of slavery by Jefferson, in his draft of the declaration of independence, was rejected by the congress of 1776, in deference to South Carolina and Georgia.

The antagonism between the northern and southern states, founded on climate, pursuits, and labor, broke out on the first effort to unite them permanently. When members from the north spoke freely of the evils of slavery, a member from South Carolina answered that, "if property in slaves should be questioned, there must be an end of confederation." In the same month, the vote on taxing persons claimed as property laid bare the existence of a territorial division of parties; the states north of Mason and Dixon's line voting compactly on the one side, and those south of that line, which were duly represented, on the other.

The clashing between the two sections fastened the attention of reflecting observers. In August, 1778, soon after the reception at Philadelphia of an envoy from France, he reported to Vergennes: "The states of the south and of the north, under existing subjects of division and estrangement, are two distinct parties, which at present count but few deserters. The division is attributed to moral and philosophical causes." He further reported that the cabal against Washington found supporters exclusively in the north.

The French minister desired to repress the ambition of congress for the acquisition of territory, because it might prove an obstacle to connection with Spain; and he found support in northern men. Their hatred of slavery was not an impulse of feeling, but an earnest conviction. No one could declare himself more strongly for the freedom of the negro than Gouverneur Morris of New York, a man of business and a man of pleasure. His hostility to slavery brought him into some agreement with the policy of Gerard, to whom, one day in October, he said that Spain would have no cause to fear the great body of the confederation, for reciprocal jealousy and separate interests would never permit its members to unite against her; that several of the most enlightened of his colleagues were struck with the necessity of establishing a law *de coercendo imperio,* setting bounds to their jurisdiction; that the provinces of the south already very much weakened the confederation; that further extension on that side would immeasurably augment this inconvenience; that the south was the seat of wealth and weakness; that the poverty and vigor of the north would always be the safeguard of the republic; and that on this side lay the necessity to expand and to gain strength; that the navigation of the Mississippi below the mouth of the Ohio should belong exclusively to Spain, as the only means of retaining the numerous population which would be formed between the Ohio and the lakes; that the inhabitants of these new and immense countries, be they English or be they Americans, having the outlet of the river St. Lawrence on the one side and that of the Mississippi on the other, would be in a condition to domineer over the United States and over Spain, or to make themselves independent,—that on this point there was, therefore, a common interest. Some dread of the relative increase of the south may have mixed with the impatient earnestness with which two at least of the New England states demanded the acquisition of Nova Scotia as indispensable to their safety, and therefore to be secured at the pacification with England. The leader in this policy was Samuel Adams, whom the French minister always found in his way.

The question of recruiting the army by the enlistment of black men forced itself on attention. The several states em-

ployed them as they pleased, and the slave was enfranchised
by the service. Once congress touched on the delicate subject;
and in March, 1779, it recommended Georgia and South Carolina to raise three thousand active, able-bodied negro men
under thirty-five years of age; and the recommendation was
coupled with a promise of "a full compensation to the proprietors of such negroes for the property." The resolution appears to have been adopted without opposition, North and
South Carolina having both been represented in the committee
that reported it. But South Carolina refused by great majorities to give effect to the scheme.

So long as Jefferson was in congress, he kept Virginia and
Massachusetts in a close and unselfish union, of which the
unanimous assertion of independence was the fruit. When he
withdrew to service in his native commonwealth, their friendship lost something of its disinterestedness. Virginia manifested its discontent by successive changes in its delegation,
and the two great states came more and more to represent different classes of culture and ideas and interests. On observing
congress thus "rent by party," Washington "raised his voice
and called upon George Mason and Jefferson to come forth to
save their country."

In 1779, when the prosperity of New England was thought
to depend on the fisheries, and when its pathetic appeals, not
unmingled with menaces, had been used prodigally and without effect, Samuel Adams said rashly that "it would become
more and more necessary for the two empires to separate." On
the other hand, when the north offered a preliminary resolution, that the country, even if deserted by France and Spain,
would continue the war for the sake of the fisheries, we have
seen four states read the draft of a protest declaring peremptorily that, if the resolution should be adopted, they would
withdraw from the confederation.

In the assertion of the sovereignty of each separate state,
there was no distinction between north and south. Massachu-

setts expressed itself as absolutely as South Carolina. As a consequence, the confederation could contain no interdict of the slave-trade, and the importation of slaves would therefore remain open to any state according to its choice. When on the seventeenth of June, 1179, a renunciation of the power to engage in the slave-trade was proposed as an article to be inserted in the treaty of peace, all the states, Georgia alone being absent, refused the concession by the votes of every member except Jay and Gerry.

Luzerne, the French envoy who succeeded Gerard, soon came to the conclusion that the confederacy would run the risk of an early dissolution if it should give itself up to the hatred which began to show itself between the north and south.

Vermont, whose laws from the first rejected slavery, knocked steadily at the door of congress to be taken in as a state. In August, 1781, its envoys were present in Philadelphia, entreating admission. Their papers were in order; New York gave up its opposition; but the states of the south held that the admission of Vermont would destroy "the balance of power" between the two sections of the confederacy, and give the preponderance to the north. The idea was then started that the six states south of Mason and Dixon's line should be conciliated by a concession of a seventh vote which they were to exercise in common; but the proposal, though it formed a subject of conversation, was never brought before congress; and Vermont was left to wait till a southern state could simultaneously be received into the union.

In regard to the foreign relations of the country, congress was divided between what the French envoy named "Gallicans" and "anti-Gallicans:" the southerners were found more among the "Gallicans;" the north was suspected of a partiality for England.

There was no hope of the delivery of the country from slavery by congress. It was but a minority of them who kept in mind that an ordinance of man can never override natural law, and that in the high court of the Eternal Providence justice forges her weapon long before she strikes. What part was chosen by each separate state must be recounted.

Nowhere was slavery formally established in the organic law as a permanent social relation; the courts of Virginia did not recognise a right of property in the future increase of slaves; in no one state did its constitution abridge the power of its legislature to abolish slavery. In no one constitution did the words "slave" and "slavery" find a place, except in that of Delaware, and there only by way of a formal and perpetual prohibition. They are found as little in that of South Carolina, which was the champion of negro bondage, as in that of Massachusetts.

In the north, the severity of the climate, the poverty of the soil, and the all-pervading habit of laborious industry among its people, set narrow limits to slavery; in the states nearest the tropics, it throve luxuriously, and its influence entered into their inmost political life. Virginia, with soil and temperature and mineral wealth inviting free and skilled labor, yet with lowland where the negro attained his perfect physical development, stood as mediator between the two. Many of her statesmen—George Mason, Patrick Henry, Jefferson, Wythe, Pendleton, Richard Henry Lee—emulated each other in confessing the iniquity and the inexpediency of holding men in bondage. We have seen the legislature of colonial Virginia in 1772, in their fruitless battle with the king respecting the slave-trade, of which he was the great champion, demand its abolition as needful for their happiness and their very existence. In January, 1773, Patrick Henry threw ridicule on the clergy of Virginia for their opposition to emancipation. In the same year, George Mason foretold the blight that was to avenge negro slavery.

When the convention of Virginia adopted their declaration of rights as the foundation of government for themselves and their posterity, they set forth that all men are by nature equally free and have inherent rights to the enjoyment of life and liberty, the means of acquiring property and pursuing happiness; yet the authoritative proclamation of the equal rights of all men brought no relief to the enslaved.

In 1778, Virginia prohibited what, under the supremacy of England, she could not have prohibited,—the introduction of any slave by land or sea, and ordered the emancipation of every slave introduced from abroad. But the bill respecting resident slaves, prepared by the commissioners for codifying the laws, was a mere digest of existing enactments. Its authors agreed in wishing that the assembly might provide by amendment for universal freedom; and it is the testimony of Jefferson that an amendatory bill was prepared with the concurrence of himself, Pendleton, and Wythe, "to emancipate all slaves born after passing the act;" but the proposal was blended with the idea of their deportation, and nothing came of it. The statute drafted by Jefferson, and in 1779 proposed by Mason, to define who shall be citizens of Virginia, declared the natural right of expatriation in opposition to the English assertion of perpetual allegiance, and favored naturalization; but it confined the right of expatriation and citizenship to white men.

In 1780, Madison expressed the wish that black men might be set free and then made to serve in the army. This was often done by individuals; but, before the end of the same year, Virginia offered a bounty, not of money and lands only, but of a negro, to each white man who would enlist for the war.

In May, 1782, just thirteen years after Jefferson had brought a bill giving power of unconditional emancipation to the masters of slaves, the measure was adopted by the legislature of Virginia. Under this act, more slaves received their freedom than were liberated in Pennsylvania or in Massachusetts. Even had light broken in on Jefferson's mind through the gloom in which the subject was involved for him, Virginia would not have accepted from him a plan for making Virginia a free commonwealth; but there is no evidence that he ever reconciled himself to the idea of emancipated black men living side by side with white men as equal sharers in political rights and

duties and powers. The result of his efforts and reflections he
uttered in these ominous forebodings: "Nothing is more certainly written in the book of fate than that these people are to
be free; nor is it less certain that the two races, equally free,
cannot live in the same government."

In the helplessness of despair Jefferson, so early as 1782,
dismissed the problem from his thoughts, with these words:
"I tremble for my country when I reflect that God is just, that
his justice cannot sleep for ever. The way, I hope, is preparing, under the auspices of Heaven, for a total emancipation."

At that time, Washington was a kind and considerate master
of slaves, without as yet a title to the character of an abolition-
ist. By slow degrees, the sentiment grew up in his mind that
to hold men in bondage was a wrong; that Virginia should proceed to emancipation by general statute of the state; that, if
she refused to do so, each individual should act for his own
household.

Next in order comes Delaware, which on the twentieth of
September, 1776, adopted its constitution as an independent
state. In proportion to its numbers, it had excelled all in the
voluntary emancipation of slaves. Its constitution absolutely
prohibited the introduction of any slave from Africa, or any
slave for sale from any part of the world, as an article which
"ought never to be violated on any pretence whatever."

In the constituent convention of New York Gouverneur
Morris struggled hard for measures tending to abolish domestic slavery, "so that in future ages every human being, who
breathed the air of the state, might enjoy the privileges of a
freeman." The proposition, though strongly supported, especially by the interior and newer counties, was lost by the vote
of the counties on the Hudson. "The constitution," wrote Jay,
on its adoption in 1777, "is like a harvest cut before it is ripe;
the grain has shrunk;" and he lamented the want of a clause
against the continuance of domestic slavery. Still, the declaration of independence was incorporated into the constitution
of New York; and all its great statesmen were abolitionists.

It has already been narrated that, in 1777, the people of Vermont, in separating themselves from the jurisdiction of New York, framed a constitution which prohibited slavery.

In July, 1778, William Livingston, the governor of New Jersey, invited the assembly to lay the foundation for the manumission of the negroes. At the request of the house, which thought the situation too critical for the immediate discussion of the measure, the message was withdrawn. "But I am determined," wrote the governor, "as far as my influence extends, to push the matter till it is effected, being convinced that the practice is utterly inconsistent with the principles of Christianity and humanity; and in Americans, who have almost idolized liberty, peculiarly odious and disgraceful." Of the two Jerseys, slavery had struck deeper root in the East from the original policy of its proprietaries; the humane spirit of the Society of Friends ruled opinion in West Jersey.

The name of Pennsylvania was dear throughout the world as the symbol of freedom; her citizens proved her right to her good report by preparing to abolish slavery. The number of their slaves had grown to be about six thousand, differing little from the number in Massachusetts, and being in proportion to the whole population much less than in New York or in New Jersey. The fourteenth of April, 1775, was the day of founding the Pennsylvania society for promoting the abolition of slavery, the relief of free negroes unlawfully held in bondage, and for improving the condition of the African race. In 1777, in the heads of a bill proposed by the council, a suggestion was made for ridding the state of slavery. The retreat of the British from Philadelphia, and the restoration to Pennsylvania of peace within its borders called forth in its people a sentiment of devout gratitude. Under its influence, George Bryan, then vice-president, in a message to the assembly of the ninth of November, 1778, pressed upon their attention the bill proposed in the former year for manumitting infant negroes born of slaves, and thus in an easy mode abrogating slavery, the opprobrium of America. "In divesting the state of slaves," said Bryan, "you will equally serve the cause of humanity and policy, and offer to God one of the most proper and best returns of gratitude for his great deliverance of us and our posterity from thraldom; you will also set your character for justice and benevolence in the true point of view to all Europe, who are astonished to see a people struggling for liberty holding negroes in bondage."

On becoming president of the executive council of Pennsylvania, Joseph Reed, speaking for himself and the council, renewed the recommendation to abolish slavery gradually and to restore and establish by the law in Pennsylvania the rights of human nature. In the autumn of 1779, George Bryan had been returned as a member of the assembly. In the committee to which on his motion the subject was referred, he prepared a new preamble and the draft of the law for gradual emancipation; and on the twenty-ninth of February, 1780, it was adopted by a vote of thirty-four to twenty-one. So Pennsylvania led the way towards introducing freedom for all. "Our bill," wrote George Bryan to Samuel Adams, "astonishes and pleases the Quakers. They looked for no such benevolent issue of our new government, exercised by Presbyterians." The Friends, well pleased at the unexpected law, became better reconciled to the form of government by which they had been grievously disfranchised.

The constitution of South Carolina of 1778 contained no bill of rights, and confined political power exclusively to white men; from the settlement of the state, slavery formed a primary element in its social organization. When Governor Rutledge in 1780 came to Philadelphia, he reported that the negroes, who in the low country outnumbered the whites as six to one, offered up their prayers in favor of England, in the hope that she would give them a chance to escape from slavery. But British officers, regarding negroes as valuable spoil, defeated every plan for employing them as soldiers on the side of England. In 1769, George III in council "gave his consent to an act of Georgia, whereby slaves may be declared to be chattels;" and the war of the revolution made no change in their condition by law.

The Puritans of Massachusetts and their descendants, though they tolerated slavery, held that slaves had rights. Negroes trained with the rest of the ranks, certainly from 1651 to 1656. Laws on marriage and against adultery were applied to them; and they were allowed, like others, to give their testimony, even in capital cases. At the opening of the revolution, William Gordon, the Congregationalist minister of Roxbury, though he declined to "unsaint" every man who still yielded to the prevailing prejudice, declared with others against perpetuating slavery, and in November, 1776, published in the "Independent Chronicle" a plan sent from Connecticut for its gradual extermination out of that colony. In the same month and in the same newspaper, "a Son of Liberty" demanded the repeal of all laws supporting slavery, because they were "contrary to sound reason and revelation." In January, 1777, seven negro slaves joined in petitioning the general court "that they might be restored to that freedom which is the natural right of all men, and that their children might not be held as slaves after they arrive at the age of twenty-one years." This petition was referred to a very able committee, on which are the names of Sergeant and John Lowell, both zealous abolitionists, the latter then the leading lawyer in the state.

In May, 1777, just before the meeting of the general court at Boston, Gordon, finding in the multiplicity of business the only apology for their not having attended to the case of slaves, as a preliminary to total emancipation asked for a final stop to the public and private sale of them by an act of the state. Clothing the argument of Montesquieu in theological language, he said: "If God hath made of one blood all nations of men for to dwell on the face of the earth, I can see no reason why a black rather than a white man should be a slave." A few weeks later, the first legislature elected in Massachusetts after the declaration of independence listened to the second reading of a bill which declared slavery "without justification in a government of which the people are asserting their natural rights to freedom," and had for its object "to fix a day on which all persons above twenty-one years of age then held in slavery should be free and entitled to all the rights, privileges, and immunities that belong to any of the subjects of this state." A committee was directed to take the opinion of congress on the subject, but no answer from congress appears on record, nor any further consideration of the bill by the Massachusetts legislature.

In his presidency, Hancock had shown proclivities to the south. When on his resignation in October a motion was made to give him the thanks of congress for his impartiality in office, the three northernmost states of New England voted in the negative, while the south was unanimous in his favor. After his arrival in Boston, the two branches of the general court saw fit to form themselves into a constituent convention, for which some of the towns had given authority to their representatives. In the winter session of 1778, the draft of a plan of government was considered. One of the proposed clauses took from Indians, negroes, and mulattoes the right to vote. Against this disfranchisement was cited the example of Pennsylvania, which gave the suffrage to all freemen. "Should the clause not be reprobated by the convention," said an orator, "I still hope that there will be found among the people at large virtue enough to trample under foot a form of government which thus saps the foundation of civil liberty and tramples on the rights of man."

On the submission of the constitution to the people, objections were made that it contained no declaration of rights; that it gave the governor and lieutenant-governor seats in the senate; that it disfranchised the free negro, a partiality warmly denounced through the press by the historian, William Gordon. There was, moreover, dissatisfaction with the legislature for having assumed constituent powers without authority from the people. Boston, while it recommended a convention for framing a constitution, gave its vote unanimously against the work of the legislature; and the commonwealth rejected it by a vote of five to one.

The history of the world contains no record of a people which in the institution of its government moved with the caution which now marked the proceedings of Massachusetts. In February, 1779, the legislature of the year asked their constituents whether they desired a new form of government; and, a large majority of the inhabitants of the towns voting in the affirmative, a convention of delegates was elected for the sole purpose of forming a constitution. On the first day of September, the convention thus chosen came together in the meeting-house of Cambridge. Their forefathers, in their zeal against the Roman superstition, had carried their reverence of the Bible even to idolatry; and some of them, like Luther, found in its letter a sanction for holding slaves. On the other hand, from principle and habit, they honored honest labor in all its forms. The inconsistencies of bondage with the principle of American independence lay in the thoughts of those who led public opinion; voice against it had come from Essex, from Worcester, from Boston, from the western counties, showing that the conscience of the people was offended by its continuance.

The first act of the constituent body was "the consideration of a declaration of rights;" and then they resolved unanimously "that the government to be framed by this convention for the people of Massachusetts Bay shall be a free republic." This resolution was deemed so important that liberty was reserved for the members of a committee who were absent to record their votes upon it; and on the next morning they declared "their full and free assent." A committee of thirty, composed for the commonwealth at large and for each county excepting the unrepresented counties of Dukes and Nantucket, was appointed to prepare a declaration of rights and the form of a constitution; but the house itself continued its free conversation on these subjects till sunset of the sixth of September. The next day, it adjourned for more than seven weeks, that its committee might have time to transact the important business assigned them.

On the thirteenth of September, the committee assembled at the new court-house in Boston. Among them were Bowdoin, who was president of the convention; Samuel Adams; John Lowell; Jonathan Jackson, of Newburyport, who thought that the liberty which America achieved for itself should prevail without limitation as to color; Parsons, a young lawyer of the greatest promise, from Newburyport; and Strong, of Northampton. John Adams had arrived opportunely from France, to which he did not return till November; and was so far the "principal" agent in writing out the first draft of the constitution that it was reputed to be his work. There are no means of distributing its parts to their several authors with certainty. No one was more determined for two branches of the legislature with a veto in the governor than John Adams. To him also more than to any other may be ascribed the complete separation of both branches from appointments to office. The provisions for the total abolition of slavery mark the influence of John Lowell. To Bowdoin was due the form of some of the sections which were most admired.

On the afternoon of the twenty-eighth of October, the committee appointed to prepare a form of government reported a draft of a constitution; and on the next day the convention adopted the first article of a declaration of rights, which was couched in the spirit and almost in the language of George Mason and Virginia: "All men are born free and equal, and have certain natural, essential, and unalienable rights, among which may be reckoned the right of enjoying and defending their lives and liberties; that of acquiring, possessing, and protecting property; in fine, that of seeking and obtaining their safety and happiness." The lawyers of Virginia had not considered this declaration as of itself working the emancipation of negro slaves; to accomplish that end, the men of Massachusetts, in deciding how many of their old laws should remain in full force, excepted those parts which were "repugnant to the rights and liberties contained in this constitution."

As the delegates gave the closest attention to every line and word in the constitution, this clause did not come up for consideration till the last day of January, 1780, in an adjourned session. Roads having been made for a time impassable by deep snows, there were still many absentees; and, though a quorum was present, the consideration of this question was from its importance deferred. For a month, therefore, other clauses were discussed and settled; and, then in full convention, after deliberation and amendment, this most momentous article of all was adopted. So calm and effortless was the act by which slavery fell away from Massachusetts. Its people wrought with the power of nature, which never toils, never employs violence in arms, but achieves its will through the might of overruling law. There is in the world a force tending to improvement, and making itself felt in us and around us, with which we can work, but which it is above our ability to call into being or to destroy. The manner in which Massachusetts left slavery behind, as of the dead and irrevocable past, was the noblest that could have been devised. The inborn, inalienable right of man to freedom was written in the permanent constitution as the law of all coming legislation. The highest voice of morality speaks to the whole universe of moral being, and utters for all its one inflexible command. When by its all-persuasive force the men of Massachusetts abolished slavery, the decision had the character of primal justice and the seal of undying authority. Yet, had they remained dependent, the veto of the British king would have forbidden their abolition of slavery, as it had prevented every measure against the slave-trade.

In an able address to their constituents, the delegates explained the grounds on which their decisions rested, and called on them in their several towns and plantations to judge "whether they had raised their superstructure upon the principles of a free commonwealth." Reassembling on the first Wednesday in June, they found that the male inhabitants of twenty-one years and upwards had ratified the new constitution, and they chose the last Wednesday in October for the time on which it should take effect.

At the coming in of the twenty-fifth day of October, 1780, Massachusetts became in truth a free commonwealth. Its people shook slavery from its garments as something that had never belonged to it. The colored inhabitants, about six thousand in number, or one in seventy of the population, equally became fellow-citizens; and, if any of them possessed the required qualifications of age, residence, and property, their right to vote admitted of no question.

As to the rights of conscience, it was agreed that "religion must at all times be a matter between God and individuals;" yet all were excluded from office who believed that a foreign prelate could have a dispensing power within the commonwealth, and who would not "disclaim those principles of spiritual jurisdiction which are subversive of a free government established by the people." The legislature and magistrates were charged to cherish literature and the sciences, and all seminaries of them, especially the university at Cambridge, public schools, and grammar schools in the towns. The constitution was marked by the effort at a complete separation of the executive, legislative, and judicial powers, that it might be a government of laws and not of men. "For a power without any restraint," said the convention, "is tyranny."

"The constitution of Massachusetts," wrote Count Matthieu Dumas, one of the French officers who served in America, "is perhaps the code of laws which does most honor to man."

As if to leave to the world a record of the contrast between the contending systems of government for colonists, the British ministry, simultaneously with the people of Massachusetts, engaged in forming its model. The part of Massachusetts between the river Saco and the St. Croix was constituted a province, under the name of New Ireland. The system adopted for Quebec and for East Florida was to receive in the New England province its full development. The marked feature of the constitution was the absolute power of the British parliament; and, to make this power secure for all coming time, every landlord on acquiring land, whether by grant from the crown, or by purchase, or by inheritance, was bound to make a test declaration of allegiance to the king in his parliament, as the supreme legislature of the province. The attorney and the solicitor general of Great Britain were to report what of the laws of England would of their own authority take effect in the province, and what acts of parliament the king might introduce by his proclamation. "It has been found," said the state paper, "by sad experience, that the democratic power is predominant in all parts of British America." "To combat the prevailing disposition of the people to republicanism," there was to be by the side of the governor and council no elective assembly until the circumstances of the province should admit of it; but a middle branch of legislature, of which every one of the members was to be named by the crown, to be distinguished by titles or emoluments, or both; and, though otherwise appointed for life, to remain ever liable to be suspended or removed by royal authority.

As a farther security to aristocratic power, the lands were to be granted in large tracts, so that there might be great landlords and a tenantry. The church of England was to be the established church; the country to be divided into parishes, each with a glebe land; and the governor, the highest judge in the ecclesiastical court, to present to all benefices. A vicar-general with a power to ordain was to open the way for a bishop. No provision was made for the establishment of schools or the education of the people. This constitution was approved by the cabinet on the tenth of August, 1780, and on the next day by the king. Pleased with their work, the ministers judged the proper time might have come to digest a system of government for all America.

Here were the two models side by side. The one would have organized self-government, the other arbitrary rule; the one a people of freeholders, the other of landlords and tenants; the one public worship according to the conscience and faith of individuals, the other a state religion subordinate to temporal power; the one education of all the people, the other indifference to human culture.

It remains to be related that in the year 1780 the Methodists of the United States at their general meeting voted "slave-keeping contrary to the laws of God, man, and nature."

THE *story of Clinton, Arnold, and André had par-*
ticular appeal to American readers, far out of pro-
portion to its historical importance, and Bancroft
gave it a full chapter in Volume VI. It had every
element that his kind of historical writing needed—
villainous aristocratic enemy, hero turned traitor,
handsome hapless scapegoat, accidental discovery
by honest soldiers, painful but just judgment, ironic
final justice. André's case had already provided ma-
terials for William Dunlap's popular play, Cooper's
Spy, and other works of fiction. Bancroft treated it
as a dramatic sketch and wrote it accurately and well.

The Complot of Sir Henry Clinton and Arnold (1780)

DESULTORY movements of the British and American troops
in the north during the winter of 1780 were baffled by unwonted
cold and deep snows. The Hudson and the East River were
covered with solid ice, but Knyphausen provided for the safety
of New York by forming battalions of the loyal inhabitants
and refugees. Besides, the American army, whose pay was in
arrear and whom congress could not provide with food, was too
feeble to hazard an attack. In May, the continental troops between the Chesapeake and Canada amounted only to seven
thousand men; in the first week of June, those under the command of Washington, present and fit for duty, numbered but
three thousand seven hundred and sixty.

On the twenty-eighth of May, the official report of the surrender of Charleston was received. The refugees insisted that
the men of New Jersey, weary of compulsory requisitions of
supplies, longed to return to their old form of government; and
English generals reported so great disaffection among the
starved and half-clothed American officers and men that one
half of them would desert to the English and the other half
disperse. The moment seemed opportune for setting up the

royal standard in New Jersey. Strengthening the post at King's Bridge, and leaving only three regiments in New York, Knyphausen formed nineteen regiments into three divisions under Robertson, Tryon, and Stachenberg, with an advanced guard under general Matthews. Of artillery, he took eight pieces.

The army of Washington was encamped at Morristown. On the east of the Passaic, the Jersey brigade under General Maxwell was stationed at Connecticut Farms, and three hundred of the Jersey militia occupied Elizabethtown. On the sixth of June, the British landed at Elizabethtown Point, but very slowly, from a scarcity of boats. The brigadier who commanded the vanguard was early wounded and disabled. Seven hours were lost in bridging a marsh which stopped their way. On the morning of the seventh, the American militia, under Colonel Dayton, having had timely warning, retired before the enemy from Elizabethtown; but with the aid of volunteers from the country people, who flew to arms, and of small patrolling parties of continental troops, they harassed the British all the way on their march of five or six miles to Connecticut Farms. James Caldwell, the Presbyterian minister of that place, was known to have inspired his people with his own patriotic zeal. A British soldier, putting his gun to the window of the house where Caldwell's wife was sitting with her children, one of them a nursling, shot her fatally through the breast. Scarcely was time allowed to remove the children and the corpse from the house when it was set on fire. The Presbyterian meeting-house and the houses and barns of the village were burnt down. In the winter, the Presbyterian church at Newark had in like manner been burnt to the ground.

From Connecticut Farms, Maxwell, with the remnant of a brigade, retreated to strong ground near Springfield, where he awaited and repelled repeated attacks made by Colonel Wurmb with a Hessian regiment. Thrice did the Americans charge with fixed bayonets; and they retired only on the arrival of a British brigade, the Hessian yagers alone having lost more than fifty killed or wounded. Instead of men eager to return to their old allegiance, the British encountered a people risking all to preserve their independence; suffered losses all the day from determined troops; and at five in the afternoon found that Washington, on hearing that they were out in force, had brought in front of them a brave and faithful army, formed on ground of his own choice. Knyphausen, though his command outnumbered the Americans two to one, declined to attack, where victory must have cost dearly, and defeat would have been disastrous. Learning at this moment that Clinton with a large force might be expected at New York within a week, he resolved to attempt nothing more; and at nine o'clock in the evening his army began a retreat to Elizabethtown Point. An American detachment, sent at break of day in pursuit, drove the twenty-second English regiment out of Elizabethtown and returned without being molested. In general orders, Dayton "received particular thanks." At this time, a committee from congress was in the American camp, to whom Washington explained the hardships of his condition. Not only had congress accomplished nothing for the relief and re-enforcement of his army, it could not even tell how far the several states would comply with the requisitions made on them. While awarding liberal praise to the militia of New Jersey, he renewed his constant plea for regular troops: "Perseverance in enduring the rigors of military service is not to be expected from those who are not by profession obliged to it. Our force, from your own observation, is totally inadequate to our safety."

On the nineteenth of June, two days after his arrival in New York, Clinton repaired to New Jersey. He had now at his disposition nearly four times as many regular troops as were opposed to him; but he fretted at "the move in Jersey as premature," and what he "least expected." With civil words to the German officers, he resolved to give up the expedition; but he chose to mask his retreat by a feint, and to give it the air of a military manœuvre.

Troops sent up the Hudson River, as if to take the Americans in the rear, induced Washington to move his camp to

Rockaway bridge, confiding the post at Short Hills to two brigades under the command of Greene. Early on the twenty-third, the British advanced in two compact divisions from Elizabethtown Point to Springfield. The column on the right had to ford the river before they could drive Major Lee from one of the bridges over the Passaic. At the other, Colonel Angel with his regiment held the left column in check for about forty minutes. Greene prepared for action; but the British army, though it was drawn up and began a heavy cannonade, had no design to engage; and at four in the afternoon, after burning the houses in Springfield, it began its return. All the way back to Elizabethtown, it was annoyed by an incessant fire from American skirmishers and militia. Its total loss is not known; once more the Hessian yagers lost fifty in killed or wounded, among the latter one colonel, two captains and a lieutenant. From Elizabethtown Point the fruitless expedition crossed to Staten Island by a bridge of boats, which at midnight was taken away. Clinton was never again to have so good an opportunity for offensive operations as that which he now rejected.

On the return of D'Estaing from America, he urged the French ministry to send twelve thousand men to the United States, as the best way of pursuing the war actively; and La-fayette had of his own motion given the like advice to Ver-gennes, with whom he had formed relations of friendship. The cabinet adopted the measure in its principle, but vacillated as to the number of the French contingent. For the command, Count de Rochambeau was selected, not by court favor, but from the consideration in which he was held by the troops. On the tenth of July, Admiral de Ternay with a squadron of ten ships-of-war, three of them ships of the line, convoyed the detachment of about six thousand men with Rochambeau into the harbor of Newport. To an address from the general assembly of Rhode Island, then sitting in Newport, the count answered: "The French troops are restrained by the strictest discipline; and, acting under General Washington, will live with the Americans as their brethren. I assure the general assembly that, as brethren, not only my life, but the lives of the troops under my command, are entirely devoted to their service." Washington in general orders desired the American officers to wear white and black cockades as a symbol of affection for their allies.

The British fleet at New York having received a large re-enforcement, so that it had now a great superiority, Sir Henry Clinton embarked about eight thousand men for an expedition to Rhode Island. Supported by militia from Massachusetts and Connecticut, the French longed for the threatened attack; but the expedition proceeded no further than Huntington Bay in Long Island, where it idled away several days, and then returned to New York. Of the incapacity of Arbuthnot, the admiral, Clinton sent home bitter complaints, which were little heeded. There were those who censured the general as equally wanting energy. The sixth summer during which the British had vainly endeavored to reduce the United States was passing away, and after the arrival of French auxiliaries the British commander in chief was more than ever disheartened.

On the twenty-fifth of August, Clinton, knowing well that he had in Cornwallis a favored rival eager to supplant him, reported officially from New York: "At this new epoch in the war, when a foreign force has already landed and an addition to it is expected, I owe to my country, and I must in justice to my own fame declare to your lordship, that I become every day more sensible of the utter impossibility of prosecuting the war in this country without re-enforcements. The revolutions fondly looked for by means of friends to the British government I must represent as visionary. These, I well know, are numerous, but they are fettered. An inroad is no countenance, and to possess territory demands garrisons. The accession of friends, without we occupy the country they inhabit, is but the addition of unhappy exiles to the list of pensioned refugees. A glance at the returns of the army divided into garrisons and reduced by casualties on the one part, with the consideration of the task yet before us on the other, would, I fear, renew the too just reflection that we are by some thousands too weak to subdue this formidable rebellion." Yet for the moment the only regiments sent to the United States were three to re-enforce Lord Cornwallis.

Hopeless of success in honorable warfare, Clinton stooped to fraud and corruption. From the time when officers who stood below Arnold were promoted over his head, discontent rankled in his breast and found expression in threats of revenge. After the northern campaign, he complained more than ever that his services had not been sufficiently rewarded. While he held the command in Philadelphia, his extravagant mode of living tempted him to peculation and treasonable connections; and towards the end of February, 1779, he let it be known to the British commander in chief that he was desirous of exchanging the American service for that of Great Britain. His open preference for the friends of the English in Pennsylvania disgusted the patriots. The council of that state, after bearing with him for more than half a year, very justly desired his removal from the command; and, having early in 1779 given information of his conduct, against their intention they became his accusers. The court-martial before which he was arraigned, on charges that touched his honor and integrity, dealt with him leniently, and sentenced him only to be reprimanded by the commander in chief. The reprimand was marked with the greatest forbearance. The French minister, to whom Arnold applied for money, put aside his request and added wise and friendly advice. In the course of the winter of 1778–79, he was taken into the pay of Clinton, to whom he gave on every occasion most material intelligence.

The plot received the warmest encouragement from Lord George Germain, who, towards the end of September, 1779, wrote to Clinton: "Next to the destruction of Washington's army, the gaining over officers of influence and reputation among the troops would be the speediest means of subduing the rebellion and restoring the tranquillity of America. Your commission authorizes you to avail yourself of such opportunities, and there can be no doubt that the expense will be cheerfully submitted to."

In 1780, the command at West Point needed to be changed. Acting in concert with Clinton and supported by the New York delegation in congress, Arnold, pleading his wounds as an excuse for declining active service, solicited and obtained orders to that post, which included all the American forts in the Highlands. Clinton entered with all his soul into the ignoble plot, which, as he believed, was to end the war. After a correspondence of two months between him and the British commander in chief, through Major John André, adjutant-general of the army in North America, on the thirtieth of August, Arnold, insisting that the advantages which he expected to gain for himself by his surrender were "by no means unreasonable," and requiring that his conditions should "be clearly understood," laid a plan for an interview at which a person "fully authorized" was to "close with" his proposals.

The rendezvous was given by him within the American lines, where Colonel Sheldon held the command; and that officer was instructed to expect the arrival "at his quarters of a person in New York to open a channel of intelligence." On the same day, André, disguising his name, wrote to Sheldon from New York, by order of Clinton: "A flag will be sent to Dobb's Ferry on Monday next, the eleventh, at twelve o'clock. Let me entreat you, sir, to favor a matter which is of so private a nature that the public on neither side can be injured by it. I trust I shall not be detained, but I would rather risk that than neglect the business in question, or assume a mysterious character to carry on an innocent affair and get to your lines by stealth." To this degree did the British commander in chief prostitute his word and a flag of truce, and lull the suspicions of the American officer by statements the most false. The letter of André being forwarded to Arnold, he "determined to go as far as Dobb's Ferry and meet the flag." As he was approaching

the vessel in which André came up the river, the British guard-
boats, whose officers were not in the secret, fired upon the barge
and prevented the interview.

Clinton became only more interested in the project, for of a
sudden he gained an illustrious assistant. At the breaking out
of the war between France and England, Sir George Rodney, a
British naval officer, chanced to be detained in Paris by debt.
But the aged Marshal de Biron advanced him money to set
himself free, and he hastened to England to ask employment
of the king. He was not a member of parliament, and was devoted to no political party; he reverenced the memory of Chatham, and yet held the war against the United States to be just.
A man of action, quick-sighted, great in power of execution,
he was the very officer whom a wise government would employ,
and whom by luck the British admiralty of that day, tired of
the Keppels and the Palisers, the mutinous and the incompetent, put in command of the expedition that was to relieve
Gibraltar and rule the seas of the West Indies. One of the king's
younger sons served on board his fleet as midshipman. He took
his squadron to sea on the twenty-ninth of December, 1779.
On the eighth of January, 1780, he captured seven vessels of
war and fifteen sail of merchant-men. On the sixteenth, he encountered off Cape St. Vincent the Spanish squadron of Lan-
guara, very inferior to his own, and easily took or destroyed a
great part of it. Having victualled the garrison of Gibraltar and
relieved Minorca, on the thirteenth of February he set sail for
the West Indies. At St. Lucia, he received letters from his wife,
saying: "Everybody is beyond measure delighted as well as
astonished at your success;" from his daughter: "Everybody
almost adores you, and every mouth is full of your praise;
come back when you have done some more things in that part
of the world you are in now."

The thanks of both houses of parliament reached him at
Barbados. In April and May, Rodney had twice or thrice en-
counters with the French fleet of Admiral Guichen, and with
such success that in a grateful mood the British parliament

thanked him once more. Yet he did not obtain a decided superiority in the West Indian seas, and he reported to the admiralty as the reason, that his flag had not been properly supported by some of his officers.

With indifference to neutral rights, he sent frigates to seize or destroy all American vessels in St. Eustatius. In June, he received a check by a junction of the Spanish squadron under Solano with the French. But the two admirals could not agree how their forces should be employed. Contagious fever attacked the Spaniards, and reached the French. Solano returned to Havana; Guichen, whose squadron was anxiously awaited in the north, sailed for France. Rodney alone, passing to the north and recapturing a ship from Charleston, anchored off Sandy Hook, where he vexed the weak Admiral Arbuthnot by taking command of the station of New York during his short stay. To the vast superiority of the British on land was now added the undisputed dominion of the water. In aid of the enterprise by which Sir Henry Clinton expected to bring the war to an immediate close, Rodney contributed his own rare powers; and perfect harmony prevailed between the two branches of the service.

On the eighteenth of September, Washington crossed the North River on his way from headquarters near Tappan to Hartford, where, attended by Lafayette and Hamilton, he was to hold his first interview with General Rochambeau. He was joined on the river by Arnold, who accompanied him as far as Peekskill, and endeavored, though in vain, to obtain his consent for the reception of an agent on pretended business relating to confiscated property. Had the consent been given, the interview with André would have taken place under a flag of truce, seemingly authorized by the American commander in chief.

Time pressed on. Besides, Sir George Rodney had only looked in upon New York, and would soon return to the West Indies. On the evening of the eighteenth, Arnold, giving information that Washington on the following Saturday night was expected to be his guest at West Point, proposed that André should immediately come up to the "Vulture" ship-of-war, which rode at anchor just above Teller's Point in Haverstraw Bay, promising on Wednesday evening "to send a person on board with a boat and a flag of truce."

This letter of Arnold reached Clinton on Tuesday evening, and he took his measures without delay. Troops were embarked on the Hudson River under the superintendence of Sir George Rodney, and the embarkation disguised by a rumor of an intended expedition into the Cheasapeake.

On the morning of the twentieth, the British adjutant-general, taking his life in his hand, prepared to carry out his orders. To diminish the dangers to which the service exposed him, "the commander in chief, before his departure, cautioned him not to change his dress, and not to take papers." At Dobb's Ferry, he embarked on the river, and, as the tide was favorable, reached the "Vulture" at about an hour after sunset, and declared to its captain "that he was ready to attend General Arnold's summons when and where he pleased."

"The night the flag was first expected, he expressed much anxiety for its arrival," and, as it did not come, on the morning of the twenty-first by an ingenious artifice he let Arnold know where he was. On the ensuing night, one Smith, in a boat with muffled oars, went off from the western shore of the Hudson to the "Vulture." "The instant André learned that he was wanted, he started out of bed and discovered the greatest impatience to be gone. Nor did he in any instance betray the least doubt of his safety and success." The moon, which had just passed into the third quarter, shone in a clear sky when the boat pushed for the landing-place near the upper edge of the Haverstraw Mountains. It was very near the time for day to appear, when André, dressed in regimentals, which a large blue cloak concealed, landed at the point of the Long Clove, where Arnold was waiting in the bushes to receive him. The general had brought with him a spare horse; and the two rode through the village of Haverstraw within the American lines to the house of Smith, which lay a few miles from the river. At the dawn of day, the noise of artillery was heard. An American party had brought field-pieces to bear on the "Vulture;" and Arnold, as he looked out from the window, saw her compelled to shift her anchorage. The negotiations of the two parties continued for several hours. Clinton was in person to bring his army to the siege of Fort Defiance, which enclosed about seven acres of land. The garrison was to be so distributed as to destroy its efficiency. Arnold was to send immediately to Washington for aid, and to surrender the place in time for Sir Henry Clinton to make arrangements for surprising the re-enforcement, which it was believed Washington would conduct in person. It was no part of the plan to risk an attempt to capture Washington while a guest at West Point. The promises to Arnold were indemnities in money and the rank of brigadier in the British service. The American general returned to his quarters. Late in the afternoon, André, changing his dress for the disguise of a citizen, provided with passes from Arnold and attended by Smith, set off by land for New York.

Four years before, Washington had sailed between the Highlands, where nature blends mountains and valleys, the primeval forests, and the deep river, in exceeding beauty, and had marked with his eye the positions best adapted to command the passage. Until 1778, West Point was a solitude, nearly inaccessible; now it was covered by fortresses with numerous redoubts, constructed chiefly under the direction of Kosciuszko as engineer, and so connected as to form one system of defence, which was believed to be impregnable. Here were the magazines of ammunition, for the use not of the post only, but of the whole army. The fortifications built by a nation just rising into notice seemingly represented a vast outlay of money; but the prodigious labor of piling on the steep heights huge trunks of trees and enormous hewn blocks had been executed by the hands of the American soldiers, who received for their toil not the smallest gratification, even when their stated pay remained in arrear. And these works, of which every stone was a monument of humble, disinterested patriotism, were to be betrayed to the enemy, with all their garrison.

On that same evening, Washington, free from suspicion, was returning to his army. He had met General Rochambeau and Admiral de Ternay at Hartford. "The interview was a genuine festival for the French, who were impatient to see the hero of liberty. His noble mien, the simplicity of his manners, his mild gravity, surpassed their expectations and gained for him their hearts." All agreed that, for want of a superiority at sea, active operations could not be begun; so that the meeting served only to establish friendship and confidence between the officers of the two nations. Washington on his return was accompanied a day's journey by Count Dumas, one of the aids of Rochambeau. The population of the town where he was to spend the night went out to meet him. A crowd of children, repeating the acclamations of their elders, gathered around him, stopping his way, all wishing to touch him and with loud cries calling him their father. Pressing the hand of Dumas, he said to him: "We may be beaten by the English in the field; it is the lot of arms: but see there the army which they will never conquer."

At this very time, André, conducted by Smith, crossed the Hudson River at King's ferry. It was already dark before they passed the American post at Verplanck's Point, under the excuse that they were going up the river, and to keep up that pretence they turned in for the night near Crompond. Very early on the twenty-third, they were in the saddle. Two miles and a half north of Pine's bridge over the Croton, Smith, assuring André that the rest of the way he would meet only Birtish parties or cow-boys as they were called, and having charged him to take the inner route to New York through the valley of the Bronx by way of White Plains, near which the British had an outpost, bade him farewell and rode up to dine with Arnold at his quarters. At a fork in the road about six miles below the Croton, André, quitting the road to White Plains, took that which led over the hills, and entered the highway from Albany to New York at a short distance above Tarrytown. He now thought himself beyond all danger, and according to his own account he fully believed that he was the bearer of a plan which would bring the civil war to an immediate end. The British troops, embarked by Sir George Rodney, lay waiting for Clinton to give the word and to lead them in person.

It happened that John Paulding, a poor man, then about forty-six years old, a zealous patriot who engaged in the service of his country at the breaking out of the war and was twice made captive, had lately escaped from New York and had formed a little corps of partisans to annoy roving parties taking provisions to New York, or otherwise doing service to the British. On that morning, after setting a reserve of four to keep watch in the rear, he and David Williams of Tarrytown and Isaac van Wart of Greenburg seated themselves in the thicket by the wayside just above Tarrytown and whiled away the time by playing cards. At an hour before noon, André was just rising the hill out of Sleepy Hollow, within fifteen miles of the strong British post at King's Bridge, when Paulding got up, presented a firelock at his breast, and asked which way he was going. Full of the idea that he could meet none but friends to the English, he answered: "Gentlemen, I hope you belong to our party?" "Which party?" asked Paulding. "The lower party," said André. Paulding answered that he did. Then said André: "I am a British officer, out on particular business, and I hope you will not detain me a minute." Upon this, Paulding ordered him to dismount. Seeing his mistake, André showed his pass from Arnold, saying: "By your stopping me, you will detain the general's business." "I hope," answered Paulding, "you will not be offended; we do not mean to take any thing from you. There are many bad people going along the road; perhaps you may be one of them;" and he asked if he had any letters about him. André answered: "No." They took him into the bushes to search for papers, and at last discovered three parcels under each stocking. Among these were a plan of the fortifications of West Point; a memorial from the engineer on the attack and defence of the place; returns of the garrison, cannon, and stores in the handwriting of Arnold. "This is a spy," said Paulding. André offered a hundred guineas, any sum of money, if they would let him go. "No," cried Paulding, "not for ten thousand guineas." They then led him off, and, arriving in the evening at North Castle, they delivered him with his papers to Lieutenant-colonel Jameson who commanded the post, and then went their way, not asking a reward for their services, nor leaving their names.

What passed between André and Jameson is not known. The result of the interview was that on the twenty-fourth the prisoner was ordered by Jameson to be taken to Arnold; but on the sharp remonstrance of Major Tallmadge, the next in rank, the order was countermanded, and he was confined at Old Salem, yet with permission to inform Arnold by letter of his arrest.

His letter was received on the twenty-fifth, too late for an order to be given for his release, and only in time for Arnold himself to escape down the river to the "Vulture." Washington, who had turned aside to examine the condition of the works at West Point, arrived a few hours after his flight.

The first care of the commander in chief was for the safety of the post. The extent of the danger appeared from a letter of the twenty-fourth, in which André avowed himself to be the adjutant-general of the British army, and offered excuses for having been "betrayed into the vile condition of an enemy in disguise" within his posts. He added. "The request I have to make to your excellency, and I am conscious I address myself well, is that, in any rigor policy may dictate, a decency of conduct towards me may mark that, though unfortunate, I am branded with nothing dishonorable, as no motive could be mine but the service of my king, and as I was unvoluntarily an impostor." This request was granted in its full extent, and in the whole progress of the affair he was treated with the most scrupulous delicacy. André further wrote: "Gentlemen at Charleston on parole were engaged in a conspiracy against us; they are objects who may be set in exchange for me, or are persons whom the treatment I receive might affect." The charge of conspiracy against Gadsden and his fellow-sufferers was ground-less; and had been brought forward only as an excuse for shipping them away from the city, where their mere presence kept the love of independence alive. To seek security by a threat of retaliation on innocent men was an unworthy act, which re-ceived no support from Sir Henry Clinton.

André was without loss of time conducted to the head-quarters of the army at Tappan. His offence was so clear that it would have justified the promptest action; but, to prevent all possibility of complaint from any quarter, he was, on the twenty-ninth, brought before a numerous and very able board of offi-cers. On his own confession and without the examination of a witness, the board, on which sat Greene, second only to Wash-ington in the service; Saint-Clair, afterwards president of con-gress; Lafayette, of the French army; Steuben, from the staff of Frederic II; Parsons, Clinton, Glover, Knox, Huntingdon, and others, all well known for their uprightness,—made their unani-mous report that Major André, adjutant-general of the British army, ought to be considered as a spy from the enemy and to suffer death. Throughout the inquiry, André was penetrated with the liberality of the members of the court, who showed him every mark of indulgence, and required him to answer no inter-rogatory which could even embarrass his feelings. He acknowl-edged their generosity in the strongest terms of manly grati-tude, and afterwards remarked to one who visited him that, if there were any remains in his mind of prejudice against the Americans, his present experience must obliterate them.

On the thirtieth, the sentence was approved by Washington, and ordered to be carried into effect the next day. Clinton had already in a note to Washington asked André's release, as one who had been protected by "a flag of truce and passports granted for his return." André had himself, in his examination before the board of officers, repelled the excuse which Clinton made for him; and indeed to have used a flag of truce for his purposes would have aggravated his offence. Washington re-plied by enclosing to the British commander in chief the report of the board of inquiry, and observed "that Major André was employed in the execution of measures very foreign to flags of truce, and such as they were never meant to authorize."

At the request of Clinton, who promised to present "a true state of facts," the execution was delayed till the second day of October; and General Robertson, attended by two civilians, came up the river for a conference. The civilians were not allowed to land; but Greene was deputed to meet the officer. Instead of presenting facts Robertson, after compliments to the character of Greene, announced that he had come to treat with him. Greene answered: "The case of an acknowledged spy admits no official discussion." Robertson then proposed to free André by an exchange. Greene answered: "If André is set free, Arnold must be given up;" for the liberation of André could not be asked for except in exchange for one who was equally implicated in the complot. Robertson then forgot himself so far as to deliver an open letter from Arnold to Washington, in which, in the event André should suffer the penalty of death, he used these threats: "I shall think myself bound by every tie of duty and honor to retaliate on such unhappy persons of your army as may fall within my power. Forty of the principal inhabitants of South Carolina have justly forfeited their lives; Sir Henry Clinton cannot in justice extend his mercy to them any longer, if Major André suffers."

Meantime, André entreated with touching earnestness that he might not die "on the gibbet." Washington and every other officer in the American army were moved to the deepest compassion; and Hamilton, who has left his opinion that no one ever suffered death with more justice and that there was in truth no way of saving him, wished that in the mode of his death his feelings as an officer and a man might be respected. But the English themselves had established the exclusive usage of the gallows. At the beginning of the war, their officers in America threatened the highest American officers and statesmen with the cord. It was the only mode of execution authorized by them. Under the orders of Clinton, Lord Cornwallis in

South Carolina had set up the gallows for those whom he styled deserters, without regard to rank. Neither the sentence of the court nor the order of Washington names death on the gallows; the execution took place in the manner that was alone in use on both sides.

In going to the place of execution, a constrained smile hid the emotions of André. Arrived at the fatal spot, the struggle in his mind was visible; but he preserved his self-control. "I am reconciled," he said, "to my fate, but not to the mode." Being asked at the last moment if he had any thing to say, he answered: "Nothing but to request you to witness to the world that I die like a brave man."

Tried by the laws of morals, it is one of the worst forms of dissimulation to achieve by corruption and treachery what cannot be gained by honorable arms. If we confine our judgment within the limits of the laws of war, it is a blemish on the character of André that he was willing to prostitute a flag, to pledge his word, even under the orders of his chief, for the innocence and private nature of his design, and to have wished to make the lives of faultless prisoners hostages for his own. About these things a man of honor and humanity ought to have had a scruple; "but the temptation was great, let his misfortunes cast a veil over his errors." The last words of André committed to the Americans the care of his reputation; and they faithfully fulfilled his request. The firmness and delicacy observed in his case was exceedingly admired on the continent of Europe. His king did right in offering honorable rank to his brother, and in granting pensions to his mother and sisters; but not in raising a memorial to his name in Westminster Abbey. Such honor belongs to other enterprises and deeds. The tablet has no fit place in a sanctuary, dear from its monuments to every friend to genius and mankind.

As for Arnold, he had not feeling enough to undergo mental torments and his coarse nature was not sensitive to shame. Bankrupt and escaping from his creditors, he preferred claims to indemnity, and received between six and seven thousand pounds. He suffered only when he found that baffled treason is paid grudgingly; when employment was refused him; when he could neither stay in England nor get orders for service in America; when, despised and neglected, he was pinched by want. But the king would not suffer his children to starve, and eventually their names were placed on the pension list.

Sir George Rodney returned to the West Indies, and, so far as related to himself, let the unsuccessful conspiracy sink into oblivion. For Clinton, the cup of humiliation was filled to the brim. "Thus ended," so he wrote in his anguish to Germain, "this proposed plan, from which I had conceived such great hopes and imagined such great consequences." He was, moreover, obliged to introduce into high rank in the British army, and receive at his council table, a man who had shown himself so sordid that British officers of honor hated to serve under him or with him, or over him. Arnold, on his part, had the effrontery to make addresses to the American people respecting their alliance with France; to write insolent letters to Washington; to invite all Americans to desert the colors of their country like himself; to advise the breaking up of the American army by wholesale bribery. Nay, he even turned against his patron as wanting activity, assuring Germain that the American posts in the Highlands might be carried in a few days by a regular attack. No one knew better than Clinton that André was punished justly; yet in his private journal he aimed a stab at the fair fame of his signally humane adversary, whom he had been able to overcome neither in the field nor by intrigue; and attributed an act of public duty to personal "rancor," for which no cause whatever existed. The false accusation proves not so much malignity in its author as feebleness.

Washington sought out the three men who, "leaning only on their virtue and an honest sense of their duty," could not be tempted by gold; and on his report congress voted them annuities in words of respect and honor.

WITH *the war in the North virtually at a stalemate, General Clinton in 1781 sent Cornwallis and a large force to Virginia to occupy the coastal areas and to capture a small group of Americans serving under Lafayette. When Lafayette escaped, Cornwallis entrenched his army at Yorktown. Washington, reinforced by French troops under Count Rochambeau, immediately took advantage of Cornwallis' inactivity and started for Virginia, a move that Clinton believed a feint to draw him out of New York. At the same time Admiral de Grasse, in a superbly co-ordinated plan, sailed from the West Indies for Chesapeake Bay with a strong French naval squadron. Washington's move was not a feint, however, and Cornwallis suddenly found himself pinned between a larger allied army on land and De Grasse's ships at sea. His army was doomed and though he held out for several weeks, Cornwallis surrendered his entire force on October 19, 1781. When the news reached Britain Lord North's ministry tottered and fell, replaced in early 1782 by those of Rockingham and later Shelburne, which were much more favorably inclined to discuss peace terms.*

Bancroft's account of Yorktown confines itself rather closely to the military action, since he apparently preferred to save his rhetoric for the actual close of hostilities, still some two years and many diplomatic maneuverings away. Noticeably, he praises Lafayette, one of his favorite Revolutionary leaders, whom he had met in Paris and who had later visited Round Hill School. Almost certainly Bancroft, in writing of Yorktown, had the benefit of the famous Frenchman's personal reminiscences. Noticeably, too, Bancroft took care to acknowledge the crucial role played in the war's final phases by the French, though he must have been aware of the anomaly of the coonies, in their war against one king, accepting assistance from another. Earlier in Volume IX of the first edition, Bancroft explained that "the movement of intellectual freedom" and "the spirit of liberty" which swept through the world in the latter part of the eighteenth century "impelled" the Bourbon monarchs of France and Spain, despite their "dull reluctance", to join the American cause, as in this chapter he em-

phasizes the "love of freedom" which "inflamed" the French at Yorktown and made each of them "proud of being a defender of the young Republic."

Campaign in Virginia (1781)

CLINTON had himself resolved to hold a station in the Chesapeake Bay; and on the second of January, 1781, Arnold, with sixteen hundred men, appeared by his order in the James River. The generous state had sent its best troops and arms to the southern army. Nelson had received timely orders from Governor Jefferson to call out the militia of the low country; but, in the region of planters with slaves, there were not freemen enough at hand to meet the invaders; and Steuben, thinking Petersburg the object of attack, kept his small force on the south side of the river. Arnold offered to spare Richmond, if he might unmolested carry off its stores of tobacco; the proposal being rejected with scorn, on the fifth and sixth, all ·its houses and stores, public and private, were set on fire. In the hope of capturing Arnold and his corps Washington detached Lafayette with about twelve hundred rank and file to Virginia; and, repairing to Newport, persuaded the French naval commander to send to the Chesapeake ten ships-of-war to co-operate with him. They were followed by the British squadron, and twelve leagues east of the bay an action took place. The French were compelled to return to Newport, while Arbuthnot entered the Chesapeake.

On the twenty-sixth of March, General Phillips, who brought from New York a re-enforcement of two thousand picked men, took the command in Virginia. All the stores of produce which its planters in five quiet years had accumulated were now carried off or destroyed. Their negroes, so desired in the West Indies, formed the staple article of plunder.

By a courier from Washington, Lafayette received informa-

Vol. VI, Chap. LIV.

tion that Virginia was about to become the centre of active operations, and was instructed to defend the state as well as the weakness of his means would permit. His troops were chiefly from New England, and dreaded the unwholesome and unknown climate of lower Virginia. Besides, they were destitute of every thing. To prevent desertion, Lafayette, as soon as he found himself on the south side of the Susquehannah, in an order of the day offered leave to any of them to return to the north; and not one would abandon him. At Baltimore, he borrowed two thousand pounds sterling, supplied his men with shoes and hats, and bought linen, which the women of Baltimore made into summer garments. Then, by a forced march of two hundred miles, he arrived at Richmond on the twenty-ninth of April, the evening before Phillips reached the opposite bank of the river. Having in the night been joined by Steuben with militia, Lafayette was enabled to hold in check the larger British force. Wayne should have accompanied Lafayette with the Pennsylvania line, but they were detained week after week for needful supplies. Meantime, Clinton, stimulated by Germain's constant praises of the activity of Cornwallis, sent another considerable detachment to Virginia.

On the thirteenth of May, General Phillips died of malignant fever. Arnold, on whom the command devolved, though only for seven days, addressed a letter to Lafayette. The young man returned it with scorn, refusing to correspond with a traitor; upon which Arnold threatened to send to the Antilles all American prisoners, unless a cartel should be immediately concluded. But on the twentieth Cornwallis arrived at Petersburg; and, to free his camp of one whom he despised, he ordered Arnold back to New York.

Clinton had little reason to be satisfied with an officer who had represented to the ministry that he might have taken the American posts in the Highlands in a few days by a regular attack. Nevertheless, he detached him once more, and this time against his native state.

Crossing from Long Island, the troops under his command,

on the sixth of September, landed on each side of New London. The town, which offered little resistance, was plundered and burnt. After a gallant defence of forty minutes by Colonel Ledyard, with about one hundred and fifty ill-armed militia-men, Fort Griswold was carried by storm, the Americans having lost not more than six men. When Ledyard had surrendered, the British officer in command ran him through with his sword, and refused quarter to the garrison. Seventy-three of them were killed, and more than thirty wounded; about forty were carried off as prisoners. With this expedition, Arnold disappears from history.

Cornwallis now found himself where he had so ardently desired to be;—in Virginia at the head of seven thousand effective men, with not a third of that number to oppose him by land, and with undisputed command of the water.

The statesmen of Virginia, in the extremity of their peril, were divided in opinion. "Wanting a rudder in the storm," said Richard Henry Lee, "the good ship must inevitably be cast away;" and he proposed to send for General Washington immediately, and invest him with "dictatorial powers." But Jefferson, on the other hand, reasoned: "The thought alone of creating a dictator is treason against the people; is treason against mankind in general, giving to their oppressors a proof of the imbecility of republican government in times of pressing danger. The government, instead of being braced and invigorated for greater exertions under difficulties, would be thrown back." As governor of Virginia, speaking for its people and representing their distresses, he wrote to Washington: "Could you lend us your personal aid? It is evident, from the universal voice, that the presence of their beloved countryman would restore full confidence, and render them equal to whatever is not impossible. Should you repair to your native state, the difficulty would then be how to keep men out of the field." These words sunk deeply into Washington's mind.

During the summer, congress improved the methods of administration. Against the opinion of Samuel Adams, and without aid from Massachusetts, it substituted for its own executive committees a single head of each of the most important departments. Robert Morris was placed in charge of the finances of the confederation; in conformity with the wish of the French minister, which was ably sustained by Sullivan, the conduct of foreign affairs was intrusted to Robert Livingston of New York. Washington would have gladly seen Schuyler elected to the war department.

Outside of congress, Hamilton persevered in recommending an efficient government. His views were so identical with those of Robert Morris that it is sometimes hard to say in whose mind they first sprung up. Many who agreed with them in wishing a stronger union might think they laid too much stress on the institution of a national bank; the opinion that a national debt, if not excessive, would be a national blessing, a powerful cement to union and a spur to industry, did not rise out of the best traditions of the country, and was carried, at least by the elder of the two, to a most perilous extreme.

Meantime, the conduct of the war continued to languish for the want of a central government. In the states from which the most was hoped, Hancock of Massachusetts was vain and neglectful of business; the president of Pennsylvania was more ready to recount what the state had done than what it meant to do: so that the army was not wholly free from the danger of being disbanded for want of subsistence. Of the armed vessels of the United States, all but two frigates had been taken or destroyed.

Madison still persevered in the effort to obtain power for congress to collect a revenue and that body named a committee to examine into the changes which needed to be made in the articles of confederation. "The difficulty of continuing the war under them," so wrote Luzerne, on the twenty-seventh of August, "proves equally the necessity of reforming them, produced, as they were, at an epoch when the mere name of authority inspired terror, and by men who thought to make themselves agreeable to the people. I can scarcely persuade myself that they will come to an agreement on this matter. Some persons even believe that the actual constitution, all vicious as it is, can be changed only by some violent revolution."

The French government declined to furnish means for the siege of New York. After the arrival of its final instructions, Rochambeau, attended by Chastellux, in a meeting with Washington at Weathersfield on the twenty-first of May, settled the preliminaries of the campaign. The French land force was to march to the Hudson River, and, in conjunction with the American army, be ready to move to the southward. De Grasse was charged anew on his way to the north to enter the Chesapeake. In the direction of the war for the coming season, there would be union; for congress had lodged the highest power in the northern and southern departments in the hands of Washington, and France had magnanimously placed her troops as auxiliaries under his command.

Before his return the American general called upon the governors of the four New England states, "in earnest and pointed terms," to complete their continental battalions, to hold bodies of militia ready to march in a week after being called for, and to adopt effective modes of supply. Governor Trumbull, of Connecticut, cheered him with the opinion that he would obtain all that he needed.

In June, the French contingent, increased by fifteen hundred men, newly arrived in ships-of-war, left Newport for the Hudson River. The inhabitants crowded around them on their march, glad to recognize in them allies and defenders, and, mingling at their encampments with officers and soldiers, listened with delight to the bands of their regiments. The rights of private property were most scrupulously respected, and the petty exigencies of local laws good-naturedly submitted to.

Cornwallis began his career in Virginia by seizing the fine horses on the James River, and mounting a gallant and most effective cavalry, five or six hundred in number. He then started in pursuit of Lafayette, who, with about one thousand continen-

tal troops, was posted between Wilton and Richmond, waiting
for re-inforcements from Pennsylvania. "Lafayette, I think,
cannot escape him," wrote Clinton to Germain. The youthful
commander warily kept to the north of his pursuer; passing
South and North Anna went through the wilderness across
the Rapidan; and on the seventh of June made a junction with
Wayne not far from Raccoon ford. Small as was his force, he
compared the British in Virginia to the French in Hanover at
the time of the seven years' war, and confidently predicted
analogous results. Cornwallis advanced as far as Hanover
courthouse, then crossed South Anna, and, having failed in his
first object, he sent out two detachments: one of cavalry under
Tarleton to capture or break up the Virginia assembly, then in
session at Charlottesville; the other of mixed troops under Sim-
coe to proceed to the Point of Fork, where Steuben, with five
hundred Virginians of the line and a few of the militia, kept
guard over large stores intended for the south. The main body
of his army, in its camp on the James River, just below Byrd
Creek, awaited the return of the expeditions. For the next ten
days, Cornwallis established his head-quarters at Elk Hill on a
plantation belonging to Jefferson.

With one hundred and eighty dragoons and forty mounted
infantry, Tarleton rode seventy miles in twenty-four hours,
destroying public stores on the way; but the assembly, having
received warning, had adjourned, and Jefferson had gone to
the mountains on horseback. The dragoons overtook seven of
the legislature; othedwise, the expedition was fruitless.

Steuben had transported his magazine across the Fluvanna,
and was safe, the water being too deep to be forded; but Sim-
coe made him believe that the whole British army was in pursuit of him; and he fled, leaving behind him some of his stores.

The two detachments rejoined the camp of Cornwallis,
which extended along the James River from the Point of Fork
to a little below the mouth of Byrd Creek. Tarleton had suffered nothing of Jefferson's at Monticello to be injured. At Elk
Hill, under the eye of Cornwallis, all the barns and fences

were burnt; the growing crops destroyed; the fields laid absolutely waste; the throats cut of all the horses that were too
young for service, and the rest carried off. He took away about
thirty slaves, but not to give them freedom. The rest of the
neighborhood was treated in like manner, but with less of destructive fury.

In the march of the British army from Elk Hill down the
river to Williamsburg, where it arrived on the twenty-fifth of
June, all dwelling-houses were plundered. The trusty band of
Lafayette hung upon its rear but could not prevent its depreda-
tions. The Americans of that day computed that Cornwallis, in
his midsummer marching up and down in Virginia, destroyed
property to the value of three million pounds sterling. He nowhere gained a foothold, and he obtained no supplies except
through the terror of his arms. His long travels had only taught
him that the bulk of the people were bent on independence.

At Williamsburg, to his amazement and chagrin, he received
from his chief orders to send back about three thousand men.
Clinton's letter of the eleventh expressed his fear of being attacked in New York by more than twenty thousand; there was,
he said, no possibility of reestablishing order in Virginia, so
general was the disaffection to Great Britain. Cornwallis
should therefore take a defensive situation in any healthy station he might choose, be it at Williamsburg or Yorktown. On
the fifteenth, he added: "I do not think it advisable to leave
more troops in that unhealthy climate at this season of the year
than are absolutely wanted for a defensive and a desultory
water expedition." "De Grasse," so he continued on the nineteenth, "will visit this coast in the hurricane season, and bring
with him troops as well as ships. But, when he hears that your
lordship has taken possession of York River before him, I think
that their first efforts will be in this quarter. I am, however,
under no great apprehensions, as Sir George Rodney seems to
have the same suspicions of De Grasse's intention that we have,
and will of course follow him hither."

From this time, the hate which had long existed between the

lieutenant-general and the commander in chief showed itself without much reserve. The former was eager to step into the chief command; the latter, though he had threatened to throw up his place, clung to it tenaciously, and declared that he would not be "duped" by his rival into resigning.

"To your opinions it is my duty implicitly to submit," was the answer of Cornwallis to the orders of Clinton; and on the fourth of July he began his march to Portsmouth. On that day, the royal army arrived near James Island, and in the evening the advanced guard reached the opposite bank of the James River. Two or three more days were required to carry over the stores and the troops. The small American army followed at a distance. Beside fifteen hundred regular troops, equal to the best in the royal army, Lafayette drew to his side as volunteers gallant young men mounted on their own horses from Maryland and Virginia. Youth and generosity, courage and prudence, were his spells of persuasion. His perceptions were quick; his vigilance never failed; and in his methods of gaining information of the movements of the enemy he excelled every officer in the war except Washington and Morgan. All accounts bear testimony to his caution, and that he never once committed himself during a very difficult campaign. Of his self-possession in danger he was now called upon to give proof.

On the sixth, Lafayette judged correctly that the great body of the British army was still on the north side of the James River; but Wayne, without his knowledge, detached a party under Colonel Galvan to carry off a field-piece of the enemy which was said to lie exposed. The information proved false. The party with Galvan found themselves suddenly in front of the advancing British line; and they retreated in column till they met Wayne with the Pennsylvania brigade. It suited the character of that officer to hazard an encounter. The British moved on with loud shouts and incessant fire. Wayne discovering that he had been tempted to engage a greatly superior force, saw his only safety in redoubling his courage; and he kept up the fight, till Lafayette, braving the hottest fire, in which his horse was killed under him, brought up the light infantry, and rescued the Pennsylvanians from their danger. Two of Wayne's field-pieces were left behind. In killed and wounded, each side lost about one hundred and twenty. The action took its name from the Greene Springs farm, about eight miles above Jamestown, where Lafayette encamped for the night.

After passing the river, Cornwallis, on the eighth, wrote orders to Tarleton with mounted troops to ravage Prince Edward's and Bedford counties, and to destroy all stores, whether public or private. The benefit derived from the destruction of property was not equal to the loss in skirmishes on the route and from the heats of midsummer.

From his camp on Malvern Hill, Layfayette urged Washington to march to Virginia in force; and he predicted in July that, if a French fleet should enter Hampton Roads the English army must surrender. In like manner, on the eighth of the same month, Cornwallis in reply to Clinton reasoned earnestly against a defensive post in the Chesapeake: "It cannot have the smallest influence on the war in Carolina: it only gives us some acres of an unhealthy swamp, and is for ever liable to become a prey to a foreign enemy with a temporary superiority at sea." Thoroughly disgusted with the aspect of affairs in Virginia, he asked leave to transfer the command to General Leslie, and go back to Charleston. Meantime, transport ships arrived in the Chesapeake; and, in a letter which he received on the twelfth, he was desired by his chief so to hasten the embarkation of three thousand men that they might sail for New York within forty-eight hours; for, deceived by letters which were written to be intercepted, he believed that the enemy would certainly attack that post.

But the judgment of Clinton was further confused by another cause. The expectation of a brilliant campaign in Virginia had captivated the minds of Lord George Germain and the king; and, now that Cornwallis was thoroughly cured of his own presumptious delusions, they came back to Clinton in the shape of orders from the American secretary, who dwelt on the vast importance of the occupation of Virginia, and on the wisdom of the present plan of pushing the war in that quarter. It was a great mortification to him that Clinton should think of leaving only a sufficient force to serve for garrisons in the posts that might be established there, and he continued: "Your ideas of the importance of recovering that province appearing to be so different from mine, I thought it proper to ask the advice of his majesty's other servant upon the subject, and their opinion concurring entirely with mine, it has been submitted to the king; and I am commanded by his majesty to acquaint you that the recovery of the southern provinces and the prosecution of the war from south to north is to be considered as the chief and principal object for the employment of all the forces under your command which can be spared from the defense of the places in his majesty's possession."

On Cornwallis he heaped praises, writing to him in June: "The rapidity of your movements is justly a matter of astonishment to all Europe." To Clinton he repeated in the same month: "Lord Cornwallis's opinion entirely coincides with mine;" and on the seventh of July: "The detachments sent to Virginia promise more towards bringing the southern colonies to obedience than any offensive operation of the war;" a week later: "You judiciously sent ample re-enforcements to the Chesapeake;" and on the second of August: "As Sir George Rodney knows the destination of De Grasse, and the French acknowledge his ships sail better than theirs, he will get before him and be in readiness to receive him when he comes upon the coast. I see nothing to prevent the recovery of the whole country to the king's obedience." So the troops in Virginia which were already embarked were ordered to remain there. "As to quitting the Chesapeake entirely," wrote Clinton in a letter received by Cornwallis on the twenty-first of July, "I cannot entertain a thought of such a measure. I flatter myself you will at least hold Old Point Comfort, if it is possible to do it without York." And four days later Clinton urged again: "It ever has been, is, and ever will be, my firm and unalterable opinion that it is of the first consequence to his majesty's affairs on the continent that we take possession of the Chesapeake, and that we do not afterwards relinquish it." "Remain in Chesapeake, at least until the stations I have proposed are occupied and established. It never was my intention to continue a post on Elizabeth River." Now the post of Portsmouth on Elizabeth River had, as Lafayette and Washington well understood, the special value that it offered in the last resort the chance of an escape into the Carolinas.

The engineers, after careful and extensive surveys reported that a work on Point Comfort would not secure ships at anchor in Hampton Roads. To General Phillips on his embarkation in April, Clinton's words had been: "With regard to a station for the protection of the king's ships, I know of no place so proper as Yorktown." Nothing therefore remained but, in obedience to the spirit of Clinton's orders, to seize and fortify York and Gloucester. Cornwallis accordingly, in the first week of August, embarked his troops successively, and, evacuating Portsmouth, transferred his whole force to Yorktown and Gloucester. Yorktown was then but a small village on a high bank, where the long peninsula dividing the York from the James River is less than eight miles wide. The water is broad, bold and deep; so that ships of the line may ride there in safety. On the opposite side lies Gloucester, a point of land projecting into the river and narrowing its width to one mile. These were occupied by Cornwallis, and fortified with the utmost diligence; though, in his deliberate judgment, the measure promised no honor to himself and no advantage to Great Britain.

On the other hand, Lafayette, concentrating his forces in a strong position at a distance of about eight miles indulged in the happiest prophecies, and wrote on the twenty-fourth of August to Maurepas: "I owe you so much gratitude, and feel for you so much attachment, that I wish sometimes to recall to your recollection the rebel commander of the little Virginia army. Your interest for me will have been alarmed at the dangerous part which has been intrusted to me in my youth. Separated by five hundred miles from every other corps and without any resources, I am to oppose the projects of the court of St. James and the fortunes of Lord Cornwallis. Thus far, we have encountered no disaster." On the same day, his words to Vergennes were: "In pursuance of the immense plan of his court, Lord Cornwallis left the two Carolinas exposed, and General Greene has largely profited by it. Lord Cornwallis has left to us Portsmouth, from which place he was in communication with Carolina, and he now is at York, a very advantageous place for one who has the maritime superiority. If by chance that superiority should become ours, our little army will participate in successes which will compensate it for a long and fatiguing campaign. They say that you are about to make peace. I think that you should wait for the events of this campaign."

On the very day on which Cornwallis took possession of York and Gloucester, Washington, assured of the assistance of De Grasse, turned his whole thoughts towards moving with the French troops under Rochambeau and the best part of the American army to Chesapeake. While hostile divisions and angry jealousies increased between the two chief British officers in the United States, on the American side all things conspired happily together. De Barras, who commanded the French squadron at Newport, wrote as to his intentions: "M. de Grasse is my junior; yet, as soon as he is within reach, I will go to sea to put myself under his orders." The same spirit insured unanimity in the mixed council of war. The rendezvous was given to De Grasse in Chesapeake Bay; and, at the instance of Washington, he was to bring with him as many land troops as could be spared from the West Indies. Clinton was so certain in his own mind that the siege of New York was the great object of Washington, that, although the force under his command, including militia, was nearly eighteen thousand, he suffered the Hudson River to be crossed on the twenty-third and twenty-fourth of August without seizing the opportunity to give annoyance. Von Wurmb, a Hessian colonel, who had commanded at King's Bridge again and again reported that the allied armies were obviously preparing to move against Cornwallis; but the general insisted that the appearances were but a stratagem. On the second of September, it first broke on his mind that Washington was moving southward.

In the allied camp, all was joy. The love of freedom took possession not of the French officers only, but inflamed the soldiers. Every one of them was proud of being a defender of the young republic. The new principles entered into their souls, and became a part of their nature. On the fifth of September, they encamped at Chester. Never had the French seen a man penetrated with a livelier or more manifest joy than Washington, when he there learned that, on the last day but one in August, the Count de Grasse, with twenty-eight ships of the line and nearly four thousand land troops, had entered the Chesapeake, where without loss of time he had moored most of the fleet in Lynnhaven Bay, blocked up York River, and without being in the least annoyed by Cornwallis, had disembarked at James Island three thousand men under the command of the Marquis de Saint-Simon. Here, too, prevailed unanimity. Saint-Simon, though older in military service as well as in years, placed himself and his troops as auxiliaries under the orders of Lafayette, because he was a major-general in the service of the United States. The combined army in their encampment could be approached only by two passages, which were in themselves difficult and were carefully guarded, so that Cornwallis could not act on the offensive, and found himself effectually blockaded by land and by sea.

One more disappointment awaited Cornwallis. If a bad king or a bad minister pursues bad ends, he naturally employs bad men. No great naval officer wished to serve against the United States. Lord Sandwich, after the retirement of Howe, gave the naval command at New York to officers without ability; and the aged and imbecile Arbuthnot was succeeded by Graves, a coarse and vulgar man, of mean ability and without skill in his profession. Rodney should have followed De Grasse to the north; but he had become involved in pecuniary perils by his indiscriminate seizures at St. Eustatius, and laid himself open to censure for his inactivity during the long-continued sale of his prize-goods. Pleading ill-health, he escaped from uncongenial cares by sailing for England, and sent in his stead Sir Samuel Hood, with fourteen sail of the line, frigates and a fire-ship into the Chesapeake, where a junction with Graves would have given the English the supremacy. But Graves, who was of higher rank than Hood, was out of the way on a silly cruise before Boston, which had no purpose unless to pick up a few prizes. Meantime, De Barras, with eight ships of the line, sailed from Newport, convoying ten transports, which contained the ordnance for the siege of Yorktown.

There was no want of information at New York, yet the British fleet did not leave Sandy Hook until the day after De Grasse had arrived in the Chesapeake. Early on the fifth of September, Graves discovered the French fleet at anchor in the mouth of that bay. De Grasse, though eighteen hundred of his seamen and ninety officers were on duty in James River, ordered his ships to slip their cables, turn out from the anchorage ground, and form the line of battle. The action began at four o'clock in the afternoon, and continued till about sunset. The British sustained so great a loss that after remaining five days in sight of the French, they returned to New York. On the first day of their return voyage, they evacuated and burned "The Terrible," a ship of the line, so much had it been damaged in the engagement. De Grasse, now undisturbed master of the Chesapeake, on his way back to his anchoring ground captured two British ships, each of thirty-two guns, and he found De Barras safely at anchor in the bay.

Leaving the allied troops to descend by water from Elk River and Baltimore, Washington, with Rochambeau and Chastellux, riding sixty miles a day, on the evening of the ninth reached his "own seat at Mount Vernon." It was the first time in more than six years that he had seen his home.

From its lofty natural terrace above the Potomac, his illustrious guests commanded a noble river, a wide expanse, and the heights, then clothed in forest, within a generation to become the capital of the united republic.

Two days were given to domestic life. On the fourteenth, the party arrived at Williamsburg, where Lafayette, recalling the moment when in France the poor rebels were held in light esteem, and when he nevertheless came to share with them all their perils, had the pleasure of welcoming Washington, as generalissimo of the combined armies of the two nations, to scenes of glory.

The first act of Washington was to repair to the "Ville de Paris," to congratulate De Grasse on his victory. The system of co-operation between the land and naval forces was at the same time concerted.

At this moment, Gerry wrote from Massachusetts to Jay: "You will soon have the pleasure of hearing of the capture of Lord Cornwallis and his army." "Nothing can save Cornwallis," said Greene, "but a rapid retreat through North Carolina to Charleston." On the seventeenth, Cornwallis reported to Clinton: "This place is in no state of defense. If you cannot relieve me very soon, you must be prepared to hear the worst." On that same day, a council of war, held by Clinton at New York, decided that Cornwallis must be relieved; "at all events before the end of October." The next day Rear-admiral Graves answered: "I am very happy to find that Lord Cornwallis is in no immediate danger."

One peril yet menaced Washington. Count de Grasse, hearing of a re-enforcement of the fleet at New York, was bent on keeping the sea, leaving only two vessels at the mouth of the York River. Against this, Washington addressed the most earnest remonstrance :"I should esteem myself deficient in my duty to the common cause of France and America, if I did not persevere in entreating you to resume the plans that have been so happliy arranged." The letter was taken by Lafayette, who joined to it his own explanations and reasonings; and De

Grasse, though reluctant, was prevailed upon to remain within the capes. Washington wrote in acknowledgment: "A great mind knows how to make personal sacrifices to secure an important general good."

The troops from the north having been safely landed at Williamsburg, on the twenty-eighth the united armies marched for the investiture of Yorktown, drove every thing on the British side before them, and lay on their arms during the night.

The fortifications of Yorktown, which were nothing but earthworks freshly thrown up, consisted on the right of redoubts and batteries, with a line of stockade in the rear, which supported a high parapet. Over a marshy ravine in front of the right, a large redoubt was placed. The morass extended along the centre, which was defended by a stockade and batteries. Two small redoubts were advanced before the left. The ground in front of the left was in some parts level with the works, in others cut by ravines; altogether very convenient for the besiegers. The space within the works was exceedingly narrow and except under the cliff was exposed to enfilade.

The twenty-ninth was given to reconnoitring, and forming a plan of attack and approach. The French entreated Washington for orders to storm the exterior posts of the British; in the course of the night before the thirtieth, Cornwallis ordered them all to be abandoned, and thus prematurely conceded to the allied armies ground which commanded his line of works in a very near advance, and gave great advantages for opening the trenches.

At Gloucester, the enemy was shut in by dragoons under the Duke de Lauzun, Virginia milita under General Weedon, and eight hundred marines. Once, and once only, Tarleton and his legion, who were stationed on the same side, undertook to act offensively; but the Duke de Lauzun and his dragoons, full of gayety and joy at the sight, ran against them and trampled them down. Tarleton's horse was taken; its rider barely escaped.

In the night before the sixth of October, every thing being

in readiness, trenches were opened at six hundred yards' distance from the works of Cornwallis,—on the right by the Americans, on the left by the French; and the labor was executed in friendly rivalry with so much secrecy and despatch that it was first revealed to the enemy by the light of morning. Within three days, the first parallel was completed, the redoubts were finished, and batteries were employed in demolishing the embrasures of the enemy's works and their advanced redoubts. On the night before the eleventh, the French battery on the left, by red-hot shot, set on fire the frigate "Charon" of forty-four guns, and three large transport ships which were entirely consumed.

On the eleventh, at night the second parallel was begun within three hundred yards of the lines of the besieged. This was undertaken so much sooner than the British expected, that it could be conducted with the same secrecy as before; and they had no suspicion of the working parties till daylight discovered them to their pickets.

All day on the fourteenth, the American batteries were directed against the abattis and salient angles of two advanced redoubts of the British, both of which needed to be included in the second parallel; and breaches were made in them sufficient to justify an assault. That on the right bank near York River was garrisoned by forty-five men, that on the left by thrice as many. The storming of the former fell to the Americans under the command of Lieutenant-colonel Hamilton; that of the latter to the French, of whom four hundred grenadiers and yagers of the regiments of Gratinois and of Deux Ponts, with a large reserve, were intrusted to Count William de Deux Ponts and to Baron de l'Estrade.

At the concerted signal of six shells consecutively discharged, the corps under Hamilton advanced in two columns without firing a gun,—the right composed of his own battalion, led by Major Fish and of another commanded by Lieutenant-colonel Gimat; the left, of a detachment under Lieutenant-colonel Laurens, destined to take the enemy of reverse and intercept their retreat. All the movements were excuted with exactness, and the redoubt was at the same moment enveloped and carried in every part. Lieutenant Mansfield conducted the vanguard with coolness and punctuality, and was wounded with a bayonet as he entered the work. Captain Olney led the first platoon of Gimat's battalion over the abattis and palisades, and gained the parapet, receiving two bayonet wounds in the thigh and in the body, but not till he had directed his men to form. Laurens was among the foremost to climb into the redoubt, making prisoner of Major Campbell, its commanding officer. Animated by his example, the battalion of Gimat overcame every obstacle by their order and resolution. The battalion under Major Fish advanced with such celerity as to participate in the assault. Incapable of imitating precedents of barbarity, the American spared every man that ceased to resist; so that the killed and wounded of the enemy did not exceed eight. The conduct of the affair brought conspicuous honor to the talents and gallantry of Hamilton.

Precisely as the signal was given, the French on the left, in like manner, began their march in the deepest silence. At one hundred and twenty paces from the redoubt, they were challenged by a German sentry from the parapet; they pressed on at a quick time, exposed to the fire of the enemy. The abattis and palisades, at twenty-five paces from the redoubt being strong and well preserved, stopped them for some minutes and cost them many men. So soon as the way was cleared by the brave carpenters, the storming party threw themselves into the ditch, broke through the fraises, and mounted the parapet. Foremost was Charles de Lameth, who had volunteered for this attack, and who was wounded in both knees by two different musket-balls. The order being now given, the French leaped into the redoubt, and charged the enemy with bayonet. At this moment, the Count de Deux Ponts raised the cry of "Vive le roi," which was repeated by all of his companions who were able to lift their voices. De Sireuil, a very young captain of yagers who had been wounded twice before, was now wounded for the third time and mortally. Within six minutes, the redoubt was mastered and manned; but in that short time nearly one hundred of the assailants were killed or wounded.

On that night, "victory twined double garlands around the banners" of France and America. Washington acknowledged the emulous courage, intrepidity, coolness, and firmness of the attacking troops. Louis XVI distinguished the regiment of Gatinois by naming it the "Royal Auvergne."

By the unwearied labor of the French and Americans both redoubts were included in the second parallel in the night of their capture. Just before the break of day of the sixteenth, the British made a sortie upon a part of the second parallel and spiked four French pieces of artillery and two of the American; but, on the quick advance of the guards in the trenches, they retreated precipitately. The spikes were easily extracted; and in six hours the cannon again took part in the fire which enfiladed the British works.

On the seventeenth, Cornwallis, who could neither hold his post nor escape into the country, proposed to surrender. On the eighteenth, Colonel Laurens and the Viscount de Noailles as commissioners on the American side met two high officers of the army of Cornwallis, to draft the capitulation. The articles were the same as those which Clinton had imposed upon Lincoln at Charleston. All the troops were to be prisoners of war; all public property was to be delivered up. Runaway slaves and the plunder taken by officers and soldiers in their marches through the country might be reclaimed by their owners; with these exceptions, private property was to be respected. All royalists were abandoned to trial by their own countrymen. But, in the packet which took the despatches to Sir Henry Clinton, Cornwallis was permitted to convey away such persons as were most obnoxious to the laws of Virginia.

Of prisoners, there were seven thousand two hundred and forty-seven regular soldiers, the flower of the British army in America, beside eight hundred and forty sailors. The British loss during the siege amounted to more than three hundred and fifty. One hundred and six guns were taken, of which seventy-five were brass. The land forces and stores were assigned to the Americans, the ships and mariners to the French. At four o'clock in the afternoon of the nineteenth, Cornwallis remaining in his tent, Major-general O'Hara marched the British army past the lines of the combined armies, and, not without signs of repugnance, made his surrender to Washington. His troops then stepped forward decently and piled their arms on the ground.

Nor must impartial history fail to relate that the French provided for the siege of Yorktown thirty-seven ships of the line, and the Americans not one; that while the Americans supplied nine thousand troops, of whom fifty-five hundred were regulars, the contingent of the French consisted of seven thousand.

Among the prisoners were two battalions of Anspach, amounting to ten hundred and seventy-seven men; and two regiments of Hesse, amounting to eight hundred and thirty-three. On the way to their camp, they passed in front of the regiment of Deux Ponts. At the sight of their countrymen, they forgot that they had been in arms against each other, and embraced with tears in their eyes. The English soldiers affected to look at the allied army with scorn; their officers conducted themselves with decorum, yet felt most keenly how decisive was their defeat.

When the letters of Washington announcing the capitulation reached congress, that body, with the people streaming in their train, went in procession to the Dutch Lutheran church to return thanks to Almighty God. Every breast swelled with joy. In the evening, Philadelphia was illuminated with greater splendor than at any time before. Congress voted honors to Washington, to Rochambeau, and to De Grasse with special thanks to the officers and troops. A marble column was to be erected at Yorktown, with emblems of the alliance between the United States and his most Christian majesty.

The Duke de Lauzun, chosen to take the news across the Atlantic, arrived in twenty-two days at Brest, and reached

Versailles on the nineteenth of November. The king, who had just been made happy by the birth of a dauphin, received the glad news in the queen's apartment. The very last sands of the life of the Count de Maurepas were running out; but he could still recognize De Lauzun, and the tidings threw a halo round his deathbed. The joy at court penetrated the whole people, and the name of Lafayette was pronounced with veneration. "History," said Vergennes, "offers few examples of a success so complete." "All the world agree," wrote Franklin to Washington, "that no expedition was ever better planned or better executed. It brightens the glory that must accompany your name to the latest posterity."

The first tidings of the surrender of Cornwallis reached England from France about noon on the twenty-fifth of November. "It is all over," said Lord North many times, under the deepest agitation and distress. Fox—to whom, in reading history, the defeats of armies of invaders, from Xerxes' time downwards gave the greatest satisfaction—heard of the capitulation of Yorktown with wild delight. He hoped it might become the conviction of all mankind, that power resting on armed force is invidious, detestable, weak, and tottering. The official report from Sir Henry Clinton was received the same day at midnight. When on the following Tuesday parliament came together, the speech of the king was confused, the debates in the two houses augured an impending change in the opinion of parliament, and the majority of the ministry was reduced to eighty-seven. A fortnight later, the motion of Sir James Lowther to give up "all further attempts to reduce the revolted colonies" was well received by the members from the country, and the majority of the ministry after a long and animated debate dwindled to forty-one. The city of London entreated the king to put an end to "this unnatural and unfortunate war." Such, too was the wish of public meetings in Westminster, in Southwark, and in the counties of Middlesex and Surrey.

The house of commons employed the recess in grave reflection. The chimes of the Christmas bells had hardly died away, when the king wrote as stubbornly as ever; "No difficulties can get me to consent to the getting of peace at the expense of a separation from America."

Yet Lord George Germain was compelled to retire ingloriously from the cabinet. It was sought to palliate his disgrace with a peerage; but, when for the first time he repaired to the house of lords, he was met at its threshold by the unsparing reprobation of his career of cowardice and blindly selfish incapacity.

BANCROFT *once said that he tried to make no important statement in his* History *"without reference to an original document." His chapter on the peace negotiations of 1782, the most authoritative written to his time, furnishes an example of the staggering amounts of original materials he employed to validate his aim. In addition to the usual published sources, Bancroft used among others the unpublished papers of all the American, French, and English representatives; the reports of the French minister at Philadelphia to his government; and the papers of Shelburne, Townshend, Oswald, and Starchey, many unpublished, including some hitherto unknown letters of George III. He was the first American historian to be granted full access to the records of the British Foreign Office, and Secretaries of State Seward and Fish granted him similar use of the State Department Archives. He could write with pardonable pride in the preface to Volume X in 1874, "With regard to the peace between the United States and England, I think I might say that my materials in their completeness are unique."*

Peace between the United States and Great Britain (1782)

DE GRASSE, as he passed through London on parole, brought from Shelburne to Vergennes suggestions which left Spain the only obstacle in the way of peace. To conciliate that power, Jay was invited to Versailles, where, on the fourth of September, Rayneval the most confidential assistant of Vergennes, sought to persuade him to resign for his country all pretensions to the eastern valley of the Mississippi, and with it the right to the navigation of that stream. Jay was inflexible. On the sixth, Rayneval sent him a paper containing a long argument against the pretensions of America to touch the Mississippi or the great lakes; and on the next morning, after an interview with the Spanish ambassador, he set off for England, to establish a good understanding with Shelburne.

On the ninth, the departure of Rayneval came to the knowledge of Jay. On the tenth, a translation of an intercepted despatch from Marbois, the French secretary of legation at Philadelphia against conceding a share in the great fishery to the Americans, was communicated to Jay and Franklin. Jay was thrown from his equipoise. Having excited the distrust of Shelburne by peremptorily breaking off the negotiation, he now, through an English agent, sent to the British minister, with whom he was wholly unacquainted, a personal request that he would for the present take no measures with Rayneval; giving as the reason, that it was the obvious interest of Britain immediately to cut the cords which tied the Americans to France. Franklin, who had vainly labored with his colleague to finish at once the treaty with England, strove as ever before to defeat all intrigues by hastening its consummation; and to this end he urged on the British government a compliance with the demand of a new commission for Oswald. Lord Grantham had assured him by letter that "the establishment of an honorable and lasting peace was the system of the ministers." "I know it to be the sincere desire of the United States," Franklin replied, on the day after reading the paper of Marbois; "and with such dispositions on both sides there is reason to hope that the good work in its progress will meet with little difficulty. A small one has occurred, with which Mr. Oswald will acquaint you. I flatter myself that means will be found on your part for removing it, and my best endeavors in removing subsequent ones (if any should arise) may be relied on;" but Franklin neither criminated France, nor compromised himself, nor his country, nor his colleague.

Rayneval passed through London directly to Bow Wood, the country seat of Shelburne, in the west of England. "I trust what you say as much as if Mr. de Vergennes himself were speaking to me," were the words with which he was welcomed. "Gibraltar," observed Rayneval, "is as dear to the king of Spain

as his life." Shelburne answered: "Its cession is impossible: I
dare not propose it to the British nation." "Spain wishes to become complete mistress of the Gulf of Mexico," continued
Rayneval. On this point, Shelburne opened the way for concession saying: "It is not by way of Florida that we carry on
our contraband trade, but by way of Jamaica." Shelburne
owned reluctantly the necessity of conceding independence to
the United States, but was resolved to concede it without any
reservation. "As to the question of boundaries and fisheries,"
observed Rayneval, "I do not doubt of the earnest purpose of
the king to do every thing in his power to restrain the Americans within the limits of justice and reason. Be their pretensions to the fisheries what they may, it seems to me that there
is one sure principle to follow on that subject; namely, that the
fishery on the high seas is *res nullius,* the property of no one,
and that the fishery on the coast belongs of right to the proprietaries of the coasts, unless there have been derogations
founded upon treaties. As to boundaries, the British minister
will find in the negotiations of 1754, a relative to the Ohio, the
boundaries which England, then the sovereign of the thirteen
United States, thought proper to assign them." To these insin-
uations, Shelburne, true to his words to Franklin, made no response.

With regard to the mediation offered by the northern powers,
he said: "We have no need of them: they can know nothing
about our affairs, since it is so hard for us to understand them
ourselves; there is need of but three persons to make peace,—
myself, the Count de Vergennes, and you." "I shall be as pacific
in negotiating as I shall be active for war, if war must be continued," he added, on the fourteenth. Rayneval replied: "Count
de Vergennes will, without ceasing, preach justice and moderation. It is his own code, and it is that of the king." On the fifteenth, they both came up to London, where, on the sixteenth,
Rayneval met Lord Grantham. Nothing could be more decided
than his refusal to treat about Gibraltar. On the seventeenth,
in bidding farewell to Rayneval, Shelburne said, in the most

serious tone and the most courageous manner: "I have been deeply touched by every thing you have said to me about the character of the king of France, his principles of justice and moderation, his love of peace. I wish, not only to re-establish peace between the two nations and the two sovereigns, but to bring them to a cordiality which will constitute their reciprocal happiness. Not only are they not natural enemies, as men have thought till now, but they have interests which ought to bring them nearer together. We have each lost consideration in our furious desire to do each other harm. Let us change principles that are so erroneous. Let us reunite, and we shall stop all revolutions in Europe." By revolutions he meant the division of Poland, the encroachments on Turkey, and the attempt of the court of Vienna to bring Italy under its control by seizing the fine harbors of Dalmatia.

"There is another object," continued Shelburne, "which makes a part of my political views; and that is the destruction of monopoly in commerce. I regard that monopoly as odious, though the English nation, more than any other, is tainted with it. I flatter myself I shall be able to come to an understanding with your court upon this subject, as well as upon our political amalgamation. I have spoken to the king on all these points. I have reason to believe that when we shall have made peace, the most frank cordiality will be established between the two princes." Rayneval reciprocated these views, and added: "Your principles on trade accord exactly with those of France; Count de Vergennes thinks that freedom is the soul of commerce."

The British ministry were so much in earnest in their desire for peace with the United States that a new commission was drafted for Oswald to conclude a peace or truce with commissioners of the thirteen United States of America, which were enumerated one by one. This concession was made after consultation with Lord Ashburton, who held that it was a matter of indifference whether the title chosen by the American commissioners should be accepted by Oswald under the king's authority, or directly by the king. The acknowledgment of independence was still reserved to form the first article of the treaty of peace. The change of form was grateful and honorable to the United States; but the delay had given time to British creditors and to the refugees to muster all their strength and embarrass the negotiation by their importunities. The king was subdued, and said: "I am so much agitated with a fear of sacrificing the interests of my country, by hurrying peace on too fast, that I am unable to add any thing on that subject but the most frequent prayers to Heaven to guide me so to act that posterity may not say the downfall of this once respectable empire to my door; and that, if ruin should attend the measures that may be adopted, I may not long survive them."

On purely Spanish questions, Jay appears to the best advantage. On the twenty-sixth of September, Aranda, in company with Lafayette, encountered him at Versailles. Aranda asked: "When shall we proceed to do business?" Jay replied: "When you communicate your powers to treat." "An exchange of commissions," said Aranda, "cannot be expected, for Spain has not acknowledged your independence." "We have declared our independence," said Jay; "and France, Holland, and Britain have acknowledged it." Lafayette came to his aid, and told the ambassador that it was not consistent with the dignity of France that an ally of hers like the United States should treat otherwise than as independent. Vergennes pressed upon Jay a settlement of claims with Spain. Jay answered: "We shall be content with no boundaries short of the Mississippi."

So soon as Oswald received his new commission, the negotiation, after the loss of a month, moved forward easily and rapidly. At the request of Franklin, Jay drew up the articles of peace. They included the clauses relating to boundaries and fisheries, which Franklin had settled with Oswald in July; to these, Jay added a clause for reciprocal freedom of commerce, which was equally grateful to Franklin and Oswald, and a concession to the British of the free navigation of the Mississippi. He repeatedly insisted with Oswald that West Florida should not be left in the hands of the Spaniards, but should be restored to England; and he pleaded "in favor of the future commerce of England, as if he had been of her council, and wished to make some reparation for her loss," not duly considering the dangers threatening the United States, if England should hold both East and West Forida and the Bahama Islands.

Shelburne had hoped to make a distinction between the jurisdiction over the western country and property in its ungranted domain, so that the sales of wild lands might yield some compensation to the loyal refugees; but Jay insisted that no such right of property remained to the king. Oswald urged upon him the restoration of the loyalists to their civil rights; but Jay answered that the subject of pardon was one with which "congress could not meddle. The states being sovereigns, the parties in fault were answerable to them and to them only." Oswald yielded on both points.

On sending over the draft of the treaty to the secretary of state, the British plenipotentiary wrote: "I look upon the treaty as now closed." Both Franklin and Jay had agreed that, if it should be approved, they would sign it immediately. Towards the French minister, they continued their reserve, not even communicating to him the new commission of Oswald.

After the capture of Minorca by the Duke de Crillon, the French and Spanish fleets united under his command to reduce Gibraltar; and Count d'Artois, the brother of the king, passed through Madrid to be present at its surrender. But danger inspired the British garrison with an unconquerable intrepidity. By showers of red-hot shot, and by a most heroic sortie under General Elliot, the batteries which were thought to be fire-proof were blown up or consumed, and a fleet under Lord Howe was close at hand to replenish the stores of the fortress. The news of the catastrophe made Paris clamorous for peace. France, it was said, is engaged in a useless war for thankless allies. She has suffered disgrace in the West Indies while undertaking to conquer Jamaica for Spain, and now shares in the defeat before Gibraltar. Vergennes saw that she needed and demanded repose. To obtain a release from his engagement to Spain, he was ready to make great sacrifices on the part of his own country, and to require them of America. Congress was meanwhile instructing Franklin "to use his utmost endeavors to effect the loan of four millions of dollars through the kind and generous exertions of the king of France;" and on the third of October it renewed its resolution to hearken to no propositions for peace except in confidence and in concert with its ally.

On the fourteenth of the same month, Vergennes explained to the French envoy at Philadelphia the policy of France: "If we are so happy as to make peace the king must then cease to subsidize the American army, which will be as useless as it has been habitually inactive. We are astonished at the demands which continue to be made upon us, while the Americans obstinately refuse the payment of taxes. It seems to us much more natural for them to raise upon themselves, rather than upon the subjects of the king, the funds which the defense of their cause exacts." "You know," continued Vergennes, "our system with regard to Canada. Every thing which shall prevent the conquest of that country will agree essentially with our views. But this way of thinking ought to be an impenetrable secret for the Americans. Moreover, I do not see by what title the Americans can form pretensions to lands on Lake Ontario. Those lands belong to the savages or are a dependency of Canada. In either case, the United States have no right to them whatever. It has been pretty nearly demonstrated that to the south of the Ohio their limits are the mountains following the shed of waters, and that every thing to the north of the mountain range, especially the lakes, formerly made a part of Canada. These notions are for you alone; you will take care not to appear to be informed about them, because we so much the less wish to intervene in the discussions between the Count de Aranda and Mr. Jay, as both parties claim countries to which neither of them has a right, and as it will be almost impossible to reconcile them."

When the draft of the treaty with the United States, as agreed to by Oswald, came back to England, the offer of Jay of the free navigation of the Mississippi was gladly accepted; but that for a reciprocity of navigation and commerce was reserved. The great features of the treaty were left unchanged; but the cabinet complained of Oswald for yielding every thing and gave him for an assistant Henry Strachey, Townshend's under-secretary of state. On the twentieth of October, both of the secretaries of state being present, Shelburne gave Strachey three points specially in charge; no concession of a right to dry fish on Newfoundland; a recognition of the validity of debts to British subjects contracted by citizens of the United States before the war; but, above all, adequate indemnity for the con-fiscated property of the loyal refugees. The last demand touched alike the sympathy and the sense of honor of England. The previous answer that the commissioners had no power to treat on the business of the loyalists was regarded as an al-legation that, though they claimed to have full powers, they were not plenipotentiaries; that they were acting under thir-teen separate sovereignties, which had no common head. To meet the exigence, Shelburne proposed either an extension of Nova Scotia to the Penobscot or the Kennebec or the Saco, so that a province might be formed for the reception of the loyalists; or that a part of the money to be received from sales of the Ohio lands might be applied to their subsistence. To the ministry, it was clear that peace, if to be made at all, must be made before the coming together of parliament, which had been summoned for the twenty-fifth of November.

While the under-secretary of state was sent to re-enforce Oswald, the American commission was recruited by the arrival of John Adams. He had prevailed on the United Provinces to acknowledge the independence of the United States, and to form with them a treaty of commerce. He was greatly elated at his extraordinary success, and he loved to have it acknowl-edged; but flattery never turned him aside from public duty, for he looked upon the highest praise as no more than his due, and as investing him with new rights to stand up fearlessly for his country. He left Vergennes to find out his arrival through the police. Franklin had hitherto warded off the demand that the treaty of peace should guarantee to English merchants the right to collect debts that had been due to them in the United States, because the British armies had themselves in many cases robbed the merchants of the very goods for which the debts were incurred; and had, wantonly and contrary to the laws of war, destroyed the property which could have furnished the means of payment. The day after Strachey's arrival in Paris, Adams, encountering him and Oswald at the house of Jay, to their surprise and delight blurted out his assent to the proposed stipulation for the payment of debts. In the evening of the same day, Adams called for the first time on Franklin, who at once put him on his guard as to the British demands relating to debts and compensation of tories; but he could not recall his word.

On the thirtieth, the American commissioners met Oswald and Strachey, and for four several days they discussed the unsettled points of the treaty. Jay and Franklin had left the northeastern boundary to be settled by commissioners after the war. It is due to John Adams, who had taken the precaution to obtain from the council of Massachusetts authenticated copies of every document relating to the question, that it was definitively established in the treaty itself. In the north-west, it was agreed that the line should be drawn through the centre of the water communications of the great lakes to the Lake of the Woods. The British commissioners denied to the Americans the right of drying fish on Newfoundland. This was, after a great deal of conversation, agreed to by John Adams as well as his colleagues, upon condition that the American fishermen should be allowed to dry their fish on any unsettled parts of the coast of Nova Scotia. Franklin said further: "I observe as to catching fish you mention only the banks of Newfoundland. Why not all other places, and among others the Gulf of St. Lawrence? Are you afraid there is not fish enough, or that we should catch too many, at the same time that you know that we shall bring the greatest part of the money we get for that fish to Great Britain to pay for your manufactures?" And this advice was imbodied in the new article on the fisheries.

On the fourth of November, Adams and Jay definitively overruled the objections of Franklin to the recognition by treaty of the validity of debts contracted before the war. Pluming himself exceedingly on having gained this concession, Strachey wrote to the secretary of state that Jay and Adams would likewise assent to the indemnification of the refugees rather than break off the treaty upon such a point. On the other hand, Franklin, in reply to a letter which he had received from the secretary, Townshend, gave an earnest warning: "I am sensible you have ever been averse to the measures that brought on this unhappy war; I have, therefore, no doubt of the sincerity of your wishes for a return of peace. Mine are equally earnest. Nothing, therefore, except the beginning of the war, has given me more concern than to learn at the conclusion of our conferences that it is not likely to be soon ended. Be assured no endeavors on my part would be wanting to remove any difficulties that may have arisen, or, even if a peace were made, to procure afterwards any changes in the treaty that might tend to render it more perfect and the peace more durable;" and then, having in his mind the case of the refugees, he deprecated any instructions to the British negotiators that would involve an irreconcilable conflict with those of America. At the same time, he persuaded Adams and Jay to join with him in letters to Oswald and to Strachey, expressing in conciliatory language their unanimous sentiments that an amnesty more extensive than what had already been agreed to could not be granted to the refugees.

Before Strachey reached London with the second set of articles for peace, the friends of Fox had forgotten their zeal for American independence. All parties unanimously demanded amnesty and indemnity for the loyalists. Within the cabinet itself, Camden and Grafton were ill at ease; Keppell

and Richmond inclining to cut loose. The king could not avoid
mentioning "how sensibly he felt the dismemberment of America from the empire:" "I should be miserable indeed," said he,
"if I did not feel that no blame on that account can be laid at
my door." Moreover, he thought so ill of its inhabitants that
"it may not," he said, "in the end be an evil that they will become aliens to this kingdom."

In the general tremulousness among the ministers, Townshend and William Pitt remained true to Shelburne; and a third
set of articles was prepared, to which these three alone gave
their approval. There was no cavilling about boundaries. All
the British posts on the Penobscot, at New York and in Carolina, at Niagara and at Detroit, were to be given up to the
United States and the country east of the Mississippi and
north of Florida was acknowledged to be theirs. The article on
the fishery contained arbitrary restrictions copied from former
treaties with France; so that the Americans were not to take
fish within fifteen leagues of Cape Breton, or within three
leagues of any other British isle on the coast in America. Not
only indemnity for the estates of the refugees, but for the proprietary rights and properties of the Penns and of the heirs of
Lord Baltimore, was to be demanded. "If they insist in the
plea of the want of power to treat of these subjects," said
Townshend, "you will intimate to them in a proper manner
that they are driving us to a necessity of applying directly to
those who are allowed to have the power."

"If the American commissioners think that they will gain
by the whole coming before parliament, I do not imagine that
the refugees will have any objections," added Shelburne. Fitzherbert, the British minister in Paris, was instructed to take
part in the American negotiations; and, with his approval and
that of Strachey, Oswald was empowered to sign a treaty.
Authority was given to Fitzherbert to invoke the influence of
France to bend the Americans. Vergennes had especially
pleaded with them strongly in favor of the refugees. In the hope
of a settlement, parliament was prorogued to the fifth of December.

On the same day on which the final instructions to Oswald were written, Vergennes declared in a letter to Luzerne: "There exists in our treaties no condition which obliges the king to prolong the war in order to sustain the ambitious pretensions which the United States may form in reference to the fishery or the extent of boundaries." "In spite of all the cajoleries which the English ministers lavish on the Americans, I do not promise myself they will show themselves ready to yield either in regard to the fisheries, or in regard to the boundaries as the American commissioners understand them. This last subject may be arranged by mutual sacrifices and compensations. But as to the first, in order to form a settled judgment on its probable issue, it would be necessary to know what the Americans understand by fishery. If it is the drift fishery on banks remote from the coast it seems to me a natural right; but, if they pretend to the fisheries as they exercised them by the title of English subjects, do they, in the name of justice, think to obtain rights attached to the condition of subjects which they renounce?" France would not prolong the war to secure to the Americans the back lands and the fisheries; the Americans were still less bound to continue the war to obtain Gibraltar for Spain.

Early in the morning of the twenty-fifth, the king was urging Shelburne to confide to Vergennes his "ideas concerning America," saying, "France must wish to assist us in keeping the Americans from a concurrent fishery, which the looseness of the article with that people as now drawn up gives but too much room to apprehend." Before Shelburne could have received the admonition, Adams, Franklin, and Jay met Oswald and Strachey at Oswald's lodgings. Strachey opened the parley by an elaborate speech, in which he explained the changes in the article on the fisheries, and that "the restitution of the property of the loyalists was the grand point upon which a final settlement depended. If the treaty should break off, the whole business must go loose, and take its chance in parliament." Jay wished to know if Oswald could now conclude the treaty; and Strachey answered that he could, absolutely. Jay desired to know if the propositions he had brought were an ultimatum. Strachey seemed loath to answer, but at last said "no." That day, and the three following ones, the discussion was continued.

On the twenty-ninth, Strachey, Oswald, and Fitzherbert on the one side, Jay, Franklin, Adams, and, for the first time, Laurens on the other, came together for their last word, at the apartments of Jay. The American commissioners agreed that there should be no future confiscations nor prosecutions of loyalists; that all pending prosecutions should be discontinued; and that congress should recommend to the several states and their legislatures, on behalf of the refugees, amnesty and the restitution of their confiscated property. Strachey thought this article better than any of the modifications proposed in Engand, and congratulated himself on his triumph. The question of the fisheries more nearly concerned Oswald. Against the British draft, John Adams spoke with the more effect as it rested not on the principle of the law of nations, but created an arbitrary restriction; and, with the support of every one of his colleagues, he declared he would not set his hand to the treaty unless the limitations were stricken out. After long altercations, the article was reduced to the form in which it appears in the treaty, granting to the United States equal rights with British fishermen to take fish on the coast of Newfoundland, and on the coasts, bays, and creeks of all other British dominions in America.

At this stage, Strachey and Fitzherbert gave the opinion that it would be necessary to consult the government at home. "We can wait," answered Adams, "till a courier goes to London." The reference would have carried the whole matter into parliament, and so would have been fatal to the treaty. Franklin saw the danger, and interposed: "If any further delay should be made, the clause insuring to the subjects of Great Britain the right of recovering their debts in the United States must also be reconsidered." But on this article Strachey prided himself as his greatest success; and, rather than expose it to risk, he joined with Oswald. Fitzherbert, now left alone reflected that peace with the United States would be the best means of forcing France and Spain to declare their ultimatum; and he, too, gave his consent.

Thus far, no word in the convention had, except indirectly, alluded to the existence of slavery in the United States. On the thirtieth, at the demand of Laurens, in the engrossed copies of the convention a clause was interlined, prohibiting, on the British evacuation, the "carrying away any negroes or any other property of the inhabitants." So the instrument, which already contained a confession that the United States were not formed into one nation, made known that in their confederacy man could be held as a chattel; but, as interpreted alike in America and England, it included free negroes among their citizens. By a separate article, the line of north boundary between West Florida and the United States had been concerted, in case Great Britain at the conclusion of the war should recover that province. Out of respect to the alliance between the United States and France, the treaty was not to be concluded, until terms of peace should have been agreed upon between Great Britain and France. With this reservation the articles which were to be inserted in and to constitute the treaty of peace between the United States of America and Great Britain were signed and sealed by the commissioners of both countries. In the hope of preventing the possibility of future dispute, the boundaries were marked interchangeably by a strong line on copies of the map of America by Mitchell.

Friends of Franklin gathered around him; and as the Duke de la Rochefoucauld kissed him for joy. "My friend," said Franklin, "could I have hoped at such an age to have enjoyed so great happiness?" The treaty was not a compromise, nor a compact imposed by force, but a free and perfect solution and perpetual settlement of all that had been called in question. By doing an act of justice to her former colonies, England rescued her own liberties at home from imminent danger, and opened the way for their slow but certain development. The narrowly selfish colonial policy which had led to the cruel and unnatural war was cast aside and for ever by Great Britain, which was henceforward as the great colonizing power to sow all the oceans with the seed of republics. For the United States, the war, which began by an encounter with a few husbandmen embattled on Lexington green, ended with their independence, and possession of all the country from the St. Croix to the south-western Mississippi, from the Lake of the Woods to the St. Mary's. In time past, republics had been confined to cities and their dependencies, or to small cantons; and the United States avowed themselves able to fill a continental territory with commonwealths. They possessed beyond any other portion of the world the great ideas of their age, and enjoyed the practice of them by individual man in uncontrolled faith and industry, thought and action. For other communities, institutions had been built up by capitulations and grants from authoritative power; the United States of America could shape their coming relations wisely only through the widest and most energetic exercise of the right inherent in humanity to deliberation, choice, and assent. While the constitutions of their separate members, resting on the principle of self-direction, were, in most respects, the best in the world, they had no general government; and, as they went forth upon untried paths, the routine statesmen of Europe looked to see the confederacy fly into fragments, or lapse into helpless anarchy. But, notwithstanding the want of a government, their solemn pledge to one another of mutual citizenship and perpetual union made them one people; and that people was superior to its institutions, possessing the vital force which goes before organization, and gives to it strength and form. Yet for success the liberty of the individual must know how to set to itself bounds; and the states, displaying the highest quality of greatness, must learn to temper their separate rule by their own moderation.

"THE order of time," wrote Bancroft in the preface to his constitutional history in 1882, "brings us to the most cheering act in the political history of mankind, when thirteen republics, of which at least three reached from the sea to the Mississippi, formed themselves into one federal commonwealth." The framing and adoption of the Constitution, in Bancroft's view of the pattern of American history, put the last piece into place. The Constitution, by its imposition of order and union on a political society already made free, marked the completion of God's design for America. Though he published it separately in two volumes, he intended the History of the Formation of the Constitution of the United States of America to be a part of his total History and included it as such in the author's last revision of 1883–85. He was, incidentally, the only living constitutional historian who could draw upon firsthand information obtained from one of its signers, for he had interviewed James Madison in 1836 and had access to Madison's own convention records.

There was a powerful "love of union" inherent in the American people from the beginning, wrote Bancroft, coexistent with a parallel love of freedom and independence, both brought to full fruition by the Revolution. After the failure of the Confederation, which "missed the plain road of English and American experience," the peoples' representatives at Philadelphia, "by calm mediation and friendly councils," framed a government which "in the union of freedom with strength and order, excelled every one known before." The Constitution represented "the sublime achievement . . . of a people led by statesmen of earnestness, perseverance, and public spirit, instructed by the widest experience in the forms of representative government, and warmed by the mutual love which proceeds from ancient connections, harmonious effort in perils, and common aspirations."

Bancroft considered the constitutional period as a five-act drama—"The subject was perfect unity," he remarked, "and falls of itself into five epochs; The Confederation; On the Way to a Federal Convention; The Federal Convention; The People of the United

*States in Judgment on the Constitution; The Federal
Government." In effect, he treated the years 1783–89
as a kind of political melodrama, with the specters of
states' rights and secession lurking in the wings while
the Federalists and their "plainly misguided" opponents struggled in debate. Out of this, "in the
happy morning of their existence as one of the powers
of the world," the American people evolved a plan
and style of government which still remained "the
only hope for renovating the life of the civilized
world."*

The Constitution (1787)

THE American constitution is the most wonderful work ever
struck off at a given time by the brain and purpose of man;"
but it had its forerunners.

England had suffered the thirteen colonies, as free states, to
make laws each for itself and never for one of the others; and
had established their union in a tempered subordination to the
British crown. Among the many guides of America, there had
been Winthrop and Cotton, Hooker and Haynes, George Fox
and William Penn, Roger Williams and John Clarke; scholars
of Oxford and many more of Cambridge; Gustavus Adolphus
and Oxenstiern; the merchants of the United Netherlands;
Southampton and Baltimore, with the kindliest influences of
the British aristocracy; Shaftesbury with Locke, for evil as
well as for good; all the great slave-traders that sat on thrones
or were fostered by parliament; and the philanthropist Ogle-
thorpe, who founded a colony exclusively of the free on a territory twice as large as France, and though he had to mourn
at the overthrow of his plans for liberty, lived to see his plantation independent.

There were other precursors of the federal government; but
the men who framed it followed the lead of no theoretical writer

Vol. II, Chap. I, of *History of the Formation of the Constitution of the
United States of America* (New York: D. Appleton & Co., 1882).

of their own or preceding times. They harbored no desire of revolution, no craving after untried experiments. They wrought from the elements which were at hand, and shaped them to meet the new exigencies which had arisen. The least possible reference was made by them to abstract doctrines; they moulded their design by a creative power of their own, but nothing was introduced that did not already exist, or was not a natural development of a well-known principle. The materials for building the American constitution were the gifts of the ages.

Of old, the family was the rudiment of the state. Of the Jews, the organization was by tribes. The citizens of the commonwealth of the Hellenes were of one blood. Among the barbarous tribes of the fourth continent, the governments and the confederacies all rested on consanguinity. Nations, as the word implied, were but large communities of men of one kin; and nationalities survive to this day, a source of strength in their unity, and yet of strife, where they exist in their original separateness and are nevertheless held in subjection under one ruler. Rome first learned to cherish the human race by a common name and transform the vanquished into citizens.

The process of assimilation which Rome initiated by war, received its perfect development in the land where the Dutch and the Swedes, and in the country north-west of the Ohio the French, competed in planting colonies; where the English, the Irish, the Scotch for the most part came over each for himself never reproducing their original nationality; and where from the first fugitives from persecution of all nations found a safe asylum. Though subjects of the English king, all were present in America as individuals.

The English language maintained itself without a rival, not merely because those speaking it as their mother tongue very gradually outnumbered all others, and because all acknowledged English supremacy; but for the simplicity of its structure; its logical order in the presentment of thought; its suitableness for the purposes of every-day life; for the discussion of abstract truths and the apprehension of Anglo-Saxon political ideas; for use as the instrument of the common law; for science and description; for the debates of public life; for every kind of poetry, from humor to pathos, from nature to the heart and mind.

But the distinctive character of the new people as a whole, their nationality, so to say, was the principle of individuality which prevailed among them as it had nowhere done before. This individuality was strengthened by the remoteness from the abodes of ancient institutions, by the war against the traditions of absolute power and old superstitions, till its developed itself into the most perfect liberty in thought and action; so that the American came to be marked by the readiest versatility, the spirit of enterprise, and the faculty of invention. In the declaration of independence the representatives of the United States called themselves "the good people of these colonies." The statesmen who drew the law of citizenship in 1776 made no distinction of nationalities, or tribes, or ranks, or occupations, or faith or wealth, and knew only inhabitants bearing allegiance to the governments of the several states of the union.

Again, this character of the poeple appeared most clearly in the joint action of the United States in the federal convention, where the variant prejudices that still clung to separate states eliminated each other.

The constitution establishes nothing that interferes with equality and individuality. It knows nothing of differences by descent, or opinions, of favored classes, or legalized religion, or the political power of property. It leaves the individual alongside of the individual. No nationality of character could take form, except on the principle of individuality, so that the mind might be free, and every faculty have the unlimited opportunity for its development and culture. As the sea is made up of drops, American society is composed of separate, free, and constantly moving atoms, ever in reciprocal action, advancing, receding, crossing, struggling against each other and with each other; so that the institutions and laws of the country rise out of the masses of individual thought, which, like the waters of the ocean, are rolling evermore.

The rule of individuality was extended as never before. The synod of the Presbyterians of New York and Philadelphia, a denomination inflexibly devoted to its own creed, in their pastoral letter of May, 1783, published their joy that "the rights of conscience are inalientably secured and interwoven with the very constitutions of the several states." Religion was become avowedly the attribute of man and not of a corporation. In the earliest states known to history, government and religion were one and indivisible. Each state had its special deity, and of these protectors one after another might be overthrown in battle, never to rise again. The Peloponnesian war grew out of strife about an oracle. Rome, as it sometimes adopted into citizenship those whom it vanquished, introduced in like manner, and with good logic for that day, the worship of their gods. No one thought of vindicating religion for the conscience of the individual till a voice in Judea, breaking day for the greatest epoch in the life of humanity by establishing a pure, spiritual and universal religion for all mankind, enjoined to render to Caesar only that which is Caesar's. The rule was upheld during the infancy of the gospel for all men. No sooner was this religion adopted by the chief of the Roman Empire, than it was shorn of its character of universality and enthralled by an unholy connection with the unholy state; and so it continued till the new nation—the least defiled with the barren scoffings of the eighteenth century, the most general believer in Christianity of any people of that age, the chief heir of the reformation in its purest form—when it came to establish a government for the United States, refused to treat faith as a matter to be regulated by a corporate body, or having a headship in a monarch of a state.

Vindicating the right of individuality even in religion, and in religion above all, the new nation dared to set the example of accepting in its relations to God the principle first divinely

ordained in Judea. It left the management of temporal things
to the temporal power; but the American constitution, in harmony with the people of the several states, withheld from the
federal government the power to invade the home of reason, the
citadel of conscience, the sanctuary of the soul; and not from
indifference, but that the infinite spirit of eternal truth might
move in its freedom and purity and power.

With this perfect individuality extending to conscience, freedom should have belonged to labor. What though slavery existed and still exists in the older states known to history, in
Egypt, in China, coming down continuously from an unknown
date; what though Aristotle knew no mode of instituting a republican household but with a slave; and Julius Caesar, when
Italy was perishing by the vastness of its slave estates, crowded
them with new hordes of captives? What though the slave-
trade was greedily continued under the passionate encouragement of the British parliament, and that in nearly all of the
continent of Europe slavery in some of its forms prevailed? In
America, freedom of labor was the moral principle of the majority of the people; was established, or moving towards immediate establishment, in a majority of the states; was by the
old confederation, with the promptest and oft-repeated sanction of the new government, irrevocably ordained in all the
territory for which the United States could at that time make
the law. The federal convention could not interfere with the
slave laws of the separate states; but it was careful to impose
no new incapacitation on free persons of color; it maintained
them in all the rights of equal citizenship; it granted those
rights to the emancipated slave; and it kept to itself the authority to abolish the slave-trade instantly in any territory that
might be annexed; in all other states and lands, at the earliest
moment for which it had been able to obtain power.

The tripartite division of government into legislative, executive, and judicial, enforced in theory by the illustrious
Montesquieu, and practiced in the home government of every
one of the American states, became a part of the constitution

of the United States, which derived their mode of instituting it from their own happy experience. It was established by the federal convention with a rigid consistency that went beyond the example of Britain, where one branch of the legislature still remains a court of appeal. Each one of the three departments proceeded from the people, and each is endowed with all the authority needed for its just activity. The president may recommend or dissuade from enactments and has a limited veto on them; but whatever becomes a law he must execute. The power of the legislature to enact is likewise uncontrolled except by the paramount law of the constitution. The judiciary passes upon every case that may be presented, and its decision on the case is definitive; but without further authority over the executive or the legislature, for the convention had wisely refused to make the judges a council to either of them.

Tripartite division takes place not only in the threefold powers of government; it is established as the mode of legislation. There, too, three powers, proceeding from the people, must concur, except in cases provided for, before an act of legislation can take place. This tripartite division in the power of legislation—so at the time wrote Madison, so thought all the great builders of the constitution, so asserted John Adams with vehemence and sound reasoning—is absolutely essential to the success of a federal republic; for if all legislative powers are vested in one man or in one assembly, there is despotism; if in two branches, there is a restless antagonism between the two; if they are distributed among three, it will be hard to unite two of them in a fatal strife with the third. But the executive, and each of the two chambers, must be so chosen as to have a character and strength and popular support of its own. The government of the United States is thoroughly a government of the people. By the English aristocratic revolution of 1688, made after the failure of the popular attempt at reform, the majority of the house of commons was in substance composed of nominees of the house of lords so that no ministry could prevail in it except by the power of that house;

and as the prime minister and cabinet depend on the majority in the house of commons, the house of lords directly controlled the government not only in its own branch but in the commons, and through the commons in the nomination of the ministry. All three branches of the government were in harmony, for all three branches represented the aristocracy.[1] In the United States, on the other hand, all the branches of power—president, senators, and representatives—proceed directly or indirectly from the people. The government of the United States is a government by the people, for the people.

To perfect the system and forever prevent revolution, power is reserved to the people by amendments of their constitution to remove every imperfection which time may lay bare, and adapt it to unforeseen contingencies. But no change can be hastily made. An act of parliament can at any time alter the constitution of England; no similar power is delegated to the congress of the United States, which, like parliament, may be swayed by the shifting majorities of party. As to the initiation of amendments, it could not be entrusted to the president; still it might lead him to initiate changes for his own advantage; still less to a judiciary holding office for life, for, such is human nature a tribunal so constituted and deciding by a majority, by whatever political party its members may have named, cannot safely be invested with so transcendent a power. The legislature of the states or of the United States are alone allowed to open the "constitutional door of amendments;" and these can be made valid only through the combined intervention of the state legislatures and of congress or a convention of all the states elected expressly for the purpose by the people of the several states. In this way no change of the constitution can be made in haste or by stealth, but only by the consent of three quarters of the states after a full and free and often-repeated discussion. There is no legal road to amendment of the con-

[1] The period to which this refers must be kept in mind; the British constitution is very different now after the various reforms in the mode of electing the house of commons.

stitution but through the consent of the people given in the form prescribed by law. America, being charged with the preservation of liberty, has the most conservative polity in the world, both in its government and in its people.

The new nation asserted itself as a continental republic. The discovery was made that the time had passed for little commonwealths with a single city and its environs. The great Frederick, who had scoffed at the idea of attempting to govern an imperial domain without a king, was hardly in his grave when a commonwealth of more than twenty degrees in each direction, containing from the first an area of six or seven times as large as the whole of Great Britain and Ireland, fifty or sixty times as great as the Netherlands or Switzerland, able to include more than a thousand confederacies as large as the Achaian, and ready to admit adjoining lands to fellowship, rose up in the best part of the temperate zone on a soil that had been collecting fertility for untold centuries. The day of the Greek commonwealth had passed forever; and, after the establishment of the representative system, it was made known that a republican government thrives best in a vast territory. Monarchy had held itself a necessity for the formation of large states; but now its was found out that monarchy can be dispensed with; and the world was summoned to gaze at the spectacle of a boundless society of republican states in union.

The United States of America are not only a republic, they are "a society of societies" "a federal republic." Toward foreign powers the country has no seam in its garment; it exists in absolute unity as a nation, with full and undisputed national resources. At home it is "a union," or "one out of many;" but still, within its own sphere, is supreme and self-supporting. For this end it has its own legislature to make enactments; its own functionaries to execute them; its own courts; its own treasury; and it alone may have an army and a navy. All-sufficient powers are so plainly given that there is no need of striving for more by straining the words in which they are granted beyond their plain and natural import.

The constitution, the laws of the United States made in pursuance of it, and all treaties framed by their authority, are the supreme law of the land, binding the judges in every state even if need be in spite of the constitution and the laws of the state; and all executive, legislative, and judicial officers, both of the United States and of the several states, are to be sworn to its support. The constitution provides within itself for the redress of every wrong. The supreme court offers relief in a "case" of injustice or conflict with the constitution; the remedy for a bad law is to be sought through the freedom and frequency of elections, a fault in the fundamental law through an amendment.

Aside of the sphere of the federal government, each state is in all things supreme, not by grace, but of right. The United States may not interfere with any ordinance or law that begins and ends with a state. The supremacy of the states in the powers which have not been granted is as essentially a part of the system as the supremacy of the general government in its sphere. The states are at once the guardians of the domestic security and the happiness of the individual, and they are the parents the protectors, and the stay of the union. The states and the United States are members of one great whole; and the one is as needful as the other. The powers of government are not divided between them; they are distributed; so that there need be no collision in their exercise. The union without self-existent states is a harp without strings; the states without union are as chords that are unstrung. But for state rights the union would perish from the paralysis of its limbs. The states, as they gave life to the union, are necessary to the continuance of that life. Within their own limits they are the guardians of industry, of property, of personal rights, and of liberty. But state rights are to be defended inside of the union; not from an outside citadel from which the union may be struck at or defied. The states and the United States are not antagonists; the states in union form the federal republic; and the system can have life and health and strength and beauty only by their harmonious action. In short, the constitution knows nothing of United States alone, or states alone; it adjusts the parts harmoniously in an organized unity. Impair the relations or the vigor of any part, and disease enters into the veins of the whole. That there may be life in the whole, there must be healthy life in every part. The United States are the states in union; these are so inwrought into the constitution that the one cannot perish without the other.

Is it asked who is the sovereign of the United States? The words "sovereign" and "subjects" are unknown to the constitution. There is no place for princes with unlimited power, or conquering cities, or feudal chiefs, or privileged aristocracies, ruling absolutely with their correlative vassals or subjects.

The people of the United States have declared in their constitution that the law alone is supreme; and have defined that supreme law. Is it asked who are the people of the United States that instituted the "general government"? The federal convention and the constitution answer, that it is the concurring people of the several states. The constitution is constantly on its guard against permitting the action of the aggregate mass as a unit, lest the whole people, once accustomed to acting together as an individual, might forget the existence of the states, and the states now in union succumb to centralization and absolutism. The people of the states demanded a federal convention to form the constitution; the congress of the confederation, voting by states, authorized that federal convention; the federal convention, voting likewise by states, made the constitution; at the advice of the federal convention the federal congress referred that constitution severally to the people of each state; and by their united voice taken severally it was made the binding form of government. The constitution, as it owes its life to the concurrent act of the people of the several states, permits no method of amending itself except by the several consent of the people of the states; and within the constitution itself, the president, the only officer who has an equal relation to every state in the union, is elected not by the aggregate people of all the states, but by the people of the several states according to the number of votes allotted to each of them.

Finally, there is one more great and happy feature in the constitution. Rome, in annexing the cities around itself, had not given them equal influence with itself in proportion to their wealth and numbers, and consequently there remained a cause of dissatisfaction never healed. America has provided for admission of new states upon equal terms with the old ones.

For Europe, there remained the sad necessity of revolution. For America the gates of revolution are shut and barred and bolted down, never again to be thrown open; for it has found a legal and a peaceful way to introduce every amelioration. Peace and intercitizenship and perfect domestic free trade are to know no end. The constitution is to the American people a possession for all ages; it creates an indissoluble union of imperishable states.

The federal republic will carry tranquillity, and freedom, and order throughout its vast domain. Will it, within less than a century, extend its limits to the capes of Florida, to the mouth of the Mississippi, to the region beyond the Mississippi, to California, to Oregon, to San Juan? Will it show all the Spanish colonies how to transform themselves into independent republics stretching along the Pacific till they turn Cape Horn? Will it be an example to France, teaching its great benefactor how to gain free institutions? Will it assist the liberal statesmen of the country from which it broke away to bring parliament more nearly to a representation of the people? Will it assist the birthplace of the reformation to gather together its scattered members and become once more an empire, with a government so entirely the child of the nation that it shall have but one hereditary functionary, with a federal council or senate representing the several states, and a house elected directly by universal suffrage? Will it teach England herself how to give peace to her groups of colonies, her greatest achievement, by establishing for them a federal republican dominion, in one continent at least if not in more? And will America send manumitted dark men home to their native continent, to introduce there an independent republic and missions that may help to civilize the races of Africa?

The philosophy of the people of the United States was neither that of optimism nor of despair. Believing in the justice of "the Great Governor of the world," and conscious of their own honest zeal in the cause of freedom and mankind, they looked with astonishment at their present success and at the future with unclouded hope.

Bibliographical Note

T HE three editions of the *History* are as follows:

The History of the United States from the Discovery of the American Continent. 10 vols. Boston: Little, Brown & Co., 1834–74.

The History of the United States of America from the Discovery of the Continent. 6 vols. Boston: Little, Brown & Co., 1876–79. The Centenary Edition.

The History of the United States of America from the Discovery of the Continent. 6 vols. New York: D. Appleton & Co., 1883–85. The author's last revision.

None of these is in print. The edition which seems to be most easily obtainable at second-hand is the Centenary Edition.

Index